Spiders & Spinsters
Women and Mythology

Marta Weigle

SUNSTONE
PRESS

ocn 137324948

Sunstone books may be purchased for educational, business, or sales promotional use. For information please write: Special Markets Department, Sunstone Press, P.O. Box 2321, Santa Fe, New Mexico 87504-2321.

Library of Congress Cataloging-in-Publication Data

Weigle, Marta.
  [Spiders & spinsters]
  Spiders and spinsters : women and mythology / by Marta Weigle.
      p. cm.
  Originally published: Spiders & spinsters. Albuquerque : University of
New Mexico Press, c1982.
  Includes bibliographical references and index.
  ISBN 978-0-86534-587-4 (softcover : alk. paper)
  1. Women--Folklore. 2. Women--Mythology. 3. Women--America--Folklore.
4. Women--America. I. Title.

GR470.W44 2007
398'.352--dc22

                        2007016866

WWW.SUNSTONEPRESS.COM
SUNSTONE PRESS / POST OFFICE BOX 2321 / SANTA FE, NM 87504-2321 /USA
(505) 988-4418 / ORDERS ONLY (800) 243-5644 / FAX (505) 988-1025

Sources

Margot Adler, from *Drawing Down the Moon*, Viking Penguin Inc. Copyright © 1979 Margot Adler. Reprinted by permission of the publisher.
Paula Gunn Allen, "Grandmother." Copyright © 1977 by Paula Gunn Allen. By permission of the author.
Edwin Ardener, from "Belief and the Problem of Women," in *Perceiving Woman*, edited by Shirley Ardener, J. M. Dent & Sons Ltd., Publishers, 1975. Reprinted by permission of the publisher.

(continued on page 325)

Contents

Preface

Women *and* mythology, women *in* mythology: we know more about the latter. As generally understood and undertaken, mythology—the study of sacred symbols, texts, rites, and their dynamic expression in human psyches and societies—concerns *men's* myths and rituals. Most extant documents, field data, and interpretations come from male scribes, scholars, artists, and "informants." Thus we know a fair amount about women *in* mythology, about the female figures who people men's narratives, enactments, philosophies and analyses, and almost nothing about women *and* mythology, or women's mythologies—the stories they recount among themselves and in the company of young children, the rituals they perform, and their elaboration, exegesis, and evaluation of their own and men's profoundly moving and significant symbolic expressions.

It should not come as a surprise, then, if the major portion of this book shows how men have treated women mythologically. How women have treated men and each other in mythological terms we can only strongly suggest.

Spiders & Spinsters is a sourcebook that focuses on mythology of the Americas and the major European "transplants"—classical and Judeo-Christian. There are more narratives, rites, customs, and beliefs from Western (folk, popular, and elite) than Native American traditions, in part because comparatively little has been published on non-Western women's expressive culture and in part because we first need to know what symbols and sociocultural forces have propelled and compelled us before we can intelligently and sensitively interact and investigate elsewhere. Thus, contemporary interpretations of the verbal and visual texts are drawn from a variety of sources, primarily anthropology, folklore, literature, classics, comparative religion, theology, and psychology, for the most part Freudian and Jungian.

The first chapter, "Spiders & Spinsters: Myth and Symbol," encapsulates the book's design and theme. The spider is not simply a biological specimen but a being with a panoply of mythological associations and psychological connotations. Spiders appear as powerful male and female symbols in myths, poems, images, dreams, popular beliefs, and tales. By extension, those who spin and weave—*spinsters*—are also viewed as persons with or in need of special powers, benevolent and/or malevolent. Only in Western tradition has the role spinster acquired so many derogatory, negative overtones, and the wizened, barren old maid must be recelebrated as a wise, creative spinner-weaver, a task in which she ought to be joined by brother as well as sister spinsters.

On the whole, goddesses have received short shrift in the world's mythologies. Perhaps because, as we know them, most have been defined and celebrated by males, they appear more often as monstrous and dangerous than as primary creators and gift-bearing culture heroines. In chapter 2, "Goddesses: Myth as Rorschach," creative and destructive Native American deities are joined by classical "loathly ladies," the Olympians (Athena, Artemis, Aphrodite, Hestia, and Hera), and the Virgin Mary in Catholic and Protestant guises.

By the same token, women can inspire, impart mysteries and enlighten men, but, in Western culture at least, they become suspect when they take too active a role in this process or themselves seek inspiration and spiritual enlightenment. Although it includes examples of strong women guides from Native American traditions, most of chapter 3, "Guides: Myth and Mystery," revolves around the Eleusinian Mysteries (which for women can be both enlightening and terrifying, being based on rape), Sophia, and the question of women's and men's muses/guides.

The moon is a very ancient guide who is often viewed and worshipped with ambivalence. Chapter 4, "Moon, Menstruation, Menopause: Myth and Ritual," explores both male and female lunar symbolism. It includes various myths and rituals associated with women's menstrual cycles. Many women's comparative freedom after menopause, a state both extolled and denounced in the wise old woman/witch figure, who in Western tradition fares so poorly in comparison with the wise old man, is also reviewed and reconsidered.

The disparity holds with respect to younger figures as well. At least in Western cultures, heroes are more often male and active, heroines female and passive. Available epics and *Märchen* (magic tales) tend to uphold this generalization. However, there are active heroines in various traditions, notably many whose heroic adventures begin at marriage, often to a beast. Some of these women's stories are sung in chapter 5, "Heroines: Myth as Model."

Amazons are regarded as the most active—and the most repugnant— women. Theirs and other matriarchies are often viewed with horror by men but, recently, with hope by women. Ultimately, however, it is probably a culture's myth about the origin of human beings that has the most far-reaching effect on its views and treatment of women, for myth "ratifies" existing social order. Thus, in chapter 6, "Origins and Matriarchy: Myth as Charter," Wonder Woman and her fellow Amazon-matriarchs are joined by Pandora,

Eve, Lilith, the man and woman created by Elohim in *Genesis* 1, and their Native American counterparts.

For the most part, the voices assembled here spin and weave their own story. It is, admittedly, more a man's story, or his view of that story. In chapter 7, "Appreciating the Mundane: Women and Mythology," some of the reasons why this is so are sketched, and women's stories—possibly many heretofore dismissed as gossip and old wives' tales—are suggested. Much work remains to be done. Until more women engage themselves and other women within and beyond their own culture and society, the imbalance can be clarified but not redressed.

Reader's Guide

In each chapter of this sourcebook the reader will find many kinds of materials: author's text; field-collected or historically sound myths and tales (verbatim or occasionally paraphrased—with indications to that effect); facsimile pages from printed versions of myths and tales; poems; pertinent illustrations, often with captions; instances of popular beliefs and customs, usually indicated with a star; historical and descriptive accounts, indicated with a double dagger; and critical, interpretive statements, indicated with a diamond. Some additional bibliography is noted in the text, but most elaboration is found in the footnotes. The bibliography is not exhaustive; it includes all sources used in the main text and further selected resources bearing on women and/in mythology and religion.

Acknowledgments

Spinning and weaving provide the theme and style for this book. Many voices (verbal and visual) are juxtaposed and interwoven—women's, men's, popular, folk, tribal, historical, contemporary, scholars', critics', psychologists', artists', and so on. My own is among them, but I have tried to orchestrate rather than marshal. Perhaps it is unfair and damaging to tear them from their original contexts. For that, I apologize. But I would also maintain that all these voices have a larger context in contemporary life, namely: in their profound, pervasive, daily influence on the relationship of women to themselves, to each other, and to their society and culture. It is that larger context which is woven into the "fabric" that follows.

My debt to all those from whom I quote is obvious. The matter of obtaining permissions for a sourcebook like this has been particularly arduous and expensive. So it is a joy to encounter the generosity of institutions like *CoEvolution Quarterly,* Dover Publications, Ann Elmo Agency, *Heresies,* the Marvel Comics Group, *Ms. Magazine,* Raines and Raines, Spring Publications, and *Western Folklore,* and of persons like Paula Gunn Allen, Sharon Barba, Carol P. Christ, Judy Grahn, Rayna Green, Nor Hall, Rosan Jordan, Wolfgang Lederer, Ursula Le Guin, Barbara Myerhoff, Benjamin Paul, Carol Sheehan, Gloria Steinem, Stan Steiner, Kay Stone, Barre Toelken, and, especially, Kay Turner.

Most of the illustrations come from Dover reprints or design and illustration books in the Dover Pictorial Archives Series. I am very grateful for the generosity of Dover Publications, Inc., in permitting me to make extensive use of this valuable visual material.

I would also like to acknowledge everyone connected with the Women's

Section of the American Folklore Society, who supported me during my tenure as editor of the *Folklore Women's Communication* (1977–79) and whose ideas on these subjects have helped so much to shape this work. My students, particularly in the undergraduate seminar courses on women and folklore and women in/and mythology, have also contributed many thoughts and evaluations. Jennifer Martínez helped with permissions and texts. Lois Vermilya-Weslowski found some of the myth texts, and I mark invaluable conversations about these matters with her, Jean Hess, Kyle Fiore, Vera John-Steiner, Elissa Melamed, and, especially, Reina Attias.

A 1979 grant from the Exxon Education Foundation, Educational Research and Development Program, made it possible for me to produce a first version of this book, a 300-page photocopied limited edition which was published by the English Department at the University of New Mexico in 1980. The Exxon grant that I and David Johnson received was for a project entitled "Mythology of the Americas: An Interdisciplinary Approach to Cultural Identity." We produced two other books during that time: *Lightning & Labyrinth: An Introduction to Mythology* (1979) and *At the Beginning: American Creation Myths* (1980). Both the Department of English and the administration of the University of New Mexico provided full campus support throughout.

Marta Field has seen this through the labyrinth and the emergence and now delivered safely to Spider Woman in all her multifarious forms. Although it more often seemed to me that unraveling would prevail, she had faith in the spinning, for which I am most grateful.

Three women were crucial in the transformation of the first version of this book. Jean Howells ably copyedited a complicated, bulky manuscript. Emmy Ezzell designed the book. Her perception of its nature, solutions to its thorny graphic and spatial problems, and conviction of its importance amazed and heartened me. Joanna Cattonar played the major editorial role, as reader and astute critic. I relied on her skills throughout but perhaps most in the beginning, when she was midwife to the rebirth of what had been a very recalcitrant child.

Spiritually, I owe an incalculable debt to all four of my grandparents. In the end, though, this book is for one Joan and four Mary's—Mary Grace, Mary Martha, Mary Angela, and, especially, Mary Elizabeth.

Chapter 1
Spiders & Spinsters:
Myth and Symbol

Out of her body she pushed
silver thread, light, air
and carried it carefully on the dark, flying
where nothing moved.

Out of her body she extruded
shining wire, life, and wove the light
on the void.

From beyond time,
beyond oak trees and bright clear water flow,
she was given the work of weaving the strands
of her body, her pain, her vision
into creation, and the gift of having made it,
to disappear.

After her,
the women and the men weave blankets into tales of life,
memories of light and ladders,
Infinity-eyes, and rain.
After her I sit on my laddered rain-bearing rug
and mend the tear with string.

—Paula Gunn Allen, "Grandmother" (1977).[1]

[1]For this poem's reprint in *The Third Woman: Minority Women Writers of the United States* (Fisher 1980:126), Allen notes, apropos of the oak tree mentioned in the third stanza, that: "I am a member of Oak Clan." She is identified as a Laguna Pueblo Indian, born in Albuquerque, New Mexico, but in the list of contributors to *Southwest: A Contemporary Anthology* edited

Spider designs on gorgets from prehistoric mounds in Missouri and Illinois (Naylor 1975:34, figs. B [above], A).

Who is the spider and who the spinster? Deity/insect? Female/male? Benevolent/malevolent? Exalted/despicable? The answers depend upon culture and time. In sampling and surveying Native American, classical, folk and contemporary myths, tales, poems, popular beliefs and images, we can see reflected and refracted our own attitudes and answers, as well as those of various artists, critics, and analysts.

Γ. Allwork Chaplin, *The Studio* 32
(Grafton 1980:125, fig. 550).

Little Miss Muffet
Sat on a tuffet,
Eating her curds and whey;
There came a big spider,
Who sat down beside her
And frightened Miss Muffet away.

  —Nursery rhyme
   (Opie 1952:323).[2]

'Will you walk into my parlour?' said the Spider to the Fly,
"Tis the prettiest little parlour that ever you did spy;
The way into my parlour is up a winding stair,
And I have many curious things to show when you are there.'

(Crawhall 1974:74)

---

by Karl and Jane Kopp (Albuquerque: Red Earth Press, 1977), in which the poem first appeared (p. 184), she is called a "poet, Lebanese-Sioux-Laguna" (p. 410). Also see the discussion of Allen's poem and other such literature and lore in Helen M. Bannan, "Spider Woman's Web: Mothers and Daughters in Southwestern Native American Literature" (1980).

[2]Iona and Peter Opie claim that the first written record of this rhyme appears in *Songs for the Nursery Collected from the Works of the Most Renowned Poets,* Tabart and Co., 1805. Apropos of this verse and variants such as "Little Mary Ester sat upon a tester" (1812) and "Little Miss Mopsey, Sat in the shopsey" (1842), they note: "Miss Muffet probably sat on a grassy hillock, though *tuffet* has also been described as a 'three-legged stool'. When she sits on a *buffet* she is certainly on a stool, and may come from the north country. Whether Mary Ester perched on a sixpence, a bed canopy, or a piece of armour for the head is a moot point" (1952:324).

'Oh no, no,' said the little Fly, 'to ask me is in vain,
For who goes up your winding stair can ne'er come down again.'

* * *

The Spider turned him round about, and went into his den,
For well he knew the silly Fly would soon come back again;
So he wove a subtle web, in a little corner sly,
And set his table ready, to dine upon the Fly.
Then he came out to his door again, and merrily did sing:
'Come hither, hither, pretty Fly, with the pearl and silver wing;
Your robes are green and purple—there's a crest upon your head;
Your eyes are like the diamond bright, but mine are dull as lead.'

Alas, alas! how very soon this silly little Fly,
Hearing his wily, flattering words, came slowly flitting by;
With buzzing wings she hung aloft, then near and nearer drew,
Thinking only of her brilliant eyes, and green and purple hew;
Thinking only of her crested head—poor foolish thing! At last,
Up jumped the cunning Spider, and fiercely held her fast.
He dragged her up his winding stair, into his dismal den,
Within his little parlour—but she ne'er came out again!

—Mary Howitt, from "The Spider and the Fly," 1829
(Opie 1973:158–59).[3]

Ethel Larcombe, *The Studio* 37 (Grafton 1980:127, fig. 555).

The frightful, cunning and dangerous spiders in these well-known children's verses stand in marked contrast to the helpful holy figures who in Zuni and Navajo mythology are said to have taught both children and adults how to manipulate diverting and instructive string figure "webs." In his classic 1907 study, *Games of the North American Indians,* anthropologist Stewart Culin notes: "My informant in Zuñi stated that the cat's cradle was called pichowaini of pishkappoa, the netted shield, figures 1067 and 1068 [below], actually representing this shield, which was supposed to have been carried by the War God. The idea is borrowed from the spider web, and cat's cradle was taught

[3]Despite her Quaker background, Mary (Botham) Howitt (1799–1888) became a writer, editor and translator. The mother of twelve, she wrote numerous pieces for children, including "The Spider and the Fly," which first appeared in *The New Year's Gift, and Juvenile Souvenir,* 1829 (Opie 1973:368).

"Fig. 1067. Cat's cradle, pich-owaini, netted shield; Zuñi Indians, Zuñi, New Mexico; cat. no. 22604, Free Museum of Science and Art, University of Pennsylvania."

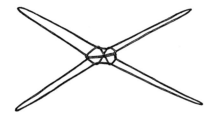

"Fig. 1068. Cat's cradle, pish-kappoa pichowainai, netted shield; Zuñi Indians, Zuñi, New Mexico; cat. no. 22605, Free Museum of Science and Art, University of Pennsylvania" (Culin 1975:777).

to the little boys, the twin War Gods, by their mother, the Spider Woman, for their amusement" (1975:779).

Father Berard Haile, noted Franciscan scholar of Navajo language and culture, wrote Culin "a personal letter" about the Navajo version of cat's cradle:

Cat's cradle owes its origin to the Spider people. They, the spiders, who in the Navaho's belief were human beings, taught them the game for their amusement. The holy spiders taught the Navaho to play and how to make the various figures of stars, snakes, bears, coyotes, etc., but on one condition—they were to be played only in winter, because at that season spiders, snakes, etc., sleep and do not see them. To play the cat's cradle at any other time of the year would be folly, for certain death by lightning, falling from a horse, or some other mishap were sure to reach the offender. Otherwise no religious meaning is said to attach to the game. Even the above information was only extracted with much patience and scheming. I may add that one Navaho claimed that the cat's cradle is a sort of schooling by which the children are taught the position of the stars, etc. Though this might be a satisfactory explanation, it was not approved by the medicine man from whom I obtained the above. Na'atlo, it is twisted, is the term for cat's cradle. (Culin 1975:766–67)

Father Haile's last observations would seem to be contradicted by the following field account from contemporary folklorists Barre Toelken, Jan Brunvand and John Wilson Foster, who recently visited a Navajo family in southeastern Utah during late December:

"Where did you learn those designs?" we ask. The children confer with their father for a while, then answer, "I don't know. I guess it's all from Spider Woman. They say if you fall into Spider Woman's den she won't let you out unless you can do all these. And then if you do these in the summer you won't get out at all anyway."

"Why is that?"

"Well, we're only supposed to do it in the winter when the spiders are hibernating, because it's really their kind of custom to do things with string." During this conversation, the mother has gone back to weaving momentarily, and the other children are still doing string figures.

"The Spider Woman taught us all these designs as a way of helping us think. You learn to think when you make these. And she taught us about weaving, too," a teen-age daughter puts in.

"If you can think well," the first boy adds, "you won't get into trouble or get lost. Anyway, that's what our father says."

Toelken: "But Spider Woman didn't teach *you* those things, right? Where did *you* learn them?"

"Well, we probably picked them up from each other and from our father, but they were already around, you know. All the people know about them. Spider Woman taught us."

The father speaks now for the first time and, taking the string, makes a tight design. "Do you know what this is?" he asks us. We do not. He shows his children and they all respond: "So' Tso" (Big Star). He nods with satisfaction and makes another figure; he holds it up to us, and we shake our heads. He holds it up to the children, and they respond, "Dilyehe." Since I have never heard the term I ask one of the children to translate it; everyone looks blank. "That's the only word there is for it." Suddenly, in an attempt to explain, the father motions us all outside. There, shivering in the night wind, we watch him carefully hold the string figure above his head and point beyond it with pursed lips to the Pleiades.

Back inside, the father helps cover our embarrassment at not knowing our astronomy by making string figure caricatures of those present: a face with vague glasses to represent Brunvand, another with a loop hanging down for Foster's beard, another with a piece of string trailing down to depict the power cord on Toelken's tape recorder.

Finally, the father puts the string down and says seriously, "These are all matters we need to know. It's too easy to become sick, because there are always things happening to confuse our minds. We need to have ways of thinking, of keeping things stable, healthy, beautiful. We try for a long life, but lots of things happen to us. So we keep our thinking in order by these figures and we keep our lives in order with the stories. We have to relate our lives to the stars and the sun, the animals, and to all of nature or else we will go crazy, or get sick." (Toelken 1979:95–96)

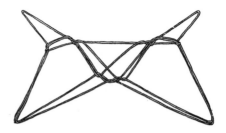

"Fig. 1040. Cat's cradle, dilyehe, Pleiades, Navaho Indians, St. Michael, Arizona; cat. no. 22717, Free Museum of Science and Art, University of Pennsylvania" (Culin 1975:764).

Spider Woman instructed the Navajo women how to weave on a loom which Spider Man told them how to make. The crosspoles were made of sky and earth cords, the warp sticks of sun rays, the healds [sic; heddles] of rock crystal and sheet lightning. The batten was a sun halo, white shell made the comb. There were four spindles: one a stick of zigzag lightning with a whorl of cannel coal; one a stick of flash lightning with a whorl of turquoise; a third had a stick of sheet lightning with a whorl of abalone; a rain streamer formed the stick of the fourth, and its whorl was white shell. *(Navajo Legend)* (Reichard 1934: frontispiece)[4]

The Spider Man said: "Now you know all that I have named for you. It is yours to work with and to use following your own wishes. But from now on when a baby girl is born to your tribe you shall go and find a spider web which is woven at the

[4]Anthropologist Gladys Reichard presumably refers to Washington Matthews, *Navaho Legends,* Memoirs of the American Folklore Society, Vol. 5 (Boston and New York, 1897). Folklorist Barre Toelken includes good insights about Navajo weaving and women's perspectives on it in "A Circular World: The Vision of Navajo Crafts" *(Parabola,* vol. 1, no. 1, winter 1976, pp. 30–37) and "Seeing with a Native Eye: How Many Sheep Will It Hold?" (in *Seeing with a Native Eye: Essays on Native American Religion,* ed. Walter Holden Capps [New York: Harper & Row, 1976], pp. 17–18, 19–21). According to anthropologist Gary Witherspoon in his valuable *Language and Art in the Navajo Universe:* "Where Navajo music, singing, and poetry are artistic endeavors common to both men and women, the other two major domains of Navajo aesthetics, weaving and sandpainting, are sexually bifurcated. Weaving is primarily an activity of women, and sandpainting is primarily an activity of men. Some Navajo men weave, but this associates them with the category of *nádlééhí,* 'transvestite.' Such a person, however, is usually held in high esteem and is not normally the object of ridicule or unkind behavior. . . . Sandpainting is exclusively a male activity. Even female singers do not do sandpainting, although they may supervise the creation of sandpainting" (Ann Arbor: University of Michigan Press, 1977, p. 160). For examples of sandpainting see chapters 2 and 3 below. Witherspoon also notes that "in contrast, among the Pueblos, weaving is primarily a male activity" (ibid, p. 205). In this regard, note Herbert Joseph Spinden's translation of a Tewa Pueblo Indian song which he calls "Song of the Sky Loom" *(Songs of the Tewa* [New York: Exposition of Indian Tribal Arts, Inc., 1933], p. 94).

mouth of some hole; you must take it and rub it on the baby's hand and arm. Thus, when she grows up she will weave, and her fingers and arms will not tire from the weaving." To this day that is done to all baby girls. (O'Bryan 1956:38)

Small Navajo blanket "with design in gaudy colors made of native yarns. This type of blanket was commonly used by a woman" (Naylor 1975:219, fig. A).

The Toba Indians of Argentina recount a similar myth about the origin of weaving. During field visits in 1933 and 1939, anthropologist Alfred Métraux collected myths and tales from several Toba and Pilagá Indians, one of them a young man named Kido'k (Jaguar). Métraux describes his informant as "ambitious," with standing in both white and tribal worlds, but "not very conversant with native lore." Hence, Kido'k turned to his mother, "who had remained faithful to the Toba past and who was probably the best storyteller in the group," listening to her during the day and regaling Métraux with narratives laced with "a vein of humor and realism" in the evening (1946:xi).

One of the stories Kido'k's old mother told was an origin myth recounting how "Spider taught the women how to weave [when] formerly sheep did not exist because the Master of Sheep [Partridge] was stingy." At the suggestion of a man, an old woman and a young woman set out to discover what kind of threads Spider used to weave. They spied on Spider at work and when she went to sleep in her hole at noon stole her bag of thread.

The people argued about whether the thread was made of yuchan tree (*Chorisia insignis*) pods or sheep's wool. They settled on the former and gathered many, but when the old woman attempted to spin "her threads broke continually." Sheep's wool was necessary but there were no sheep. The women then conferred with Fox, "who had arrived just that day." He boastfully set out to call upon his friend Partridge but returned emptyhanded and told them to call Toad.

The chief commissioned Toad to approach Partridge, who "snapped" that he would never give his sheep to anyone whosoever. Toad then asked to be shown the water. Uttering the cry "May you fly low! May the water in your jars disappear!" he dove into the pool, swallowed its contents and left.

A worried Partridge finally contacted Fox, renewed their friendship and agreed to exchange sheep for water. Partridge demanded the water first, but when Fox dove into the empty pool he broke his neck. Partridge briefly bemoaned his friend but, since he was still thirsty, decided to call on Toad.

The remainder of the origin myth goes as follows:

. . . Toad arrived, his stomach swollen with water. He asked, "If I bring back the water in this country, will you give me all your flock?" "Yes," said Partridge. "I want all the flock; otherwise I shall make the country dry forever." They picked up a cactus thorn. Partridge pricked Toad's stomach. First the water fell in small drops, then it ran faster and faster until it filled all the pools, the lagoons, and the wells of the land as they were before. As soon as he had quenched his thirst, Partridge said, "Let's go home. I'll give you the flock. You may take it." Toad and his friends drove the flock home, leaving Partridge without a single sheep. Thereafter women could spin wool. First they had unspun wool, but when they saw how Spider used it for spinning, they spun like Spider, and made a poncho. The first woven poncho was given to Toad. (Métraux 1946:113–15)

Anthropologist A. L. Kroeber admits that material on the Chibcha Indians of Colombia is "limited," claiming: "Chibcha mythology is confused, partly because of conflicting or misunderstood Spanish renditions, more largely because *Chibcha* culture had not achieved systematic organization in any field. The tales are like the rest of the culture in being highly localized" (1946:907). Nevertheless, he pieces together an account of a male figure who brought spinning and weaving, among other boons.

The most famous myth personage is the culture hero Bochica, also called Xue (lord), or Nebterequetoba, or Chimi-sapagua as "messenger" of Chimi-ni-gagua [creator deity]. According to one statement, he lived on earth 20 generations before the Spaniards arrived, according to another, 4. He came to *Chibcha*-land from the plains of the Far East. . . .

Bochica is described as old and bearded; a white complexion is ascribed to him only by late authors; and various traits of costume mentioned—long hair, headdress, knotted mantle, bare feet—are merely standard *Chibcha* attire. He is always said to have preached and taught, especially virtue, charity, and observance of custom law. His specific civilizing instruction is exemplified chiefly by the teaching of spinning, weaving, and cloth painting.

Bochica was worshipped with offerings. In Iraca, he was known as Sugu-monxe and Sugu-n-sua, invisible or disappearing person and sun, respectively. Iraca also had tales of one of its rulers, Idaca-n-sás, who "inherited" the powers of Bochica, and could produce rains, droughts, epidemics, and the like. (Kroeber 1946:908–909)

Significantly, the word "spider" is derived from an Old English verb *spinnan,* "to spin." According to the *Oxford English Dictionary,* "the cunning, skill, and industry of the spider, as well as its power of secreting or emitting poison, are frequently alluded to in literature," while the epithet "spider" is "applied to persons as an opprobrious or vituperative term." *Webster's New World Dictionary of the American Language* identifies the spider as "any of a number of

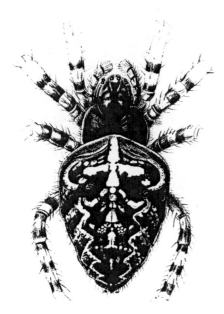

(Haeckel 1974:66)

small, eight-legged animals having a body composed of two divisions, a cephalothorax bearing the legs and an abdomen bearing two or more pairs of spinnerets, whose function is to spin silk threads from which they make nests, cocoons, or webs for trapping insects: the spider is an arachnid and not an insect." The Linnaean classification "arachnid," which includes spiders, scorpions and mites, is derived from *arachne,* the Greek word for spider. In his *Metamorphoses* (ca. 8 A.D.), Roman poet Ovid recounts a prettified classical version of the origin of spiders from Minerva (Pallas Athena)'s transformation of her talented rival, the weaver Arachne.

> Pallas had listened closely, borne along
> In admiration of the Muses' song.
> Approving of their righteous anger too,
> She thought: "'Tis well to praise what others do:
> But let me earn the praise I give, nor see
> Too cheaply scorned my own divinity."
> And as she pondered thus, her mind was bent
> To plan Arachne's destined punishment—
> Her Lydian rival, who was said to claim
> Of all who worked in wool the foremost name;
> Yet lowly born: to skill her fame was due:
> Her father, Idmon, gave her wools their hue;
> To dye the drinking fleeces was his trade
> With purple from Phocaean murex made;
> A Colophonian he: her mother, bred,
> Like him, of no patrician stock, was dead.
> Of humble home and humble native place,
> She lacked advantage drawn from rank or race;
> Yet, not alone in small Hypaepa heard,
> Through Lydia was her name a household word.
> The nymphs of Tmolus left their vine-clad hills,
> Pactolian nymphs forsook their native rills,
> And watched, enchanted not alone to view
> The product, but the expert process too.
> Did she, first stage of all, prepare to spin,
> Bunching the fleecy wool upon the pin,
> And twist, with fingers' rhythmic rise and fall,
> The thread that lengthened from the cloudlike ball,
> And thumb the whirling spindle; or, to end,
> With needle o'er her fine embroidery bend—
> She showed the school of Pallas; yet denied
> Her teacher, for such greatness irked her pride.
> "Let her compete with me: I will refuse
> No forfeit" (so she challenged) "if I lose."
>
>   Acting old age, with fringe of false white hair
> And stick to prop her limbs, came Pallas there;
> And soon she fell conversing, and addressed
> Arachne thus: "In some things age is best:
> Years bring experience: heed what I advise:
> Of mortal weavers claim the foremost prize:
> Challenge the world—but give a goddess place;
> Take back your boasts, and humbly ask her grace,

Which she, when asked, will give." Arachne's eyes
Blazed, and she dropped her spindle in surprise,
And raised her hand to strike, and scarce refrained,
While in her face was anger unrestrained;
And back to Pallas, though she little knew
To whom she spoke, her sharp rejoinder flew:
"Must you come doddering here, with wits gone wrong,
The curse of age on those who live too long?
Have you no daughters, are your sons unwed,
That these your ramblings must to me be said?
I take my own advice, and think it sound:
Yours, be assured, will leave me as it found.
Why comes she not herself, why does she fear
This contest?" Pallas answered: "She is here,"
And with the word she dropped her masquerade,
And let the form of Pallas be displayed.
While nymphs and country girls and all who saw
Dropped on their knees, Arachne showed no awe.
She flushed, but not with fear: the sudden red
Dyed her unwilling cheeks, and quickly fled,
As, with the stir of dawn, the atmosphere
Turns red, then whitens as the sun breaks clear.
She stood her ground, nor let her thirst abate
For foolish fame, but rushed upon her fate.
Nor did Jove's daughter, for her part, demur,
Repeat her warnings, or the test defer.

(Harter 1978b: 108)

  No more delay: each to her corner gone,
They set their looms, and stretch the warp-threads on;
Fast to the beam the fine-spun threads are tied,
Which, parted by the reed, stand side by side;
And when the shed divides them, fingers deft
Make fly the pointed shuttle with the weft
Between the warp-threads; they they use the comb,
Deep notched with heavy teeth, to drive it home.
Both work with speed, and, sashed beneath the breast,
Move expert arms, and have no thought of rest.
Purples of price are there, that felt the fire,
And took their temper, in the vats of Tyre;
And woven in the web are hues that range
From shade to shade by undetected change;
As, after rainstorms, when the bow will dye
With its huge arc the longest reach of sky,
A thousand tints are there, distinct and bright,
Yet the transition will elude the sight;
So wholly, where they meet, they merge in one,
Yet to such difference at the rims they run.
And there, inwrought, were strands of ductile gold,
And woven in the piece, a tale of old.

  By Pallas, Cecrops' citadel was wrought—
The rock of Mars, where once the suit was fought
To name the city. Twelve celestials here,
Reverend and grave, on lofty seats appear

Poseidon (Roman Neptune)
(Lehner 1969:23, fig. 48).

(The likeness writes their names); and clearly shown,
Jove in the midst, by regal aspect known.
She makes the sea-god stand, and with the shock
Of his tall trident wound the flinty rock;
And from the cleft, to give the wondrous sign
That claims the city his, has gushed the brine.
Herself with shield and sharp-tipped spear she dressed;
A casque her head, the aegis armed her breast.
It seemed that, smitten by her spear, the earth
To the hoary olive, with its fruit, gave birth.
The gods look wondering on: the suit is won:
And the main labor of her loom is done.
Then, that her rival might by samples know,
What wages may to such rash ventures go,
Four contests in the corners four she drew,
In tiny scale but realistic hue.
First Rhodope and Haemus, who in Thrace
Now ice-capped peaks, but once of mortal race,
Usurped the names of gods; and next was seen
The piteous fate of that Pygmaean queen
Outmatched, and made a crane, whom Juno bade
Cry war upon the tribes that once she swayed;
The third, Antigone, whom boldness drove
To try conclusions with the queen of Jove;
Nor could her city, Ilion, or its king,
Laomedon, her sire, deliverance bring:
By Juno changed, she wears the stork's white quill,
And clacks, in self-applause, a noisy bill.
In one last corner, Cinyras lay prone,
Embracing, as he wept upon the stone,
The temple steps, his daughter's flesh and bone.
Olives of peace she wove, for border, round,
And when her tree closed all, art reached its bound.
  Arachne shows the gods in various guise;
And first the bull that cheats Europa's eyes,
So skillfully depicted, you would swear
A living bull, a moving sea, was there.
The girl herself was seen to watch dismayed
The fast-receding shore, and call for aid,
And draw her feet back, fearing to be caught
By mounting waves—so well the weaver wrought.
She made the eagle to Asterië cling,
And Leda couch beneath the swan's white wing;
And added, how Antiope the fair
To Jove, in satyr's guise, twin children bare.
Jove, as Amphitryon, to Alcmena came;
As gold, to Danaë; to Aegina, flame;
A shepherd's semblance tricked Mnemosyne;
To Deo's child a speckled snake was he.
Thy changes, Neptune, too were there displayed:
Now a fierce bull beside the Aeolian maid;
Now false Enipeus, sire of twins, and now

Charolaise Bull
(Rice 1979:7).

To cheat Bisaltis' eyes, a ram art thou;
Now to the gracious harvest-queen a horse:
Thus did the golden goddess feel thy force;
And now the bird that with Medusa lies,
The snake-haired mother of the steed that flies;
And now the dolphin that Melantho knew—
These, with their backgrounds, to the life she drew.
There too did Phoebus like a rustic stride;
Or wear the falcon's wings, or lion's hide;
Or lurk in shepherd's semblance, to seduce
Too-simple Isse, child of Macareus.
Bacchus, as pictured, seemed again to be
A bunch of grapes, to cheat Erigone;
While Saturn fathered Chiron, who began
The wondrous interbreed of horse and man.
A narrow border rims the whole design,
Where flowers and trailing ivy intertwine.
    Such was Arachne's work: not envy's eyes
Could find a flaw, nor Pallas criticize.
The girl's achievement galled her, and she tore
The faultless fabric, with the scenes it bore
Impeaching heaven, a crime in every strand;
And as her boxwood shuttle lay to hand
Of wood from mount Cytorus, brought it down
Blow after blow upon her rival's crown;
Who, mad with pain and dashed in spirit, tied
A noose about her neck, and so had died;
But Pallas, who observed her, and conceived
Some pity, raised her up, and thus reprieved:
"Live, Mischief, live and hang: this sentence be
On you and yours to far posterity
Without remission." As she went, she spilled
The noxious juice from Hecate's herb distilled.
Gone at the touch are hair and ears and nose;
A tiny head on tiny body shows;
Long feelers at the sides for legs are spread;
The rest is belly, whence she spins her thread;
And as a spider, with her ancient skill,
Arachne plies her tireless weaving still.

    —*Metamorphoses,* Book VI, lines 1–147;
       trans. Watts 1980:116–21.[5]

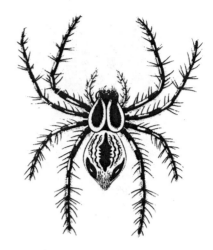

(Haeckel 1974:66)

[5]Minerva, here translated as Pallas, a name Athena assumed to honor a girl friend whom she accidentally killed while practicing war arts, makes her successful contest with Neptune (Poseidon) at the Acropolis for sovereignty over Attica and Athens the central part of her tapestry. The four corner scenes depict instances of mortals' attempts to usurp immortals' powers, while the whole is bordered by the olive tree, a symbol of victory and fertility long associated with Athena. For her part, Arachne presents a catalogue of the gods who seduced and raped goddesses and mortal women. The bordering ivy was associated with Dionysus (Bacchus). (Interestingly, in an Orphic version of Dionysus's birth, Persephone is weaving in a cave sacred to Pallas Athena when her father Zeus impregnates her in the form of a snake [Kerényi 1979: 252–54].) Also see Susan Stern's story, "Arachne" (1981).

Intertwined Crescents (Hornung 1946: plate 3, fig. 27).

Still other spinners play important roles in classical mythology and art. Poet, novelist and scholar Robert Graves summarizes the various attributes of the Moirai or Fates as described in the works of Homer, Hesiod, Aeschylus, Herodotus, Plato, Simonides, Pausanias and Virgil:

There are three conjoined Fates, robed in white, whom Erebus begot on Night: By name Clotho, Lachesis, and Atropos. Of these, Atropos is the smallest in stature, but the most terrible.

Zeus, who weighs the lives of men and informs the Fates of his decisions can, it is said, change his mind and intervene to save whom he pleases, when the thread of life, spun on Clotho's spindle, and measured by the rod of Lachesis, is about to be snipped by Atropos's shears. . . .

Others hold, on the contrary, that Zeus himself is subject to the Fates, as the Pythian priestess once confessed in an oracle: because they are not his children, but parthenogenous daughters of the Great Goddess Necessity, against whom not even the gods contend, and who is called 'The Strong Fate'. (1960:48)[6]

Historian of religions Mircea Eliade generalizes the relationship between spiders, spinning, weaving, destiny and the moon:

The moon, however, simply because she is mistress of all living things and sure guide of the dead, has "woven" all destinies. Not for nothing is she envisaged in myth as an immense spider—an image you will find used by a great many peoples. For to weave is not merely to predestine (anthropologically), and to join together differing realities (cosmologically) but also to *create*, to make something of one's own substance as the spider does in spinning its web. And the moon is the inexhaustible creator of all living forms. But, like everything woven, the lives thus created are fixed into a pattern; they have a destiny. The Moirai, who spin fates, are lunar deities. . . .

Needless to say, in those cultures in which Great Goddesses have absorbed the powers of the moon, the earth and vegetation, the spindle and distaff with which they spin the fates of man become two more of their many attributes. . . . Destiny, the thread of life, is a long or short period of *time*. The Great Goddesses consequently become mistresses of time, of the destinies they create according to their will. (1958:181–82)

Bestiaries combine what is now called natural history with theological and popular beliefs, homilies, legends, allegories, and myths about various real

---

[6]According to Graves' first note: "This myth seems to be based on the custom of weaving family and clan marks into a newly-born child's swaddling bands, and so allotting him his place in society . . .; but the Moerae, or Three Fates, are the Triple Moon-goddess—hence their white robes, and the linen thread which is sacred to her as Isis. Clotho is the 'spinner', Lachesis the 'measurer', Atropos is 'she who cannot be turned, or avoided'. *Moera* means 'a share' or 'a phase', and the moon has three phases and three persons: the new, the Maiden-goddess of the spring, the first period of the year; the full moon, the Nymph-goddess of the summer, the second period; and the old moon, the Crone-goddess of autumn, the last period. . . ." (1960:48–49).

and imaginary animals. A twelfth-century Latin bestiary translated by T. H. White classifies spiders with "Reptiles and Fishes":

Vermis the Worm is an animal which is mostly germinated, without sexual intercourse, out of meat or wood or any earthly thing. People agree that, like the scorpion, they are never born from eggs. There are earth worms and water worms and air worms and flesh worms and leaf worms, also wood worms and clothes worms.

A Spider is an air worm, as it is provided with nourishment from the air, which a long thread catches down to its small body. Its web is always tight. It never stops working, cutting out all loss of time without interruption in its skill. (White 1954:191; also see Mercatante 1974:131–34)

The Desana Indians of the Northwest Amazon in Colombia single out a different characteristic of a particular spider—its sting—and derive its significance from its actions and position in mythological times. Part of the lengthy Desana creation myth tells about the life of the Daughter of Aracú, herself an aracú fish. This fish is recognized as the primary mythical ancestor of the Desana, and she cohabited with the first men of the tribe.

When the Daughter of Aracú gave birth to her child, there were also some animals watching. The bat was a bird then and was watching and singing. Then the Daughter of Aracú said to it: "I at least have my offspring where I should give birth, but you will defecate by mouth from now on." The centipede and a large, black, poisonous spider came to lick the blood of the childbirth, and from that time on the centipede looks like an umbilical cord and the spider like a vagina. Also the scorpion and a large black ant licked the blood, and from that time on the bite of these two makes one vomit and produces great pains similar to those of childbirth. The stingray is the placenta of the Daughter of Aracú, and its poisonous sting produces the same pains. (Reichel-Dolmatoff 1971:30–31)[7]

The Tenetehara Indians of Brazil believe spiders to be immortal. During field trips in 1941–42 and 1945, anthropologists Charles Wagley and Eduardo Galvão collected myths and tales "related to us freely in the native language and translated into Portuguese for us either by the narrator himself or by an interpreter" and later published these texts "freely transcribed for their content alone . . . to remain faithful to detail and to episode but we have not attempted

[7]Anthropologist Gerardo Reichel-Dolmatoff also notes that: "The only mythical beings who have the characteristics of cultural heroes, even though very weakly developed, are the Daughter of the Sun and the Daughter of Aracú. There is no male personification in Desana mythology that represents a model or an example" (1971:31). Elsewhere, he summarizes "the symbolic value of nature," including: "*Spider*. The black, hairy kind, which inflicts a painful bite, licked the blood of the first birth of the Daughter of Aracú and ever since its bite produces strong pains. It symbolizes the vagina, in a sense of latent danger. The spiderweb is compared to the placenta" (ibid:99).

Javeline Vampire Bat
(Rice 1979:89).

to transmit any of the colorful Tenetehara narrative style" (1949:130). The following tale is one of a number which "generally point out a moral to the Tenetehara—even though that moral is not always readily apparent to the outsider" (ibid).

A young Tenetehara woman met a snake while she was walking through the forest. She returned frequently to the forest to make love to the snake. He built a house where they could lie down together. Finally she became pregnant. Since her family did not know about her lover, she did not tell them that she was pregnant. One day she gave birth to a son; he was already a youth when he was born and he went at once to the forest where he spent the day making arrows for his mother. At sundown each day he returned to his mother and reentered her womb. After several days, the girl's brother discovered her secret. He waited until after Snake's son had left for the day, to talk with his sister. After hearing her story, the brother advised her to let the youth leave her womb next day and, while he was away, to hide. Her brother helped her hide a great distance away. When Snake's son returned that evening to enter his mother's womb, she could not be found.
The snake son immediately went to talk with his snake grandfather who advised him to hunt for his father. Snake's son did not wish to do this, so that evening, transforming himself into a ray of lightning, he climbed into the sky carrying with him his bow and arrow. As soon as he arrived he broke the bow and arrow in pieces and they became stars in the sky. Everyone was asleep and no one except the spider saw this take place. For this reason, the spiders do not die nowadays when they get old but simply change their shells. Before this, men and animals also changed skin when they were old, but from this day until now they die when they are old.
(Wagley and Galvão 1949:149)

Although many cultures revere spider deities as culture heroes and helpers, few consider them primary creators. Nevertheless, spider figures may serve important functions during the early stages of creation. According to the Pima Indians of southern Arizona, Earth Doctor consciously crafted the world from dust he "took from his breast." He danced upon this "flat dust cake" to shape the mountains and mesas of this world.

Next Earth Doctor created some black insects, tcotcĭk tâtâny, which made black gum on the creosote bush. Then he made hiapitc, the termite, which worked upon and increased the small beginning until it grew to the proportions of our present earth. As he sang and danced the wonderful world developed, and then he made a sky to cover it, that was shaped like the round house of the Pimas. But the earth shook and stretched so that it was unfit for habitation. So Earth Doctor made a gray spider, which he commanded to spin a web around the unconnected edges of earth and sky. When this was done the earth grew firm and solid. (Russell 1975:207)[8]

The Sinkyone Indians of the Eel River in northwestern California believe that in the beginning Spider, a male deity, kept fire from their world. According to anthropologist A. L. Kroeber, Mrs. Tom Bell from Garberville told him that a small lizard child, "of a species living in rotten wood," cried so much it was thrown out of the house. Coyote heard its cries and understood them, thus discovering the existence of fire. In the "fragmentary mythic tale" Kroeber collected from George Burt of Dyerville in 1902, the people hear the inconsolable child (not specifically a lizard) crying "I fear the fire."

. . . At last they found out what it was crying for. It saw fire that no one else could see. Then the people discussed how they would get the fire from him who kept it. This was the Spider. He kept the fire inside of himself. This is what made his body large. Coyote told them how to obtain the fire. He gathered many kinds of animals and birds. They went to where Spider was. They made a large crowd. After it became night, the Spider took the fire out from his body. During the day he would put it back. The people played, doing whatever was most ridiculous. If they could cause the Spider to laugh, the fire would shoot out of his mouth, and they could get it. All tried, but could not make him laugh. At last the Skunk

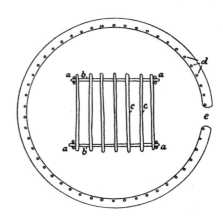

"Fig. 76. Diagram of house. Scale: 1 inch = 10 feet" (Russell 1975:154).[9]

[8]Anthropologist Frank Russell collected this version of the Pima creation myth (referred to as "smoke talk") during 1901–1902. According to his account, published as the *Twenty-Sixth Annual Report of the Bureau of American Ethnology to the Secretary of the Smithsonian Institution, 1904–1905:*

> The traditions of the Pimas are kept by those who show special aptitude in remembering them and who gradually become recognized as the tribal historians. To them the boys are regularly sent that they may listen for four nights to the narratives of how the world was made and peopled: whence the Pimas came and how they struggled with demons, monsters, and savage enemies. These tales are not usually told in the presence of women, and consequently they know only imperfect fragments of them. (1908, in Russell 1975:206)

[9]According to Russell: "The central supporting framework is usually entirely of cottonwood, though other timber is sometimes used. The lighter framework shown in plate XXV, *a,* is of willow, on which is laid the arrowwood, cattail reeds, wheat straw, cornstalks, or similar material that supports the outer layer of earth. The roof is supported by four crotched posts set in the ground 3 or 4 m. apart, with two heavy beams in the crotches. Lighter cross poles are set half a meter in the ground around the periphery of the circle, their tops are bent in to lap over the central roof poles, and horizontal stays are lashed to them with willow bark. The frame is then ready for a covering of brush or straw. Although the earth is heaped upon the roof to a depth of 15 to 20 cm. it does not render it entirely waterproof. When finished the ki is very strong and capable of withstanding heavy gales or supporting the weight of the people who may gather on the roof during festivals" (1975:154).

Framework of Pima house
(Russell 1975: pl. XXXV, a).

came dancing in with his tail stuck up. All laughed, and the Spider laughed too. Then fire shot out of his mouth. All the people were sitting about, holding pitch or tinder in order to catch the fire; but the eel-tail caught fire first. At once it was thrown out of doors. There stood swift runners to take it. The Buzzard flew with it, zigzag, over the dry grass. Wherever he went, he fired the grass, and the flames spread. Thus fire was obtained on earth. If it had not been for the child, there would have been no fire. (Kroeber 1919:347)

The Cherokee Indians, who once inhabited the entire Allegheny region before being removed to Oklahoma, tell an opposite story about the origin of fire through the industry and imagination of the female Water Spider. During 1887–90, anthropologist James Mooney collected myths from the few remaining "East Cherokee living upon the Qualla reservation in North Carolina and in various detached settlements between the reservation and the Tennessee line," as well as from some "in the Cherokee Nation in Indian Territory, chiefly from old men and women who had emigrated from what is now Tennessee and Georgia" (1900:12). Mooney claims that almost "every myth here given has been obtained directly from the Indians, and in nearly every case has been verified from several sources" (ibid:236).

In the beginning there was no fire, and the world was cold, until the Thunders (Ani'-Hyûñ'tĭkwălâ'skĭ), who lived up in Gălûñ'lătĭ, sent their lightning and put fire into the bottom of a hollow sycamore tree which grew on an island. The animals knew it was there, because they could see the smoke coming out at the top, but they could not get to it on account of the water, so they held a council to decide what to do. This was a long time ago. . . .

[Raven, Screech-owl, Hooting Owl, Horned Owl, the black racer snake, and the great blacksnake in turn volunteered to secure the fire, and each failed, scorching themselves to the blackness they now exhibit.]

Now they held another council, for still there was no fire, and the world was cold, but birds, snakes, and four-footed animals, all had some excuse for not going, because they were all afraid to venture near the burning sycamore, until at last Kănăne'skĭ Amai'yĕhĭ (the Water Spider) said she would go. This was not the water spider that looks like a mosquito, but the other one, with black downy hair

16   CHAPTER 1

and red stripes on her body. She can run on top of the water or dive to the bottom, so there would be no trouble to get over to the island, but the question was, How could she bring back the fire? "I'll manage that," said the Water Spider; so she spun a thread from her body and wove it into a *tusti* bowl, which she fastened on her back. Then she crossed over to the island and through the grass to where the fire was still burning. She put one little coal of fire into her bowl, and came back with it, and ever since we have had fire, and the Water Spider still keeps her tusti bowl. (Mooney 1900:240–42)

(Haeckel 1974:66)

Among the "charms" in a Cherokee shaman's notebook that anthropologists Jack Frederick Kilpatrick and Anna Gritts Kilpatrick translated and interpreted is the following "for a spider bite":

ghanani:sgi	saɨgho:nige	ghanani:sgi	uné:gv	ghaɪ	niga:da
spider	blue, it	spider	white	it now	a

Free Translation
Blue Spider! White Spider!
Now! Both of You!

Commentary
As Mooney and Olbrechts (1932, p. 19) have pointed out, "As a rule the spirit who has caused the disease is never prevailed upon to take the disease away; the office of another, rival, spirit is called upon to do this." The i:gawé:sdi [medical or magical text] for a spider bite that appears here cannot be offered in contradiction to this statement: it was not a spirit spider that created the condition that made therapeutic measures necessary, but a real arachnid.

As is the case of the conjuration for the centipede sting, this is a text that any layman might know. . . .

The curing procedure which incorporates the foregoing i:gawé:sdi may be effected by the victim of the spider bite himself, and it is similar to that for a centipede sting: the therapist recites the conjuration four times, and then expectorates upon and rubs with saliva the locus of the bite. Tobacco is not used, and the treatment is customarily administered only once.

The significance of the colors attributed to the spider spirits appears to be this: there is progression—in fact, quick transition—from blue, the symbol of trouble and illness, to white, the symbol of relief and well-being. (Kilpatrick and Kilpatrick 1970:96)

In many native and colonial folk medical traditions throughout North America spider webs are considered efficacious in stopping blood, a crucial skill which everyone, not just curing specialists, needed to know. Historian Virgil J. Vogel reports that spider webs were used to stop bleeding by "such widely scattered groups as the Mohegans, Kwakiutls, Mescalero Apaches, and white settlers from Tennessee to Oregon" (1970:224). In French Canada as elsewhere in the Catholic New World, priests serving parishes without doctors also acted as physicians, often to good effect, as in the case of "Father Pierre-Joseph Compain (1740–1806) [who] wrote down for the nuns of the Hôtel-Dieu of Quebec in 1799 his cure for cancer and a remedy for cankers in which spider webs played an important role" (Lacourcière 1976:206).

(Haeckel 1974:66)

★ Some of the old-time remedies are known by everybody [in French Louisiana] and widely praised. Among them are the following: spider webs to stop bleeding; baking soda and vinegar for a wasp bite; quid of tobacco for insect bites; sassafras tea used as a tonic; whiskey camphré for sprains and cricks in the neck; garlic for worms; dew water for skin; grease of toads, rattlesnakes, or alligators for rheumatic pains; a little bag made of red flannel and filled with camphor or asafetida to ward off disease; brass or copper rings and bracelets to relieve rheumatism; a key on a string around a person's neck to stop a nosebleed. (Brandon 1976:218)

Anthropologist J. Owen Dorsey translated the following "Spider-Lore" from the Teton Sioux manuscripts of George Bushotter and presented the material in a paper read before the Anthropological Society of Washington in November 1888:

The Tetons pray to gray spiders, and to those with yellow legs. When a person goes on a journey, and a spider passes, one does not kill it in silence. For should one let it go, or kill it without prayer, bad consequences must ensue. In the latter case, another spider would avenge the death of his relation. When the spider is met the person must say to it, "Ikto'mi Tun-kan'-shi-la, Wa'kin'-yan ni'-kte-pe lo', O Grandfather Spider, the Thunderers kill you!" The spider is crushed at once, and his spirit believes what has been told him. His spirit probably tells this to the other spiders, but they cannot harm the Thunderers. If one prays thus to a spider as he kills it, he will never be bitten by other spiders.

Ikto or Iktomi (in Teton) and Unktomi (in Santee) are the names now given to the spider by the Dakotas, but the name belonged to a mythical hero, the Ictinike of the Omahas and Ponkas, and the Ictcinke of the Iowas and Otos. Ikto, say the Tetons, was the first being who attained maturity in this world. He is more cunning than human beings. He named all people and animals, and he was the first to use human speech. Some call him the "Mocker" or "Monkey" (with which compare an African belief about monkeys having the gift of human speech). If we see any peculiar animals at any place, we know that Ikto made them so. All the animals are his kindred, and they are obliged to act just as he commanded them at the beginning. Though Ikto was very cunning, he was sometimes deceived by other beings. One day he caught the Rabbit, and the latter was about to fare hard, when a thought occurred to him. He persuaded Ikto to release him on condition that he taught his captor one of his magic arts. Said he, "Elder brother, if you wish snow to fall at any time, take some hair such as this (pulling out some rabbit fur), and blow it in all directions, and there will be a blizzard." The Rabbit made a deep snow in this manner, though the leaves were still green. This surprised Ikto, who thought that he had learned a wonderful accomplishment. But the foolish fellow did not know that rabbit fur was necessary, and when he tried to make snow by blowing his own hair, he was disappointed. (Dorsey 1889:134–35)

Among the Kiowa of the southern Great Plains, Spider Woman is a culture hero who continues to help her people. Folklorist Elsie Clews Parsons collected tales "in November-December, 1927, from Kiowa met haphazardly in Oklahoma over the sixty miles or so from Anadarko to Hobart." Fifty-five-year-old Kiabǫ (Rescued) lived at Red Stone, seven miles south-west of Anadarko. He gave her the name Spider Old Woman, and his family also called her that.

It rained for ten days and the water covered all the land. It killed all the people. There was a woman who had for her dâ'kya [spirit] the spider. After the water covered the land, she turned into a spider. She floated about until the water dried up. Then she became a woman again. After the water soaked in, soft, soggy places were left. Spider Old Woman (Konatąsǫhi) could stay on top of them. So she is safe on water and land and in the air.

"As you will be," smiled Kiabǫ, "when you travel." (Parsons 1929:9)[10]

Myths and tales from other traditions also portray spiders who help imperiled protagonists escape—either up from beneath or down from on high. The classical myth of Ariadne, daughter of King Minos of Crete, and the Athenian hero Theseus exemplifies the spinster whose thread helps the hero emerge from the depths. According to Greek accounts, King Minos prayed for Poseidon to send him a sacrificial bull from the sea and then kept it for himself. The enraged god of the sea caused Minos' wife Pasiphae to fall in love with the bull, with whom she mated after climbing into a hollow likeness of a cow constructed by Daedalus. She later gave birth to the Minotaur, a monster with a man's body and a bull's head. In his *Metamorphoses,* Roman poet Ovid gives an abbreviated version of the story of Theseus' encounter with the Minotaur in the labyrinth on Crete and his subsequent abduction and abandonment of Ariadne.

> King Minos, landing on the Cretan shore,
> Discharged his vows to Jove with bulls fivescore.
> The palace blazed with trophies; but within
> Was scandal dark and hideous fruit of sin,
> The household shame, full-grown and foul to see,
> The illicit half-and-half monstrosity.
> To rid his roof of such a stain, the king
> Commissioned Daedalus to house the thing;
> And he, the world-famed architect, designed
> A multiplex of courts and cloisters blind,
> Where misdirections led, in mazes long,
> The cheated eye circuitously wrong.
> In Phrygian fields Maeander, winding through,
> Plays fast and loose, and wanders fro and to;
> And runs to meet himself, and with a glance
> Up river views his waters in advance;
> And now drives seaward his capricious course,
> Now points his wayward waters to their source:
> So endless error filled the winding ways,
> And he that made could scarcely thread the maze.
> In this enclosure Minos kept confined
> The hybrid blend of man and bull combined;
> And each nine years the lots were drawn to feed
> With blood of Attic youth the monster's greed.

Minotaur
(Lehner 1969: 135, fig. 799).

[10]Grandmother Spider and various spider images appear throughout N. Scott Momaday's aesthetic recreation of the Kiowas' mythology, history and imagination in *The Way to Rainy Mountain* (1969).

The third time brought him death, when through the aid
Which Ariadne gave, though but a maid,
The thread rewound disclosed the door again,
Which those who sought before had sought in vain;
And Theseus set his sails, and with him bore
The Cretan royal maid to Naxos' shore;
But when love cooled, he steeled his heart to fly,
Leaving his comrade there, to weep and sigh.
But Bacchus soon arrived to bring relief:
He took her in his arms, and hushed her grief;
And then, to make her fame and beauty shine
For ever, with a star to be her sign,
He sent her crown aloft: the jewels grew
To burning fires, and sparkled as they flew;
And now, a crown of stars, their place they take
'Twixt him that kneels, and him that holds the snake.

—*Metamorphoses*, Book VIII, lines 156–84;
trans. Watts 1980:169–70.[11]

The Coeur d'Alene Indians of northern Idaho recount a tale, in which Spider people help the hero down from on high, with widespread variations in the greater northwest. Anthropologist James A. Teit conducted research on the interior Salish tribes for over ten years during the late nineteenth and early twentieth centuries. When anthropologist Gladys Reichard arrived in 1929, little Coeur d'Alene culture remained except "the language which survived among the old people and was preserved in the mythology which also has many evidences of white influence." Reichard worked with Dorothy Nicodemus, wife of Teit's chief informant. Their daughter-in-law, Mrs. Julia Antelope Nicodemus, acted as translator and interpreter. Commenting on Coyote's Son's spider-like descent in the following tale from Teit's collection, Reichard notes: "There is no indication of a taboo in this story. It is merely the way the spiders move, as Julia says, 'Like an elevator,' making four regular stops" (Reichard 1947:2,80).

Jealous of his son Tô'rtôrsEmstEm, Coyote "induced" him to climb a tall tree to obtain tail-feathers from young eagles in a nest there. High in the tree, the son looked down to see his father blinking his eyes. Coyote claimed it was because dust might get into them, but the tree grew with each blink until it reached the sky:

[11]For a discussion of the various stories about Ariadne, see Morford and Lenardon 1977: 387–90. Also see Otto 1965:181–88. In *The Glory of Hera: Greek Mythology and the Greek Family*, psychologist Philip E. Slater sees Theseus' treatment of Ariadne as another example of the Greeks' pervasive gynephobia: "Theseus must flee Ariadne because she is tainted with maternal attributes: she knows the secret of the Labyrinth. Furthermore, her feeling for Theseus is so intense that she is willing to betray her father and sacrifice the life of her brother (the Minotaur); such depth of feminine passion had little appeal for the Greek male. Jason deserts Medea who makes a similar sacrifice, Minos himself kills Scylla for her love-inspired parricide, and Amphitryon similarly rewards Comaetho . . ." (1968:392). For a Jungian, feminist interpretation of "Ariadne, Mistress of the Labyrinth," see Downing 1980.

. . . Here Tô'rtôrsEmstEm found himself in a new country. He travelled about, and at last came to a lodge where he heard talking. There were two Spider people inside who were quarrelling about Indian-hemp. One said it grew one way, and the other said it grew another way. One said it belonged to him, and the other said it belonged to him. He addressed them, saying, "Grandchildren, I want you to take me back to my country." They paid no attention. He spoke again, and offered them some beads, but they paid no heed. Then he offered them necklaces, but still they paid no heed. He thought to himself, "They are only interested in Indian-hemp." Then he offered them each two fathoms of Indian-hemp. At once they ceased their quarrelling and became attentive. They promised to let him down to his country by a rope. They put him into a basket, to which they fastened the end of the rope. They said, "You will stop four times on your way down. You must not rise, but turn over. Then the basket will proceed. When the basket stops the fourth time, you will be on the earth; and when you hear the grass, you will know that you are in your own country. Then step out of the basket and tug the rope, and we will pull it up." He did as directed, and they pulled it up. Tô'rtôrsEmstEm went home, found his father, and killed him. (Teit 1917:120–21)

Spiders and their webs are also depicted as relatively benevolent signs in many popular beliefs. Mexican Americans interviewed at Austin, Texas, in 1948 and 1949 believed that six- or eight-legged spiders foretold good news and good luck, those with five or seven legs bad news and bad luck (Pérez 1951:117). Folklorist J. Frank Dobie reports that, along the Texas-Mexican border, spider webs were thought to signal rain and that "in the mesquite country, at times, the spaces between bushes are all interlaced with them so thick that they appear like stringy clouds" (1923:94–95).[12]

★ It is good luck for a spider to spin its web down in front of you. It is bad luck to kill a spider. (Coffin and Cohen 1966:135–36)[13]

★ If you find your initials in spider webs near the door of a new home, it is a sign that you will be lucky as long as you live there. (Randolph 1947:75)[14]

[12]Dobie notes that: "In Letter LXV of Gilbert White's *Natural History of Selborne* (Bohn's Library) there is a vivid description of the phenomenon together with some accounts of folk superstitions attached thereto" (1923:95).

[13]These Anglo-American beliefs were "collected by Lelah Allison 'in the Wabash region in southeastern Illinois,' a region settled by the English and former residents of southern states who were of English descent," and published originally in the *Journal of American Folklore*, 1950, pp. 318–23.

[14]Randolph also notes that "very few of the mountain people would intentionally kill a spider, since such an act is supposed to bring misfortune in its wake" (1947:259). In mountain Virginia, the so-called "writing spider has also been used as a means of prognostication, particularly . . . seeking the name or initials of a future mate. Females could watch the spider web for any possible evidence of letters; this was done most often after a rain or in the early morning after a heavy dew" (Elmer L. Smith, "Communicating with Critters," *Folklore and Folklife in Virginia*, vol. 1, 1979, p. 56).

Flat stamp from the State of Mexico depicting a spider (Enciso 1953:63, fig. V).

★ North American Chippewa Indians hang spiderwebs on the hoop of infants' cradleboards "to catch the harm in the air." (Leach 1972:1074)

The Aztecs viewed spiders as malevolent. Jungian analyst Erich Neumann cites the Codex Borgia as his source for the observation that: "The souls of women who, having died in childbirth, become demons combining death and birth also belong to the symbolism of the west. As spiders, hostile particularly to men, they dangle from the heavens; and as the demonic powers of primordial darkness, they escort the sun down from the zenith to its place of death in the west" (1963:184). This belief is amplified in art historian Ferdinand Anton's *Woman in Pre-Columbian America:*

The woman who died in childbirth deserved the same honours as the warrior fallen in battle. An equal heaven awaited them, an equally honourable task. The fallen warriors accompanied the sun god Tonatiuh from the house of the god in the eastern sky to the zenith, with songs and dances, and then, disguised as precious birds and butterflies, fluttered down to the earth to refresh themselves with honey and the juice of blossoms; similarly the souls of the "warriors in female shape" *(mociuaquetzque),* the women who died in childbirth, met the sun in the zenith and accompanied it to its setting in the western sky. The living, however, were afraid of them, because they were no friendly ghosts, like the male warriors, but night ghosts *(tzitzimime)* which lay in wait at crossroads, wished epilepsy on children and incited men to lewdness. (1973:19)[15]

Contemporary psychoanalysts also interpret the spider as a basically malevolent symbol when it appears in myths, tales, dreams, beliefs and behaviors. For example, in a 1922 paper on "The Spider as a Dream Symbol" (1927: 326–32), psychoanalyst Karl Abraham demonstrated how, in three dreams of a male patient, the spider represented the wicked mother, its web her pubic hair and the single hanging thread the male organ attributed to her. In a postscript, he also cited work by Viennese psychoanalyst Nunberg, who emphasized a spider's killing its victim by blood-sucking—and hence the evil mother's capacity to castrate and kill "during incestuous intercourse"! According to Abraham, "Prof. Freud" also drew his attention to "a remarkable biological fact," namely, the female spider's superiority in copulation and the real dangers to the male's survival of it.

In *Childhood and Folklore: A Psychoanalytic Study of Apache Personality,* L. Bryce Boyer claims that Apaches' spider lore also reflects such "ambivalence

Ancient Mexican flat stamp depicting a spider. From Veracruz. (Enciso 1953:63, fig. 11)

[15]According to George C. Vaillant: "The east was the home of warriors, whose death in battle or sacrifice nourished the sun, and the west the home of women who died in childbirth, thus sacrificing themselves in the bearing of potential warriors" (1962:179). For another version see Miguel León-Portilla (1963:126). Also see book VI, chap. 20, of the fifteenth-century *Florentine Codex Book VI,* Arthur J. O. Anderson and Charles E. Dibble, eds. (Santa Fe, New Mexico: School of American Research and Salt Lake City: University of Utah Press, 1950), pp. 161–65, partially reprinted as "The Mociuaquetzque: Aztec Goddess," in *Lady-Unique-Inclination-of-the-Night,* Cycle 3, Autumn 1978, pp. 62–64.

toward the mother," and "frequently the spider represents the castrating or cannibalistic vagina, and its web is seen as a trap." However, Boyer further states that in some instances the strand of the web "seems to denote the umbilical cord, the sustaining symbol of rebirth" (1979:108). This positive dimension to the otherwise negative interpretation of the spider as symbol is generally uncharacteristic of more orthodox Freudian analysts, though not of Jungian ones, who tend to develop both the positive and negative aspects of symbols, paying particular attention to their unclear, undeveloped or "shadow" dimensions (e.g., the positive, "light" aspects of an apparently negative or "dark" symbol, and vice versa).

This analytic stance may be illustrated by accounts of Hopi Indian beliefs about their female spider deity. Folklorist Elsie Clews Parsons summarizes the positive aspect in her two-volume study of Pueblo Indian religion.

Sun and spider symbols on prehistoric Hopi pottery. "In Hopi mythology the spider and the sun are associated, the former being the symbol of an earth goddess." (Fewkes 1973:150; plate 87c)

Hopi. "Spider is our mother," says the Antelope chief of Shipaulovi; "she is the mother of all." . . . She has her own stone image (Walpi) and her own shrine, where the Antelope society chief asks her to keep away storm and sickness and sand rain (Mishonognovi). She is the patroness of the Spider clan and Blue Flute society of Oraibi. . . . When the Hopi girl, Cactus Flower, is being tested by the Kachina, one of the tests is not to weep at a song they sing about her unhappy experience in leaving home. She does weep, but Spider Grandmother is sitting on her cheek in her familiar role of ear prompter or monitor, and this time swallows the tears as they fall. (1939:192–93)[16]

Hopi Indian Don Talayesva's autobiography, *Sun Chief,* tells of a powerful "negative" encounter:

When I was four or five I was captured by the Spider Woman and nearly lost my life. One morning in May as I played in the plaza in my shirt my father said that he was going to his field. I wanted to go. But as he filled his water jar he said, "You had better stay here, my jar does not hold enough for us both." I began to cry. As he started down the south side of the mesa I followed along the narrow path between two great stones and came to the bottom of the foothill near the Spider Woman's shrine. My father had disappeared among the rocks. I happened to look to my left at a rock by the shrine where some clay dishes had been placed as offerings to the Spider Woman. There sat the old woman herself, leaning forward and resting her chin in her hands. Beside her was a square hole in the ground. She

[16]Parsons cites the following sources, in order: Alexander M. Stephen, *Hopi Journal,* Columbia University Contributions to Anthropology, vol. 23 (New York, 1936), pp. 744–45; G. A. Dorsey and H. R. Voth, *The Mishongnovi Ceremonies of the Snake and Antelope Fraternities,* Field Columbian Museum Pub. 66, Anthropological Series, vol. 3, no. 3 (Chicago, 1902), p. 205; H. R. Voth, *The Oraibi Summer Snake Ceremony,* Field Columbian Museum Pub. 83, Anthropological Series, vol. 3, no. 4 (Chicago, 1903), p. 350, n.2. For other versions of Spider Woman stories and beliefs, see, e.g.: Frank Waters, *Book of the Hopi* (New York: Viking Press, 1963); and G. M. Mullett, selector and interpreter, *Legends of the Hopi Indians: Spider Woman Stories* (1979). Mullett worked with Jesse Walter Fewkes at the Smithsonian from 1910 to 1928. The stories have been edited by her daughter, and there is a valuable foreword by anthropologist Fred Eggan.

said, "You are here at the right time. I have been waiting for you. Come into my house with me." I had heard enough about the Spider Woman to know that no ordinary person ever sits by the shrine. I stood helpless, staring at her. "Come into my house," she repeated. "You have been walking on my trail, and now I have a right to you as my grandson." (Simmons 1942:47–48)[17]

In *The Great Mother: An Analysis of the Archetype,* Jungian theorist Erich Neumann claims such encounters are crucial to the individual's development of consciousness:

On the other hand, the Great Mother in her function of fixation and not releasing what aspires toward independence and freedom is dangerous. This situation constellates essential phases in the history of consciousness and its conflict with the Archetypal Feminine. To this context belongs a symbol that plays an important role in myth and fairy tale, namely, captivity. This term indicates that the individual who is no longer in the original and natural situation of childlike containment experiences the attitude of the Feminine as restricting and hostile. Moreover, the function of ensnaring implies an aggressive tendency, which, like the symbolism of captivity, belongs to the witch character of the negative mother. Net and noose, spider, and the octopus with its ensnaring arms are here the appropriate symbols. The victims of this constellation have always acquired some element of independence, which is endangered; to them containment in the Great Mother is no longer a self-evident situation; rather, they have already become "strugglers." (1963:65–66)

Whether or not interpretations such as Neumann's pertain equally to the "contemporary" psychology of men and of women is certainly moot. However, his characterization of the "negative mother" who ensnares an individual like the young Talayesva may be compared with Jungian analyst Marie-Louise von Franz's interpretation of an Eskimo myth involving a spider woman and a female protagonist from a woman's perspective. In her lectures on "Problems of the Feminine in Fairytales," von Franz presents a synopsis of the origin myth from one of Knud Rasmussen's ethnological reports, which she does not identify. In the following synopsis I have paraphrased and abbreviated her version, preserving her wording only in those sections indicated by quotation marks:

A girl refuses to marry, exasperating her parents. One day while the girl was out walking, "suddenly a head jumped out of the earth among the hills, a head without a body, but the face was that of a very handsome man." She took the head home with her and was happy with it until her father discovered

[17]Don Talayesva was sick for four days. His grandfather was unable to cure him, so his parents carried him to see a specialist in Shongopavi. The man told his father to make a prayer feather for Spider Woman, which he had neglected to do. According to Talayesva's recollection: "As my father returned from the shrine walking along the corn-meal path, I heard him talking to my spirit. He said, 'Now, my son, I am taking you back home. Don't ever follow me off the mesa, or some bad spirit will get you and take you away'" (Simmons 1942:50). Thereafter, the child obeyed, and stayed away from the shrine as well.

his son-in-law's identity. Enraged, "he took a meat skewer and thrust it through the young man's eye and then threw the head out into the rubbish heap, crying, 'I have no use for a son without a body who could not hunt for us when we are old!' " The head rolled away and into the sea, leaving a bloody track which the girl followed upon her return. She was unable to enter the sea, however, until she had secured a white lemming which magically parted the waters.

The one-eyed head refused to recognize her. "The girl was very much depressed and without knowing what she was doing, she ran three times round the house in the same direction as the sun circles round in the heavens. Then she saw two ways—one led straight ahead and to the earth, and the second went up to heaven." She chose the latter, and the head called out his regretful warnings too late. After entering the sky through a hole, she sat dejectedly beside a lake until startled by a boatman with kayak, oars and harpoon of copper. The man sang a song and magically undressed and abducted her.

In the man's dreary big house, a small woman who "wore extraordinary clothes made out of the gut of a bearded seal" warned her to escape and led the hapless girl to her own house, where she lived with a little girl. Offering aid, "she gave her a small cask filled with water in which were four small pieces of whaleskin [and] . . . told her that when the strange man came she should hide at the entrance to the house and throw the pieces of whaleskin in his face, for the woman had sung a magic song over her present, so as to make it strong." The man returned and flew toward the woman's house. The girl did as instructed, and the man fell out of the air, powerless.

"Then the three women went into his house, which was the house of the moon spirit, and it was the Man in the Moon himself . . . [who] is incalculable and can become dangerous; he takes but he also gives, and man must sacrifice to him in order to share in the things over which he rules." In one corner of the house was a huge water barrel filled with whales, walruses and seals. The three women pushed aside a whale's shoulder blade in the middle of the floor and were able to look down on the earth and the people entreating the new moon for a good catch. The girl became homesick, and the sympathetic old woman and little girl helped her plait a rope of animal sinews. The old woman then told her she must shut her eyes on the way down and open them the moment she touched the earth.

"The young girl fastened the end of the rope tight in the heavens and took the great ball of plaited sinews and began to let herself down. She thought it would be a very long way, but she felt the ground beneath her feet sooner than she had expected. It happened so quickly that she didn't open her eyes quickly enough, and she was changed into a spider. From her come all the spiders of the world, all come from the girl who let herself down from heaven to the earth by a rope of plaited sinews." (von Franz 1972:95–100)

Von Franz views the Eskimo girl's encounter with the Man in the Moon as a confrontation with her animus, her "masculine," which in its negative forms can, she maintains, separate a woman from life, whether emotionally, intellectually or spiritually. In looking down on the earth from above, von Franz claims, the girl "is a visionary and is in danger of becoming a clairvoyant with a tinge of madness, and it is because of this danger that her female in-

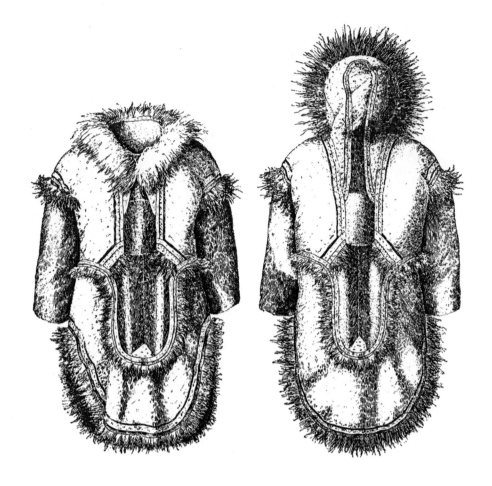

"Unusually handsome Point Barrow (Alaska) Eskimo woman's dress made of shanks and bellies of reindeer pieced together to form light and dark stripes. It is hemmed with white mountain sheep, fawnskin and red worsted (trade cloth), and fringed with wolfskin" (Naylor 1975:99, figs. B, C).

stinct, the spider woman, arouses in her the wish to return to earth." In completing her interpretation, however, von Franz perhaps unconsciously denigrates both the girl's transformation and, by implication, her tutelary deity-"instinct":

The spider woman provides the other with a rope with which she can get to earth again. (Most women are prone from time to time to muse about their own lives and to lose themselves in a vapoury whirl of speculation, but if one can touch reality one gains a standpoint outside of these fantasies. One way of doing this is to write down what one is musing about, and by giving it expression one is no longer identical with it. This has the effect of reducing such animus-fed fantasies and no longer being at their mercy. When one is confronted with one's own thoughts in black and white, one can discover how much is mere opinion and how much is valid; to do this means an inner strengthening.) The woman is told that when she gets to earth she must open her eyes quickly—that is, she must make a supreme effort to be aware and conscious of her actual state—but tragically she fails to do this. So she turns into a spider. She becomes a spinster, having had an inner religious experience but being unable to make this experience fruitful for her tribe and for herself. (von Franz 1973:136)[18]

In characterizing the Eskimo girl turned spider as a barren spinster, von Franz calls upon a commonly held definition of the noun, which has many negative connotations for contemporary women. The primary definition of the term, according to the *Oxford English Dictionary,* is "a woman (or, rarely, a man) who spins, *esp.* one who practices spinning as a regular occupation." However, the *Webster's New World Dictionary of the American Language* drops the reference to men and gives as the first definition "a woman who spins thread or yarn."[19] Nevertheless, it is the second definition in both dictionaries which is more usual and more value-laden:

2. Appended to names of women, originally in order to denote their occupation, but subsequently (from the 17th century) as the proper legal designation of one still unmarried; b. a woman still unmarried; esp. one beyond the usual age for marriage, an old maid. *(OED)*

2. an unmarried woman; especially, an elderly woman who has never married; old maid. *(New World)*

Sociolinguist Robin Lakoff amplifies these connotations in *Language and Woman's Place:*

Also relevant here are the connotations (as opposed to the denotative meanings) of the words *spinster* and *bachelor.* Denotatively, these are . . . parallel to "cow" versus "bull": one is masculine, the other feminine, and both mean "one who is not married." But there the resemblance ends. *Bachelor* is at least a neutral term, often used as a compliment. *Spinster* normally seems to be used pejoratively, with connotations of prissiness, fussiness, and so on. . . . A man may be considered a bachelor as soon as he reaches marriageable age: to be a bachelor implies that one has the choice of marrying or not, and this is what makes the idea of a bachelor existence attractive, in the popular literature. He has been pursued and has successfully eluded his pursuers. But a spinster is one who has not been pursued, or at least not seriously. She is old unwanted goods. . . . The metaphorical connotations of "bachelor" generally suggest sexual freedom; of "spinster," puritanism or celibacy. (1975:32–33; also see Key 1975:39–44; Schulz 1975; Boulding 1976:649; Miller and Swift 1976:89; Foote 1977; Stannard 1977; McConnell-Ginet 1980:5–7)

[18]In this discussion, von Franz identifies the source of her synopsis as Knud Rasmussen, *Die Gabe des Adlers,* Frankfort, n.d. given (1973:107).

[19]Texas lawyer Hermes Nye identifies a more masculine spinner in the contemporary "folksay of the drag strip," where *"knock-offs* or *spinners* are wheel-caps designed for quick, easy changes." Although sported by various street and custom rods and sports cars, they are "purely a status symbol" in drag racing, which has no pit stops ("T-Bones and Cheater Slicks: The Folksay of the Drag Strip," in Wilson M. Hudson, ed., *Tire Shrinker to Dragster,* Publications of the Texas Folklore Society No. 34 [Austin: Encino Press, 1968], p. 16).

The Lovely Spinner

(Bowles & Carver 1970:88)

"The Witch," by Hans Weiditz, from Petraca's *Von der Artzney Beider Glück* (1532) (Lehner 1969:102, fig. 558). This is identified as Holbein's "The Old Maid Witch" in Haining 1975:63, fig. 90.

Historically, in European and European-derived American traditions, the spinster is also associated with witchcraft as well as womanhood. Marie-Louise von Franz surveys these associations, interpreting the spinster's spindle as:

. . . a symbol of femininity. In medieval Germany one speaks of "spindle kinship," just as one speaks of the "distaff side of the family" in referring to relations on the mother's side. It was the sign of St. Gertrude in the Middle Ages, who took most of the qualities of the pre-Christian mother-goddesses such as Freja Hulda, Perchta, and others. The spindle is also the symbol of the wise old woman and of witches. Flax was also regarded as having to do with feminine activities. In many countries women used to expose their genitals to the growing flax and say, "Please grow as high as my genitals are now." It was thought the flax would grow better for that. In many countries flax is planted by the women, for it is linked up with their lives. Therefore, sowing of the flax and spinning and weaving are the essence of feminine life with its fertility and sexual implications. (1972:38; also see Garbáty 1968)[20]

[20]In a study of South American spindle whorls, Johannes Wilbert contends that the spindle symbolizes the cycle of life and death, and "when full, the spindle resembled a mandorla, the symbol of dualism and inversion" *(The Thread of Life,* Studies in Pre-Columbian Art and Archaeology, No. 12 [Washington, D.C.: Dumbarton Oaks, 1974], pp. 7, 30–32). A mandorla, "the *vesica piscis,* or *ichthus,* the almond-shaped aureole, the 'mystical almond' which depicts divinity; holiness; the sacred; virginity; the vulva, . . . also denotes an opening or gateway and the two sides represent the opposite poles and all duality" (J. C. Cooper, *An Illustrated Encyclopaedia of Traditional Symbols* [London: Thames and Hudson, 1978], pp. 103–104).

SPINDLE, SHUTTLE, AND NEEDLE

ONCE upon a time there lived a girl who lost her father and mother when she was quite a tiny child. Her godmother lived all alone in a little cottage at the far end of the village, and there she earned her living by spinning, weaving, and sewing. The old woman took the little orphan home with her and brought her up in good, pious, industrious habits.

When the girl was fifteen years old, her godmother fell ill, and, calling the child to her bedside, she said: 'My dear daughter, I feel that my end is near. I leave you my cottage, which will, at least, shelter you, and also my spindle, my weaver's shuttle, and my needle, with which to earn your bread.'

Then she laid her hands on the girl's head, blessed her, and added: 'Mind and be good, and then all will go well with you.' With that she closed her eyes for the last time, and when she was carried to her grave the girl walked behind her coffin weeping bitterly, and paid her all the last honours.

After this the girl lived all alone in the little cottage. She worked hard, spinning, weaving, and sewing, and her old godmother's blessing seemed to prosper all she did. The flax seemed to spread and increase; and when she wove a carpet or a piece of linen, or made a shirt, she was sure to find a customer who paid her well, so that not only did she feel no want herself, but she was able to help those who did.

Now, it happened that about this time the King's son was making a tour through the entire country to look out for a bride. He could not marry a poor woman, and he did not wish for a rich one.

'She shall be my wife,' said he, 'who is at once the poorest and the richest.'

When he reached the village where the girl lived, he inquired

who was the richest and who the poorest woman in it. The richest was named first; the poorest, he was told, was a young girl who lived alone in a little cottage at the far end of the village.

The rich girl sat at her door dressed out in all her best clothes, and when the King's son came near she got up, went to meet him, and made him a low curtsey. He looked well at her, said nothing, but rode on further.

When he reached the poor girl's house he did not find her at her door, for she was at work in her room. The Prince reined in his horse, looked in at the window through which the sun was shining brightly, and saw the girl sitting at her wheel busily spinning away.

She looked up, and when she saw the King's son gazing in at her, she blushed red all over, cast down her eyes and span on. Whether the thread was quite as even as usual I really cannot say, but she went on spinning till the King's son had ridden off. Then she stepped to the window and opened the lattice, saying, 'The room is so hot,' but she looked after him as long as she could see the white plumes in his hat.

Then she sat down to her work once more and span on, and as she did so an old saying which she had often heard her godmother repeat whilst at work, came into her head, and she began to sing:

> 'Spindle, spindle, go and see,
> If my love will come to me.'

Lo, and behold! the spindle leapt from her hand and rushed out of the room, and when she had sufficiently recovered from her surprise to look after it she saw it dancing merrily through the fields, dragging a long golden thread after it, and soon it was lost to sight.

The girl, having lost her spindle, took up the shuttle and, seating herself at her loom, began to weave. Meantime the spindle danced on and on, and just as it had come to the end of the golden thread, it reached the King's son.

'What do I see?' he cried; 'this spindle seems to wish to point out the way to me.' So he turned his horse's head and rode back beside the golden thread.

Meantime the girl sat weaving, and sang:

> 'Shuttle, weave both web and woof,
> Bring my love beneath my roof.'

The positive association of spinning and womanhood is illustrated in several magic tales from the well-known collection by the Brothers Grimm. The first volume of Jacob (1785–1863) and Wilhelm (1786–1859) Grimm's *Kinder- und Haus-Märchen* ("Children's and Household Tales") was published in Berlin in 1812. A second volume appeared in 1815 and a third in 1822. Later editions included additional variants and notes on the 210 narratives, most of which the two brothers collected from friends, neighbors and servants in their native Hesse-Cassel.

Grimm's "Spindle, Shuttle, and Needle" (no. 188), e.g., has Irish, German, Hungarian, and Russian variants, according to Antti Aarne and Stith Thompson's index, *The Types of the Folktale* (1973), where it is classified as tale type number 585, a narrative involving magic objects. The text above and on next page is reproduced from Andrew Lang's *The Green Fairy Book,* published in London ca. 1892 (1965:286–89). The illustration is by H. J. Ford.

The shuttle instantly escaped from her hand, and with one bound was out at the door. On the threshold it began weaving the loveliest carpet that was ever seen. Roses and lilies bloomed on

both sides, and in the centre a thicket seemed to grow with rabbits and hares running through it, stags and fawns peeping through the branches, whilst on the topmost boughs sat birds of brilliant plumage and so life-like one almost expected to hear them sing. The shuttle

flew from side to side and the carpet seemed almost to grow of itself.

As the shuttle had run away the girl sat down to sew. She took her needle and sang:

> ' Needle, needle, stitch away,
> Make my chamber bright and gay,'

and the needle promptly slipped from her fingers and flew about the room like lightning. You would have thought invisible spirits were at work, for in next to no time the table and benches were covered with green cloth, the chairs with velvet, and elegant silk curtains hung before the windows. The needle had barely put in its last stitch when the girl, glancing at the window, spied the white plumed hat of the King's son who was being led back by the spindle with the golden thread.

He dismounted and walked over the carpet into the house, and when he entered the room there stood the girl blushing like any rose. ' You are the poorest and yet the richest,' said he: ' come with me, you shall be my bride.'

She said nothing, but she held out her hand. Then he kissed her, and led her out, lifted her on his horse and took her to his royal palace, where the wedding was celebrated with great rejoicings.

The spindle, the shuttle, and the needle were carefully placed in the treasury, and were always held in the very highest honour.

Grimm.

The highly valued skills of stitchery, spinning and weaving were not necessarily easily mastered by all women. Considerable tensions must have been generated—doubts about one's womanly competence, anger at difficult or dreary tasks, fear of failure or of not winning a mate. Both Aarne-Thompson tale type number 500, "The Name of the Helper (Titeliture, Rumpelstilzchen [below], Tom-Tit-Tot)," and type number 501, "The Three Old Women Helpers," suggest that this anxiety was expressed in narratives, which were told by and to both women and men. In such tales, a girl is given an impossible spinning assignment. In type 501, three old women, deformed by too much spinning, help her and ask to be repaid with an invitation to the wedding. When they appear, the prince is so disgusted by their deformity that he vows never to let his wife spin (Thompson 1973:167–69; also see Thompson 1946:47–49).

"So the poor miller's daughter sat down, and didn't know what in the world she was to do. She hadn't the least idea of how to spin straw into gold, and became at last so miserable that she began to cry. Suddenly the door opened, and in stepped a tiny little man and said: 'Good-evening, Miss Miller-maid; why are you crying so bitterly?' 'Oh!' answered the girl, 'I have to spin straw into gold, and haven't a notion of how it's done.' 'What will you give me if I spin it for you?' asked the manikin."

—Illustration for "Rumpelstiltzkin," Grimm's no. 55, Aarne-Thompson tale type no. 500, in Andrew Lang, ed., *The Blue Fairy Book,* published in London, ca. 1889 (1965:97; also see Opie 1974:195–98).

Legends collected in the New World also reflect such fears. Folklorist Frank C. Brown collected a "ghost story" (apparently a family legend) from Mrs. Gertrude Allen Vaught of Alexander County, North Carolina, in 1922–23:

My great-great-grandfather Mays took my grandmother to an old home known as the "Flowers House" near York Institute, where people had been hearing a wheel spinning. He told it to spin and it began. Grandmother said it sounded exactly like the noise made by a spinning wheel. I have often heard her tell this story and of how frightened she was at the time. (White 1952:678)

Journalist Charles M. Skinner popularized numerous legends from nineteenth-century America (for an assessment see Dorson 1971). In the second volume of his *Myths and Legends of Our Own Land,* he recounts the stories told by "a pious old woman" lodger in the home of one Marie Louise Thebault, "more usually called Kennette," whom "old [Detroit] residents remembered when she was one of the quaintest figures and most assertive spirits in the town, for until a few years before her death [in 1868] she was rude of speech, untidy in appearance, loved nothing or respected nothing unless it might be her violin and her money, and lived alone in a little old house on the river-road to Springwells." An hermetic, miserly sort, Kennette's "love of gain, not of company, induced her to lease one of her rooms":

When the pious [lodger] tried to win her to the church it angered her, and then, too, she had a way of telling ghost stories that Kennette laughed at. One of these narratives that she would dwell on with especial self-conviction was that of Lieutenant Muir, who had left his mistress, when she said No to his pleadings, supposing that she spoke the truth, whereas she was merely trying to be coquettish. He fell in an attack on the Americans that night, and came back, bleeding, to the girl who had made him throw his life away; he pressed her hand, leaving the mark of skeleton fingers there, so that she always kept it gloved afterward. Then there was the tale of the two men of Detroit who were crushed by a falling tree: the married one, who was not fatally hurt, begged his mate to call his wife, as soon as his soul was free, and the woman, hearing the mournful voice at her door, as the spirit passed on its way to space, ran out and rescued her husband from his plight. She told, too, of the *feu follet,* or will-o'-the-wisp, that led a girl on Grosse Isle to the swamp where her lover was engulfed in mire and enabled her to rescue him. There was Grandmere Duchene, likewise, who worked at her spinning-wheel for many a night after death, striking fear to her son's heart, by its droning, because he had not bought the fifty masses for the repose of her soul, but when he had fulfilled the promise she came no more. (Skinner 1896:143–44)

A familiar magic tale depicts spinning as dangerous to young women. *"La Belle au bois dormant"* ("The Sleeping Beauty in the Wood") was the first tale published in Charles Perrault's 1697 *Histoires ou Contes du temps passé. Avec des Moralitez,* which first appeared in English in 1729, with a second corrected edition of the R. S. Gent [Robert Samber] translation of *Histories or Tales of Passed Times With Morals* in 1737. This literary folktale by retired civil servant and *Académie Française* member Perrault (1628–1703) influenced the version published by the Grimm brothers as *"Dornröschen,"* or "Little

Briar-Rose," number 50 in their collection, Aarne-Thompson tale type number 410. The following text is from Margaret Hunt's two-volume 1884 translation and edition of the *Grimm's Household Tales with the Author's Notes,* which included an introduction by Scottish mythographer and man of letters Andrew Lang.[21]

A long time ago there were a King and a Queen who said every day, "Ah, if only we had a child!" But they never had one. But it happened that once when the Queen was bathing, a frog crept out of the water onto the land and said to her, "Your wish shall be fulfilled; before a year has gone by you shall have a daughter."

What the frog had said came true, and the Queen had a little girl who was so pretty that the King could not contain himself for joy, and ordered a great feast. He invited not only his kindred, friends, and acquaintances, but also the Wise Women, in order that they might be kind and well-disposed towards the child. There were thirteen of them in his kingdom, but, as he had only twelve golden places for them to eat out of, one of them had to be left at home.

The feast was held with all manner of splendour and when it came to an end the Wise Women bestowed their magic gifts upon the baby; one gave virtue, another beauty, a third riches, and so on with everything in the world that one can wish for.

When eleven of them had made their promises, suddenly the thirteenth came in. She wished to avenge herself for not having been invited and without greeting, or even looking at any one, she cried with a loud voice, "The King's daughter shall in her fifteenth year prick herself with a spindle and fall down dead." And, without saying a word more, she turned round and left the room.

They were all shocked; but the twelfth, whose good wish still remained unspoken, came forward, and as she could not undo the evil sentence but only soften it, she said, "It shall not be death, but a deep sleep of a hundred years, into which the Princess shall fall."

The King, who would fain keep his dear child from the misfortune, gave orders that every spindle in the whole kingdom should be burnt. Meanwhile, the gifts of the Wise Women were plenteously fulfilled in the young girl, for she was so beautiful, modest, good-natured, and wise, that everyone who saw her was bound to love her.

It happened that on the very day when she was fifteen years old, the King and the Queen were not at home, and the maiden was left in the palace quite alone. So she went round into all sorts of places, looked into rooms and bedchambers just as she liked, and at last came to an old tower. She climbed up the narrow winding-staircase and reached a little door. A rusty key was in the lock and when she turned it the door sprang open, and there in a little room sat an old woman with a spindle, busily spinning her flax.

[21]For a brief history of this magic tale, see Iona and Peter Opie, *The Classic Fairy Tales* (1974:81–92), and Max Lüthi, "Sleeping Beauty: The Meaning and Form of Fairy Tales" (1970:21–34). For a concise discussion of the brothers Grimm and their influence, see Richard M. Dorson, "Foreword" to Kurt Ranke, ed., *Folktales of Germany* (Chicago: University of Chicago Press, 1966), pp. v–xxv. "Little Briar-Rose" is No. 50 in the final (1856) set of 210 narratives. An excellent edition of *The Complete Grimm's Fairy Tales* (New York: Pantheon Books, 1944) contains a revised text (by James Stern) of Margaret Hunt's 1884 translation, an introduction by Padraic Colum, folkloristic commentary by Joseph Campbell, and illustrations by Josef Scharl.

(Bowles & Carver
1970:51)

"Good day, old dame," said the King's daughter, "what are you doing there?" "I am spinning," said the old woman and nodded her head. "What sort of thing is that, that rattles round so merrily?" said the girl, and she took the spindle and wanted to spin, too. But scarcely had she touched the spindle when the magic decree was fulfilled, and she pricked her finger with it.

And in that very moment when she felt the prick, she fell down upon the bed that stood there, and lay in a deep sleep. And this sleep extended over the whole palace; the King and Queen who had just come home, and had entered the great hall, began to go to sleep, and the whole of the court with them. The horses, too, went to sleep in the stable, the dogs in the yard, the pigeons upon the roof, the flies on the wall; even the fire that was flaming on the hearth became quiet and slept, the roast meat left off frizzling, and the cook, who was just going to pull the hair of the scullery boy, because he had forgotten something, let him go and went to sleep. And the wind fell, and on the trees before the castle not a leaf moved again.

But round about the castle there began to grow a hedge of thorns, which every year became higher, and at last grew close up round the castle and all over it, so that there was nothing of it to be seen, not even the flag upon the roof. But the story of the beautiful sleeping "Briar-Rose," for so the Princess was named, went about the country, so that from time to time Kings' sons came and tried to get through the thorny hedge into the castle.

But they found it impossible, for the thorns held fast together, as if they had hands, and the youths were caught in them, could not get loose again and died a miserable death.

After long, long years a King's son came again to that country, and heard an old man talking about the thorn hedge and that a castle was said to stand behind it in which a wonderfully beautiful princess, named Briar-Rose, had been asleep for a hundred years; and that the King and the Queen and the whole court were asleep likewise. He had heard, too, from his grandfather, that many King's sons had already come, and had tried to get through the thorny hedge, but they had remained sticking fast in it and had died a pitiful death. Then the youth said, "I am not afraid, I will go and see the beautiful Briar-Rose." The good old man might dissuade him as he would, he did not listen to his words.

But by this time the hundred years had just passed, and the day had come when Briar-Rose was to awake again. When the King's son came near to the thorn hedge, it was nothing but large and beautiful flowers, which parted from each other of their own accord, and let him pass unhurt, then they closed again behind him like a hedge. In the castle yard he saw the horses and the spotted hounds lying asleep; on the roof sat the pigeons with their heads under their wings. And when he entered the house, the flies were asleep upon the wall, the cook in the kitchen was still holding out his hand to seize the boy, and the maid was sitting by the black hen which she was going to pluck.

He went on farther, and in the great hall he saw the whole of the court lying asleep, and up by the throne lay the King and Queen.

Then he went on still farther, and all was so quiet that a breath could be heard, and at last he came to the tower, and opened the door into the little room where Briar-Rose was sleeping. There she lay, so beautiful that he could not turn his eyes away; and he stooped down and gave her a kiss. But as soon as he kissed her Briar-Rose opened her eyes and awoke and looked at him quite sweetly.

Then they went down together, and the King awoke and the Queen and the whole court and they all looked at each other in great astonishment. And the horses in the courtyard stood up and shook themselves; the hounds jumped up and wagged their tails; the pigeons upon the roof pulled out their heads from under their wings, looked around and flew into open country; the flies on the wall crept again; the fire in the kitchen burned up and flickered and cooked the meat; the joint began to turn and frizzle again, and the cook gave the boy such a box on the ear that he screamed and the maid plucked the fowl ready for the spit.

And then the marriage of the King's son with Briar-Rose was celebrated with all splendour and they lived contented to the end of their days. (Hunt 1905, in Travers 1975:67–71)

(Fox 1979:7)

> He kissed Briar Rose
> and she woke up crying:
> Daddy! Daddy!
> Presto! She's out of prison!
> She married the prince
> and all went well
> except for the fear—
> the fear of sleep.
>
> Briar Rose
> was an insomniac . . .
> She could not nap
> or lie in sleep
> without the court chemist
> mixing her some knock-out drops
> and never in the prince's presence.
>
> If it is to come, she said,
> sleep must take me unawares
> while I am laughing or dancing
> so that I do not know that brutal place
> where I lie down with cattle prods,
> the hole in my cheek open.
> Further, I must not dream
> for when I do I see the table set
> and a faltering crone at my place,
> her eyes burnt by cigarettes
> as she eats betrayal like a slice of meat.
>
> —Anne Sexton, from "Briar Rose
> (Sleeping Beauty),"
> *Transformations* (1971).[22]

Psychoanalyst Julius E. Heuscher's view of Sleeping Beauty's plight is remarkably similar to Marie-Louise von Franz's interpretation of the Eskimo girl's peril (above):

[22]The seventeen poems in Anne Sexton's *Transformations* retell and recast various Grimm's tales in contemporary and "classic" terms. Also see the Sleeping Beauty poems by Josef Wittmann, Jochen Jung, and Vera Ferra-Mikurra at the beginning of Jack Zipes, *Breaking the Magic Spell: Radical Theories of Folk and Fairy Tales* (1979:xiv–xvi).

It is justifiable to see a symbolic meaning in the place where the temptation of the princess occurs: high up in the castle's tower, in a little cubbyhole behind a little door which can be opened with a rusty key. Is it not up in the belfry, in the head, where we spin the intellectual threads which are deadening our feelings and deep beliefs, especially if the mental processes in the brain are shut off from the rest of our soul for such a long time that the key to the door (between heart and brain) has become rusty?

It must be added that in the German language "spinning" refers not only to the mechanical operation of a spinning wheel, but also to a type of reasoning which is detached from active life, as well as to the thought processes of the mentally ill. (1974:164–65)

Psychoanalyst Bruno Bettelheim poses a somewhat more teleological interpretation of the spinning, one which applies to adolescent girls and boys alike:

While many fairy tales stress great deeds the heroes must perform to become themselves, "The Sleeping Beauty" emphasizes the long, quiet concentration on oneself that is also needed. During the months before the first menstruation, and often also for some time immediately following it, girls are passive, seem sleepy, and withdraw into themselves. While no equally noticeable state heralds the coming of sexual maturity in boys, many of them experience a period of lassitude and of turning inward during puberty which equals the female experience. It is thus understandable that a fairy story in which a long period of sleep begins at the start of puberty has been very popular for a long time among girls and boys.

In major life changes such as adolescence, for successful growth opportunities both active and quiescent periods are needed. The turning inward, which in outer appearance looks like passivity (or sleeping one's life away), happens when internal mental processes of such importance go on within the person that he has no energy for outwardly directed action. Those fairy tales which, like "The Sleeping Beauty," have the period of passivity for their central topic, permit the budding adolescent not to worry during his inactive period: he learns that things continue to evolve. The happy ending assures the child that he will not remain permanently stuck in seemingly doing nothing, even if at the moment it seems as if this period of quietude will last for a hundred years. (1976:225)

Nevertheless, feminist culture historian and philosopher Simone de Beauvoir emphasizes that it is the *girl's* waiting and passivity which is popularly perceived and remembered about magic tale protagonists like Sleeping Beauty:

. . . True it is that the little girl experiences in the presence of her confessor, and even when alone at the foot of the altar, a thrill very similar to what she will feel later in her lover's embrace. . . .

Head bowed, face buried in her hands, she knows the miracle of renunciation: on her knees she mounts toward heaven; her surrender to the arms of God assures her an Assumption fleecy with clouds and angels. It is from this marvelous experience that she copies her earthly future. The child can find it also through many other roads: everything invites her to abandon herself in daydreams to men's arms in order to be transported into a heaven of glory. She learns that to be happy she must be loved; to be loved she must await love's coming. Woman is the Sleeping Beauty, Cinderella, Snow-White, she who receives and submits. In song and story the young man is seen departing adventurously in search of woman; he slays the dragon, he battles giants; she is locked in a tower, a palace, a garden, a cave, she is chained to a rock, a captive, sound asleep: she waits. (1961:271–72)

The effects of such conditioning are generally evident in the contrast between most heroes and heroines. The males are more active, powerful, and innovative than their passive, powerless, and accepting female counterparts. This difference is vividly shown by the two illustrations and texts that follow:

"The Princess was looking at the poor creatures in dismay, when the Enchanter suddenly entered, wearing a long black robe and with a crocodile upon his head. In his hand he carried a whip made of twenty long snakes, all alive and writhing, and the Princess was so terrified at the sight that she heartily wished she had never come. Without saying a word she ran to the door, but it was covered with a thick spider's web, and when she broke it she found another, and another, and another. In fact, there was no end to them; the Princess's arms ached with tearing them down, and yet she was no nearer to getting out, and the wicked Enchanter behind her laughed maliciously."

—Illustration by Lancelot Speed for "The Golden Branch," a literary fairy tale by Madam d'Aulnoy, in Andrew Lang, ed., *The Red Fairy Book,* published in London, 1890 (1966:232).

"Scarce had he advanced towards the wood when all the great trees, the bushes, and brambles gave way of themselves to let him pass through; he walked up to the castle which he saw at the end of a large avenue which he went into; and what a little surprised him was that none of his people could follow him, because the trees closed again as soon as he had passed through them. However, he did not cease from continuing his way; a young and amorous prince is always valiant."

—Illustration for "The Sleeping Beauty in the Wood," by Charles Perrault, in Andrew Lang, ed., *The Blue Fairy Book,* published in London, ca. 1889 (1965:58).

In many respects, comics serve as contemporary magic tales, but their heroines are not always as passive as Cinderellas and Sleeping Beauties. According to comic-book creator Stan Lee, the "superhero women" invented for Marvel Comics were *not* "written primarily for female readers," but:

Each and every one is an integral part of the Marvel mythos, intended to be selected and savored by anyone who loves fantasy and adventure. But, for too many years the emphasis has been on the men of action. For too many years the females have been relegated to more supporting roles. We think it's time to change all that.

It's time for the Super Women! (1977:8)

As a result he and his colleagues have created heroines like Medusa, Red Sonja, the Invisible Girl, the Wasp, the Cat, Ms. Marvel, Hela, Shanna the She Devil, Crystal, Phoenix, Enchantress, Storm, Tigra, Satanna, and others, including the Black Widow (Lee 1977:231–51) and Spider-Woman.

In Volume 1, Number 20, November 1979, of the Spider-Woman Marvel Comics series, Spider-Woman—Jessica Drew in ordinary life—comes "At Last! Face-to-Face With Spider-Man." This confrontation prompts her to ponder her childhood and the origins of her superhuman powers, as we see above.

Fittingly, one of Spider-Woman's early (and continuing) adversaries is Brother Grimm, who is introduced in the following illustration:

(Lee 1979:57)

While creators of comic books and other forms of pop culture expand the popular imagination regarding heroines, feminist critics such as Madonna Kolbenschlag explore ways to *Kiss Sleeping Beauty Good-Bye: Breaking the Spell of Feminine Myths and Models.* She finds the traditional passivity in the story's symbolism as well as another, more promising clarion:

Thus, at the universal level of meaning, Sleeping Beauty is most of all a symbol of *passivity,* and by extension a metaphor for the spiritual condition of women—cut off from autonomy and transcendence, from self-actualization and ethical capacity in a male-dominated milieu. But this is to restrict the meaning of the metaphoric image to its descriptive content. Its very persistence in the cultural ashes suggests that the story has a phoenixlike aspect. Out of the ashes of cultural memory, out of the recognition of the metaphor as descriptive of a universal condition that is passing, arises a dynamic symbol calling women forth to an "awakening" and to spiritual maturity. (1979:5–6)

There is a hint of this promise in Jungian therapist Nor Hall's focus on the thirteen fairies, whom she calls "medial women" who assist as "midwives to the psyche" during "times of difficult passage." Such women have "not only the power to inspire, but also the power to intoxicate or induce stupor or sleep," which can nonetheless heal and yield powerful dreams. Hall is less concerned with the prince than with Sleeping Beauty herself, "whose going under and coming out were mediated by the feminine principle active in fairies, who are little and look young but in fact are ageless beings (like the Moirai or Graiai, the Greek spinners, who were 'fair-cheeked' but had the gray hair of a spinster). To sleep for a hundred years because a spindle or distaff was turned against you would mean that you were 'cursed' by the feminine side of the family. Although sleep is classically close to death (brothers Hypnos and Thanatos), the curse of sleep is not literally death-dealing, which indicates some hope for girls who fade into a sleep state at fifteen. Like Persephone, they can come up again out of their phase of sleep-in-season" (1980:197).

In revaluing such wise old women and their knowledge, the full span of women's lives can be enhanced and the longstanding opprobrium attached to age and barrenness alleviated. Unfortunately, a sordid tradition of persecution and prosecution of witches—usually female—fuels this fear and loathing even today. Instances are legion from all manner of traditions. In 1926, for example, folklorist Newbell Niles Puckett reported that some southern blacks believed:

A hag may be caught in a properly conjured bottle and if this bottle is then hidden in the ashes under the fire, she will die in agony. Some say that the bottle should be simply put down on its side with the mouth open. Whatever you find within the bottle in the morning—roach, cricket, spider, gnat, or other insect or animal—represents the witch, and whatever is done to the thing captured will be done to the witch as well. (1926:161)

Self-taught folklorist Cleofas M. Jaramillo recalled that in her turn-of-the-century northern New Mexico Hispano community of Arroyo Hondo:

Old women who lived alone were usually suspected of being witches. La Chon was one of these women in our village. She was usually found sitting on a sheepskin in the corner of her fireplace, smoking a *cigarrito* and poking the fire with a stick to keep her pots of beans boiling. A low door, always kept covered with a ragged patch quilt, led into her storeroom. No one was allowed to enter this secret room, where bunches of dried herbs hung in a corner. From the pumpkin rinds, Chon made the *guejas,* into which she crawled and sailed through the air to places she wanted to visit. Once La Chon was met walking through the park in Santa Fe by a lady who knew her well. The lady asked Chon if she would take a package to her mother who lived in the same village. La Chon called for the package and delivered it to the lady's mother the next morning. In those days [late 1800s] it took three days to make the trip from Arroyo Hondo to Santa Fe, and her

Illustration by John D. Batten for "The Story of Deirdre" in Joseph Jacobs, ed., *Celtic Fairy Tales,* 1892 (reprint, New York: Dover Publications, 1968), between pages 68 and 69.

Public hanging of witches, from Sir George Mackenzie's *Law and Customs of Scotland in Matters Criminal,* Edinburgh, 1678. The man at the right is the witch-finder being paid for turning in the women. (Lehner 1971:81, fig. 119)

neighbors could never find out who had brought the old woman to town. Many stories were told of how she was met at night in the form of a dog, cat, or some other animal. (1972:99)[23]

Philosopher-theologian Mary Daly radically condemns all such traditions, whether in folk, popular or elite culture, warning: "Spinsters must also constantly unweave the ghostly false images of ourselves which have been deeply embedded in our imaginations and which respond like unnatural reflexes to the spookers' unnatural stimuli. Unweaving involves undoing our conditioning in femininity. This means unraveling the hood of patriarchal woman-hood" (1978:409). In *Gyn/Ecology: The Metaethics of Radical Feminism,* Daly challenges longstanding and cherished conceptions of the feminine and celebrates spinsters spinning primal, primary, ludic creations:

. . . This entire book is asking the question of movement, of Spinning. It is an invitation to the Wild Witch in all women who long to spin. This book is a declaration that it is time to stop putting answers before the Questions. It is a declaration/Manifesto that in our chronology (Croneology) it is time to get moving again. It is a call of the wild to the wild, calling Hags/Spinsters to spin/be beyond the parochial bondings/bindings of any comfortable "community." (1978:xv)

[23]For more on witches in this area, see Marc Simmons, *Witchcraft in the Southwest: Spanish and Indian Supernaturalism on the Rio Grande* (Flagstaff, Arizona: Northland Press, 1974). For notes and references on why "in nearly every society that believes in witches . . . the vast majority of suspected individuals [are] women," see Clarke Garrett, "Women and Witches: Patterns of Analysis" (1977), and later responses (Balfe 1978, Honegger 1979, Moia 1979, Garrett 1979). Also see Matalene 1978.

Industrial Spinsters
(Harter 1978b:37).

◆ Spinsters spin and weave, mending and creating unity of consciousness. In doing so we spin through and beyond the realm of multiply split unconsciousness. In concealed workshops, Spinsters unsnarl, unknot, untie, unweave. We knit, knot, interlace, entwine, whirl, and twirl. Absorbed in Spinning, in the ludic celebration which is both work and play, Spinsters span the dichotomies of false consciousness and break its mindbinding combinations. (ibid:386)[24]

> I watch her in the corner there,
> As, restless, bold, and unafraid,
> She slips and floats along the air
> Till all her subtile house is made.
>
> Her home, her bed, her daily food
> All from that hidden store she draws;
> She fashions it and knows it good,
> By instinct's strong and sacred laws.
>
> No tenuous threads to weave her nest,
> She seeks and gathers there or here;

[24]Daly's challenge is metaphoric. Other feminists have attempted to unravel the conditioning by becoming literal spinsters—a process detailed by Susan Hill and Judy Chicago in *Embroidering Our Heritage: The Dinner Party Needlework* (1980). Still others have reconsidered and celebrated the creative joys in, e.g., lacemaking (Boetti n.d.; Feinberg et al. 1978), weaving (Johnson and Boyd 1978; Feinberg et al. 1978; Burnside 1978), quilting (Roach and Weidlich 1974; Cooper and Buferd 1977), and, in the case of the editorial collective involved in Cycle 3 (Autumn 1978) of the feminist journal of mythology, *Lady-Unique-Inclination-of-the-Night*, "all the traditional weaving arts of women" in whatever media. Also see other articles in *Heresies* 4, Winter 1978, an issue devoted to "Women's Traditional Arts: The Politics of Aesthetics."

(Harter 1978b:75)

But spins it from her faithful breast,
Renewing still, till leaves are sere.

Then, worn with toil, and tired of life,
In vain her shining traps are set.
Her frost hath hushed the insect strife
And gilded flies her charm forget.

But swinging in the snares she spun.
She sways to every wintry wind:
Her joy, her toil, her errand done,
Her corse the sport of storms unkind.

Poor sister of the spinster clan!
I too from out my store within
My daily life and living plan,
My home, my rest, my pleasure spin.

I know thy heart when heartless hands
Sweep all that hard-earned web away:
Destroy its pearled and glittering bands,
And leave thee homeless by the way.

I know thy peace when all is done.
Each anchored thread, each tiny knot,
Soft shining in the autumn sun;
A sheltered, silent, tranquil lot.

I know what thou hast never known,
—Sad presage to a soul allowed;—
That not for life I spin, alone,
But day by day I spin my shroud.

> —Rose Terry Cooke, "Arachne,"
> 1860 (in Pearson and Pope 1976:208–09).

10.
This is what I am: watching the spider
rebuild—"patiently", they say,

But I recognize in her
impatience—my own—

the passion to make and make again
where such unmaking reigns

the refusal to be a victim
we have lived with violence so long

Am I to go on saying
for myself, for her

*This is my body,
take and destroy it?*

> —Adrienne Rich, from
> "Natural Resources," 1977 (in 1978:64–65).

Chapter 2
Goddesses:
Myth as Rorschach

Our mother of the growing fields, our mother of the streams, will
have pity upon us. For whom do we belong? Whose seeds are we? To
our mother alone do we belong.

 —Cágába Indian prayer.

Hail Mary, full of grace, the Lord is with thee. Blessed art thou
among women and blessed is the fruit of thy womb Jesus. Holy Mary,
Mother of God, pray for us sinners now and at the hour of our death.
Amen.

 —Roman Catholic prayer.

Female Creator Deities

Creatress, creatoress, creatrix—these cumbersome, unfamiliar terms suggest the
difficulties in identifying creators who are portrayed as female rather than
male or bisexual/androgynous (in which case the male aspect tends to pre-
dominate linguistically and/or mythologically). Quite simply: such female
creator deities are rare.[1] On the whole, goddesses play second fiddle to gods
in cosmogonic and origin myths dealing with the early stages of creation. Only
when creation myths tell of a cosmos generated through natural reproductive
processes do female creator deities enact significant roles.

 The Cágába Indians of northern Colombia described their *creatrix* as a universal *genitrix* when talking to German anthropologist K. T. Preuss:

The mother of our songs, the mother of all our seed, bore us in the beginning of
things and she is the mother of all types of men, the mother of all nations. She is

---

[1] As part of her cross-cultural study of *Female Power and Male Dominance: On the Origins of
Sexual Inequality*, anthropologist Peggy Reeves Sanday examined 112 creation stories world-
wide. According to her: "Creative agents depicted as feminine are usually associated with the
water or the earth" and "create from the body" rather than "magically" (1981:58). Only 18%
of the 112 myths could be classified as "feminine" (ibid:59). In an appended "Analysis of the
relationship between environment, father's proximity to infants, and origin symbolism," she
selected 61 societies and was able to analyze 39 origin myths—only 6 of which (the African
Shilluk and Tuareg, the South Asian Semang and Lepcha, the North American Copper Eskimo and the South American Nambicuara) featured a "female creator or ancestress," rather
than a sexless creator, couple creators or ancestors, male culture-hero or ancestor, animal creator or ancestor, or supreme being or force (ibid:241).

the mother of the thunder, the mother of the streams, the mother of trees and of all things. She is the mother of the world and of the older brothers, the stone-people. She is the mother of the fruits of the earth and of all things. She is the mother of our youngest brothers, the French and the strangers. She is the mother of our dance paraphernalia, of all our temples and she is the only mother we possess. She alone is the mother of fire and the Sun and the Milky Way. She is the mother of the rain and the only mother we possess. And she has left us a token in all the temples,—a token in the form of songs and dances.

Anthropologist Paul Radin, who translated these quotations for his 1927 study of *Primitive Man as Philosopher,* claims this constitutes "a female supreme deity and a profession of faith that should satisfy even the most exacting monotheist." Nevertheless, Preuss was able only to record the single prayer above because "she has no cult, and no prayers are really directed to her, [although] when the fields are sown and the priests chant their incantations the Kagaba [sic] say, 'And then we think of the one and only mother of the growing things, of the mother of all things' " (Radin 1957:357–58).

Particularly in agricultural societies, the earth is seen as a mother, cyclically giving birth to all life. Belief in such an earth mother is often coupled with a belief that certain *places*—rocks, caves, trees, rivers, etc.—engender children, whose souls are actually conceived and carried in the womb of their "real" Mother, the Earth, and only later enter human mothers. Such beliefs foster what Mircea Eliade calls "the mystical experience of autochthony, the profound feeling of having come from the soil, of having been born of the Earth." According to him, "perfect autochthony" involves a complete cycle from "dust to dust"; "the mother did no more than to bring to completion the creation of the Earth-Mother: and, at death, the great desire was to return to the Earth-Mother, to be interred in the native soil—that 'native soil' of which we can now see the profound meaning" (1960:164, 165).

Emergence myths tell how in the beginning people, animals, seeds, and so on ascended through and emerged from the womb or wombs of the earth mother (Rooth 1957:502–03; Wheeler-Voegelin and Moore 1957). One such myth, collected by anthropologist Leslie A. White from Acoma Pueblo Indians of the Southwest in 1926 and 1927, explicitly portrays the first beings as infants who mature rapidly:

They came out of the earth, from Iatik'ᵘ, the mother. They came out through a hole in the north called Shipap. They crawled out like grasshoppers; their bodies were naked and soft. It was all dark; the sun had not yet risen. All of the little people had their eyes closed; they hadn't opened them yet. Iatikᵘ lined them all up in a row, facing east. Then she had the sun come up. When it came up and shone on the babies' eyes they opened. They crawled around. In eight days they were bigger and stronger. They walk around now. There was a lake at Shipap. There was an island in the center of the lake, and there was a building on the island. Iatikᵘ left her people when they got big enough to take care of themselves and went to live in this building. Before she went she told the people how to get food to eat. She also told them about the k'a·'tsina who lived out west at Wenimatsⁱ. She told them that the k'a·'tsina would come to dance for them. She told the people that they must respect these spirits, for they were very powerful. Iatikᵘ told her children to multiply and to teach their children to live as Iatik[u] wished. She said that she would always be near them to help them and to take care of them. (White 1932:142)[2]

Anthropologist Washington Matthews calls all such narratives "myths of gestation and parturition"—even claiming that the vine or tree by which, according to some versions, the people ascend through the underworld "wombs" into this world are, like the world tree Yggdrasil in Scandinavian mythology, "nothing more poetic than [the funis,] that which every midwife beholds when she performs her special functions"! (1902:742)

Whether or not one wishes to be as literal as Matthews, it is clear that peoples who view the earth as the *Terra Mater* (Earth Mother) and Universal *Genetrix* (female begetter) maintain a strong and sacred relationship to their lands. In June 1884, Major J. W. MacMurray began interviewing Indians along the Columbia River who were angered by the homestead laws and the Northern Pacific Railroad's usurpation of their lands. During his northwestern travels, MacMurray spoke with the Wanapûm prophet, priest and chief Smohalla, who vigorously objected to the "bad word" from the government in Washington:

Acoma pottery design. "In the pottery of Acoma one will find designs of trees, leaves, birds, and flowers, combined with geometric patterns; the colors used are black, red, and a creamy gray. The ware of Acoma is highly prized for its thinness and lightness, as well as for the wide range of its charming decoration" (Sides 1961: plate 25, fig. b.).

You ask me to plow the ground! Shall I take a knife and tear my mother's bosom? Then when I die she will not take me to her bosom to rest.
You ask me to dig for stone! Shall I dig under her skin for her bones? Then when I die I can not enter her body to be born again.
You ask me to cut grass and make hay and sell it, and be rich like white men! But how dare I cut off my mother's hair?
It is a bad law, and my people can not obey it. I want my people to stay with me here. All the dead men will come to life again. Their spirits will come to their bodies again. We must wait here in the homes of our fathers and be ready to meet them in the bosom of our mother. (quoted in Mooney 1896:721)

This intense relationship obtains even when the earth mother neither is given nor gives birth to in a strictly natural way, as in the beginning of the following Northwestern Indian Okanagon myth told to anthropologist James A. Teit in the early 1900s by Red-Arm, an old Nespelim (western division of the Sanpoil) man related to the Okanagon:

Old-One, or Chief, made the earth out of a woman, and said she would be the mother of all the people. Thus the earth was once a human being, and she *is* alive yet; but she has been transformed, and we cannot see her in the same way we can

[2]A different and much longer version was collected by Bureau of American Ethnology chief Matthew W. Stirling from a group of Acoma Indians visiting Washington in 1928. In this, two sisters— female culture heroes—emerge from the underworld and are instructed in survival skills by a tutelary spirit called Tsichtinako (Stirling 1942). Leslie A. White also includes a variant myth involving two sisters but cautions that, although such a duo is found "in Keresan tradition, I feel that this particular version is largely the product of some individual fantasy, perhaps the informant's" (1932:147–48).

see a person. Nevertheless she has legs, arms, head, heart, flesh, bones, and blood. The soil is her flesh; the trees and vegetation are her hair; the rocks, her bones; and the wind is her breath. She lies spread out, and we live on her. She shivers and contracts when cold, and expands and perspires when hot. When she moves, we have an earthquake. Old-One, after transforming her, took some of her flesh and rolled it into balls, as people do with mud or clay. These he transformed into the beings of the ancient world, who were people, and yet at the same time animals. (Teit in Boas 1917:80)

In some myths, the earth mother is portrayed as giving birth unaided, by parthenogenesis; in others, the sky fathers her children. According to Eliade, hierogamy precedes and insures fertility, and "it is probable that this sacred marriage between heaven and earth was the primeval model both of the fertility of the land and of human marriage" (1958:257). In many agricultural societies, public ritual intercourse as well as orgies in the plowed fields or elsewhere symbolize and stimulate this cosmic hierogamy, "arousing" the fertilizing rain from the sky. During periods of drought, women might also run naked through the fields to stir the heavens' desire (ibid:356–61). In any case, parthenogenesis seems to be the older notion, stemming from a time when the man's role in conception was either unknown or minimized and when agriculture was more a woman's province. When the true causes of conception are understood and agriculture considered more a male than a female activity, the plow is often identified with the phallus, the furrow with the woman, and tilling the soil with the sexual act (Eliade 1978:40–41; 1958:259–60). Sometimes, even "the procreative characteristics of the mother goddess have been transferred to the male god who has thus fully assumed her role as agrarian deity" (Hultkrantz 1979:55).

In many non-agrarian cultures and certainly in contemporary technological society, creation and procreation are dissociated and differently valued. "To create" is then not the same as "to give birth to" or "to mother," and (symbolic or spiritual) creation is not equivalent to (natural or biological) procreation. Indeed, much psychoanalytic theory about the so-called compensatory nature of the creative process in both men and women—womb or parturition envy for the former (e.g. Montagu 1953; Hand 1957; Bettelheim 1962; Dundes 1962; Hays 1964; Gilbert and Gubar 1979:3–44; Kris and Kurz 1979:115–16), a substitute for barrenness or lack of children in the latter (e.g. Horney 1967:61–62, 115; Chesler 1972:30–31, 94, 96)—is predicated on this distinction. In any case, whether either creation or procreation is more esteemed, or whether they are considered equally valuable, varies from culture to culture and from era to era.

Ordinary contemporary English usage applies the verb "to create" to *creatio ex nihilo* ("creation from nothing") by thought, dream, breath, spirit, laughter, speech, and the like, or to the crafting of a world and its inhabitants by an artisan or architect. In most mythological traditions such creations are the work of male creator deities (see, e.g. Maclagan 1977; Sproul 1979; Van Over 1980; Weigle and Johnson 1980). Nevertheless, the following Native American myths portray equally "creative" female deities.

Anthropologist C. F. Voegelin reports that "during field work among the Shawnee in 1933 and 1934, it was found that mention of a female deity was

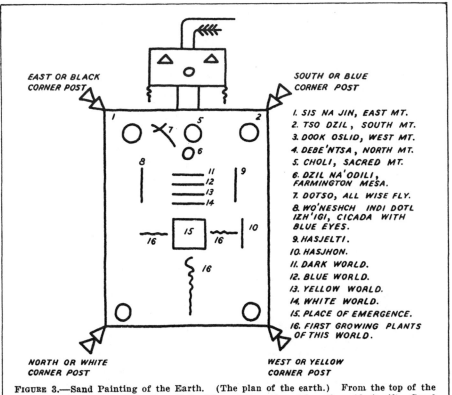

EAST OR BLACK
CORNER POST

SOUTH OR BLUE
CORNER POST

1. SIS NA JIN, EAST MT.
2. TSO DZIL, SOUTH MT.
3. DOOK OSLID, WEST MT.
4. DEBE'NTSA, NORTH MT.
5. CHOLI, SACRED MT.
6. DZIL NA'ODILI,
   FARMINGTON MESA.
7. DOTSO, ALL WISE FLY.
8. WO'NESHCH INDI DOTL
   IZH'IGI, CICADA WITH
   BLUE EYES.
9. HASJELTI.
10. HASJHON.
11. DARK WORLD.
12. BLUE WORLD.
13. YELLOW WORLD.
14. WHITE WORLD.
15. PLACE OF EMERGENCE.
16. FIRST GROWING PLANTS
    OF THIS WORLD.

NORTH OR WHITE
CORNER POST

WEST OR YELLOW
CORNER POST

FIGURE 3.—Sand Painting of the Earth. (The plan of the earth.) From the top of the mask projects a breath feather, tied with a white cotton string, the spider's gift. Coral and turquoise ear pendants are indicated. The body is dark gray. Borders, mask, neck, etc. The two arms and two legs are kos ischin, triangles set upon one another and symbolizing forming clouds or cloud terraces. (Sam Ahkeak and Gerald Nailor got this from medicine men at Shiprock.)

Navajo sandpainting of the female earth, showing the underworlds (nos. 11–14) through which the first people emerged (O'Bryan 1956:22).[3]

forever on the lips of informants from all three bands of Shawnee in Oklahoma [the Absentee Shawnee, the Cherokee Shawnee, and the Eastern Shawnee]." This well known and revered figure, commonly called Our Grandmother, was definitely a Supreme deity and creator (1936:3). She is an anthropomorphic female, variously described as of immense size or small stature, with gray or white hair, with "good" or separated teeth. "That she wears short skirts may be seen when she is reflected in the full moon. In the Rescue

[3]According to this version of the Navajo emergence myth (for details see chapter 4 below), after raising the sky, the Holy Ones "planned just how the earth should be. They made the face of the earth white, with eyes and nose and mouth. They made earrings of turquoise for the ears; and for a border they placed a black ring, a blue ring, a yellow ring, and a white ring, which is the earth's edge. These rings are for the earth's protection; no power shall harm her" (O'Bryan 1956:23). Numbers 1–6 (3 and 4 are not marked) are the sacred mountains which bound the Navajo cosmos, guarding it from the chaos outside. Dotso (no. 7) often acts as a messenger for the gods in mythology, while the cicada (no. 8) or locust is usually thought to have emerged first from the fourth underworld into this fifth world. In O'Bryan's version, Hasjelti (no. 9) and Hasjohon (not Hasjhon, no. 10) are powerful supernatural figures associated with healing ceremonies known as mountain chants. Also see Wyman 1970:65–102, and a color reproduction of a similar sandpainting in Sandner 1979:between 132 and 133.

of Corn tale, she is painted with round spots on her cheeks and her hair is parted down the middle by Shawnee attendants" (ibid:4). Voegelin summarizes the creation myths associated with Our Grandmother thus:

> It was during this first period . . . that the Creator descended from the void above and created the basis of the earth, a turtle, the earth to rest upon the turtle, bodies of water to rest upon the earth, and successively other observable features of heaven and earth. Most of the cosmic creations were performed while the Creator and her grandson and little dog were living on the recently completed earth. Some variants note the presence of the devil. People are taken for granted rather than specified. The earthly residence of a presumably small group before the flood marks the second period. During this period Our Grandmother permits her grandson, and in some variants the devil, unwholesome license. The third period is the time after the flood when Our Grandmother was still on this earth. The fourth period extends to the present time and is marked by the residence of Our Grandmother above the earth, from which place she dispenses medicine and other benefits to mortal visitors.
>
> During the first three periods, Our Grandmother originates nothing bad, only beneficial things. Evil origins and happenings are ascribed to her grandson and constant companion, Rounded-side, or to another grandson introduced in some variants, the devil, over whom she has little control; also, the Creator herself occasionally bungles in her creations. But once she retires to her present residence, her creations or rather instructions are without the least suggestions of bungling. Her grandson, Rounded-Side, no longer originates catastrophes, but innocently plays with cumulus cloud formations. When the devil punishes, he does so under her auspices. She tolerates the nonsense of her Silly Boys, but without question has firm control over them. But she herself is less given to continuing the creation of good things. Rather she guards jealously her accomplished work, boasts about her power in a way calculated to arouse awe, plays the role of policewoman rather than benevolent deity, and on occasion metes out punishment. (Voegelin 1936:8–9)[4]

Our Grandmother is a later supreme deity and creator in Shawnee culture, which as recently as 1924 acknowledged a male Great Spirit creator. Anthropologists C. F. and E. W. Voegelin think that the change likely resulted from contacts with Iroquoian-speaking groups, because "there run through Iroquois mythology, especially Huron mythology, quite occasional references to a female divinity. Ataentsic, and her son, Iouskaha; the female divinity is accredited with the creation of heaven, earth, and mankind; and both she and

---

[4]Like many creator deities, Our Grandmother also controls the end of the cosmos. Voegelin summarizes these myths, which exhibit a strong missionary influence. In them, Our Grandmother becomes a spinster/weaver: "Mythologic punishments include a purgatory, with obvious Christian influences, which is administered by the devil as well as by the Creator. The dead who are not virtuous do not choose the proper path, which is a narrow one, in the bifurcation of the road to the land of the dead. Those who arrive safely find the creator weaving a basket. During the night her little dog (with her grandson, in a Cherokee Shawnee version) unravels the weaving of the previous day and thus prevents the Creator from completing her basket. Some day, not too distant now say the present day Shawnee, Our Grandmother will complete this basket. Then the virtuous living will be gathered into the basket, and those who are remaining will be destroyed with the world, but those in the basket will be used to repopulate a new world" (Voegelin 1936:21).

her son superintend the world after creation" (1944:374; also see Converse 1908; Leach 1972:87). The following version is the opening section of a Huron myth collected by Horatio Hale from a man named Clarke, who "was about seventy-five years of age in 1874, and as he had heard the myth in his youth from the elders of his people, their joint recollections would carry it back to the middle of the last century, when the customs and traditions of the Wendat were retained in their full vigor."

Ataensic
(Lehner 1969:28, fig. 72).

In the beginning there was nothing but water, a wide sea, which was peopled by various animals of the kind that live in and upon the water. It happened that a woman fell down from the upper world. It is supposed that she was, by some mischance, pushed down by her husband through a rift in the sky. Though styled a woman, she was a divine personage. Two loons, which were flying over the water, happened to look up and see her falling. To save her from drowning they hastened to place themselves beneath her, joining their bodies together so as to form a cushion for her to rest on. In this way they held her up, while they cried with a loud voice to summon the other animals to their aid. The cry of the loon can be heard at a great distance, and the other creatures of the sea heard it, and assembled to learn the cause of the summons. Then came the tortoise (or "snapping turtle," as Clarke called it), a mighty animal, which consented to relieve the loons of their burden. They placed the woman on the back of the tortoise, charging him to take care of her. The tortoise then called the other animals to a grand council, to determine what should be done to preserve the life of the woman. They decided that she must have earth to live on. The tortoise directed them all to dive to the bottom of the sea and endeavor to bring up some earth. Many attempted it,—the beaver, the musk-rat, the diver, and others,—but without success. Some remained so long below that when they rose they were dead. The tortoise searched their mouths, but could find no trace of earth. At last the toad went down, and after remaining a long time rose, exhausted and nearly dead. On searching his mouth the tortoise found in it some earth, which he gave to the woman. She took it and placed it carefully around the edge of the tortoise's shell. When thus placed, it became the beginning of dry land. The land grew and extended on every side, forming at last a great country, fit for vegetation. All was sustained by the tortoise, which still supports the earth. [This opening is followed by the woman's giving birth to twin sons, whose struggles kill their mother and eventually shape and create the earth as we know it today.] (Hale 1888:180)[5]

Although the old woman Cō'tsi'pamā'pöt shares some of the creation with her daughter and son-in-law, she is definitely a more perspicacious and powerful creator than they appear to be in this Southern Paiute myth collected by anthropologist Robert H. Lowie in 1915, from an unidentified Moapa informant in southern Nevada.

Long ago an old woman, named Cō'tsi'pamā'pöt, made the whole country. No one lived here at all anywhere except this old woman, her son, and her daughter.

[5]A Seneca version of this myth collected by Jeremiah Curtin and J. N. B. Hewitt attributes much less "creativity" in the sense of activity to the woman, who apparently does not herself mold the earth on the turtle's back (reprinted with useful comparative notes in Thompson 1929:14–15). Sanday (1981:24–28) discusses still another Seneca version and relates it to Iroquoian female power (ibid: 117–18, 141–43). Also see Shimony 1980.

Deer (burnt umber, 18 x 17 mm). On spindle whorl or bead from central coast of Ecuador, 500–1500 A.D. (Shaffer 1979: 14, fig. 39).

The entire country was flooded with water except one little spot where Cō'tsi'pamā'pöt stayed. At last she scattered earth all over, seed-fashion. Then she sent her daughter to see how much land there was. When the girl came back, she said, "It is not enough yet." Her mother kept sending her, and the girl always came back reporting that there was not yet enough. At last the girl went a great distance and when she came back she said there was now enough land. The old woman said, "See whether you can find some people, look everywhere, go to the mountains, and see." So the girl went and looked everywhere but she saw nothing. The old woman said to her, "I don't think you looked very much." So she went again and found just one man. She traversed the entire country in a very short time. She returned and told her mother, "I have found only one man."—"Well, that will be well, get him." The girl went to the man and said, "My mother wants you to come to where we live." He agreed to come.

Cō'tsi'pamā'pöt lived in the middle of a wide stretch of water. The girl laid a stick across from the shore and walked ahead. When she was nearly across, she tipped the stick so as to topple the man into the water, but he flew up, unseen by her, and reached camp first. When the girl arrived, she told her mother, "I called him and he was drowned." She had one lodge while her mother lived in another. Her mother said, "That man is in your lodge." The girl did not know that he had flown there.

Cō'tsi'pamā'pöt made deer, cottontail rabbits, bears, antelope, and every kind of animal out of mud, threw them off and bade them take to the mountains. She said to her daughter, "You had better stay with him, you can't find anyone else, keep him for a husband." So the man and the girl lay together, but the man, though eager to possess her, was afraid. The old woman said to him, "Since you can do nothing with her, you had better go get some deer; kill it and bring the first vertebra." The man went off, killed a deer and brought the first hard vertebra. "Well," said Cō'tsi'pamā'pöt, "you had better use this, don't let her see this. This may fix it, perhaps she will bite it, then you can have your will of her." Night fell. He took the vertebra and put it by his *membrum virile*. The girl had a toothed vagina, but the teeth could not bite the bone and broke off. Then he had his will of her and she bit no more. He lay with her every night now.

After a while the young woman was big with child. Her mother made a big sack and into this the daughter dropped her children so that the bag was full of them. Cō'tsi'pamā'pöt said to the man, "You had better take this bag to the center of the world. Don't open it till you get there, no matter what noise you may hear from within." So the man set out with the sack and went on. After a while his load grew heavy and he heard a noise inside. He thought he would like to see the inside. He took off the bag, sat down and listened to the noise. He was eager to see what it was. At last he opened the bag and saw nothing. The babies got out and scattered all over the country. Most of them escaped. When he tied up the sack again, there were only a few left. He sat down and gave tribal names to the different babies. "You go up there, you shall be called by such a name," and so forth. To these few that remained at the bottom he said, "These are my people." All the babies in the sack were Indians.

The man had a long stone knife and an awl of hard bone. He had a rabbitskin blanket wide enough for two to sleep under. He had nothing with which to start fire, except a rock on which he would place his food. After a while he saw ashes falling down. "Where did this come from?" He sent several men far up, but they could see no fire anywhere. Others went higher still, and yet they could find no fire. Finally one of them went higher still and reported, "It looks like fire over there."—"Well, I think we had better all go and get that fire by gambling or some other way." He got all of them to come with him. They went to the people who had fire and gambled with them. Before daylight Cüna'waʙ' took a piece of bark, tied it round his head, stuck it into the fire, and then ran off. The people who owned the fire ran after him, but did not catch him. Then he took some root and said, "Make fire out of this." So he made fire from it, and after a while he threw away the rock he had used to cook on. He cooked seeds in the fire now.

He named all the hills and waters and rocks and bushes, so that people knew what to call them. He was the first to name them.

After a while the people who had come from the sack fought among themselves.

Cö'tsi'pamā'pöt, the old woman who made the earth, is still living. She made all the tribes speak different languages. She saw what all the people were doing. When Indians died they went to her, and she made new ones. People did not know where the dead went to; we don't know it, but she knows it all. . . .

The old woman gave people all kinds of seed to eat. She thought of the seeds and the people went to the place she pointed out and would find the seeds and eat them. "Live on this, boys," she would say; "this is yours to eat." (Lowie 1924:157–59; compare ibid: 103–104)

Female Culture Heroes

Culture heroes, whether human or animal, female or male, bring or bring about valuable objects, teachings and natural changes which make possible human society and survival. "The typical culture hero steals or liberates the sun, fire, or summer for his people, regulates the winds, originates corn, acorns, beans, and other foods, marks the animals and plants with their characteristic marks, determines the course of rivers, teaches men how to plant and plow, hunt, hold their ceremonies with efficacious songs and dances, invents shepherds, gives to men their medicines and magic, and usually sometime before the world becomes as it is now, he goes away into the west to await a certain time appointed for his return" (Leach 1972:268).

In "culture hero" as in "creator," the feminine form is the marked term, one which is used so seldom that it sounds strained at best. "Creatoress," "creatrix" and "culture heroine" are awkward and almost meaningless designations, reflecting the relatively weaker roles women play in creation, transformation and origin myths—when they appear at all in such narratives about ordering the world. Despite the fact that goddesses, women, and female animals do give birth to all manner of creatures, female figures in most of the mythology on record are much more likely to be depicted as destructive monsters rather than creative benefactors.

Vegetation goddesses, especially those associated with corn, are among the most prevalent "culture heroines" in the broadest sense. Åke Hultkrantz, Swedish scholar of comparative religions, summarizes the beliefs about this deity in the Americas:

The vegetation goddess (or the mother goddess in her role as vegetation goddess) appears to have her strongest foothold in the agrarian areas of North and Central America. She is here a corn goddess, corn being the predominant grain. The corn goddess may also rule over grass and herbs, bushes and trees, as in a story told by the Arikara on the Missouri River. Among the Hopi in Arizona and the central Algonkin, the latter being hunters rather than cultivators, the corn mother is

An ancient Mexican flat stamp depicting an ear of corn, found in Veracruz (Enciso 1953:50, fig. 111).

replaced by a male corn spirit—undoubtedly a secondary notion adapted to the interests of the patrilinear hunters. . . . The functions of the corn goddess may be shared by a number of corn goddesses, as among the Pueblo Indians. Among the Iroquois three sisters are mentioned: the Corn Sister, the Bean Sister, and the Squash Sister, each one embodying the prolific power of the cultivated domestic plants. . . .

The corn goddess may occasionally appear in the myth as a corncob, among the Seminole in Florida and the Cochiti in New Mexico, for instance. It is therefore interesting to observe that in the cult she is represented by a corncob among the Indians in Central America, Mexico, the southwestern United States, and on the plains. The Cochiti generally plant a superb specimen of a corncob, evidently symbolizing the power of vegetation or the goddess herself. Other rites involving the corncob include the flesh sacrifices by the Arikara at certain festivals, during which the "mother" is called upon to yield an abundant harvest.

The concept of the corncob as the symbol of the vegetation goddess recurs in Peru, where it plays a significant part in the harvest ritual; the corncob is then wrapped in clothes. Elsewhere in South America, outside the Andes, there is naturally little evidence of corn goddesses. From the tropical forest areas, however, we have some information about a corn spirit who is sometimes appeased with dances, as among the Cashinawa on the Purus River [Amazon]. Along with the corn spirit the cassava spirit is present in these areas. This spirit is also cherished in the cult, since the cassava or manioc plant is used for breadmaking. Thus the Mundurucú [interior Amazon] hold an annual celebration during which the mothers of corn and manioc are honored and reconciled. . . . The earth goddess of the Jívaro [northern Peru] is also the guardian of vegetation. When the Jívaro plant manioc, they call upon this goddess, Nungui, the soul of the manioc, who is represented by a stone of remarkable shape. The women who plant the manioc are themselves seated on manioc roots and one of them caresses a red-painted manioc in her lap. (Hultkrantz 1979:56, 57–58)

The Wabanaki (Abanaki, Abenaki, or Abnaki) Indians of what is now northern New England and eastern Canada tell about a beautiful woman who brought corn and cultivation. This version was collected by Mrs. W. Wallace Brown of Calais, Maine, whom Garrick Mallery called "the highest authority" on such mythology (1893:468; see "Female Monsters" below).

A long time ago, when Indians were first made, there lived one alone, far, far from any others. He knew not of fire, and subsisted on roots, barks, and nuts. This Indian became very lonesome for company. He grew tired of digging roots, lost his appetite, and for several days lay dreaming in the sunshine; when he awoke he saw something standing near, at which, at first, he was very much frightened. But when it spoke, his heart was glad, for it was a beautiful woman with long *light* hair, very unlike any Indian. He asked her to come to him, but she would not, and if he tried to approach her she seemed to go further away; he sang to her of his loneliness and besought her not to leave him; at last she told him, if he would do just as she should say, he would always have her with him. He promised that he would. She led him to where there was some very dry grass, told him to get two very dry sticks, rub them together quickly, holding them in the grass. Soon a spark flew out; the grass caught it, and quick as an arrow the ground was burned over. Then she said, "When the sun sets, take me by the hair and drag me over the burned ground." He did not like to do this, but she told him that wherever he dragged her something like grass would spring up, and he would see her hair

Pumpkin vine, as represented in a Navajo sandpainting of the Mountain chant (Matthews 1887: 448, plate xvii; in Sides 1961: plate 49, f).

coming from between the leaves; then the seeds would be ready for his use. He did as she said, and to this day, when they see the silk (hair) on the cornstalk, the Indians know she has not forgotten them. (Brown 1890:214; for useful comparative notes see Thompson 1929:293)

The beautiful woman whose hair yields corn in the Wabanaki myth contrasts with the filthy old woman whose body dirt becomes corn in a tale collected between 1908 and 1914 by anthropologist John R. Swanton from Koasati Indians living near Kinder, Louisiana.

An old woman was traveling about. She was covered with sores and was very dirty, so that wherever she went people did not want to see her. Finally she came to where some orphan children were living and remained there to take care of them. They said, "Stay with us." Then the old woman said, "Set out the things you use when you cook," and they set them before her. She was Corn. She rubbed herself as one rubs roasting ears and made bread of what came off, which they continued to eat.
By and by she said, "The corn is now getting hard." An old corncrib stood near, and she said, "Sweep this out, shut it up, and go to sleep. I am your mother. You can eat bread made out of white corn." When night came they lay down, and they heard a rapping noise in the corncrib, which presently ceased. Next day they went to it and opened the door and it was full of corn. (Swanton 1929:168)

Swanton collected a similar version during the same years from "one of the few remaining speakers of the ancient Natchez tongue residing near Braggs, Okla., a man named Watt Sam. This informant had drawn not merely upon his own people but upon his Cherokee and Creek neighbors, and it would now be impossible to say how much of the collection is pure Natchez, or, indeed, whether any of it may be so denominated" (ibid:1).

Corn-woman lived at a certain place in company with twin girls. When the corn was all gone she went into the corn house, taking two baskets, and came out with the baskets full. They lived on the hominy which she made from this.
One time the girls looked into this corn house and saw nothing there. They said to each other, "Where does she get it? Next time she goes in there we will creep up and watch her."
When the corn was all gone she started to go in and they saw her. So they crept after her and when she entered and closed the door they peeped through a crack. They saw her set down the basket, stand astride of it and rub and shake herself, and there was a noise, tsàgak, as if something fell off. In this way she filled one basket with corn. Then she stood over the other, rubbed herself and shook, the noise tsàgak was heard and that basket was full of beans. After that the girls ran away.
"Let us not eat it," they said. "She defecates and then feeds us with the excrement." So when the hominy was cooked they did not eat it, and from that she knew they had seen her. "Since you think it is filthy, you will have to help yourselves from now on. Kill me and burn my body. When summer comes things will spring up on the place where it was burned and you must cultivate them, and when they are matured they will be your food."
They killed Corn-woman and burned her body and when summer came corn, beans, and pumpkins sprang up. They kept cultivating these and every day, when

Stalk of corn, as represented in a Navajo sandpainting of the Mountain chant (Matthews 1887: 448, plate xvii; in Sides 1961: plate 49, d).

they stopped, stuck their hoes in the ground and went away. But on their return more ground would be hoed and the hoes would be sticking up in different places.

They said, "Let us creep up and find out who is hoeing for us," and they did so. When they looked they saw that the hoes were doing it of themselves and they laughed. Immediately the hoes fell down and did not work for them any more. They did not know that it was just those two hoes which were helping them and they themselves spoiled it. (Swanton 1929:230)

Other myths are associated with rituals involving corn. During the summer of 1924, anthropologist Ruth Benedict collected the following text from a "well-known" woman narrator, a Cochiti Pueblo Indian who "held an important ceremonial position."

All the women of the Corn Grinding Society (Kuya') were to grind on that day. They shelled all their baskets of corn and they put aside the sooted ears. The head of the Corn Grinding Society called together all the members of her society, and three women stayed in the house of the head of the society and slept there in order to begin to grind before sunrise. Daylight came and all the girls and women of the village shelled baskets of corn to take with them to the Corn Grinding Society to grind so that they might always have plenty. Everybody said, "Don't put the sooted ears in with the good corn." The girls and women of that village all went to grind and the head of the society and the three women who had slept in her house were already grinding. They sang their songs. One of the women heard somebody crying. She said, "Listen, somebody is crying." Just then the door opened and Corn Soot Woman came in crying. She said, "Nobody likes me to be with the corn they are to grind. I am fat but nobody has any use for me." The head woman of the society said to Corn Soot Woman, "Why are you crying?" "I am crying because they don't ever put me among the good ears. I am not rotten." The head woman of the society said, "Don't ever separate her from the good corn. She is fat; that is why she is what she is. She is the mother of the corn soot and you must put her in with the good corn whenever you shell it, in order that that too may be fat, as she is." They gave her a new name, Ioashkanake (shuck), and they gave the soot a ceremonial name, Wesa. (Benedict 1931:14–15)[6]

White Buffalo Maiden brought the Sioux Indians of the northern Plains their important ceremonial pipe and instructed them in its ritual use. With the help of interpreter Mr. Robert P. Higheagle, ethnomusicologist Frances Densmore conducted fieldwork on the Standing Rock Reservation in North and South Dakota between July 1911 and 1914. Although recorded in Higheagle's words, the narrative was told by the prominent Teton Sioux warrior Lone Man (Iśna'la-wića), who had battled Custer at Little Big Horn. "Preceding this recital by Lone Man, the subject had been discussed with other informants for more than two years. A summary of this story was read to Lone Man and discussed with him, after which he was requested to give the narrative in connected form, incorporating therewith material which he wished to add" (Densmore 1918:63).

In the olden times it was a general custom for the Sioux tribe (especially the Teton band of Sioux) to assemble in a body once at least during the year. This gathering took place usually about that time of midsummer when everything looked beautiful and everybody rejoiced to live to see nature at its best—that was

Tobacco plant, as represented in a Navajo sandpainting of the Mountain chant (Matthews 1887: 448, plate xvii; in Sides 1961: plate 49, e).

Hopi doll of Calako (Salako) Mana, or Maiden. The band marked with bars across her forehead, with feathers at both ends, represents an ear of corn. (Naylor 1975:207)[7]

[6]According to Charles H. Lange's 1946–53 anthropological investigations: "At present there are four members of the Women's Society (Ko'yawē) at Cochiti. . . . The principal function of the group is the ceremonial grinding of corn to make prayer meal for the cacique" *(Cochiti: A New Mexico Pueblo, Past and Present* [Carbondale: Southern Illinois University Press, 1959], p. 283). Lange further claims that Edward S. Curtis was wrong to call this an informal "pseudo-society" *(The North American Indian,* vol. XVI [Norwood, Massachusetts: Plimpton Press, 1926], p. 88). For more on Ruth Benedict's approach to folklore and mythology see Briscoe 1979, and for more on her Cochiti experiences see Alfonso Ortiz's introduction to the reprint of her 1931 BAE Bulletin (Albuquerque: University of New Mexico Press, 1981, pp. v–viii).

[7]According to Naylor, who does not specify her sources: "Hopi katcina, a doll of the Calako Mana (Corn Maiden), a female deity wearing a stepped headdress. This doll represents a katcina that appeared in the Palulukonti [Palolokonti, or Water Serpent Ceremony, in February or March] rites in Tusayan in 1893 [presumably, as reported by Jesse Walter Fewkes]" (1975:207). However, according to Alfonso Ortiz, the Salako Mana, or maiden, appeared with an "identically named male counterpart" in Salako dances infrequently held in connection with the July *Niman* ceremonies ("Of Kachinas and Men," in *Hopi Kachina Dolls,* exhibition catalogue, Moore College of Art Gallery in Philadelphia, 1975, p. 21; photo, p. 5). Jesse Walter Fewkes says about a drawing of a similar Hopi Calako Mana (Plate LVI): "The tablet represents terraced rain clouds. . . . Across the forehead is a symbol of an ear of corn, with two feathers attached to each end. The ring hanging over the forehead represents a fragment of Haliotis shell. There are imitation flowers made of wood represented in the hair . . . [with] chevrons on the cheek" ("Hopi Katcinas Drawn by Native Artists," in *Twenty-First Annual Report of the Bureau of American Ethnology to the Secretary of the Smithsonian Institution, 1899–1900,* by J. W. Powell, Director [Washington: Government Printing Office, 1903], p. 177). Although Fewkes claims that the Calako Mana is a "being not called katcina," such carved wooden dolls were designed to teach children and were/are still brought by the kachinas to distribute to the young during dances. Also see Laughlin 1977.

the season when the Sun-dance ceremony took place and vows were made and fulfilled. Sometimes the tribal gathering took place in the fall when wild game was in the best condition, when wild fruits of all kinds were ripe, and when the leaves on the trees and plants were the brightest.

One reason why the people gathered as they did was that the tribe as a whole might celebrate the victories, successes on the warpath, and other good fortunes which had occurred during the year while the bands were scattered and each band was acting somewhat independently. Another reason was that certain rules or laws were made by the head chiefs and other leaders of the tribe, by which each band of the tribe was governed. For instance, if a certain band got into trouble with some other tribe, such as the Crows, the Sioux tribe as a whole should be notified. Or if an enemy or enemies came on their hunting grounds the tribe should be notified at once. In this way the Teton band of Sioux was protected as to its territory and its hunting grounds.

After these gatherings there was a scattering of the various bands. On one such occasion the Sans Arc band started toward the west. They were moving from place to place, expecting to find buffalo and other game which they would lay up for their winter supply, but they failed to find anything. A council was called and two young men were selected to go in quest of buffalo and other game. They started on foot. When they were out of sight they each went in a different direction, but met again at a place which they had agreed upon. While they were planning and planning what to do, there appeared from the west a solitary object advancing toward them. It did not look like a buffalo; it looked more like a human being than anything else. They could not make out what it was, but it was coming rapidly. Both considered themselves brave, so they concluded that they would face whatever it might be. They stood still and gazed at it very eagerly. At last they saw that it was a beautiful young maiden. She wore a beautiful fringed buckskin dress, leggings, and moccasins. Her hair was hanging loose except at the left side, where was tied a tuft of shedded buffalo hair. In her right hand she carried a fan made of flat sage. Her face was painted with red vertical stripes. Not knowing what to do or say, they hesitated, saying nothing to her.

(Harter 1980a:98)

She spoke first, thus: "I am sent by the Buffalo tribe to visit the people you represent. You have been chosen to perform a difficult task. It is right that you should try to carry out the wishes of your people, and you must try to accomplish your purpose. Go home and tell the chief and headmen to put up a special lodge in the middle of the camp circle, with the door of the lodge and the entrance into the camp toward the direction where the sun rolls off the earth. Let them spread sage at the place of honor, and back of the fireplace let a small square place be prepared. Back of this and the sage let a certain frame, or rack, be made. Right in front of the rack a buffalo skull should be placed. I have something of importance to present to the tribe, which will have a great deal to do with their future welfare. I shall be in the camp about sunrise."

While she was thus speaking to the young men one of them had impure thoughts. A cloud came down and enveloped this young man. When the cloud left the earth the young man was left there—only a skeleton. The Maiden commanded the other young man to turn his back toward her face and in the direction of the camp, then to start for home. He was ordered not to look back.

When the young man came in sight of the camp he ran in a zigzag course, this being a signal required of such parties on returning home from a searching or scouting expedition. The people in the camp were on the alert for the signal, and preparations were begun at once to escort the party home. Just outside the council lodge, in front of the door, an old man qualified to perform the ceremony was waiting anxiously for the party. He knelt in the direction of the coming of the party to receive the report of the expedition. A row of old men were kneeling behind him. The young man arrived at the lodge. Great curiosity was shown by the people on account of the missing member of the party. The report was made, and the people received it with enthusiasm.

The special lodge was made, and the other requirements were carried out. The crier announced in the whole camp what was to take place on the following morning. Great preparations were made for the occasion. Early the next morning, at daybreak, men, women, and children assembled around the special lodge. Young men who were known to bear unblemished characters were chosen to escort the Maiden into camp. Promptly at sunrise she was in sight. Everybody was anxious. All eyes were fixed on the Maiden. Slowly she walked into the camp. She was dressed as when she first appeared to the two young men except that instead of the sage fan she carried a pipe—the stem was carried with her right hand and the bowl with her left.

The chief, who was qualified and authorized to receive the guest in behalf of the Sioux tribe, sat outside, right in front of the door of the lodge, facing the direction of the coming of the Maiden. When she was at the door the chief stepped aside and made room for her to enter. She entered the lodge, went to the left of the door, and was seated at the place of honor.

The chief made a speech welcoming the Maiden, as follows:

"My dear relatives: This day Wakan'tanka has again looked down and smiled upon us by sending us this young Maiden, whom we shall recognize and consider as a sister. She has come to our rescue just as we are in great need. Wakan'tanka wishes us to live. This day we lift up our eyes to the sun, the giver of light, that opens our eyes and gives us this beautiful day to see our visiting sister. Sister, we are glad that you have come to us, and trust that whatever message you have brought we may be able to abide by it. We are poor, but we have a great respect to visitors, especially relatives. It is our custom to serve our guests with some special food. We are at present needy and all we have to offer you is water, that falls from the clouds. Take it, drink it, and remember that we are very poor."

Dakota (Sioux) Thunderpipe, one to which is attached the wings of a thunder-bird (Mallery 1893:486, fig. 682).

Crossed pipes—a conventional device indicating peace (Mallery 1893:651, fig. 1018).

Then braided sweet grass was dipped into a buffalo horn containing rain water and was offered to the Maiden. The chief said, "Sister, we are now ready to hear the good message you have brought." The pipe, which was in the hands of the Maiden, was lowered and placed on the rack. Then the Maiden sipped the water from the sweet grass.

Then, taking up the pipe again, she arose and said:

"My relatives, brothers and sisters: Wakan'tanka has looked down, and smiles upon us this day because we have met as belonging to one family. The best thing in a family is a good feeling toward every member of the family. I am proud to become a member of your family—a sister to you all. The sun is your grandfather, and he is the same to me. Your tribe has the distinction of being always very faithful to promises, and of possessing great respect and reverence toward sacred things. It is known also that nothing but good feeling prevails in the tribe, and that whenever any member has been found guilty of committing any wrong, that member has been cast out and not allowed to mingle with the other members of the tribe. For all these good qualities in the tribe you have been chosen as worthy and deserving of all good gifts. I represent the Buffalo tribe, who have sent you this pipe. You are to receive this pipe in the name of all the common people [Indians]. Take it, and use it according to my directions. The bowl of the pipe is red stone—a stone not very common and found only at a certain place. This pipe shall be used as a peacemaker. The time will come when you shall cease hostilities against other nations. Whenever peace is agreed upon between two tribes or parties this pipe shall be a binding instrument. By this pipe the medicine-men shall be called to administer help to the sick."

Turning to the women, she said:

"My dear sisters, the women: You have a hard life to live in this world, yet without you this life would not be what it is. Wakan'tanka intends that you shall bear much sorrow—comfort others in time of sorrow. By your hand the family moves. You have been given the knowledge of making clothing and of feeding the family. Wakan'tanka is with you in your sorrows and joins you in your griefs. He has given you the great gift of kindness toward every living creature on earth. You he has chosen to have a feeling for the dead who are gone. He knows that you remember the dead longer than do the men. He knows that you love your children dearly."

Turning to the children:

"My little brothers and sisters: Your parents were once little children like you, but in the course of time they became men and women. All living creatures were once small, but if no one took care of them they would never grow up. Your parents love you and have made many sacrifices for your sake in order that Wakan'tanka may listen to them, and that nothing but good may come to you as you grow up. I have brought this pipe for them, and you shall reap some benefit from it. Learn to respect and reverence this pipe, and above all, lead pure lives. Wakan'tanka is your great grandfather."

Turning to the men:

"Now my dear brothers: In giving you this pipe you are expected to use it for nothing but good purposes. The tribe as a whole shall depend upon it for their necessary needs. You realize that all your necessities of life come from the earth below, the sky above, and the four winds. Whenever you do anything wrong against these elements they will always take some revenge upon you. You should reverence them. Offer sacrifices through this pipe. When you are in need of buffalo meat, smoke this pipe and ask for what you need and it shall be granted you. On you it depends to be a strong help to the women in the raising of children. Share

Dakota using a ceremonial pipe to raise a war party (Mallery 1893: 540, fig. 767).

the women's sorrow. Wakan'tanka smiles on the man who has a kind feeling for a woman, because the woman is weak. Take this pipe, and offer it to Wakan'tanka daily. Be good and kind to the little children."

Turning to the chief:

"My older brother: You have been chosen by these people to receive this pipe in the name of the whole Sioux tribe. Wakan'tanka is pleased and glad this day because you have done what it is required and expected that every good leader should do. By this pipe the tribe shall live. It is your duty to see that the pipe is respected and reverenced. I am proud to be called a sister. May Wakan'tanka look down on us and take pity on us and provide us with what we need. Now we shall smoke the pipe."

Then she took the buffalo chip which lay on the ground, lighted the pipe, and pointing to the sky with the stem of the pipe, she said, "I offer this to Wakan'tanka for all the good that comes from above." (Pointing to the earth:) "I offer this to the earth, whence come all good gifts." (Pointing to the cardinal points:) "I offer this to the four winds, whence come all good things." Then she took a puff of the pipe, passed it to the chief, and said, "Now my dear brothers and sisters, I have done the work for which I was sent here and now I will go, but I do not wish any escort. I only ask that the way be cleared before me."

Then, rising, she started, leaving the pipe with the chief, who ordered that the people be quiet until their sister was out of sight. She came out of the tent on the left side, walking very slowly; as soon as she was outside the entrance she turned into a white buffalo calf. (Densmore 1918:63–66)[8]

Bluejay is the culture heroine in a Snuqualmi myth told by Little Sam to Dr. Hermann Haeberlin while the latter was on an expedition to the Puget Sound area. He told how, in the beginning, "before the world had changed," five women—dog salmon, tyee salmon, silver salmon, steelhead salmon and rainbow salmon—traveled from the west and came to the Falls on the Snuqualmi River. There they stole a baby from a sleeping old woman and returned to the west. The people could not find the missing child, so its grandmother, Bluejay, flew westward to the "end of the world," where she encountered a

Chief-Boy of the Oglala Sioux. The large pipe is their conventional device indicating a chief (Mallery 1893:652, fig. 1023).

[8]According to Densmore's final note: "It is interesting to observe that the identity of a dream object often is unrecognized until it turns to depart" (1918:66). She also cites Alice C. Fletcher, "The White Buffalo Festival of the Unepapas," *Peabody Museum Reports,* vol. III, nos. 3 and 4 (Cambridge, Massachusetts, 1884), pp. 260–75. For a slightly different version, see "The Gift of the Sacred Pipe," in Joseph Epes Brown, ed., *The Sacred Pipe: Black Elk's Account of the Seven Rites of the Oglala Sioux* (1953), chap. 1.

Densmore continues her account thus: "It is said that the chief who received the pipe from the White Buffalo Maiden was Buffalo Stands Upward (Tatan'ka-woslal'-naźin). The pipe has been handed down from one generation to another, and is said to be now in the possession of Elk Head (Heña'ka-pa) who lives at Thunder Butte, on the Cheyenne River Reservation. He is said to be of 'about the third generation' which has kept the pipe, and is 98 years of age [Her note 2: "Elk Head died in January, 1916. . . ."]. Each preceding keeper of the pipe lived to be more than a hundred years old.

"The Indians named the pipe the White Buffalo Calf pipe. Duplicates of it were made, and soon every male member of the tribe carried a similar pipe. The stem was made to resemble the windpipe of a calf. Whenever this pipe is used in a smoking circle, or even when two men are smoking together, the rule is that the pipe be passed to the left, because that was the direction taken by the White Buffalo Maiden when she went away. The one who lights this pipe is required to make an offering" (1918:66–67).

Fish in a net pattern from an Olmec ceramic stamp found at Las Bocas, in present-day Puebla, Mexico (Field 1974:88, fig. 15).[9]

Eskimo finger mask from Big Lake, lower Yukon River. "It is used by women in ceremonial dances; otherwise its significance is unknown" (Nelson 1899:412, plate CIV; in Naylor 1975:84, fig. B).[10]

Symplegades, "two big rocks . . . always opening and closing" onto a darkness beyond. Bluejay managed to get through but the back of her head was flattened in the process.

When Bluejay got through the rock she met a man who made all kinds of fish nets. This was the stolen boy whom the salmon women had reared, and when he was grown to manhood they had married him. Bluejay flew past him and as she did so the man took up some dust and threw it into her face. Bluejay began to cry and said: "I have been looking for you for years, and now you throw dust in my face." Then the man who was Dō'kᵘibEɬ showed Bluejay all the salmon who were his children and he taught her how to make all kinds of nets. Bluejay brought all this information to her people, the Snuqualmi.

As Bluejay was returning through the opening and closing rock she put the net gauge which DōkᵘibEɬ had given her for the fish nets in between the rocks and in this way kept them open, until she had passed through.

DōkᵘibEɬ returned to this world and he brought all his salmon children with him so that they could spawn in the rivers. Before DōkᵘibEɬ came, there were no salmon in this world, and when he brought all the species of salmon the humpbacked salmon were forgotten and so this kind of salmon comes only every second year. (Haeberlin 1924:372)

Sedna (also known as Arnaknagsak) is the Central Eskimo culture heroine whose misfortunes at the hands of her father Anguta brought whales and seals into the world. Sedna now rules Adlivun, the underworld, to which Anguta conducts souls past the guardian dog. These souls must spend at least a year there sleeping beside Anguta, who pinches them (Leach 1972:11, 58, 979; Wardle 1900). The following narrative was prepared by anthropologist Franz

[9]Field cites Carlo T. E. Gay's 1971 study of Olmec iconography, *Chalca-cingo*, for the suggestion that such designs indicate "rain propitiation themes" rather than fishing or hunting. Field claims that "it is not difficult to see in the fish within the net of #15 another water motif, along with the clouds, especially since, as Gay has pointed out to me, the eyes of the fish are so disproportionately enlarged into the circles also used as water symbols" (1974:81). He also cites Gay's suggestion that "it is conceivable that the Olmecs shared with other ancient Mexican peoples the belief that the moon goddess was the 'first person to weave'; hence, the weaver par excellence. If so, her symbolic weaving in the sky is well described by the net pattern representing clouds" (ibid). The moon as first weaver comes from J. Eric S. Thompson's *Maya Hieroglyphic Writing* (Norman: University of Oklahoma Press, 1960).

[10]According to Dorothy Jean Ray: "In early times women danced fully clothed, stripped to the waist, or naked, covered only by a translucent intestine parka . . . in the South [between the Yukon and Nushagak Rivers] they waved carved geometric pieces of wood or miniature masks decorated with feathers or caribou fur. These objects, traditionally called finger masks, were used to extend or emphasize the flowing movements of shoulders and arms, as well as to incorporate symbolism into the dance" (1967:31). Even though some copied face masks, finger masks were *not* "true masks," which "always partially or wholly covered a face to transform a human being into a spirit, a thing, an animal, or another human being," for "women, except in certain secular dances, did not wear masks . . . [and] even a female shaman's experiences were interpreted by a male carver" (ibid:73–74). Women usually used pairs of finger masks, one in each hand, although "occasionally circlets of fur or feathers, or upright wands, were used instead . . ." (ibid:200).

Boas from "the particulars of the myth as I received it from the Oqoniut and the Akudnirmiut [southern Baffin Island]."

Once upon a time there lived on a solitary shore an Inung with his daughter Sedna. His wife had been dead for some time, and the two led a quiet life. Sedna grew up to be a handsome girl, and the youths came from all around to sue for her hand, but none of them could touch her proud heart. Finally, at the breaking up of the ice in the spring, a fulmar flew from over the ice and wooed Sedna with enticing song. "Come to me," it said; "come into the land of the birds, where there is never hunger, where my tent is made of the most beautiful skins. You shall rest on soft bearskins. My fellows, the fulmars, shall bring you all your heart may desire; their feathers shall clothe you; your lamp shall always be filled with oil, your pot with meat." Sedna could not long resist such wooing and they went together over the vast sea. When at last they reached the country of the fulmar, after a long and hard journey, Sedna discovered that her spouse had shamefully deceived her. Her new home was not built of beautiful pelts, but was covered with wretched fishskins, full of holes, that gave free entrance to wind and snow. Instead of soft reindeer skins her bed was made of hard walrus hides and she had to live on miserable fish, which the birds brought her. Too soon she discovered that she had thrown away her opportunities when, in her foolish pride, she had rejected the Inuit youth. In her woe she sang: "Aja, O father, if you knew how wretched I am you would come to me and we would hurry away in your boat over the waters. The birds look unkindly upon me, the stranger; cold winds roar about my bed; they give me but miserable food. O come and take me back home, Aja."

When a year had passed and the sea was again stirred by warmer winds, the father left his country to visit Sedna. His daughter greeted him joyfully and besought him to take her back home. The father, hearing of the outrages wrought upon his daughter, determined upon revenge. He killed the fulmar, took Sedna into his boat, and they quickly left the country that had brought so much sorrow to Sedna. When the other fulmars came home and found their companion dead and his wife gone, they all flew away in search of the fugitives. They were very sad over the death of their poor murdered comrade and continue to mourn and cry until this day.

Having flown a short distance, they discerned the boat and stirred up a heavy storm. The sea rose in immense waves that threatened the pair with destruction. In this mortal peril the father determined to offer Sedna to the birds and flung her overboard. She clung to the edge of the boat with a death grip. The cruel father then took a knife and cut off the first joints of her fingers. Falling into the sea they were transformed into whales, the nails turning into whalebone. Sedna holding on to the boat more tightly, the second finger joints fell under the sharp knife and swam away as seals; when the father cut off the stumps of the fingers they became ground seals.

(Rice 1979:122)

Meantime the storm subsided, for the fulmars thought Sedna was drowned. The father then allowed her to come into the boat again. But from that time she cherished a deadly hatred against him and swore bitter revenge. After they got ashore, she called her dogs and let them gnaw off the feet and hands of her father while he was asleep. Upon this he cursed himself, his daughter and the dogs. They have since lived in the land of Adlivun, of which Sedna is the mistress. (Boas 1888:583; for useful comparative notes see Thompson 1929:272–73)

The following legend involving Sedna was collected by Harlan I. Smith from Conieossuck, the head of an Eskimo family living at Nachvak, north of the Christian mission at Rama, "through the medium of George Deer, a bright Eskimo from Rigoulette . . . the narrator reciting a few words at a time, and pausing until these were interpreted and written out." According to Smith's footnote: "The Eskimo story-teller, of which class there is usually a representative in each village, is obliged to narrate the stories correctly, as it is considered a part of the duty of the audience to correct his inaccuracies." Both the narrative and Smith's notes have been reprinted below to give a better idea of Sedna, of a "medicine woman," of the context of narration, and of nineteenth-century attitudes toward Native Americans.

Olŭngwa[a]

In the old times, Sedna[b] came up to the surface of the water, and while there was seen by an old heathen[c] woman named Olŭngwa, who had been left on an island, with two or three children, by a party of heathen, while on their way to visit other heathen.

Olŭngwa wanted Sedna to go below the water again, and so went walking out to her upon the water, and combed her hair.[d]

After Olŭngwa combed her hair, she returned to the bottom.

There was a party of heathen men talking about something in a dark house, where there was no light. In the winter, one of these men went out to the island because Olŭngwa was there. One day, Olŭngwa left the man and walked on the water to her home, where her husband gave her his leader dog. She then went back to the island in the night, and going to the door of the house, asked the man she had left on the island the day before what they had to eat.

In the winter she went home. There an old heathen[c] man (angakok?) was talking with another heathen[c] man about her. He would not believe her to be a heathen.[c] She was listening to them, but they did not know it. He said, "How is it she cannot melt solder,[e] as I can do,[f] if she is a heathen."[c] While he was talking she came in through the door. Then she went out and took a handful of sod or turf, and going in again held it out in her hand. She said to the man who did not believe she could melt solder, "Here is some turf." She smacked her other hand on top of it several times while they looked at her. She said, "Turf now," and the last time she smacked her hand on the turf, it melted, and running between her fingers fell on the floor as shining solder. The man who did not believe became ashamed, and the next day went and "hung"[g] himself, because he was wrong, and Olŭngwa could do what he could not.

a. This story seemed to be made up of several short parts, some of which are apparently incomplete and show but little relation to each other. Collected October 2, 1893. Olŭngwa, as the writer understands, was a medicine woman, perhaps an angakok, or possibly a pivdlerortok, "a mad or delirious person," able to foretell events, unfold the thoughts of others, and "even gifted with a faculty of walking upon the water, besides the highest perfection in divining, but was at the same time greatly feared." Rink's *Tales and Traditions of the Eskimo*, p. 56.

b. "Sedna" has been substituted in each case for the following words of the interpreter, "the woman whose fingers had been cut off," as it is supposed that the phrase refers to her. "Their Supreme Being is a woman whose name is Sedna." Boas, "Central Eskimo," *6th An. Rep. Bur. Ethnology*, p. 583.

When telling of Sedna, Conieossuck and his wife would clutch the top of the table, from the side, then letting go the right hand would draw it edgewise over the fingers of the left: or she would hold both hands while he struck them with the edge of his: thus representing the cutting of Sedna's fingers, the story of which, also, is related in Boas' "Central Eskimo."

c. "Heathen," was used almost invariably by the christianized Eskimo at the village, to designate those from the north of Labrador, or even their own ancestors previous to their conversion by the Moravian missionaries. In this instance, however, it was probably used by the interpreter, to signify medicine or angakok, and in note f of this tale the reference to "angakok" must be understood in this connection.

d. It is supposed that Sedna's hair was infested with vermin, that after the combing all this vermin turned to seals and her hair to flaunting seaweed, and that this was done by Olŭngwa as an atonement.

e. It was impossible to determine the exact significance of the word "solder," as used by this interpreter.

f. The following explanatory sentence inserted by Conieossuck at this point of the story suggests either that he did not believe in the angakok or that he understood some of the impositions used by them to impress the credulous. "He did not really melt solder. He stole it from the whites and made others believe he melted it."

g. The words of the Eskimo interpreter, and later of the informer, have often been remodeled and arranged to complete the sense; however, those included within quotation marks are exactly retained. In many cases where more specific words should be substituted the lack of familiarity with the exact sense of the words used will not permit a change. (Smith 1894:209–10)

Eskimo finger mask from Norton Sound, 5 x 2¾ inches. "This specimen was collected by Mr. L. M. Turner, who states that it was intended to represent a star, the feathers indicating the twinkling of light. This finger mask was used by women in certain ceremonial dances" (Nelson 1899:413, pl. CIV; in Naylor 1975:84, fig. A; also see Ray 1967:220, plate 65).

Female Monsters

It is not difficult to find myths that portray women as monstrous, unnatural, dangerous, and lethal—especially to men, but also to each other. Psychoanalysts have suggested that this is basically because myths are projective expressions, collective Rorschach tests that show an unconscious fear of women, at least on the part of men who generally maintain and proclaim a culture's myths and rituals. H. R. Hays summarizes the rationale behind his anthropological, historical and psychological study of *The Dangerous Sex* in these terms:

We have been endeavoring to show by the facts assembled in this study that male attitudes toward women and the images of women created by men are strongly influenced by deep anxieties, which are probably universal and basic as the young male grows up in the family relationship, and also shaped by the pressures of the various cultures which man has created. In other words, since men have a tendency to be afraid of women they also create situations which rationalize these fears and perpetuate them. In addition, since no human being can easily face his own compulsions, the male tends to project his fears and antagonisms in terms of derogatory attributes by insisting that women are evil, inferior and valueless (because different) and hence should be made to obey, be kept in their place, or fulfill some unreal role which neutralizes them and removes them from the sphere of competition. From all of this, traditions and stereotypes are born which can always be called upon to justify the inherent tendencies in male behavior. (1964:281)

After joint fieldwork among the Mundurucú Indians of Amazonian Brazil in 1952–53—she largely in the company of women and he largely in the company of men—anthropologists Yolanda Murphy and Robert F. Murphy drew much the same conclusion from the rituals and behavior they observed and the myths and folklore they collected. A key narrative recounted how in mythic times men wrested the karökö—sacred trumpets kept in the men's house and taboo to the sight of women—from the women, who today live in matrilocal houses surrounding the men's house and who in those times had discovered and initially owned the trumpets while occupying the men's house. This and similar myths, as well as men's casual remarks and actions toward women, indicated that among the Mundurucú, "the penis has power; it is how men dominate women." However:

The myth of the karökö is a parable of phallic dominance, of male superiority symbolized in, and based upon, the possession of the penis. But it is at best an uneasy overlordship, obtained only by expropriation from the original custody of the women. In one sense, the myth is an allegory of man's birth from woman, his original dependence upon the woman as the supporting, nurturant and controlling agent in his life, and of the necessity to break the shackles and assert his autonomy and manhood. The mother is the center of love and affect, but she is also an eternal threat to self-individuation, a figure of authority, a frustrater of urges, and a swallower of emergent identity; she can devour and reincorporate that which she issued, and the vagina, the avenue to life, is ambivalently conceived by the men as destructive. The role of the male, then, must be maintained by vigilance and continual self-assertion. (Murphy and Murphy 1974:95; also see chapter 6 below)

In their summary discussion of "Women and Men"—Mundurucú and American—the Murphys suggest:

. . . If the men's house [and its hidden sacred trumpets] symbolism has any function at all in Mundurucú society, it is to conceal from the men the fragility of their own superiority; it perpetuates an illusion. . . . Perhaps Margaret Mead (1972 [personal communication]) summed it up best when she said, in a passing remark: "If men really were all that powerful, they wouldn't need such rigamarole." (1974:226)

In his psychoanalytic study, *The Fear of Women,* Dr. Wolfgang Lederer maintains that:

In our Western culture, which reached its clearest definition during Freud's time and which today, in spite of much dilution and adulteration, still largely follows

(Harter 1980b:149)

the basic values of his time—in this our Western Culture men have seen women variously as charming or boring, as busy home-makers or emancipated discontents, as inspiring or castrating; but throughout, and in spite of everything, still basically and always as "the weaker sex." Whether dominated, tolerated, despised, adored, or protected, in any case they are to be "the Other," the appendage and foil for "the Lord of Creation," man. (1968:vi)

It is this "weaker sex" notion, Lederer claims, which "has to such an extent slanted the perception of Western man that he must, to this day, consider any fear of women as unmanly and hence unacceptable" (ibid). He assembles evidence from archeology, folklore, mythology and history—from the ancient Venus von Willendorf to contemporary "mom" as scathingly portrayed in Philip Wylie's 1942 *Generation of Vipers*—because: "We must admit and face our fear of women—and as therapists make our patients admit and face it—the way the heroes of old faced it and, facing it, conquered fear and woman and the monsters of the unconscious deep, of night and death" (ibid:283).

Once again, heroes are men and the monstrous unknown symbolically linked with women. This is perhaps still unavoidable, and indeed, maybe women fear each other with the same symbolic associations, but it may be circumstantial. Most myth texts have been collected by men from other men, and they are usually interpreted from a male's perspective. Perhaps when there have been additional joint explorations such as the Murphys' and when more women have become actively involved in the study of myths told and believed by both sexes, but particularly by other women in the company of women, complementary mythologies will emerge. Meanwhile, the following list of "viragos" is abbreviated only by temporal and spatial demands; similar examples can be multiplied almost indefinitely from mythologies worldwide.

‡   Coatlicue was the awesome and powerful mother of Huitzilopochtli, the War and Sun God, chief deity of Tenochtitlán, also known as Hummingbird Wizard. Coatlicue's statue depicts her with a head of twin serpents, clawed hands and feet, a necklace of human hands and hearts, a skull breastplate, and a skirt of writhing serpents. It "brings into a dynamic concentrate the manifold horrors of the universe" (Vaillant 1962:170, pl. 52; also see, e.g., Nicholson 1967:85, 87).

‡   "Edward Seler, the German Americanist (1849–1922), saw in the two heads of snakes the decapitated body of the goddess. Seler thinks that the conception of showing the goddess of earth decapitated stems from Aztec rites; according to tradition, in the course of feasts celebrated in the honour of the goddess, a woman representing Coatlicue was decapitated and flayed. The flaying, the stripping off the skin of sacrificial victims who represented the gods, was the symbol of the rejuvenation of nature. These vegetation rites were performed every spring" (Anton 1973:58).

Critic John Bierhorst translated the following Aztec myth about Coatlicue from a sixteenth-century French translation by André Thévet. The lost Spanish original was supposed to have been compiled by missionaries in 1543. According to Bierhorst's introductory annotation: "Quetzalcoatl and Tezcatlipoca represent the bright and dark aspects of the Creator. The earth her-

Aztec goddess Coatlicue, "Lady of the Serpent Skirt." Over eight feet high, this statue was discovered on the site of Tenochtitlán and is now in the National Museum of Anthropology in Mexico City (Lehner 1969:26, fig. 59).

self is the nourisher of life; but she is also the burial ground of the dead. One purpose of this myth is to validate the Aztec custom of sacrificing live human hearts."

The gods Quetzalcoatl and Tezcatlipoca brought the earth goddess down from on high. All the joints of her body were filled with eyes and mouths biting like wild beasts. Before they got down, there was water already below, upon which the goddess then moved back and forth. They did not know who had created it.

They said to each other, "We must make the earth." So saying, they changed themselves into two great serpents, one of whom seized the goddess from the right hand down to the left foot, the other from the left hand down to the right foot. As they tightened their grip, she broke at the middle. The half with the shoulders became the earth. The remaining half they brought to the sky—which greatly displeased the other gods.

Afterward, to compensate the earth goddess for the damage those two had inflicted upon her, all the gods came down to console her, ordaining that all the produce required for human life would issue from her. From her hair they made trees, flowers, and grasses; from her skin, very fine grasses and tiny flowers; from her eyes, wells and fountains, and small caves; from her mouth, rivers and large caves; from her nose, valleys and mountains; from her shoulders, mountains.

Sometimes at night this goddess wails, thirsting for human hearts. She will not be silent until she receives them. Nor will she bear fruit unless she is watered with human blood. (1976:50–51)

Flower design on pre-Hispanic Mexican stamp from Cuitzeo (Field 1974:132, fig. 11).

In a myth common to northern California and Oregon (Thompson 1929: 355), Loon-Woman, like Coatlicue, hangs human hearts around her neck. The first part of a Yana Indian Loon-Woman myth collected by folklorist Jeremiah Curtin in northern California betrays its nineteenth-century origins in a stilted, ornate style. Curtin's introductory note on "Personages" states: "After each name is given that of the creature or thing into which the personage was changed subsequently. *Chuhna*, spider; *Haka hasi* [sic], loon; *Hitchinna*, wildcat; *Jamuka*, acorn worm; *Juka*, silkworm; *Metsi*, coyote; *Tsanunewa*, fisher (a bird); *Tsore Jowa*, eagle" (1899:407).

At some distance east of Jigul matu lived old Juka. He had a great many sons and two daughters—a big house full of children.

Juka's two daughters were Tsore Jowa, the elder, and Haka Lasi, the younger. After a time Haka Lasi fell in love with her brother Hitchinna. One day she fell asleep and dreamed that he had married her.

Metsi lived, too, in Juka's house. He was no relative; he just lived as a guest there.

One day all the men were out hunting. It was then that Haka Lasi saw Hitchinna in a dream. She began to sing about him, and she sang: "I dream of Hitchinna; I dream that he is my husband. I dream of Hitchinna; I dream that he is my husband."

All the men came back from the hunt at night. At daylight next morning they went to swim, and Tsore Jowa made ready food for them. Haka Lasi took a very nice staff in her hand, and went on top of the sweat-house. She looked in and sang,—

"Where is my husband? Send him up here to me. I will take him away. We must go on a journey. Where is my husband? Send him up here to me."

All knew that she had no husband.

"You have no husband," said they.

Hitchinna was lying in one corner wrapped up in the skin of a wildcat.

"You have no husband in this house; all here are your brothers," said Juka.

"I have a husband and I want him to come here to me," answered Haka Lasi.

"Well," said the eldest son, "I will go up to her. Let us hear what she will say." He went up.

"You are not my husband," said Haka Lasi. "Do not come near me."

She drove that one down, and called again: "Where is my husband? Send him up to me."

"Go you," said Juka to the second son.

"I don't want you," said Haka Lasi to the second son.

She refused one after another, and drove them away until none was left but Hitchinna. Juka went then to Hitchinna and said,—

"My son, get up and go to her; it looks as though you were the one she wants."

"He is the one," said Haka Lasi; "he is my husband. I want him to go away with me."

Hitchinna said not a word, but rose, washed, dressed himself nicely, and went to the woman.

"The sun is high now," said Haka Lasi; "we must go quickly."

She was glad when taking away the one she wanted. They travelled along, and she sang of Hitchinna as they travelled, sang of him all the time. They went a long distance, and at night she fixed a bed and they lay down on it.

Young Hitchinna could not sleep, he was frightened. When Haka Lasi was asleep, he rose very quickly, took a piece of soft rotten wood, put it on her arm where she had held his head, covered it, and then ran away quickly, hurried back toward Juka's sweat-house with all his might. About daylight he was at the sweat-house.

Now Chuhna, Juka's sister, lived with him. She was the greatest person in the world to spin threads and twist ropes. She had a willow basket as big as a house, and a rope which reached up to the sky and was fastened there.

"My nephew," said she to Hitchinna, "I will save you and save all from your terrible sister. She will be here very soon; she may come any moment. She will kill all in this house; she will kill every one if she finds us here. Let all go into my basket. I will take you up to the sky. She cannot find us there; she cannot follow us to that place."

"I will lie lowest," said Metsi. "I am a good man, I will go in first, I will go in before others; I will be at the bottom of the basket."

Metsi went in first; every one in the sweat-house followed him. Then Chuhna ran up, rose on her rope, and pulled the basket after her.

Klikitat basket
(Naylor 1975:110, fig. A).

The sweat-house was empty; no one stayed behind. Chuhna kept rising and rising, going higher and higher.

When Haka Lasi woke up and saw that she had a block of rotten wood on her arm instead of Hitchinna, she said—

"You won't get away from me, I will catch you wherever you are."

She rushed back to the sweat-house. It was empty; no one there. She ran around in every direction looking for tracks, to find which way they had gone. She found nothing on the ground; then she looked into the sky, and far up, very high, close to the sun, she saw the basket rising, going up steadily.

Haka Lasi was raging; she was so awfully angry that she set fire to the house. It burned quickly, was soon a heap of coals.

The basket was almost at the sky when Metsi said to himself, "I wonder how far up we are; I want to see." And he made a little hole in the bottom of the basket to peep through and look down.

That instant the basket burst open; all came out, poured down, a great stream of people, and all fell straight into the fire of the sweat-house.

Now, Tsore Jowa was outside on top of the basket. She caught at the sun, held to it, and saved herself.

Hitchinna went down with the rest, fell into the burning coals, and was burned like his brothers.

Haka Lasi was glad that they had not escaped her; she took a stick, fixed a net on it, and watched.

All were in the fire now and were burning. After a while one body burst, and the heart flew out of it. Haka Lasi caught the heart in her net. Soon a second and a third body burst, and two more hearts flew out. She caught those as well as the first one. She caught all the hearts except two,—Juka's own heart and his eldest son's heart.

Juka's heart flew high, went away far in the sky, and came down on the island of a river near Klamath Lake. It turned into Juka himself there. He sank in the ground to his chin; only his head was sticking out.

The heart of the eldest son flew off to the foot of Wahkalu and turned to be himself again. He fell so deep into the earth that only his face was sticking out on the surface.

Now Haka Lasi put all the hearts which she had caught on a string, hung them around her neck, and went to a lake east of Jigulmatu. She wanted to live at the bottom of the lake, but could not find a place deep enough. So she went northwest of Klamath Lake to Crater Lake, where she could live in deep water. . . .

(Curtin 1899:407; also see Demetracopoulou 1933)

During the summer of 1907, anthropologist Robert H. Lowie collected a myth about a dangerous "Burr-Woman" from Stoney Assiniboine Indians of Morley, Alberta, Canada. Citing similar tales from Omaha, Fox, Arikara, and Pawnee groups, Lowie notes that "this story was said to symbolize the tenacity of the frog's nuptial embrace" (1909:180).

Frog design on pre-Hispanic Mexican stamp from Michoacán (Field 1974:69, fig. 16).

Long ago, there lived a very handsome youth. All the girls were eager to marry him, but he did not care for women. There was a good-looking girl who was living with her grandmother. She proposed to the youth, but he refused to marry her. The girl returned and complained to her grandmother. The old woman was angry, and said, "Let me stay behind when the camp moves." When the camp was broken, the old woman remained in the rear. The men went out to hunt. She allowed them to pass without saying anything. At last, when the young man came, she asked him to pack her on his back. "Why do you ask me to do this?" "I am unable to walk. Carry me on your back and put me off near the camp." Finally, the youth consented and carried her near the camp. There he tried to set her down, but she stuck tight. He tried to throw her off, running against trees, but she still stuck to him. When he saw he could not get her off, he began to cry. Some women, hearing the noise, ran up to see what was the matter. When they tried to pull her off, the hag cried, "Don't bother me, I am his wife." They could not get her down; they went to the youth's father and told him what had happened. The old man said, "Whoever pulls off the old woman, may marry my son." A number of women tried, but all failed. Whenever they caught hold of her, the old woman cried, "Let me alone, I am married to him." There were two good-looking girls who did not say anything, but thought they could rid the youth of his burden. They went there and found him lying on his stomach. One went on either side. They began to pull. Four times they pulled, and the last time they pulled the old woman off, whereupon they killed her. The youth's back had been fouled by the woman's urine. They washed him, and doctored him in a sweat-lodge. Thus they restored him to his former condition. When he was clean again, they had him for a husband. (Lowie 1909:180–81; also see Lévi-Strauss 1978:57–60)

In his 1893 "Picture-Writing of the American Indians," Col. Garrick Mallery reports that "among the hundreds of figures and characters seen by the present writer on the slate rocks that abound on the shores and island of Kejimkoojik Lake, Queen's county, Nova Scotia . . . there appears a class of incised figures illustrating the religious myths and folklore of the Indian tribes which inhabited the neighborhood within historic times." Mallery claims these were Abnaki myths, many of which "had been recently repeated to him by Mrs. W. Wallace Brown, of Calais, Maine, the highest authority in that line of study, and by other persons visited in Maine, New Brunswick, Nova Scotia, and in Cape Breton and Prince Edwards Islands, who were familiar with the Penobscot, Passamaquoddy, Amalecite, and Micmac tribes. A number of these myths and tales had before been collected in variant forms by Mr. Charles G. Leland [*The Algonquin Legends of New England*, Boston, 1884]" (1893:468).

Fig. 654 is one of the drawings mentioned, and indicates one episode among the very numerous adventures of Glooscap, the Hero-God of the Abnaki, several of which are connected with a powerful witch called by Mr. Leland Pook-jin-skwess, or the Evil Pitcher, and by Mrs. W. Wallace Brown, Pokinsquss, the Jug Woman. She is also called the toad woman, from one of her transformations, and often appeared in a male form to fight Glooscap after he had disdained her love proffered as a female. Among the multitude of tales on this general theme, one narrates how Glooscap was at one time a Pogumk, or the small animal of the weasel family commonly called Fisher (Mustela Canadensis), also translated as Black Cat, and was the son of the chief of a village of Indians who were all Black Cats, his mother being a bear. Doubtless these animal names and the attributes of the animals in the tales refer to the origin of totemic divisions among the Abnaki. Pokinsquss was also of the Black Cat village, and hated the chief and contrived long how she could kill him and take his place. Now, one day when the camp had packed up to travel, the witch asked the chief Pogumk to go with her to gather gull's eggs; and they went far away in a canoe to an island where the gulls were

Fig. 654.—Myth of Pokinsquss (Mallery 1893:469).

breeding and landed there, and then she hid herself to spy, and having found out that the Pogumk was Glooscap, ran to the canoe and paddled away singing:

Nikhed-ha Pogumk min nekuk,
Netswil sāgāmawin!

Which being translated from the Passamaquoddy language means—

I have left the Black Cat on an island,
I shall be chief of the Fishers now!

The continuation of the story is found in many variant shapes. In one of them Glooscap's friend the Fox came to his rescue, as through Glooscap's m'toulin or magic power he heard the song of appeal though miles away beyond forests and mountains. In others the Sea Serpent appears in answer to the Hero-God's call, and the latter, mounting the serpent's back, takes a load of stones as his cargo to throw at the serpent's horns when the latter did not swim fast enough. In the figure {above} the island is shown at the lower right hand as a roundish outline with Glooscap inside. The small round objects to the left are probably the gull's eggs, but may be the stimulating stones above mentioned. Pokinsquss stands rejoicing in the stern of a canoe, which points in the wavy water away from the island. The device to the left of the witch may be the dismantled camp of the Black Cats, and the one to her right is perhaps where the Fox "beyond forests and mountains" heard Glooscap's song of distress. (Mallery 1893:469–70)

Glooscap's Homeric counterpart Odysseus must combat equally dangerous and compelling female figures in the seaside Sirens. Circe warns him what to expect from them as he continues his journey home after the Trojan war:

"Next, where the Sirens dwell, you plough the seas;
Their song is death, and makes destruction please.
Unblest the man, whom music wins to stay
Nigh the cursed shore, and listen to the lay.
No more that wretch shall view the joys of life,
His blooming offspring, or his beauteous wife!
In verdant meads they sport; and wide around
Lie human bones that whiten all the ground:
The ground polluted floats with human gore,
And human carnage taints the dreadful shore.
Fly swift the dangerous coast; let every ear
Be stopp'd against the song! 'tis death to hear!"

—Homer, *The Odyssey*, book xii,
trans. Pope (1882:173).

‡ ". . . The Greeks knew nothing about the Homeric Sirens except what they found in the *Odyssey;* but they . . . were quick to supply them with a parentage, with individual names, with a geographical location, and with an end to their story.

"Their father was Phorcus; or you may prefer Achelous. Their mother was Earth, if she was not Sterope or one of the Muses. Concerning their home there was general agreement: they inhabited three island-rocks off the west coast of Italy, between Sorrento and Capri. As for the end of their story, it was fated that they must die if their charms ever failed to attract a passing vessel to its destruction; this happened once in the story of Odysseus and once in the story of the Argonauts" (Page 1973:85–86).

‡   "For everybody knew, from the beginning to the end of Greek history, what a Siren really was. . . . There are many works of art from the eighth century B.C. onwards to tell us the dismal truth about these creatures. . . . They are the demons of the underworld. The Siren is not a beautiful female but a bird with a human head. . . . It does not lure men to destruction; it waits (impatiently, perhaps) until you die, then escorts your soul (gently or violently) on its journey to the underworld. Its effigy often crowns the tomb, presumably representing the soul of the departed" (ibid:86).

◆   Denys Page, *Folktales in Homer's 'Odyssey'*: "It is easy to demonstrate that the story of the beautiful female whose singing lures the traveller, and especially the seafarer, to destruction, is common and widespread. I therefore suppose that the narrative in the *Odyssey* is based on familiar folktale, not free invention. And it is the content of the common folktale which explains why the poet might call his females 'Sirens,' and why the ancients found nothing amiss with this transfer of the name" (1973:88).

(Harter 1980b:141)

‡   "The Sirens were indeed originally terrestrial. . . . But by the sixth century the traditional habitat of the Sirens had changed. 'The Sirens,' says an anonymous work on monsters and great beasts, 'are mermaids, who by their exceeding beauty and winning song ensnare mariners; from the head to the navel they are of human and maidenly form, but they have the scaly tails of fishes' " (Lawson 1910:87; also see Benwell and Waugh 1961; Levi 1977; Costello 1979:34–58).

James Douglas Suggs (1887–1955), a gifted black storyteller, told a mermaid legend to folklorist Richard M. Dorson in Calvin, Michigan, in 1952.[11]

Before they had any steam, ships were sailing by sails, you know, across the Atlantic. The Atlantic was fifteen miles deep, and there were mermaids in those days. And if you called anybody's name on the ship, they would ax for it, say, "Give it to me." And if you didn't give it to them they would capsize the ship. So the captain had to change the men's names to different objects—hatchet, ax, hammer, furniture. Whenever he wanted a man to do something, he had to call him, "Hammer, go on deck and look out." The mermaid would holler, "Give me hammer." So they throwed the hammer overboard to her, and the vessel would proceed on. The captain might say, "Ax, you go down in the kindling room start a fire in the boiler; it's going dead." Then the mermaid says, "Give me ax." So they have to throw her an iron ax. Next day he says, "Suit of furniture, go down in the stateroom and make up those beds." And the mermaid yells, "Give me suit of furniture." So they had to throw a whole suit of furniture overboard.

One day he made a mistake and forgot and said, "Sam, go in the kitchen and cook supper." The mermaid right away calls, "Give me Sam." They didn't have anything on the ship named Sam; so they had to throw Sam overboard. Soon as Sam hit the water she grabbed him. Her hair was so long she could wrap him

By Alfred Roller (Grafton 1980: 52, fig. 159).

[11]Dorson has also published this story with notes and variants in his *American Negro Folktales* (Greenwich, Connecticut: Fawcett Publications, 1967), pp. 250–54; and in his *Folktales Told Around the World* (Chicago: University of Chicago Press, 1975), pp. 484–85. His biography of Suggs is in the 1967 volume, pp. 59–64, and a discussion of his narrating abilities in "Oral Styles of American Folk Narrators," in Dorson's *Folklore: Selected Essays* (Bloomington: Indiana University Press, 1972), pp. 99–146.

up—he didn't even get wet. And she's swimming so fast he could catch breath under the water. When she gets home she goes in, unwraps Sam out of her hair, says: "Ooooh, you sure do look nice. Do you like fish?" Sam says, "No, I won't even cook a fish." "Well, we'll get married." So they were married.

After a while Sam begin to step out with other mermaids. His girl friend became jealous of him and his wife, and they had a fight over Sam. The wife whipped her, and told her, "You can't see Sam never again." She says, "I'll get even with you." So one day Sam's girl friends asked him didn't he want to go back to his native home. He says yes. So she grabs him, wraps him in her hair, and swum the same fastness as his wife did when she was carrying him, so he could catch breath. When she come to land she put him onto the ground, on the bank. "Now if he can't do me no good he sure won't do her none." That was Sam's experience in the mermaid's house in the bottom of the sea.

Then he told the others how nice her home was, all fixed up with the furniture and other things. There weren't any men down there—guess that's why they ain't any mermaids any more. Sam said they had purple lips, just like women are painted today. You see pictures of mermaids with lips like that. In old days people didn't wear lipstick, and I think they got the idea from seeing those pictures.

Sam told the people the mermaid's house was built like the alligator's. He digs in the bank at water level; then he goes up—nature teaches him how high to go—then digs down to water level again, and there he makes his home, in rooms ten to twenty feet long. The mermaid builds in the wall of the sea like the alligator. Sam stayed down there six years. If he hadn't got to co'ting he'd a been there yet, I guess. (Dorson 1956:147–48)

> Now Thaumas married a daughter
> of deep-running Okeanos,
> Elektra, and she bore him swift-footed Iris,
>   the rainbow,
> and the Harpies of the lovely hair,
>   Okypete and Aëllo,
> and these two in the speed of their wings
>   keep pace with the blowing
> winds, or birds in flight, as they soar
>   and swoop, high aloft.
>
> —Hesiod, *Theogony*, lines 265–69,
> trans. Richard Lattimore
> (1959:138–39).

Harpies, who resemble Sirens with human heads on birds' bodies, play a minor role in the mythology surrounding Jason and his followers and their search for the golden fleece:

The next landfall was at Salmydessus on the Euxine shore of Thrace; here the Argonauts were received by King Phineus. . . . In most versions he is old, blind, and a prophet; in addition he was tormented by the Harpies, two winged monsters (their name means "the snatchers") who, every time a meal was set before Phineus, would swoop down upon it, snatch away most of the food, and render what was left untouchable. Here the winged sons of Boreas, Zetes and Calais, proved their especial value; when the Harpies next appeared they rose into the air and pursued

Harpy (16th century)
(Lehner 1969:139, fig. 818).

them with drawn swords to the Strophades Islands (i.e., the islands of turning), where Iris put an end to the chase by making the sons of Boreas return and the Harpies swear never to go near Phineus again. (Morford and Lenardon 1977:405)

Robert Graves has assembled the story of the Phorcids, among them the fearsome Gorgons, from the works of Hesiod, Apollodorus, Ovid, Scholiast on Apollonius Rhodius, and Euripides:

The Phorcids . . . children of Ceto by Phorcys, another wise old man of the sea, are Ladon, Echidne, and the three Gorgons, dwellers in Libya; the three Graeae; and, some say, the three Hesperides. The Gorgons were named Stheino, Euryale, and Medusa, all once beautiful. But one night Medusa lay with Poseidon, and Athene, enraged that they had bedded in one of her own temples, changed her into a winged monster with glaring eyes, huge teeth, protruding tongue, brazen claws and serpent locks, whose gaze turned men to stone. When eventually Perseus decapitated Medusa, and Poseidon's children Chrysaor and Pegasus sprang from her dead body, Athene fastened the head to her aegis; but some say that the aegis was Medusa's own skin, flayed from her by Athene. (1960:127)

‡ "The fifty Nereids seem to have been a college of fifty Moon-priestesses, whose magic rites ensured good fishing; and the Gorgons, representatives of the Triple-goddess, wearing prophylactic masks—with scowl, glaring eyes, and protruding tongue between bared teeth—to frighten strangers from her Mysteries. . . . The Sons of Homer knew only a single Gorgon, who was a shade in Tartarus (*Odyssey* xi. 633–5), and whose head, an object of terror to Odysseus (*Odyssey* xi. 634), Athene wore on her aegis, doubtless to warn people against examining the divine mysteries hidden behind it. Greek bakers used to paint Gorgon masks on their ovens, to discourage busybodies from opening the oven door, peeping in, and thus allowing a draught to spoil the bread. The Gorgons' names—Stheino ('strong'), Euryale ('wide roaming'), and Medusa ('cunning one')—are titles of the Moon-goddess; the Orphics called the moon's face 'the Gorgon's head' " (Graves 1960:129).

◆ Abstract of Sigmund Freud, "Medusa's Head" [1940; 1922]: "An interpretation of the decapitated head of Medusa is presented. To decapitate is synonymous with to castrate. The terror of Medusa is thus a terror of castration that is linked to the sight of something. The hair upon Medusa's head is frequently represented in works of art in the form of snakes, and these are derived from the castration complex. However frightening they may be in themselves, they serve as a mitigation of the horror, for they replace the penis, the absence of which is the cause of the horror. If Medusa's head takes the place of a representation of the female genitals, or rather if it isolates their horrifying effects from their pleasure-giving ones, it may be recalled that displaying the genitals is familiar in other connections as an apotropaic act. The erect male organ also has an apotropaic effect" (Rothgeb 1971:126).

◆ Wolfgang Lederer, *The Fear of Women:* "Nothing but terror emanates from Medusa's head; and yet it too, says Freud, stands for the female, the maternal genital,—the hairy maternal vulva seen by the son. The cut-off head itself stands for castration, the snaky hair both terrifying—as snakes, and reassuring—as so many penises; the petrifying effect: both death and erection" (1968:3).

Gnostic gem depicting a "Gorgon's head: below, the legend АРНГω ΡωΡΟΜΑΝΔΑΡΗ, 'I protect Rho-romandaros:' some Persian or Armenian, as his name attests. This singular inscription is most important, on account of its explaining the cause of the frequency of the *Gorgoneion* in personal decorations of every kind, being reputed the most efficacious of amulets. Red Jasper" (King 1864:223, pl. X, 5).

Perseus with Medusa's head. Bronze by Benvenuto Cellini, 1554, in Florence (Harter 1980a:62).

♦ Erich Neumann, *The Great Mother:* "The petrifying gaze of Medusa belongs to the province of the Terrible Great Goddess, for to be rigid is to be dead. This effect of the terrible stands in opposition to the mobility of the life stream that flows in all organic life; it is a psychic expression for petrification and sclerosis. The Gorgon is the counterpart of the life womb; she is the womb of death or the night sun" (1963:166).

Gynephobia: The Classical Model

In Western culture "mythology" has tended to mean Greek and Roman mythology, as preserved in classical art and litrature and perennially reworked and reinterpreted by (usually) men of letters and, more recently, of science, especially the behavioral sciences. Classicist Sarah B. Pomeroy points out a distinction between such myths as we have come to know them and their original cult activities:

Myths represent goddesses as hostile to women, or show them pursuing many activities foreign to the experience of mortal women. In cult, on the other hand—that is, in the ceremonial veneration of these divinities by women—attention is paid both to the fulfillment of women's needs and to the delineation of their proper roles in society. Thus, for women, Athena's patronage of weaving, Hera's of marriage, and Artemis' of childbirth were of supreme importance, but these qualities are not emphasized in myth. (1975:9)

Pomeroy astutely observes that a "whole being" with "potential" does not emerge from the myths until the characteristics of the five chief Olympian goddesses—Athena, Artemis, Aphrodite, Hestia, and Hera—are merged:

The goddesses are archetypal images of human females, as envisioned by males. . . . A fully realized female tends to engender anxiety in the insecure male. Unable to cope with a multiplicity of powers united in one female, men from antiquity to the present have envisioned women in "either-or" roles. As a corollary of this anxiety, virginal females are considered helpful, while sexually mature women like Hera are destructive and evil. The fact that modern women are frustrated by being forced to choose between an Athena—an intellectual, asexual career woman—or an Aphrodite—a frivolous sex object—or a respectable wife-mother like Hera shows that the Greek goddesses continue to be the archetypes of female existence. If the characteristics of the major goddesses are combined, a whole being with unlimited potential for development—a female equivalent of Zeus or Apollo—would emerge. (1975:8–9)

In *Women & Madness,* Phyllis Chesler uses the contemporary transformations of both classical and Christian mythic figures to explore the mental health profession and its treatment (often mistreatment) of women. In her introduction, "Demeter Revisited," psychologist Chesler observes:

Goddesses never die. They slip in and out of the world's cities, in and out of our dreams, century after century, answering to different names, dressed differently, perhaps even disguised, perhaps idle and unemployed, their official altars abandoned, their temples feared or simply forgotten. (1972:xviii)

And she asks:

What of Artemis and Athena? . . .
   Today both Artemis and Athena have increasingly been caught at violence— at crimes of passion, greed, even of honor. Most often, they do whatever is required of them, those proud and lonely two, do their jobs well, too well. Sometimes Athena, sometimes Artemis, is well known for some accomplishments—envied, admired, misunderstood—until she turns on the gas, poisons herself, drowns—and is done with it once more. (ibid:xix, xx)

It is this sort of despair which has both inspired and deterred contemporary women social scientists, scholars, and artists who might re-examine and re-fashion a mythology more meaningful and efficacious for women, who after all share the Western cultural legacy.
   The characteristics of the five main Olympian goddesses (Athena, Artemis, Aphrodite, Hestia and Hera)—as invoked in the Homeric Hymns by various classical poets writing between perhaps 600 B.C. and 400 A.D., and as culled from classical texts and artifacts by reputable scholars—are presented below. These invocations and descriptions are followed by various contemporary (primarily psychological) interpretations, most of which have profoundly shaped men's views of women and women's views of themselves in present-day Western culture.

Athena
(Roman Minerva)

Pallas Athena, illustrious goddess, I sing to begin with.
Grey are her eyes, and her wisdom is much, but her heart is unyielding;
Terrible virgin, austere and courageous protector of cities,
Tritogeneia, whom Zeus by himself in his wisdom engendered
Out of his worshipful head. She came wearing the armour of battle,
Golden and glaring all over, and awe seized on all the immortals
When they beheld her. In front of her father who carries the aegis
Issued the goddess impetuously from his immortal forehead
Shaking a sharp-pointed javelin. Mighty Olympus went reeling
dreadfully under the impact of grey-eyed Athena, and round it
Earth gave a horrible groan, and the depths of the sea were excited,
Seething with purplish waves, and the salt water swell was suspended
Suddenly. Meanwhile Hyperion's glorious son having stayed his
Swift-footed horses remained where he was for a while, until virgin
Pallas Athena removed from her immortal shoulders her god-like
Armour. Then Zeus the deviser of counsel was heartily gladdened.
Here is my greeting to you, child of Zeus who is armed with the aegis,
And I shall surely remember yourself and another song also.

   —Homeric Hymn XXVIII "To Athena,"
      trans. Daryl Hine (1972:79).

‡   Athena is usually depicted as a fully armed war goddess, whose aegis or shield may be decorated with the Gorgon Medusa's head. One of her epithets is *glaukopis*, a reference either to her eyes (gray or green) or to the kind of gaze she uses. She is

Athena Parthenos (Harter 1978b: 46). A second-century marble copy (3' 3-5/8" high, from the Varvakeion) of the original forty-foot tall ivory and gold cult image from the Parthenon sculpted by Pheidias ca. 438 B.C. The goddess is wrapped in her peplos, a shawl or robe woven for her annually by the Athenians. Her helmet carries a sphinx flanked by two griffins. Her left hand supports a shield and serpent, while the right holds the Nike, the symbol of victory.

(Crawhall 1974:61)

associated with both the owl and the snake, suggesting an origin in earlier fertility goddesses. "Athena is a goddess of many specific arts, crafts, and skills (military, political and domestic), as well as the deification of wisdom and good counsel in a more generic and abstract conception." Athenians worshipped her and Hephaestus as patrons of all arts and crafts. (Morford and Lenardon 1977:100, 101–102)

★ "As the bird of Athena (companion and attribute) the owl was auspicious in classical Greece; old Greek vases associated with the worship of Athena depict owls with breasts, and vulva represented by a circle. But in Rome the owl was a bird of ill-omen and its hooting presaged death. . . . The Talmud mentions its being bad luck to dream of owls. *Leviticus* numbers the owl among the unclean birds.
"In European and American folklore in general, the owl is also a bird of ill-omen whose hooting is an omen of death. . . .
"One of the best known folktales about the owl is the story of the baker's daughter who was turned into an owl for begrudging bread her mother had baked for Jesus. . . ." (Leach 1972:838).

★ "The city of Athens had so many owls that the proverb 'Taking owls to Athens' was an ancient equivalent of 'Coals to Newcastle' " (Mercatante 1974:156).

★ Modern Greek augury views the brown owl (κουκουβάγια) as a signal of death within days if it perches on a house roof "suggesting by its inert posture that it is waiting in true oriental fashion," but as announcing an acquaintance's arrival and stay "if it settle there for a few moments only, alert and vigilant, and then fly off elsewhere." The "tawny owl," which is "known popularly as χαροπούλι or 'Charon's bird,' is, as the name suggests a messenger of evil under all circumstances, whether it be heard hooting or be seen sitting in deathlike stillness or flitting past like a ghost in the gathering darkness" (Lawson 1910:311–12).

◆ Helene Deutsch, *The Psychology of Women:* "The intellectual woman of the nonfeminine type discussed here has no mother in the psychologic sense of the term. She is . . . like Pallas Athene, the women born out of her father's head." Deutsch distinguishes this type of woman from the "active" one who identifies with her father but has not "impoverished" her ego by eliminating her mother. Motivated by jealousy of her sisters and, like Pallas Athene allying with her brothers, the former woman "achieves superiority over her sister and dismisses her mother, her sisters, and her own femininity from her emotional life" (1944: vol. 1, 292).

◆ Carol Schreier Rupprecht, "The Martial Maid and the Challenge of Androgyny": "[The hero's] armor proclaims his heroic standing. . . . The battle dress of the martial maid has no such obvious and clear significance. Even the Gods were terrified by Pallas Athene until she removed her armor. Then they accepted her into the Olympian assemblage. But the quandry of the martial maid is not so easily settled, for true recognition never comes to her. No one ever questions her heroic stature. . . . Nor does anyone ever question [her beauty]. . . . [But] why can no one let the martial maid be both powerful and beautiful, both admired and loved?" (1974:290,291).

◆ Murray Stein, "Translator's Afterthoughts" to Karl Kerényi's *Athene:* "Athene keeps us in the 'real world'; she gives us the wherewithall to confront its problems, the joy of conquering ourselves, others, problems, and the sagacity and confidence to slay its dragons. She keeps us grounded in 'real projects,' out of vain and idle speculations. As a religious attitude, Athene is muscular and action-oriented: building, winning, marching. We can see her moving in the religion of the 'healthy-minded,' to use the phrase of William James, and not in the religion of 'sick souls' who pass through the terrors of guilt and breakdown into visions of transcendence. As philosopher she is pragmatic, giving 'wise counsel' to those who reflect on strategies for action" (1978:75–76).

♦   "Psychologically, then, Athene protects our civilized and civilizing selves from the consuming fires of the spirit (could mystics build a city?) and from the threats of our various primordial passions (look at what Dionysos did to Thebes). Like her craftsmen, the metallurgists, she 'tempers.' Athens, one of the glories of the civilized self, is, after all, her namesake" (ibid:79). [12]

Artemis
(Roman Diana)

Artemis, clamorous huntress, I celebrate: gilt are her arrows,
Terrible virgin assaulter of stags with a volley of arrows,
Sister indeed of Apollo whose ritual sabre is gilded;
She through the shadowy mountains and over the high, windy headlands
Takes her delight in the chase as she stretches her parcel-gilt bow and
Launches deplorable shots: then the towering crests of the lofty
Mountaintops tremble, the forest resounds and the underbrush echoes
Dreadfully to the complaint of the beasts, and the earth even shivers,
As does the fish-swarming deep. But the goddess is very stout-hearted;
Every-which-way that she turns she destroys generations of wildlife.
Yet, when this spotter of beasts with the shower of barbs has enjoyed her-
Self, and has gladdened her heart, then she loosens her neatly-curved bow and
Goes to the spacious abode of her only and dearly-loved brother,
Phoebus Apollo, and enters the opulent province of Delphi
Where she arranges the beautiful dance of the Muses and Graces.
There having hung up her double-bent bow on a hook with her arrows,
Artemis wearing her elegant bodily ornaments leads and
Starts off the dance, and the rest, pouring forth their ambrosial voices
Sing about Leto with beautiful ankles, how she bore these children,
Best of immortals by far both in counsel and other achievements.
Hail to you, children of Zeus and of Leto the beautifully coiffed. Now
I shall remember you both, and another about you, and sing it.

—Homeric Hymn XXVII "To Artemis," trans. Daryl Hine (1972:78).

‡   Artemis is depicted as an archer, usually clad in a short tunic. She spurns the company of men and gods, spending her time in the wilds in company with wild animals. "In her relationships with humans, Artemis is primarily concerned with

[12]In " 'Dear Grey Eyes': A Revaluation of Pallas Athene" (1981), Christine Downing considers the role Athene played in her life and the goddess as "the woman artist" and as "one who gives soul." She also heeds Mary Daly's warning that Athene must be viewed in relation to her mother and only thereby her Self (1978:39) and examines the goddess in relation to Zeus, Metis, Ares, Hephaestus, the owl, and the serpent.

From *Gli Adornatori del Libro in Italia,* published in Bologna, Italy, 1923–27 (Grafton 1980: 63, fig. 198).

females, especially the physical aspects of their life cycle, including menstruation, childbirth, and death, however contradictory the association of these with a virgin may appear. (She is also cited as the reason for the termination of female life: when swift death came to a woman, she was said to have been shot by Artemis.)" (Pomeroy 1975:5–6).

‡ Artemis wove nets *(diktuon)* for fishing and hunting. She was also known as Dictynna, "Lady of the Nets," a name also applied to the maiden Britomartis, who fled Minos' advances by jumping off a cliff. Fishermen's nets saved her. Artemis and Britomartis were often identified with one another (Simmer 1980:59).

♦ Philip E. Slater, *The Glory of Hera:* "It is the man-hating virgin huntress, Artemis, who sends the boar . . . to gore, castrate, and disembowel the flower of Greek youth [in the myth of Oeneus, his son Meleager, and Atalanta]; and the warlike and masculine heroine of the story, Atalanta, is a carbon copy of the goddess. Like Artemis, she is a virgin huntress, and punishes the attentions of would-be suitors with cruel death. Furthermore, her own history reveals the origin of this attitude, for it is said [Apollodorus:iii.9.2] that her father had wished for a boy, and had exposed her on a mountain top, where she was suckled by a bear which the goddess sent to her aid. In her refusal to marry, in her competitions with men (beating them at racing and at wrestling), and in her general masculine demeanor, Atalanta both complies with this wish and expresses her resentment of it" (1968:260; also see Allen and Hubbs 1980).

♦ Phyllis Chesler, *Women & Madness:* "In many pagan and Catholic 'downfall' myths, the male god is usually stripped of his full former powers by being sent 'earthward,' the female, by being sent 'skyward.' For example, Poseidon was sent to the sea; Pluto, as well as the Judeo-Christian Lucifer, beneath the earth. Mythologically, one expression of power loss for men is to be returned to the earth, to the concrete. Often for women, the expression of power loss is to be removed from the earth, or from their (heterosexual) bodies. Goddesses such as Athena, Diana, or the Catholic Madonna are virgins. [Chesler's note here reads: "I.e., Either unmarried or childless, (hetero)sexually uninvolved or 'innocent' of experience. In Amazon society, a 'virgin' was not chaste, but unmarried; in Catholic mythology a 'virgin' is married and chaste. The pagan Artemis (Diana), the Virgin-Huntress, is not motherless. She is raised together with her brother Apollo and, unlike Athena, is probably a lesbian goddess of Amazon origin. She requested—and received from Zeus—sixty ocean nymphs and twenty river nymphs as companions. According to one myth, she *rescues* Iphigenia from being sacrificed by her father Agamemnon. According to another myth, one of her lovers is the woman Callisto—whom Artemis' father Zeus seduces—*only by taking Artemis' form."*] Virginity, *one* form of mind-body splitting, is the price that women are made to pay in order to keep whatever other "fearful" powers they have: childbearing, wisdom, hunting prowess, maternal compassion." [Chesler's note here reads: "Of course, de-virginization via heterosexual *rape* is as maddening a split in female mind-body continuity."] (1972:24–25).

♦ René Malamud, "The Amazon Problem": "We must understand virginity in two ways. On the one hand, it connotes the characteristic detachment of youth, including uncommitedness and irresponsible wandering. . . .
   "The other form of 'being-a-maiden' occurs in the woman who is self-sufficient, whether she be wife, mother, or whatever. She is a person 'at one with herself,' as

Esther Harding puts it. This is the essence of Artemis, symbolically understood. She is precisely not the feminine counter-part to a masculine divinity; *her divinity belongs to herself*. On the level of personal feminine psychology, this form of virginity is that attitude that makes a woman independent of the 'one oughts,' those conventional beliefs and practices to which her own viewpoint does not accede. The motive force behind such an independent attitude is not personal; it is directed toward a super-personal goal, toward a relationship to the Goddess" (1980:57).

Aphrodite
(Roman Venus)

Now I shall sing the Cytherean born upon Cyprus who gives to
Mortals her gifts, which are kind; and upon her desirable face there
Always are smiles, and the bloom of desire effulgent upon it.
Hail to you, guardian goddess of pleasant Salamis, the queen of
Cyprus enisled in the sea! Yours the gift of desirable song, and
I shall remember yourself and a ballad about you and sing it.

—Homeric Hymn X "To Aphrodite,"
  trans. Daryl Hine (1972:60).

‡ Aphrodite, goddess of love, is often depicted as attended by the Graces (Charities) and Seasons (Horae). She is thought to possess a magical girdle with irresistible seductive powers. "In early Greek art she is rendered as a beautiful woman, usually clothed. By the fourth century she is portrayed in the nude (or nearly so), the idealization of womanhood in all her femininity; the sculptor Praxiteles was mainly responsible for establishing the type—sensuous in its soft curves and voluptuousness" (Morford and Lenardon 1977:107).

In *Theogony,* his eighth-century account of creation and the genealogy of the Olympians, Boeotian farmer-poet Hesiod recounts the story of Aphrodite's birth:

> And huge Ouranos came on
>   bringing night with him, and desiring
> love he embraced Gaia and lay over her
>   stretched out
> complete, and from his hiding place his son
>   reached with his left hand
> and seized him, and holding in his right
>   the enormous sickle
> with its long blade edged like teeth,
>   he swung it sharply,
> and lopped the members of his own father,
>   and threw them behind him
> to fall where they would,
>   but they were not lost away when they were flung
> from his hand, but all the bloody drops
>   that went splashing from them

(Harter 1978b:16)

Cronos (Roman Saturn), who was identified with Chronos (Roman Tempus) or time, and in the Christian era became known as Father Time (e.g., von Franz 1978:5, 11, 65, 70, 77, pl. 28; Lehner 1969:136, fig. 806).

were taken in by Gaia, the earth,
    and with the turning of the seasons
she brought forth the powerful Furies
    and the tall Giants
shining in their armor
    and holding long spears in their hands;
and the nymphs they call, on boundless earth,
    the Nymphs of the Ash Trees.
But the members themselves, when Kronos
    had lopped them with the flint,
he threw from the mainland
    into the great wash of the sea water
and they drifted a great while
    on the open sea, and there spread
a circle of white foam
    from the immortal flesh, and in it
grew a girl, whose course first took her
    to holy Kythera,
and from there she afterward made her way
    to sea-washed Cyprus
and stepped ashore, a modest lovely Goddess,
    and about her
light and slender feet the grass grew,
    and the gods call her
Aphrodite, and men do too,
    and the aphro-foam-born
goddess, and garlanded Kythereia,
    because from the seafoam
she grew, and Kythereia because she had gone
    to Kythera,
and Kyprogeneia, because she came forth
    from wave-washed Cyprus,
and Philommedea, because she appeared
    from *medea,* members.
And Eros went with her, and handsome Himeros
    attended her
when first she was born, and when she joined
    the immortal community,
and here is the privilege she was given
    and holds from the beginning,
and which is the part she plays among men
    and the gods immortal:
the whispering together of girls,
    the smiles and deceptions,
the delight, and the sweetnesses of love,
    and the flattery.

     —Lines 176–206, trans. Richard Lattimore
     (1959:133–35).

‡ Robert Graves relates Aphrodite to Near Eastern goddesses like Ishtar and Ashtaroth, claiming: "Cythera was an important centre of Cretan trade with the Peloponnese, and it will have been from here that her worship first entered Greece.

(Harter 1978a:61)

The Cretan goddess had close associations with the sea. Shells carpeted the floor of her palace sanctuary at Cnossus; she is shown on a gem from the Idean Cave blowing a triton shell, with a sea-anemone lying beside her altar; the sea-urchin and cuttle-fish . . . were sacred to her. A triton-shell was found in her early sanctuary at Phaestus, and many more in late Minoan tombs, some of these being terracotta replicas" (1960:50).

◆   Geza Róheim, "Aphrodite, or the Woman with a Penis" [1945]: "The myth evidently means that Aphrodite can only originate after the father had been killed and also points to the phallic origin of the love goddess. . . . 'Her statue on Cyprus is bearded, but wears a woman's dress, holds a scepter, and has a masculine build; they consider her both male and female. Aristophanes calls her "Aphrodition" (neuter form).' Rendel Harris actually derives Aphrodite from the mandragora of the ancients, the German *Alraun*. 'Hesychius explains the term Madragoritis (She of the Mandrake) as meaning Aphrodite.' Women wore mandrake roots next to their skin to make themselves irresistible. Its magic virtue is clear from the language of Homer. It was witchcraft and made its wearer, for the time being, into a witch. Hence Hera begs to use it that she may operate on Zeus with more than normal charms. . . .
". . . According to the traditions of medieval magic the root originates from the ejaculated semen of a thief who emitted the semen while he was hanging from the gallows. The thief should never have had anything to do with a woman. The person who wishes to dig for it must stuff something into his ears so as to prevent him from hearing the terrible piercing yell of the root—when dug out it shrieks so that a person who hears it would die of fright. The root looks like a child and helps the women to conceive and deliver their children. It becomes a kind of familiar spirit and brings its possessor money and luck. . . .
"We see that there is a striking parallelism between the origins of Aphrodite and the mandrake: there, froth from the penis of the castrated Ouranos; here, drops of semen from a man on the gallows. The child symbolism of the root goes well with its phallic significance. The Lady of the Mandrake would therefore be the woman with a penis and the great love charm she wears under her girdle is her imaginary phallus. We find her represented with helm and spear at Cyprus, in Cythera, at Akrokorinthus and Sparta. At the mysteries held in Cyprus in honor of the goddess, the initiates received a phallus and salt. Nilsson enumerates all the androgynous elements in the cult of the goddess, which finally culminated in forming a being called Hermaphroditus, a combination of the phallic Hermes and the goddess of love" (1972:169–70, 171; also see Delcourt 1961; Kerényi 1979a; chapter 6 below).

◆   Paul Friedrich, *The Meaning of Aphrodite*: ". . . My comparison of the queens of heaven . . . tries to recreate and take the point of view of an eighth- or seventh-century Greek. The central question is: What did Aphrodite mean to an appreciative and informed Greek in Homer's audience? What sort of structure of perceptions and ideas did he bring to a hearing? My approach is thus essentially a phenomenological one. . . .
". . . In such terms Aphrodite is, for example, the least lunar, the least virginal, the least specific in her kinship role. In positive terms, she is the most floral, the most insular, the most solar, the most aquatic, the most intimate with humans, the most attended by nymphs (the Graces and so forth), and the most (i.e., the only one who is) subjective in her workings, in the sense that her power consists mainly in inspiring compelling and subjective states. She is also the most golden,

the most beautiful, and the most charged with fertility and the powers of creation. In short, she is the most potent of the goddesses—the most intensely characterized or 'highly marked' of all the queens of heaven [Hera, Athena, Artemis and Aphrodite]. . . .

"Aphrodite is also the most extreme in another, more comprehensive sense. . . . While two of the other queens are to some extent mannish or masculine in terms of such conventionally male arts as war (Athena) and hunting (Artemis), Aphrodite never is. Hence she is the most 'feminine,' in the conventional sense of ancient Greek and modern American culture (senses that today would be [implicitly] sexist)" (1978:100, 101, 102–103).

Hestia
(Roman Vesta)

Hestia who as a housekeeper serves in the sacrosanct home of
Lordly Apollo the long-distance archer at excellent Pytho,
Endlessly out of the hair of your head the slick oil is exuded.
Come to this house and with the spirit take heart and come unto this dwelling.
Come with the counsellor, Zeus, and grant grace, too, to this composition.

—Homeric Hymn XXIV "To Hestia," trans. Daryl Hine (1972:75).

‡ "There is little myth about Hestia, for she was the archetypal old maid, preferring the quiet of the hearth to the boisterous banquets and emotional entanglements of the other Olympians. Moreover, she is seldom depicted in the visual arts, for instead of having an anthropomorphic conception, Hestia is commonly envisioned as the living flame" (Pomeroy 1975:6; also see Kerényi 1979:91–92).

◆ Stephanie A. Demetrakopoulos, "Hestia, Goddess of the Hearth": "Hestia could very well be called 'The Forgotten Goddess.' Studies abound on other Greek deities, but little has been written on her. This is not surprising; classicists have usually perceived her as just an allegory for that monotonous work that sustains our species, housewifery. This denigrated activity crucially needs re-sacralizing. . . ." (1979:55; also see Oakley 1974; Glazer-Malbin 1976; Meinhardt and Meinhardt 1977).

◆ "Hestia as earth means that she is the matrix, the material, the *sine qua non* of all differentiation, of self-realization, without which spirit remains suspended and never comes down. . . . The hearth altar originally signified the energy of 'the almost irresistible compulsion and urge to *become what one is,* just as every organism is driven to assume the form that is characteristic of its nature.' Thus the ideas of the circle and of original *materia* (the earth) help explain why Hesiod says she was first born: she is the ground of being.

"She is also the *last re-born* because she contains the pattern of the transcendent macrocosm that we each as microcosm contain and bear (as in 'reproduce') in the second stage of life. The source contains and reflects all; beginnings are also endings. Hestia contains the central paradox of all human life. Thus she is, as Hesiod states, the chief of all Goddesses, not only because she is most venerated day-to-day, but because she is the source of all things. . . .

"Hestia is the murky origins out of which we each issue and which always remain curiously unknown to us. She is the heat, the hearth, the center we live—and forget—in our daily rounds. Her hazy, weakly anthropomorphized form

(Lehner 1969:52, fig. 186)

84   CHAPTER 2

best articulates our beginnings to us, for she remains a virgin, unknown, a pure source with no external relatedness to interrupt the interior wholeness of beginning" (ibid:72, 73).

♦   Barbara Kirksey, "Hestia: a Background of Psychological Focusing": "Hestia's value in psychological life is her ability to mediate soul by giving a place to congregate, a gathering point. And through this point the psyche and world merge. Hestia allows *spaciality* to be a form of *psychological reality.* The Greeks never forsook this truth for a purely geometric view of space. Spaciality had a divine aspect. . . .

"Because the psychology of Hestia is a revisioning of soul in terms of spatial metaphors, the pathology of the soul through Hestia's language contains phrases related to space. 'Off base,' 'off-center,' 'unable to find a place,' 'can't settle down,' 'spaced out,' and 'off the wall' are related to Hestian values, and remind the wanderer of her power to bring the soul into a state of dwelling. Ever since antiquity, pathology has been fantasized as a 'wandering' phenomenon (*e.g.*, delirium, deviate). Cicero proclaimed that a sick soul was one which could not attain or endure and was always astray. The soul, gone astray, is a soul without psychic connection to this Goddess and her centeredness. The soul can't come home for there is no place for the homecoming. This specific lack of having a place is not equal to being an abandoned child or the wanderings of the puer. The child may still find a home and a place to nurse its abandonment within other dwelling places. But the loss of Hestia is a more severe threat to the total psyche with its multitudes of images and their influence. Without Hestia, there can be no focusing on the image, and there are no boundaries to differentiate the intimacy of the inner dwelling and the outer world, for there is no psychic house to give protective walls. There can be no joyous feasts, no celebrations of life, no food for the soul" (1980: 105–106).

Hera
(Roman Juno)

Hera I sing on her throne made of gold, her whom Rhea gave birth to,
Deathless, a queen and a goddess possessed of superior beauty,
Sister and consort of Zeus who contends with the voice of thunder,
Reverend, whom all the blessed that live upon lofty Olympus
Hold in like honour and awe as great as Zeus whose delight is in thunder.

—Homeric Hymn XII "To Hera," trans. Daryl Hine (1972:62).

✠   "In art [Hera] is depicted as regal and matronly, often with attributes of royalty. Homer describes her as ox-eyed and white-armed, both epithets presumably denoting her beauty. The peacock is associated with her. . . . Argos was a special center for her worship, and a great temple was erected there in her honor in classical times. Hera was worshipped not so much as an earth-goddess but rather as a goddess of women, marriage, and childbirth, functions that she shares with other deities" (Morford and Lenardon 1977:63).

♦   Philip E. Slater, *The Glory of Hera:* " 'The Glory of Hera' was chosen as the title of this book because it translates the name 'Heracles,' and hence captures the bitter

(Lehner 1969:22, fig. 42)

irony of the Greek mother-son relationship, inasmuch as Hera was also the hero's chief prosecutor. . . .

". . . Heracles exemplifies every mode of response to maternal threat. Like Zeus, he is a sexual athlete, and fears not to copulate with the serpent. Like Apollo, he affects a masculine antisepsis against matriarchy, femininity, and chthonic forces everywhere. Like Orestes, he attacks the mother directly—the very breast that suckled him. Like Hephaestus, he emasculates himself and plays the servant and buffoon. Like Dionysus, he identifies with the mother and becomes feminine. Like Perseus, he 'castrates' the mother. But more specifically than those others, Heracles represents a kind of compulsive assertion of strength, or, to put it the other way around, a vigorous denial of weakness in the face of maternal hostility. Even today he symbolizes exaggerated masculine differentiation, with emphasis on secondary rather than primary sex characteristics: muscularity rather than virility per se. . . ." (1968:337, 338–39).

‡ "The Stymphalians in Arcadia knew Hera by three names: *Parthenos* or *Pais* ('virgin' or 'girl'), *Teleia* ('perfect one' and 'fulfilled'), and *Chera* ('widow'). The second term, *Teleia,* refers to Hera just after her wedding, for 'in marriage she attained perfection.' In this connection Zeus was referred to as *Teleios,* 'bringer to perfection,' since as bridegroom he brought his sister-wife, Hera, to perfection.

"Besides having the effect of allowing Hera to achieve a wide appeal among women of all ages and statuses ('all women, whatever their condition, worshipped her'), these three epithets refer to a certain rhythm in the archetype. In her cults Hera underwent periodic recurring weddings. Before each of them her image would be immersed in a 'bridal bath' (traditionally the spring Kanathos), and this immersion would restore her virginity. In the subsequent wedding ritual Hera achieved her 'perfection' *(Teleia).* This high-point would then be followed by a dispute or misunderstanding with her husband Zeus, or at any rate by rupture and separation, and Hera, going into retreat or hiding from Zeus, would be referred to as *Chera* ('widow'). When it came time for the cycle to repeat itself, the image of Hera would have to be 'found,' taken to the bridal path, restored, etc." (Stein 1977:108–109).

Robert Graves abstracts this version of the legend of Io, Zeus, and Hera from Callimachus, Apollodorus, Lucian, Herodotus, Aeschylus, and Euripides, among others:

Io, daughter of the River-god Inachus, was a priestess of Argive Hera. Zeus, over whom Iynx, daughter of Pan and Echo, had cast a spell, fell in love with Io, and when Hera charged him with infidelity and turned Iynx into a wryneck [bird] as a punishment, lied: 'I have never touched Io.' He then turned her into a white cow, which Hera claimed as hers and handed over for safe keeping to Argus Panoptes, ordering him: 'Tether this beast secretly to an olive-tree at Nemea.' But Zeus sent Hermes to fetch her back, and himself led the way to Nemea—or, some say, to Mycenae—dressed in woodpecker disguise. Hermes, though the cleverest of thieves, knew that he could not steal Io without being detected by one of Argus's hundred eyes; he therefore charmed him asleep by playing the flute, crushed him with a boulder, cut off his head, and released Io. Hera, having placed Argus's eyes in the tail of a peacock, as a constant reminder of his foul murder, set a gadfly to sting Io and chase her all over the world. (1960:190)

(Crawhall 1974:61)

◆ Murray Stein, "Hera: Bound and Unbound": "It is not a question here of a patriarchal Zeus thwarting the wishes of a strong-willed Hera who must have her way in all things, nor is it a matter of a patriarchal religion dominating a matriarchal one. The nub of the issue is rather that Zeus thwarts Hera in a specific way, i.e., he will not allow her to find her 'perfection' and fulfilment in *gamos* [marriage]; he will not be married to her in more than a token way, nor allow her to be deeply married to him. It is this that makes a *Chera* ('widow') of Hera and constellates her *infernal* destructiveness. For a Hera, a token, merely official 'husband' is worse than no husband at all, and it arouses in her a far grimmer sort of destructiveness than would the sadness and disappointment of eternal maidenhood" (1977:111–12).

Misogyny: The Christian Model

Conception and birth have always been a primary human concern and wonder. In the texts which follow, both tribal and folk or popular beliefs (indicated by stars) about impregnation are interspersed with official Roman Catholic doctrines (indicated by large crosses from Lehner 1969) about the Virgin Mary, promulgated at various times in Church history. (Additional historical commentary is indicated by double daggers.) These declarations and teachings have had a profound effect on Western women, whether Catholic or Protestant. As the *idea* of virginity evolved, the *ideals* for female behavior grew increasingly difficult to emulate—a dilemma which has generated considerable feminist commentary in recent years. (Such interpretations are indicated by diamonds below.)

Printer's mark, Ulrich Zell, Koeln, 1491 (Lehner 1969: 197, fig. 1213).

Therefore the Lord himself will give you a sign. Behold, a young woman shall conceive and bear a son, and shall call his name Immanuel.

—*Isaiah* 7:14 (RSV).

Now the birth of Jesus Christ took place in this way. When his mother Mary had been betrothed to Joseph, before they came together she was found to be with child of the Holy Spirit; and her husband Joseph, being a just man and unwilling to put her to shame, resolved to divorce her quietly. But as he considered this, behold, an angel of the Lord appeared to him in a dream, saying, "Joseph, son of David, do not fear to take Mary your wife, for that which is conceived in her is of the Holy Spirit; she will bear a son, and you shall call his name Jesus, for he will save his people from their sins." . . . When Joseph woke from sleep, he did as the angel of the Lord commanded him; he took his wife, but knew her not until she had borne a son; and he called his name Jesus.

—*Matthew* 1:18–21, 24–25 (RSV).

(Lehner 1969:113, fig. 636)

‡ ". . . These are the only words from the Old Testament [*Isaiah*] applied to Mary in the New [*Matthew*]. . . . They form the lynch pin of the Christian argument for the virgin birth of Christ, which almost all Christians hold, and the virginity of his mother Mary, which Catholics and some reformed Churches believe to have continued all her life. As has been pointed out many times before, Matthew was using the Greek Septuagint translation of the Bible, where the Hebrew word *'almah* had been translated as *parthenos* in Greek. The two words are not synonymous,

for *'almah* means a young girl of marriageable age, with a primary connotation of eligibility. . . .

"Naturally, the venerable elders at work in Alexandria around 300 B.C. on the Greek version of the Hebrew Bible would expect a young, eligible woman to be a virgin; but *parthenos* carries a sense of intact virginity, of physical maidenhead far more strongly than *'almah,* which could have been translated by the Greek *neanis* (girl)" (Warner 1976:19).

Now on a certain day, while Mary stood near the fountain to fill her pitcher, the angel of the Lord appeared unto her, saying, Blessed art thou, Mary, for in thy womb thou hast prepared a habitation for the Lord. Behold, light from heaven shall come and dwell in thee, and through thee shall shine in all the world.

> —*The Gospel of Pseudo-Matthew,* chap. ix (quoted in Campbell 1968:309).

★

> *Si com en la verriere*
> *Entre et reva arriere*
> *Li solaus que n'entame*
> *Ainsi fus verge entiere*
> *Quant Diex, qui es ciex iere*
> *Fist de toi mere et dame.*
>
> (Just as the sun enters and passes back through a windowpane without piercing it, so were you *virgo intacta* when God, who came down from the heavens, made you his mother and lady.)
>
> —Hymn by thirteenth-century jongleur Rutebeuf (quoted and translated in Warner 1976:44).

(Lehner 1969:114, fig. 660)

"Fray Pedro Simón reports, in his *Noticias historiales de las conquistes de Tierra Firme en las Indias Occidentales* (Cuenca, 1627), that after work had begun among the peoples of Tunja and Sogamozzo in Colombia, South America,

'the demon of that place began giving contrary doctrines. And among other things, he sought to discredit what the priest had been teaching concerning the Incarnation, declaring that it had not yet come to pass; but that presently the Sun would bring it to pass by taking flesh in the womb of a virgin of the village of Guacheta, causing her to conceive by the rays of the sun while she yet remained a virgin. These tidings were proclaimed throughout the region. And it so happened that the head man of the village named had two virgin daughters, each desirous that the miracle should become accomplished in her. These then began going out from their father's dwellings and garden-enclosure every morning at the first peep of dawn; and mounting one of the numerous hills about the village, in the direction of the sunrise, they disposed themselves in such a way that the first rays of the sun would be free to shine upon them. This going on for a number of days, it was granted the demon by divine permission (whose judgments are incomprehensible) that things should come to pass as he had planned, and in such fashion that one of the daughters became pregnant, as she declared, by the sun. Nine months and she brought into the world a large and valuable *hacuata,* which in their language is an emerald. The woman took this, and, wrapping it in cotton, placed it between her breasts, where she kept it a number of days, at the end of which time it was transformed into a living creature: all by order of the demon. The child was named Goranchacho, and he was reared in the household of the head man, his grandfather, until he was some twenty-four years of age.' Then he proceeded in triumphant procession to the capital of the nation, and was celebrated throughout the provinces as the 'Child of the Sun' " (Lord Kingsborough, *Antiquities of Mexico,* as quoted in Campbell 1968:309–10).

★
> *Non ex virili semine*
> *Sed mystico spiramine*
> *Verbum Dei factum est caro*
> *Fructusque ventris floruit.*
>
> (Not from human seed but by the
> mystical breath of the Spirit
> was the Word of God made flesh
> and the fruit of the womb brought
> to maturity.)
>
> —Hymn by St. Ambrose
> (d. 397) (quoted and
> translated in Warner
> 1976:37).

★ Huitzilopochtli's mother Coatlicue was doing penance on Coatepec ("Serpent Mountain") when a ball of feathers fell on her. She put it in her bosom and soon became pregnant (Leeming 1981:36).

★ "According to innumerable beliefs, women became pregnant whenever they approached certain places; rocks, caves, trees or rivers. The souls of the children then entered their bodies and the women conceived. Whatever was the condition of these child-souls—whether they were or were not the souls of ancestors—one thing was certain: in order to become incarnate, they had been waiting hidden somewhere, in crevasses or hollows, in pools or woods. Already, then, they were leading some sort of embryonic life in the womb of their real Mother, the Earth. That was where children came from. And thence it was, according to other beliefs still surviving among Europeans of the nineteenth century, that they were brought by certain aquatic animals—fish, or frogs, and especially by storks" (Eliade 1960:164–65).

‡ "The influence of pagan bird metamorphoses on ideas about Christ's birth appears to have been stronger in the western, Latin world, where it endures into the late Renaissance, than in eastern Christianity, where the Holy Spirit's gender was unclear. The Apostles' Creed, developed at the end of the fourth century and finally drawn up in the eighth, expresses the idea that the Holy Spirit carried the whole child into Mary's womb to be nourished there, rather than quickening it to life. . . . In the long romance *The Acts of Thomas,* the apostle invokes the Holy Spirit: 'Come, O communion of the male . . . come . . . the holy dove that beareth the twin young, come, the hidden mother. . . .'" (Warner 1976:38).

Stork

(Bowles & Carver 1970:142)

★ Folklorist Stith Thompson surveys motifs of miraculous births in Native North American tales, including conception from rain (Southwestern), from eating ("practically all tribes except those of the Southwest"), and from "casual contact with a man" (North Pacific, Plains, Plateau). He reports the child "Dug from Ground" (California), born in a jug (California, Southwest), removed from the dead mother (Plains and elsewhere), born from a clot of blood, and "the birth from a splinter wound in the story of Splinter-Foot-Girl, but there are similar tales from the North Pacific Coast telling of birth from tears or from other secretions of the body, most frequently . . . from mucus of the nose" (Thompson 1946:340).

★
Mirentur ergo saecula
quod angelus fert semina
quod aure virgo concepit
et corde credens parturit.

(The centuries marvel therefore
that the angel bore the seed
the virgin conceived through her
ear, and, believing in her heart,
became fruitful.)

—Hymn tentatively attributed
to Venantius Fortunatus
(d. 609?) (quoted and translated
in Warner 1976:37).

★ "If a woman does not wish to become pregnant, she is very careful about letting people place babies on her bed. Here is an item from the Springfield (Missouri) *News & Leader,* Dec. 10, 1933: 'At a party in Springfield not long ago, a woman started to lay her baby down on the bed. The hostess didn't want a baby right away, so she asked the guest *to lay the baby on a chair. . . .* And if a bride is very anxious to have a baby, her friends may all take their babies and lay them on her bed. It's regarded as a sure sign of the coming stork.'

"A male visitor should always leave a cabin by the same door he entered; if he fails to do this, it may mean that there'll be an increase in the host's family. Many mountain people take this very seriously, and some women make certain that a visitor *does* go out the same way he came in. There are a lot of bawdy stories on the subject, of course.

"Every mountaineer's wife knows that if a baby's diaper is left in her house by some visiting mother, she herself will very shortly become pregnant. I've heard some good stories about that one, too" (Randolph 1947:193).

We declare, pronounce, and define that the doctrine which holds that the most blessed Virgin Mary, in the first instant of her conception, by a singular grace and privilege granted by the almighty God, in view of the merits of Jesus Christ, the Saviour of the human race, was preserved free from all stain of original sin, is a doctrine revealed by God and therefore to be believed firmly and constantly by all the faithful.

—Pius IX, Papal bull, *Ineffabilis Deus,* December 8, 1964
(in Brantl 1961:78).

(Lehner 1969:116, fig. 696)

90   CHAPTER 2

‡ "Mary has always been the paragon of virginity. In 325, the Council of Nicaea exhorted all women to follow her example: 'The Lord looked upon the whole of creation, and he saw no-one to equal Mary. Therefore he chose her for his mother. If therefore a girl wants to be called a virgin, she should resemble Mary.' It is in the homilies on the ascetic life, in the exhortations to chastity penned by the Christian Fathers from the second century onwards that the Virgin chiefly appears: in Cyprian's *On the Dress of Virgins*, in Ambrose's *Instructions of a Virgin*, in Tertullian's *On the Veiling of Virgins*, in Jerome's disciplinary letters to his circle of pupils. There has been little deviation from this theme over the centuries. The authorized prayer book of the Second Vatican Council of 1964 includes a section called 'We promise to imitate her' and recommends a modern prayer: 'Most blessed Virgin Mary . . . your life of faith and love and perfect unity with Christ was planned by God to show us clearly what our lives should be . . . you are the outstanding model of motherhood and virginity.'

(Crawhall 1974:55)

"Through the ascetic renunciation of the flesh, a woman could relieve a part of her nature's particular viciousness as the Virgin Mary had done through her complete purity. The life of self-denial was seen as a form of martyrdom, and the virgin was encouraged to suffer physically. For in times of persecution, martyrdom made amends for nature's wrongs, and proved the faith of the victim; and in untroubled times the equivalent of the arena was the cell, and the equivalent of the wild beast was the renunciation of worldly happiness and the practices of the hair shirt, the waterbowl, and the scourge. Through virginity and self-inflicted hardship, the faults of female nature could be corrected" (Warner 1976:68–69).

◆ Naomi R. Goldenberg, *Changing of the Gods:* "Some years ago, while walking along the lakeshore in Zurich, I saw a defaced statue of the Virgin Mary. Someone had painted genitals on the Virgin! I was intrigued. Whoever did the artwork probably did not realize the political statement he or she was making. Mary has certainly been desexed in Christian tradition. The painter was restoring her sexuality.

"Obsession with purifying Mary of any taint of womanhood has occupied Christian scholars for centuries. Treatises on the Holy Mother's hymen abound in every Catholic research library. Theologians have insisted that Mary remained 'intact' before, during (!) and after the birth of Jesus. Traditions also speak of how Mary's body never decayed and never gave off odors. Instead, her physical body remained perfect even after death.

"Mary is certainly the good girl of Christianity. Absolutely obedient to the male God, she derives all her status from her son. Because of her absolute purity and obedience, she is the only pinup girl who has been permitted in monks' cells throughout the ages. . . .

"Mary has been castrated by popes, cardinals, priests and theologians, by all who fear the sexual and emotional power of natural womanhood" (1979:75).

★ "UNICORNIS the Unicorn, which is also called Rhinoceros by the Greeks, is of the following nature.

"He is a very small animal like a kid, excessively swift, with one horn in the middle of his forehead, and no hunter can catch him. But he can be trapped by the following stratagem.

"A virgin girl is led to where he lurks, and there she is sent off by herself into the wood. He soon leaps into her lap when he sees her, and embraces her, and hence he gets caught" (White 1954:20–21; also see, e.g., Shepard 1979; Costello 1979: 94–103).

(Bowles & Carver 1970:36)

‡ "There was one particular attitude toward virginity that the Christian religion did inherit from the classical world: that virginity was powerful magic and conferred strength and ritual purity. Thus Hera, wife of Zeus and mother of many, renewed her maidenhead annually when she was dipped by nymphs in the spring at Canathus. . . . By extension, celebrants of sacred mysteries in the ancient world often prepared themselves by abstaining from food and drink as well as from sexual intercourse in order to acquire the condition of strength and purity appropriate to serving the gods. . . .

"But the Christian religion broadened the concept of virginity to embrace a fully developed ascetic philosophy. The interpretation of the virgin birth as the moral sanction of the goodness of sexual chastity was the overwhelming and distinctive contribution of the Christian religion to the ancient mythological formula. . . . And it was this shift, from virgin birth to virginity, from religious sign to moral doctrine, that transformed a mother goddess like the Virgin Mary into an effective instrument of asceticism and female subjection" (Warner 1976:48, 49).

Anthropologist Marigene Arnold spent sixteen months doing field research among Mexican village women for her 1973 doctoral dissertation. She found that about one in eleven never married, bore children, or cohabited with a man. Such "spinsters" were known as *muchachas ya grandes* ("old girls"). They never achieved "full social adulthood," always remaining linked with adolescent girls and "at death . . . dressed as saints and buried as *angelitas* (little angels) without a funeral mass [since] loss of virginity is tantamount to ritual loss of innocence, and thus a 60- or 70-year-old woman is buried as if she were a young girl." Many became known as *cucarachas del templo* (church cockroaches), "practically living in the church" while performing Catholicism's important ritual role of praying for the dead (Arnold 1978:50–51).

Melius ac beatus quam jungi in matrimonio ("Virginity and celibacy are better and more blessed than the bond of matrimony").

— Canon Ten, Twenty-Fourth Session, Council of Trent (1545–63)
(quoted and translated in Warner 1976:336).

(Lehner 1969:116, fig. 697)

◆ Marina Warner, *Alone of All Her Sex:* "The twin ideal the Virgin represents is of course unobtainable. Therefore, the effect the myth has on the mind of a Catholic girl cannot but be disturbing, and if it does not provoke revolt (as it often does) it deepens the need for religion's consolation, for the screen of rushes against the perpetual frost of being carnal and female. By setting up an impossible ideal the cult of the Virgin does drive the adherent into a position of acknowledged and hopeless yearning and inferiority. . . ." (1976:337).

◆ John Layard, "The Incest Taboo and the Virgin Archetype" [1945]: "For what woman, in her inmost soul, would not like to give birth to a man child without all the bother of having a husband, a child with whom she might be in complete unity of spirit without any outside interference? Many married women in fact do reach out towards this solution, but in a condition of negative participation mystique due to a largely unconscious relationship with the husband owing to a mixture of fear and pride, leading to a spiritually incestuous relationship with the son. But the archetypal conception of Mary is, on the contrary, that she was so humbly receptive in herself that she was a fitting mate for the All Highest in the form of the Holy Ghost. That is to say that she was so virginal (i.e., uncontaminated by

(Harter 1978b:7)

man's misconceptions) as to be worthy of this honour and of receiving of the heavenly spiritual semen direct without its having to pass through the body of an imperfect man" (1972:291–92).

♦ Phyllis Chesler, *Women & Madness:* "After women grasp the meaning—and limitations—of Joan of Arc, they seek protection and redemption—from the Catholic Mary, the compassionate and powerful mother. Unfortunately, Mary is no Demeter. Catholic mythology has not granted Mary either a daughter or Demeter's bartering power with men and gods. Nevertheless, women in madness wish to give birth to the world (and to themselves) anew. They wish to avoid Joan's crucifixion and can do so only by becoming Virgin-Mothers. They also wish to become their own much-needed mothers." [Chesler notes here: "The women whom I spoke with who *did* have Virgin Birth experiences all gave birth to sons. However, some experienced their *own* rebirth at the same time."] (1972:28; also see Turner 1981).

♦ Elisabeth Schüssler Fiorenza, "Feminist Spirituality, Christian Identity, and Catholic Vision": "The more the Christian understanding of God was patriarchalized—the more God became the majestic ruler and the stern judge, the more people turned to the figure and cult of Mary. The more Jesus Christ became divinized, the more it became necessary to have a mediator between the majestic-transcendent God or his Son and the Christian community. One could almost say that through the dynamics of this development of the gradual patriarchalization of the god image, Mary became the 'other face,' the Christian 'face,' of God. All the New Testament images and attributes which characterize God as loving, life giving, compassionate and caring, as being with the people of God are now transferred to the 'mother of God,' who is as accessible as was the nonpatriarchal God whom Jesus preached. Even though any Catholic school child can explain on an *intellectual-theological* level the difference between the worship of God and Christ and the veneration of Mary, on an *emotional, imaginative, experiential* level the Catholic child experiences the love of God in the figure of a woman. Since in later piety Jesus Christ becomes so transcendentalized and absorbed into his divinity, the 'human face' of God is almost solely experienced in the image of a woman. The cult of Mary thus grew in proportion to the gradual repatriarchalization of the Christian God and Jesus Christ. The Catholic tradition gives us thus the opportunity to *experience* the divine reality in the figure of a woman" (1979:138–39).

♦ Mary Daly, *Beyond God the Father:* "On a functional level, Protestant obliteration of the Virgin ideal has to some extent served the purpose of reducing 'woman's role' exclusively to that of wife and mother, safely domesticated within the boundaries of the patriarchal family. Within Catholicism, the actual living out of the Virgin model has of course been less than totally liberating. Nuns have in a limited sense been removed from male domination. . . . Yet, they have been cloistered by patriarchal power, often physically and nearly always psychologically and socially. In spite of this, some strong independent women have emerged within Catholicism . . . some women have managed to absorb from the Mary image a vision of the free and independent woman who stands alone. Thus the relational aspect of the symbol has been minimized, though seldom totally discarded.

"In contrast to this, women in Protestant Christianity appear to have been thrown back into the ambiguous situation of having only Jesus as a symbol-model—an impossible ideal especially for women. . . . Concretely, instead of having 'the nun' as religious ideal, Protestant women have been offered the picture of 'the minister's wife.' Clearly, this has hardly been a liberating image.

"It is evident, then, that women can look neither to Catholicism nor to Protestantism for adequate models of liberation" (1973:85). [*Note:* Since publication of *Beyond God the Father* the author's thinking has changed in regard to the terms "God" and "androgyny." For an explanation of her more recent thinking see the Prefact to *Gyn/Ecology: The Metaethics of Radical Feminism*, Beacon Press, 1978.]

(Crawhall 1974:54)

♦ Marina Warner, *Alone of All Her Sex:* "Although Mary cannot be a model for the New Woman, a goddess is better than no goddess at all, for the sombre-suited masculine world of the Protestant religion is altogether too much like a gentlemen's club to which the ladies are only admitted on special days. But it should not be necessary to have a goddess contrasted with a god, a divinity who stands for qualities considered the quintessence of femininity and who thus polarizes symbolic and religious thought into two irreconcilably opposed camps" (1976:338).

Toward Complementarity: Challenge, Clarion

Insofar as they express the projected fears, hopes and desires of their narrators and adherents, myths can be viewed as cultural "Rorschach tests." Unfortunately, most myths now on record apparently have little to do with women and their fears, hopes and desires. For the most part, available narratives have been collected by male researchers from male informants, later to be translated and interpreted by male scholars from their own perspectives. Thus, both gods and goddesses, culture heroes and heroines, male and female monsters—to say nothing of all the Olympians and the Virgin Mary—are largely male constructs. As the following commentators suggest, a greater range of myths and their associated ideals of behavior must now be gathered, scrutinized, compared and re-interpreted from various feminist and humanist perspectives. Only when more women have studied and participated in more myths-in-process/context with other women and lived more stories within themselves will the imagination transmute the Rorschach, and many more facets of all the goddesses emerge.

◆ Adolf Guggenbühl-Craig, *Marriage—Dead or Alive:* "A more exact study of the archetypal possibilities of human beings could contribute much to the understanding of the so-called neuroses. A too-limited vision of what man should be hinders us from understanding the countless possible archetypal variations of human behavior. Many of the so-called neurotically false attitudes are not the result of an unfavorable psychological development, as we usually understand them, but the image of a particular archetype which cannot be lived with a good conscience because it is rejected by the collective. Practically whole archetypal patterns of feminine behavior which do not relate to men are relegated to 'should not be,' and are seen as neurotic and sick" (1977:51).

◆ "Since the mother archetype and the Hera archetype are less dominant today, more room is left for other archetypes to emerge. Numerous other archetypes contain psychic energy. The contemporary woman has the opportunity to live into the most diverse archetypes.
"Significantly, the situation for men is not precisely the same. For them not much has changed. For millenia men have had more archetypal possibilities than women . . . the archetype of Ares . . . Odysseus . . . the priest, the man of God . . . the medicine man, the doctor . . . Hephaistos . . . Hermes . . . and many others were not closed to men. The fact that today's woman has more archetypal possibilities open to her does not mean automatically that today's man also has more possibilities at his disposal than in the past" (ibid:53).

◆ "The situation of women today is especially hazardous because they are detaching themselves from a small group of archetypes and approaching a larger group of them, but the new group is not yet clearly visible" (ibid:55).

◆ Naomi R. Goldenberg, *Changing of the Gods:* "Gender stereotypes will be eliminated when we recognize that women and men can have many different styles of thought, feeling and behavior. One person can live many myths in a single lifetime or, in some cases, in a single year. In this age of change for our gods we need to proliferate the ways we allow ourselves to imagine psychological and religious

(Harter 1978a:61)

styles. Let us not endorse *one* goddess or *one* image as embodying the ideals of the new age. Why not see the different people we all might become by looking at many myths and images?" (1979:78).

♦ Kay Turner: "A culture is known by its images and by the ease or difficulty any individual has in gaining access to the power those images represent. Women have been denied their right to images which define and promote female power and independence. To reclaim images of the feminine world (i.e. to discover and release the political potential of the spiritual) is a serious task which will continue to involve many women" (1976a:2).

♦ Carol P. Christ, "Why Women Need the Goddess": "The symbol of Goddess has much to offer women who are struggling to be rid of the 'powerful, pervasive, and long-lasting moods and motivations' of devaluation of female power, denigration of the female body, distrust of female will, and denial of the women's bonds and heritage that have been engendered by patriarchal religion. As women struggle to create a new culture in which women's power, bodies, will, and bonds are celebrated, it seems natural that the Goddess would reemerge as symbol of the newfound beauty, strength, and power of women" (1978:13).

Chapter 3
Guides:
Myth and Mystery

After a while you will come to tremendous perpendicular bluffs which hardly seem surmountable. Think again what your grandfather said and you will then find yourself on the other side of these bluffs and quite safe.

These bluffs mean death. As you travel along the road of life you will find yourself alone. All your relatives, all your loved ones, are dead. You will begin to think to yourself, "Why, after all, am I living?" You will want to die. Now this, my grandson, is the place where most encouragement is given for it is here most needed. This is the most difficult of all the places you will come to. Keep in the footsteps of the medicine-men and you will be safe. The teachings of the lodge are the only road; they alone will enable you to pass this point safely.

—Crashing Thunder, a Winnebago Indian (Radin 1957:88–89).

Beautiful indeed is the Mystery given us by the blessed gods: death is for mortals no longer an evil, but a blessing.

—Inscription found at Eleusis (Angus 1925:140).

15th–16th century Mixtec skull mask (6¾" high, British Museum Collection) covered with turquoise (light) and obsidian (dark) with eyes of polished pyrite. It probably represents the powerful solar god Tezcatlipoca, "Smoking Mirror," chief deity of Texococo (Vaillant 1962:187; plate 46; rendering above from Harter 1978a:27).

A mystery cannot be broadcast; its truth must remain hidden until revealed to the proper initiate, who in turn vows to guard its powerful secret. The word "mystery" comes from the Greek *myein,* "to close the lips or eyes," and certainly the Athenians maintained one of the most famous and influential mystery cults, the Eleusinian Mysteries.[1] Despite the myriads of female and male initiates from throughout the Mediterranean world and beyond, for some two thousand years these sacred rites have never been fully revealed by anyone. They remain an awesome secret whose power is evoked by George E. Mylonas in the moving conclusion to his lifelong study of them:

Whatever the substance and meaning of the Mysteries was, the fact remains that the cult of Eleusis satisfied the most sincere yearnings and the deepest longings of the human heart. The initiates returned from their pilgrimage to Eleusis full of

---

[1]Demeter's Eleusinian Mysteries were but one of a number of mystery religions in the ancient Mediterranean and Near Eastern worlds. Mystery cults were also associated with Cybele, Dionysus, Hermes-Toth, Isis, Mithra, Orpheus, and the Cabeiri-Dioscuri of Samothrace, to name but a few. Such occult rites also influenced the early forms of Christianity. According to Alan Watts: "Prior to the general practice of infant baptism, initiation into the Christian Mysteries was a tremendous solemnity involving preliminary disciplines, tests, and exorcisms of a most serious kind. For in this respect, as in many others, Christianity was following the

joy and happiness, with the fear of death diminished and the strengthened hope of a better life in the world of shadows: 'Thrice happy are those of mortals, who having seen those rites depart for Hades; for to them alone is it granted to have true life there; to the rest all there is evil,' Sophocles cries out exultantly. And to this Pindar with equal exultation answers: 'Happy is he who, having seen these rites goes below the hollow earth; for he knows the end of life and he knows its god-sent beginning.' When we read these and other similar statements written by the great or nearly-great of the ancient world, by the dramatists and the thinkers, when we picture the magnificent buildings and monuments constructed at Eleusis by great political figures like Peisistratos, Kimon, Perikles, Hadrian, Marcus Aurelius and others, we cannot help but believe that the Mysteries of Eleusis were not an empty, childish affair devised by shrewd priests to fool the peasant and the ignorant, but a philosophy of life that possessed substance and meaning and imparted a modicum of truth to the yearning human soul. That belief is strengthened when we read in Cicero that Athens has given nothing to the world more excellent or divine than the Eleusinian Mysteries. (1961:284–85)

The myth of Demeter and her daughter Persephone, which recounts the origin of these Eleusinian rites, begins with a motif important to women's mythology—rape. Such beliefs and narratives suggest a fear of men in women's mythology which may parallel the "fear of women" (see chapter 2) allegedly expressed in much male-dominated mythology. This fear is explored further (below) by comparing male beliefs about the *vagina dentata* with female ones about the vaginal serpent. Such lore constitutes the informal learning of women, which is sometimes made more formal in various initiation rites.

Historian of religions Mircea Eliade distinguishes three types of initiations into mysteries: (1) so-called "puberty rites" designed to effect a transition from childhood or adolescence to adulthood, (2) rites to enter secret societies,[2] and (3) disciplines connected with obtaining special religious status such as medicine man, shaman or mystic. The second and third types of initiation

---

pattern of the other great Mystery cults of the Graeco-Roman world. In those days the inner Mystery of the Mass was by no means a public rite which anyone might attend. It was a true *mystery,* and the actual rite was divided into two parts—the Mass of the Catechumens and the Mass of the Faithful. The Catechumens were those undergoing preparation for baptism—being catechized—and because they had not yet received initiation were permitted to attend only the introductory part of the Mass. After the reading of the Gospel for the day, the Deacon of the Mass would turn to the people and say, 'Let the catechumens depart', whereafter it was the duty of the Doorkeepers to see that no uninitiated person remained in the church. This custom prevailed so long as Christians were a minority in their society, but disappeared when Christianity had been adopted as a state-religion, and when whole societies were nominally Christian" (1968:139; also see Eliade 1965:115–21).

[2]According to Eliade: "The second category includes all types of rites for entering a secret society, a *Bund,* or a confraternity. These secret societies are limited to one sex and are extremely jealous of their respective secrets. Most of them are male and constitute secret fraternities *(Männerbünde);* but there are also some female secret societies" (1965:2). Elsewhere, he notes that: "As to the *Weiberbünde* [women's secret societies], the initiation consists of a series of specific tests followed by revelations concerning fertility, conception, and birth" (1969:115). Eliade further claims that "in the ancient Mediterranean and Near Eastern world, the mysteries were open to both sexes; and although they are a little different in type, we can put the Greco-Oriental mysteries in the category of secret confraternities" (1965:2).

are not obligatory, and "most of them are performed individually or for comparatively small groups" (1965:2). In Native American traditions, women were not always denied access to important secret knowledge, whether in medicine societies or individually.

For example, ethnomusicologist Frances Densmore collected songs "during 1907, 1908, and 1909, from Chippewa Indians on the White Earth, Leech Lake, and Red Lake reservations in Minnesota" (1910:1; also see Peterson 1980). She persuaded a woman at Red Lake to tell a story. "She consented with reluctance as it was the summer season and she said the snakes would certainly bite her at night if she told stories in the summer. After writing down a story the writer asked her to tell something about the Mīde'wīwīn [lit. "mystic doings"] and to sing one of its songs. This request was received with still greater reluctance. The woman finally consented to sing one song in some secluded place where she was sure no one would hear her. When asked what the song would be she replied that it was a love-charm song. She was a woman about sixty years of age and was the most dirty and unattractive woman with whom the writer has come in contact. In a thin, nasal tone she sang the song, which was noted down by ear, no phonograph being available. With coy shyness she said the song meant that she was as beautiful as the roses. She also drew a crude picture of the song. . . . [She] promised to come back and sing other songs the next day, but some friends who knew that she had sung a Mīde' song threatened her with calamity and she did not return" (ibid:88; also see Vennum 1978; and Landes 1968 for an account of the Midé based in part on a woman visionary, Mrs. Maggie Wilson of Ontario).

Song picture No. 71. The heart of the figure is shown. . . . (Densmore 1910:89).

Words

A'ninajun'	What are you saying to me?
Ogini'bagun'	I am arrayed like the roses
Ajina'gooyan'	And beautiful as they

On the other hand, among the Papago Indians of southern Arizona during the early 1930s:

The regular routes to dream power are not open to women, who do not kill enemies or eagles and who are never taken on the salt pilgrimage. The woman of imagination and energy sometimes manages, from a cold start, to dream enough to become a medicine woman, but this does not happen often. (Underhill 1973:125)

This is not atypical, and the stories of some Native American women who did manage to become healers, shamans and visionaries are sampled below (also see Niethammer 1977:139–63). For the most part, their initiations are more private and personal, like that of Mountain Wolf Woman, Crashing Thunder's sister:

There was an old man who was my grandfather, and I used to help him in various ways. I always gave him food. He liked to eat. That is the way old people are. If you give food to an old person and he really likes it, that is very good. The thinking powers of old people are strong and if one of them thinks good things for you, whatever he wishes for you, you will obtain that good fortune. That is what they always said. . . .

. . . Then he said, "Granddaughter, you have helped me with many things. What do you wish? You have helped me in many ways and given me many things. What is it that you want? Tell me. . . ."

"Yes, grandfather, I always liked the Indian medicines. I have a lot of children and I even have grandchildren. I do not always have money to pay for the doctor. I know it is a fact that the Indian medicines help people. I always liked the Indian medicines."

"Oh, granddaughter, you have certainly said something worthwhile. You have asked for a very good thing. You said a good thing. You are going to have something valuable. . . .

"It is good. You will prescribe Indian medicines. I used to do this; now you will do it. The power will be yours. You are not yet holy, but these medicines are holy."—I did not know what he meant by that, but he said—, "These medicines are going to talk to you. If someone sets his mind on you, that is, he is going to buy medicines from you, you will know it before they come to you. And when they come to you, say to them, 'You will be cured.' If you put your mind to it intensely, that is where you will have your power. Then you will give them Indian medicines. You are going to be a medicine woman. You are going to cure sickness. This redounds to your honor, my granddaughter."

This is what my grandfather said to me. Naqisaneingahinigra, Naqiwankwaxopiniga, he was called. I learned his medicines. He told me all of them, so I know a lot of good medicines. (Lurie 1961:61, 62, 63–64)

Even though they are frequently denied entrance into formal mysteries, in many traditions women are thought to be the source of wisdom. Indeed, in Western tradition, the female Sophia has long personified wisdom itself, at least men's wisdom. (Women's wisdom, which will be explored further in chapter 4, has more often been demeaned as witchcraft.) Furthermore, in Western tradition at least, the female muses who inspire creative individuals seem not to have an apparent male counterpart. Masculine spirits are more frequently seen as dangerous Bluebeard-like abductors than inspiriting sages, at least in terms of their relationship to women's development. This unfortunate disparity may be seen in the Jungian approach to the anima, the psyche's "female," in men, and the animus, the psyche's "male," in women. The former is more often presented favorably than the latter, as the examples in "Musings: Animus ≠ Anima, Yet" (below) suggest.

The Myth of Demeter and Persephone and the Eleusinian Mysteries

The town of Eleusis is some fourteen miles west of Athens, where the Lesser Mysteries were usually held annually in the spring. Those who participated in these ceremonies—all who had not committed homicide, men, women, children, and slaves who spoke Greek—could advance to the Greater Mysteries in Eleusis. An annual fifty-five-day truce was declared during September and October in order to accommodate worshippers from afar for these Greater

Mysteries. A preliminary day-long procession, when the caskets of sacred objects *(Hiera)* were brought from the Telesterion in Eleusis to the Eleusinion, Demeter's sanctuary in Athens, preceded the crucial eight days:

1. In assembly at the Agora, a proclamation was read inviting participation.
2. Participants purified themselves in the sea, together with a pig to be sacrificed subsequently.
3. Sacrifices and prayers were offered.
4. Asclepius (a traditional "latecomer") was honored, and late arrivers could join.
5. Grand procession to Eleusis, perhaps culminating in a night dance by women bearing sacred vessels.
6, 7. Core of the Mysteries, about which little is definitely known.
8. Concluding ceremonies.

On the ninth day, celebrants returned to Athens without a formally organized procession, and a full report about the ceremonies was delivered to the Athenian council of five hundred on the tenth day.

Initiates *(mystes),* sponsored and guided by a patron *(mystagogos),* fasted, maintained vigils, and drank the *kykeon,* the "meal" drink which, according to the Homeric hymn (below), Demeter requested Metaneira to mix in lieu of wine. A further, optional stage of initiation, the highest, was called the *Epopteia* ("the state of 'having seen' "). (cf. Morford and Lenardon 1977: 231–37)[3]

The central experience of the Mysteries, in which revelation came through words, acts and displays of sacred objects, has remained secret. At least two revelations, both basically having to do with rebirth and the soul's journey to the afterlife, have been suggested by classicist Karl Kerényi, who bases his speculation on the early Christian writer Hippolytos. The latter claims that the Hierophant (priest), officiating at night "under the great fire," shouted: "The Mistress has given birth to a holy boy, Brimo has given birth to Brimos!" Kerényi thinks that the words *brimo* and *brimos* were from northern Greece and refer to Demeter, Persephone, and Hecate in their aspect as goddesses of the underworld. The "message" to initiates, then, was that funeral pyres were vehicles of birth rather than death (Kerényi 1967:92–93; but see Mylonas 1961:306–10). He also proposes:

At Eleusis . . . it must have been the Hierophant who intoned the call for Kore. He beat the *echeion,* the instrument with the voice of thunder. The *epopteia* began; ineffable things were seen. A vision of the underworld goddess . . . a figure— *schema ti*—rose above the ground. In a second phase—how much later we do not know—the Hierophant, silent amid profound silence—displayed a mown ear of grain. . . . All who had "seen" turned, at the sight of this *concrete thing,* as though turning back from the herafter into this world, back to the world of tangible things, which includes grain. (Kerényi 1967:94)

---

[3]The best source on this subject is Mylonas 1961. A view of the Mysteries as involving hallucinogens is presented in R. Gordon Wasson, Albert Hofmann and Carl A. P. Ruck, *The Road to Eleusis: Unveiling the Secret of the Mysteries,* Ethno-mycological Studies, No. 4 (New York: Harcourt Brace Jovanovich, 1978).

Mylonas considers the latter unlikely, since grains were so frequently depicted and used throughout the rituals (1961:275–76). He suggests instead that the Hiera displayed may have been "small relics from the Mycenaean age handed down from generation to generation . . . [whose] age and unfamiliarity . . . would have lent the impression of objects used by the goddess herself during her stay in the temple within which they found themselves" (1961: 273–74).[4]

In any case, much of what little we know about the Eleusinian Mysteries comes from the myth of Demeter and Persephone as told in the second Homeric Hymn, "To Demeter," probably composed around 650 B.C. This text, which describes the Mysteries' origin and suggests certain rituals—e.g., women dancing like Iambe and imbibing a special barley drink like the one Demeter requested—which may have been observed during annual cult ceremonies, has tantalized generations of scholars and artists. Poet Daryl Hine's verse translation of this rich, complex document follows in full.

Awesome Demeter, the goddess with beautiful hair, I begin to
Sing about, her and her trim-ankled daughter whom Aidoneus
Raped or was given by Zeus the deep-thunderer widely-discerning,
When she was playing apart from her mother Demeter the golden
Giver of glorious fruit, with the deep-bosomed daughters of Ocean,
Gathering flowers, the roses and crocus that grow in the midst of
Deep grassy meadows as well as fair lilies and hyacinths, iris,
And the narcissus, which earth at the bidding of Zeus had produced to
Please the Receiver of Many, a snare for the flower-faced maiden,
Glistening miracle, marvel and wonder to all who behold it,
Whether the gods who are deathless or men who are born but to perish.
For from its root it thrust upward a glorious hundred-fold blossom,
And it exuded a fragrance so sweet that broad heaven above and
All the earth laughed with pleasure, as did the salt wave of the sea. The
Maiden was struck with amazement, and reached out with both of her hands to
Seize the desirable plaything. Then earth-the-extensively-travelled
Gaped in the prairie of Nysa, and He Who Has Several Names, the
Monarch Who Welcomes So Many, the underworld offspring of Cronus
Leapt, with his immortal horses, straight out of the chasm upon her,
Catching her up on his glittering chariot—she was unwilling—
Carried her off still complaining; she wailed at the top of her voice and
Called on her father, the Highest and Best, the successor of Cronus.
Nobody heard her, however, not one of the undying gods, nor
Men who are born but to perish, not even the rich-fruited olives,

---

[4]Also see the quote from Hippolytus (*Philosophoumena* V, 8) that "the Athenians, when they initiate in the Eleusinia exhibit in silence to the *epoptai* the mighty and marvellous and most complete epoptic mystery, an ear of cut-wheat." According to Walter F. Otto, "there can be no doubt of the miraculous nature of the event. The ear of wheat growing and maturing with supernatural suddenness is just as much a part of the mysteries of Demeter as the vine growing in a few hours is part of the revels of Dionysus" ("The Meaning of the Eleusinian Mysteries," in *The Mysteries: Papers from the Eranos Yearbooks*, 2, ed. Joseph Campbell, Bollingen Series XXX [New York, 1955], p. 25). Both these and other quotations appear in No. 128 The Eleusinian Mysteries, chap. III of Mircea Eliade, *From Primitives to Zen* (1967), pp. 148–49 of the 1974 Harper & Row paperback, *Man and the Sacred*.

(Harter 1978b:47)

No one but Persaeus' daughter, considerate Hecate, heard her,
Wearing a radiant headdress at home in the depth of her cave, and
Helios' lordship, Hyperion's glorious son: they both heard the
Maiden invoking her father the scion of Cronus who sat far
Off and apart from the gods in his worshipful temple receiving
Manifold human petitions and beautiful offerings from men.
It was with Zeus's connivance that Hades, his paternal brother,
Host and Director of Many, the Lord Who Has Several Titles,
Cronus' notorious son, had abducted the Maiden reluctant,
Driving his immortal horses. So long as the goddess beheld the
Earth and the stars in the sky and the beams of the sun and the roaring
Sea full of fish, and the maiden expected the sight of her noble
Mother as well as her kindred the gods who are ever-begotten,
Hope still enchanted her generous spirit in spite of her anguish . . .

Then did the heights of the mountains, and then did the depths of the ocean
Echo her immortal voice; she was heard by her reverend mother.
Keen was the anguish that seized on her heart so she tore off the headdress
From her ambrosial hair, and she rent it with both of her dear hands;
Shedding the coal-coloured cloak from her shoulders she fled like a sea-bird
Over the wet and the dry ways of earth in pursuit of her daughter.
No one was willing to tell her what happened exactly and fully,
Neither her undying kindred nor men who are born but to perish,
None of the birds as reliable messenger flew to Demeter.
Searching, the Reverend Mother then wandered on earth holding kindled
Torches aloft in her hands for nine days and nine nights without tasting
Either ambrosia or the sweet beverage nectar, in mourning,
Not even bathing her body. But when the tenth radiant morning
Shone upon earth she encountered dear Hecate carrying brightness
Held in her hands, who addressed her by name as if bringing her tidings,
"Holy Demeter, great bringer of seasons and glorious giver,
Which of the heavenly gods or of men who are born but to perish
Has, by abducting Persephone, thus so afflicted your dear heart?
I heard her voice, but I did not behold who it was with my own eyes.
Briefly have I told you everything that I can honestly tell you."
Thus she concluded. And never a word did the daughter of Rhea
Answer, but swiftly she darted away with her, holding the blazing
Torches on high, till they came to the sun, overseer of gods and
Men; and then standing in front of his horses the goddess addressed him.
"Helios, now, if I ever have gladdened your heart or your humour
Once, by a deed or a word perhaps, pity me, though I'm a goddess.
Her whom I bore, the superlative flower of beauty, The Maiden,
Hers was the voice that I heard as it thrilled through the harvestless aether,
As if she were being forced; but I did not observe it at first hand.
You upon every land and on every body of water
Out of the glittering atmosphere blaze down your radiant sunbeams.
Tell me exactly about my dear child if you happened to see her.
Who was it seized her and took her against her will forcibly from me?
One of the undying gods or a man who was born but to perish?"
That was her question. The son of Hyperion answered her briefly.
"Madame, Demeter, almighty and beautiful daughter of Rhea,
You shall be told, for I greatly revere you and pity your grieving
Over your trim-ankled daughter. Now nobody else is to blame, no

(Harter 1978b:54)

God but cloud-carrying Zeus, for he gave her to Hades his brother
For his intended, to call her his blossoming bride; as for Hades,
Snatching her up on his horses he bore her off loudly lamenting
Under the earth to his kingdom of murk and perennial darkness.
Nevertheless, mighty goddess, desist from extravagant mourning;
It is not proper in vain to indulge your insatiate anger.
Aidoneus the Ruler of Many is not an unlikely
Son-in-law; he is your brother. And furthermore he obtained worship
At the first triple division of worlds when their doom was decided,
Dwelling with those over whom Hades' lot once appointed him ruler."
Helios when he had spoken the foregoing called to his horses,
And they, obedient, drew the swift chariot rapidly, bird-like.
Anguish more bitter and violent entered the heart of Demeter.
Angry henceforth with the black-clouded king of the gods, she avoided
Heavenly meetings and lofty Olympus. She went in disguise from
City to city of men and the splendid achievements of mankind,
Wasting her looks a great while, so that nobody, whether of men or
Broad-girdled women would recognize her upon sight, till she reached the
Home of sharp-witted Celeus, the ruler of fragrant Eleusis.
Deo sat down at the roadside, consuming her dear heart with sorrow
Next to the Spring of the Maiden, where women who lived in the city
Came for their water, in shade, for above it there flourished an olive.
Like an old woman she was in appearance, one born in the distant
Past who has long outworn childbed and has no more part in the gifts of
Her Who Loves Wreaths, Aphrodite—of such are the nurses of children
Or, in the echoing mansions of kings who administer justice,
Housekeepers; such she appeared to the four Eleusinian maidens
Coming to fetch the available water back home in the brazen
Pitchers unto the affectionate home of their father Celeus—
Four of them, lovely as goddesses, still in the flower of girlhood.
These were their names: Callidice, and Demo and fair Cleisidice,
Plus Callithoe, the eldest. Now, none of them recognized Deo:
Difficult are the immortals for mortals to know when they see them.
Standing nearby, they addressed her in words that flew straight to their target.
"Who are you? where are you coming from, grandmother, one of the old folk?
Why have you strayed from the city? Why don't you draw near to the houses?
There, women your age and younger there are in the shadowy great halls
Ready to shew you affection not only in words but in action."
Thus they expressed themselves; reverend Deo replied to them, saying,
"Daughters, whoever you are, for I see that indeed you are women,
Greetings! I willingly tell you my story; it isn't improper
That I should tell you the truth, since you earnestly ask me to do so.
Doso my name, for my reverend mother imposed it upon me.
Recently over the breadth of the sea I unwillingly crossed from
Crete—yes, unwillingly: pirates abducted me forcibly, using
Strength of necessity. In their swift vessel they landed, soon after,
Somewhere near Thoricus. There all the women in bands went ashore, the
Menfolk accompanied them. In the shade of the prow of their ship they
Spread out their supper. My heart was not set on the tasty repast, so
Secretly slipping away in the darkness cross-country I quickly
Fled from my arrogant masters in order they might not enjoy my
Ransom who'd carried me off so, like booty unbought, or unpaid for!

104   CHAPTER 3

Wandering, I have come here, and I do not have any idea
What is the name of this country or who its inhabitants may be.
But I pray those who inhabit Olympian mansions to give you
Suitable husbands and birth of such children as mothers desire.
Pardon me, maidens, which man's or what woman's abode, my dear children,
Would I be wise to approach in my search for employment befitting
One who is no longer young? Woman's work I will gladly perform, and
Holding a newly born baby secure in my arms I should nurse him
Beautifully; I can do housework and make master's bed in the alcove
Of the well-carpentered bedroom, and see to the work of the women."
Thus spoke the goddess, and straightway replied the inviolate maiden
Fair Callidice, of Celeus' daughters the best in appearance:
"Mother, the gifts of the gods humankind must endure, though afflicted.
They are much stronger than we are. And now I shall clearly instruct you,
Naming the men hereabouts who possess greatest influence for their
Respectability, those who stand out in the populace, who keep
By their advice and their upright decisions our citadel secure.
Prudent Triptolemus, honest Dioclus, and good Polyxenus,
Blameless Eumolpus, and Dolichus, and our respectable father—
All of them eminent persons, with wives to look after their households.
And, of the women, not one on first sight would dismiss you off-hand or
Send you away from her door disrespectfully, slighting your aspect;
Rather will they all receive you because you appear like a goddess.
Now, if you like to abide here, then we will go back to our father's
House and relate to our mother the handsomely dressed Metaneira
All from beginning to end that has happened, so she will invite you
Home to our house, and you need not go making such inquiries elsewhere.
Our little brother, her last born and darling, is nursed in the palace,
Subject of much supplication and heartily welcomed at last there.
If you should bring the boy up till he came to the measure of manhood,
Anyone seeing you soon—any woman—would envy you for the
Gifts which I know that our mother would give in reward for his raising."
Such was the speech of the maiden; the goddess agreed with a nod. Then
Filling their glistening vessels with water they carried them proudly;
Soon they had come to the house of their father, and quickly related
What they had seen to their mother and what they had heard, and at once she
Bade them go summon the stranger, whatever she asked for in wages.
Then, like young hinds, or like heifers that gambol in Spring in the meadows
Once they have fed to their hearts' satisfaction, they picked up the edges
Of their impeccable shifts, and they darted along down the hollow
Chariot path, with their crocus-like hair floating over their shoulders.
Soon they discovered the reverend goddess at rest where they left her
Right by the roadside, and then they conducted her to their beloved
Father's abode, and she followed behind them consuming her dear heart,
Grief-stricken; veiled was her head, and about the dear goddess's narrow
Feet the deep fringe of her sea-coloured over-cloak rustled like water.
Soon they approached the affectionate home of their god-nurtured father.
Entering through the verandah they came on their ladylike mother
Seated, her back to a pillar that held up the tightly-made ceiling,
Holding her newly born babe to her breast, her new darling. Her daughters
Ran to their mother. The goddess, however, in crossing the threshold,
Reached to the roof with her head, filled the doorway with heavenly splendour.

Reverence, awe, and a sickening terror possessed Metaneira,
So she arose from her chair and invited her guest to be seated.
Deo, the bringer of seasons and giver of glorious gifts, not
Wishing to sit on the glittering chair, without speaking a long while
Stood with her beautiful eyes lowered, till the good-hearted Iambe
Brought her a carpentered stool, after throwing a silvery sheepskin
Over it. There sat the goddess, upholding her veil in her hands in
Front of her face, without utterance, grief-stricken, mute on the foot stool
For a long while, neither greeting by gesture or word anybody,
Silent, unsmiling, refusing to taste either liquid or solid,
Wasting away in incessant desire for her trim-ankled daughter,
Until kind-hearted Iambe by means of her many facetious
Sayings and mockery roused the most holy and reverend goddess
First to a smile, then to laughter and something resembling good humour.
Often at seasons thereafter she flattered the goddess's bad moods.
Then Metaneira presented a cup full of sweet-tasting wine which
Deo refused, for she said that she was not permitted to taste red
Wine, but she asked them to give her instead a concoction of barley
Water to drink, in a beverage flavoured with delicate mint-leaves.
So they concocted the potion the goddess requested, and brought it.
Deo accepted this drink for the sake of the sacrament, gravely.
Handsomely girt Metaneira began to attempt conversation.
"Greetings, good woman. I do not suppose you descended from base-born
Parents, but rather from noble, for dignity shines in your eyes, and
Grace, as they shine from the faces of kings who administer justice.
Ah, but we men must endure all the gifts of the gods, though we suffer!
Out of necessity, seeing their yoke has been laid on our shoulders.
Now that you've come here, whatever is mine will be yours to dispose of.
Take, then, this child unto nurse—my dear son, lately born and unlooked-for,
Whom the immortals have sent me in answer to my supplication.
If you will bring up the boy till he comes to the measure of manhood,
Anyone seeing you then, any woman, will envy you, for the
Gifts that I promise his mother will give in reward for his raising."
Thus did Demeter the goddess once gorgeously garlanded answer:
"Greetings, good woman, as well, in return: may the gods give you good things!
As for your son, I will gladly accept him to nurse as you ask me;
Yes, and I hope through no fault of his nurse will enchantment afflict him.
I know a powerful antidote for the discomfort of toothache,
I know an excellent bulwark against the most mischievous magic."
When she had said this she gathered him into her sweet-smelling bosom
With her ambrosial hands, and the heart of his mother was gladdened.
Thus it befell that Demeter brought up in the palace the brilliant
Demophoon, son of sharp-witted Celeus and fair Metaneira.
Quickly he grew and waxed strong, like a true supernatural being,
Eating no food, neither fed at the breast of his mother. Demeter
Rubbed him instead with ambrosia, like one engendered of heaven,
Fragrantly breathing upon him and holding the child in her bosom.
Nightly she buried him deep in the midst of the fire like a firebrand
All unbeknownst to his parents, to whom it appeared a great wonder
How he was growing precocious and how he resembled the gods. And
She might have made him immortal and ageless, except for the folly
Of the well-girt Metaneira who, spying one night from her chamber,

(Harter 1978b:35)

106   CHAPTER 3

Saw what the goddess was doing. She shrieked and belaboured her flanks in
Terror, hysterical over her son, and distracted in mind, and
As she lamented she uttered the following hasty expressions:
"Demophoon, darling! Behold where the outlandish woman has hid you
Right in the midst of the fire, to my grief and unbearable anguish!"
So she exclaimed in her grievance: the queen among goddesses heard her.
Angry therefore, the once gorgeously garlanded Lady Demeter
Snatched from the fire with her immortal hands the dear child Metaneira
Bore in the palace unhoped-for, and brusquely rejected the infant
From her immortal embrace to the ground, being dreadfully angry.
At the same time she admonished the handsomely girt Metaneira:
"Witless are mankind and gross, inconsiderate, thoughtless, and stupid!
Lacking foreknowledge of fate, whether evil or good will befall them.
You in your folly have erred to the highest degree, Metaneira.
Witness the pitiless waters of Styx, the great oath of the gods, that
I should have made your dear son an immortal and furthermore ageless
All of his days, and moreover had given him evergreen honour.
Now he has not any way of escaping from death and misfortune.
Nevertheless an unwithered renown will attach to him always
Since he has lain on my lap and has slept in the arms of a goddess.
But, with the full revolution of years and succession of seasons,
He shall experience much: Eleusinians, sons of their fathers,
Waging incessantly war internecine, with battle and war-cry.
I am Demeter the Venerable, to immortals and mortals
Mightiest source of delight and of physical sustenance also.
Go now and build me a sizable temple, an altar beneath it,
Let the whole populace build it, in sight of the citadel's steep walls,
Over the Spring Callichorus upon a conspicuous hillside.
I shall instruct you myself in my mysteries, so that hereafter
When you perform them you may do so piously, winning my favour."
When she had spoken the goddess transfigured her size and appearance,
Shedding old age. Circumambient beauty was wafted about her;
From her odoriferous garments diffused a delectable perfume,
From her immortal, ambrosial body a radiance shone, her
Corn-coloured hair tumbled over her shoulders; the comfortable house was
Filled with a brightness of lightning. Demeter went out through the palace.
Poor Metaneira! her knees were immediately loosened, a long while
She remained speechless, completely forgetting to pick up her darling
Child from the ground. But his sisters on hearing his piteous outcry
Leapt from their comfortable beds, and while one took him up in her arms and
Cradled the child in her bosom, another rekindled the fire,
While yet another was running on tiptoe to waken their mother.
Then they all gathered about him and, washing the struggling infant,
Cuddled and kissed him, in vain, for his heart was not comforted thereby,
Feeling inferior nurses and worse foster mothers now held him.
Nightlong while quaking with dread they placated the reverend goddess,
And at the dawn's first appearance they told the whole story to widely-
Ruling Celeus exactly as beautiful Deo commanded.
Summoning to an assembly his numerous people he bade them
Make for the richly-coiffed goddess an opulent temple and altar
On the conspicuous hillside. And they very quickly obeyed him,
Harkening to his instruction, and built it as he had enjoined them.

(Harter 1978b:60)

As for the infant, he flourished like some supernatural being.
When they'd completed the building and rested a while from their labour
Severally they went home. But Demeter whose hair is like ripe corn
Sitting apart from the blessed immortals, from all of her kindred,
Waited and wasted away with regret for her trim-ankled daughter.
Then a most terrible year over all the inhabited earth she
Caused for mankind, and a cruel. The soil did not let any seedlings
Come to the surface: Demeter, once handsomely garlanded, hid them.
Many a crescent-shaped ploughshare the oxen in vain dragged through furrows;
Much was the colourless barley that fell without fruit on the good earth.
Now were the race of articulate men altogether destroyed by
Hardship and famine, depriving the gods who inhabit Olympus
Of their invidious worship, their honours and sacrifice, had not
Zeus taken thought and considered what ought to be done to prevent it.
First he dispatched golden Iris to fly to and summon his sister,
Fair-haired Demeter whose form is admired and desired of so many.
Thus her commission, and Iris obeyed him, the black-clouded son of
Cronus, and rapidly ran on swift feet through the space intervening
Till she arrived at a citadel fragrant with incense, Eleusis,
Where in her temple she found the deep-blue-mantled goddess Demeter
Whom she addressed in this wise, using words that flew straight to their target.
"All-father Zeus, he whose thoughts are unwithered and deathless, Demeter,
Calls you to come to your kind and the gods who're engendered forever.
Go, then, and let not my message from heaven remain unaccomplished!"
Iris besought her; the heart of the earth mother was not persuaded.
Then father Zeus must dispatch all the blessed and ever-abiding
Gods, till, one after another, they came and they called upon Deo,
Giving her manifold beautiful gifts and the deference due her
Which she desired to receive at the hands of the other immortals.
No one, however, was able to sway her emotions or conscious
Mind. She was angry at heart and she sternly rejected their speeches,
Saying she never again would set foot upon fragrant Olympus,
Never would suffer the corn and the fruit of the earth to awaken
Till she beheld with her own eyes the face of her lovely daughter.
When father Zeus the deep thunderer widely discerning had heard this,
Into Erebus he sent the gold-wanded destroyer of Argus,
So that when he with soft words had talked over inflexible Hades,
He might lead holy Persephone out of the visible darkness
Into the light and the company of the immortals, so then her
Mother, Demeter, beholding her child might abate her resentment.
Hermes was not disobedient. Quitting the throne of Olympus,
He with alacrity leapt and descended to underground chasms
Where he discovered the Ruler at home in the midst of his palace
Seated upon a divan at the side of his worshipful consort.
Very unwilling she was on account of her longing for mother,
Who afar off all because of the deeds of the blessed immortals
Brooded upon her design. Then the powerful slayer of Argus
Standing in decent proximity spoke to the Ruler as follows.
"Hades with coal-coloured ringlets, dictator of those that have perished,
All-father Zeus has commanded me forthwith to fetch back the Maiden,
Noble Persephone out of Erebus to him, that her mother
May at the sight of her daughter desist from her anger and dreadful

Fury against the immortals. For know that she mediates mighty
Deeds: the destruction of feeble mankind from the face of the earth by
Hiding the seeds underground and thus utterly blasting the worship
Of the immortals. She harbours a dreadful resentment, no longer
Visits the gods, but she sits in her incense-odoriferous temple
Far away, holding the rocky acropolis over Eleusis."
When he had finished, the Lord of the Underworld, Aidoneus
Smiled with his eyebrows. But never the less he obeyed the behest of
Zeus, for he summoned and said to sharp-witted Persephone quickly,
"Go, then, Persephone, back to the arms of your sable-robed mother,
Keeping a gentle and kind disposition and heart in your bosom.
Do not indulge in excessive despondency more than is proper.
I shall, among the immortals, not prove an unsuitable husband,
Being your father's own brother, the brother of Zeus. In this kingdom
You shall be mistress of everything living and creeping and have the
Greatest proportion of honour among the immortals. Eternal
Shall be the penalties of those transgressors hereafter whoever
Fail to propitiate your mighty godhead by sacrifice and the
Pious performance of rites and the payment of suitable presents."
When he had spoken exceedingly clever Persephone was glad;
Blithely she leapt up, delighted. But Hades himself gave her something
Edible covertly, namely a sweet pomegranate seed, just one,
Peering about him suspiciously, so that she should not abide the
Rest of her days at the side of her mother, impressive Demeter.
Hades the Ruler of Many then harnessed his undying horses
Unto the front of his glittering chariot, which she ascended.
Standing beside her then Hermes the powerful slayer of Argus
Taking the whip and the reins between both of his capable dear hands
Drove through the hall of the dead, and the horses were nothing unwilling,
Flying, they quickly traversed the long journey before them, and neither
Seas nor the water of rivers nor green grassy glens in the mountains
Nor mountainpeaks ever checked the career of the undying horses—
Over all these lay their course as they cleft through the fathomless aether.
Hermes their driver drew up right in front of the sweet-smelling temple
Where the once beautifully garlanded goddess Demeter was waiting.
When she got sight of her daughter she dashed like a madwoman down the
Forested side of the mountain. Persephone, seeing the beaming
Eyes of her mother, abandoned both horses and driver, and leaping
Down from the chariot, ran to her, fell on her neck, and embraced her.
Even as Deo was holding Persephone safe in her arms, her
Mind had begun to suspect some deception. She anxiously trembled,
Checked her affectionate greeting a moment, and asked her a question.
"Darling, while you were there, underground, tell me, you did not partake, or
Did you? of any refreshment? Speak out. Do not try to conceal it.
Better that both of us know. If you didn't, now you have arisen,
Dear, from the side of detestable Hades, with me and your father,
Cronus' umbrageous successor, and honoured by all the immortals
Shall you abide. If you did, you must, fluttering back underneath the
Chasms of earth, make your dwelling a third of the year and its seasons
There; and the other seasons with me and the other immortals.
But, when the earth is abloom with the various flowers of springtime,
Then from the palpable darkness again you shall rise, a great wonder

Hades (Roman Pluto)
(Lehner 1969:23, fig. 41).

Both to the undying gods and to men who are born but to perish.
Now, tell me just by what ruse the Receiver of Many deceived you."
Then very lovely Persephone said to her mother in answer,
"Mother, to you I will tell the whole story exactly and frankly.
When the swift messenger Hermes the luck-bringer came to me saying
At the command of my father—of Zeus—and the other immortals
That I should come from Erebus so you when you saw me might cease from
Anger against the immortals, abating your terrible fury,
Blithely I leapt for delight, but my Lord surreptitiously gave me
One pomegranate seed—one—a delicious and delicate morsel
Which he compelled me by force and against my desire to swallow.
Now, how he first caught me up, by the closely laid plan of my father
Zeus, and then carried me off into vast subterranean chasms,
I shall explain, as you ask me, and tell from beginning to end. As
All of us girls were disporting ourselves in a lovely meadow—
Leucippe, Phaeno, Electra, Ianthe, Iache, Melite,
Rhode and sweet Callirhoe as well, Melobosis and Tyche,
Rhodope, darling Calypso, Urania, Styx, Galaxaure,
Pallas who rouses to battle and Artemis strewer of arrows:
All of us playing, and plucking by handfuls adorable blossoms,
Delicate crocuses mingled with iris and hyacinth, cup-shaped
Roses and lilies together, a wonderful sight to behold, and
Also the fatal narcissus that broad earth produced like a crocus.
This I was plucking for joy when the earth underneath me gaped vastly;
Out leapt that powerful lord, the Receiver of Many, and bore me
Under the earth on his gold-plated chariot. Very unwilling
Was I, I shouted aloud at the top of my voice, but in vain. And
There, though it causes me many a pang, I have told you the whole truth."
Mother and daughter the whole of the day in unanimous humour
Thereupon gladdened each other in heart and in mind very greatly,
Clinging together in love till their spirits abated their sorrows.
Mutual pleasures and joys they received and they gave one another.
Hecate, her of the glittering headdress, came into their presence,
Frequently kissed with affection the daughter of holy Demeter.
Henceforth that lady became to Persephone servant and handmaid.
Golden-haired Rhea, his mother, deep-thundering, widely-discerning
Zeus had appointed as envoy to summon the sable-cloaked goddess
Back to her kindred the gods, where he promised to give her such honours
And she desired to obtain in the company of the immortals.
Thus he decreed that her daughter should dwell a third part of the turning
Year under vaporous darkness, the other two parts with her mother
And with the other immortals; and Rhea obeyed his commission.
Down from the heights of Olympus she darted imperious till she
Came to the Rharian plain, a rich, life-giving udder of ploughland
Once, but now not at all life-giving: fallow it stood, and all leafless.
By the design of fair-ankled Demeter the barley lay hidden.
Not long thereafter the plain would be coiffed with the corn's narrow ears when
Spring turned to summer, and while the rich furrows were laden with corn stalks
Others were bound into sheaves. Such the spot where the goddess first landed
From the unharvested air. When they gladly beheld one another
Both of the goddesses' hearts were rejoiced. And then brightly crowned Rhea
Said to her, "Come here, my child, the deep-thundering, widely-discerning

(Grafton 1980a:96)

Zeus summons you to your kindred the gods, and he promises you such
Honours as you may desire in the company of the immortals.
And he decrees that The Maiden shall dwell a third part of the turning
Year under vaporous darkness, the other two parts with her mother
And with the other immortals. And thus his pronouncement, 'So be it!'
Sealed with a nod of his head. Therefore come, my dear child, and obey him,
Be not incessantly wroth with the black-clouded scion of Cronus!
Soon make the lifegiving fruits of the earth again flourish for mankind."
Rhea had spoken; Demeter, fair-garlanded, was not unwilling.
Soon from the clod-cluttered furrows she made the rich harvest of grain spring
So the whole breadth of the earth was encumbered with leaves and with flowers.
Paying a visit in turn to the kings who administer justice—
Noble Triptolemus, princely Diocles the drover of horses,
Mighty Eumolpus, Celeus the leader of people—Demeter
Shewed them her ritual service and taught them her mysteries, even
Diocles, princely Triptolemus, and Polyxenus, the solemn
Mysteries, which are unthinkable either to question or utter
Or to transgress: for a holy respect checks the utterance of them.
Happy the man who, of those that inhabit this earth, has beheld them!
The uninitiate, one without part in the ritual, never
Gets any portion of similar benefits, blessings, whatever,
Once he has perished and passed away under the vaporous darkness.
After the queen among goddesses had inculcated these matters,
She and her daughter returned to Olympus' divine congregation
Where they have ever a dwelling with Zeus who delights in the thunder:
Solemn and reverend goddesses! Happy indeed is the man whom
These ladies love, of all people who dwell on the earth, with aforethought.
Soon they will send to his fireside Plutus, the giver of riches,
Wealth and abundance and plenty to men who are born but to perish.
Goddesses holding in fee the republic of fragrant Eleusis,
Paros amid the encircling waters, and stony Antrona,
Mistress and bringer of seasons, queen, glorious giver, Demeter,
You and your excellent, beautiful daughter Persephone, Maiden,
Kindly in thanks for this poem assure me a pleasant subsistence,
And I shall try to remember another about you and sing it! (Hine 1972:4–16)

Demeter (Roman Ceres)
(Lehner 1969:23, fig. 45).

The Eleusinian rites honoring Demeter and Persephone clearly involved
revelations important to both sexes. Karl Kerényi claims that *all* participants
identified themselves with Demeter:

The separation of Mother and Daughter, with all its anguish, may in itself be
termed archetypal, characteristic of the destiny of women. If men take part in this
destiny as though it were their own, the explanation must be sought on a level
deeper than the divided existence of men and women: here only women, there only
men! The separation of Mother and Daughter, the yearning of Demeter for her own
girl-child, the Kore, must be characteristic of undivided human existence, of men
as well as women, but in one way of men and in another of women. . . .
    The Eleusinian vision . . . opened up a vision of the *feminine source of life,* of the
common source of life for men and women alike. . . . The reason for this is
probably that all human beings and not women alone bear this origin and this

duality—that *is* both the Mother and the Daughter—within themselves and are therein the heirs of an endless line, not only of fathers but of mothers as well. (1967:145–46, 147)

In other words, "by entering into the figure of Demeter we realize the universal principle of life, which is to be pursued, robbed, raped, to *fail to understand*, to rage and grieve, but then to get everything back and be born again" (Kerényi 1963:137).

Poets Penelope Shuttle and Peter Redgrove offer a somewhat more radical version of the Mystery's universal power:

Perhaps the ceremonies [at Eleusis] brought men and women alive to the baptism of blood at the birth-trauma, the pain of birth to the human baby which stands between it and the natural bliss of the womb, like an angel with a flaming sword, turning every way. Perhaps in a "birthing" they saw their own creation by body-light, womb-light. Perhaps in this way the men came into understanding of what a woman is, just as a rite of menarche (which Thomson [1965] believes the Mysteries began in) for the woman shows her that she is now beginning to be what her mother was, and there is a recognition, if possible a "heuresis". Both men and women know that they have the power to feel death and to be reborn, since they were once unborn, and recall passing this threshold. Having passed into life successfully once, there might seem no reason why they should ever really die, and one of the Eleusinian hymns praises the initiates for their awareness when all other shades after death are without existence or consciousness. (Shuttle and Redgrove 1978:200)

The Homeric Hymn to Demeter itself has also received considerable attention on its own terms. Paul Friedrich presents a very careful and useful reading of the text in his study of Aphrodite. He also proposes that "the four queens of heaven [Hera, Aphrodite, Athena and Artemis] are inadequate in some profoundly significant affective sense . . . [and] *leave an emotional gap*. This lacuna, this lack of motherhood and motherliness, is filled by the great and awesome figure of Demeter. . ." (1978:151). When Aphrodite is compared with Demeter, there is an antithesis between two kinds of love, which Friedrich explores in a final chapter on "Sex/Sensuousness and Maternity/ Motherliness."

The power of the taboo against mixing sensuousness and motherliness is shown by the fact that the early poets say little about Demeter's sensuousness in contrast to her maternity and motherliness (aside from the affair with Iasion). Aphrodite's maternal love is significant but minor compared with her erotic subjectivity. Perhaps some future titan of the novel or epic will create a full synthesis of the meanings of Demeter and Aphrodite that will recapture the archaic synthetic imagery of the early Mayans and Indo-Europeans. Perhaps, also, we can hope for a future that will recognize, accept, and encourage the deep and natural connections between sensuous sexuality and motherliness-maternity. The split between them should be healed in the world view, or by the religion, by the system of ideas, whatever it is called, that connects our concrete lives with the awesome powers beyond our control. (Ibid:191)

Still other interpreters focus on Demeter alone, on Persephone alone, or on the mother-daughter bond. The following selection of such interpretations

(Harter 1978b:12)

illustrates a variety of analytical perspectives and demonstrates the continued symbolic power of the Demeter-Persephone myth in contemporary society:

♦ Adrienne Rich, *Of Woman Born:* "The loss of the daughter to the mother, the mother to the daughter, is the essential female tragedy. We acknowledge Lear (father-daughter split), Hamlet (son and mother), and Oedipus (son and mother) as great embodiments of the human tragedy; but there is no presently enduring recognition of the mother-daughter passion and rapture.

   "There was such a recognition, but we lost it. It was expressed in the religious mystery of Eleusis, which constituted the spiritual foundation of Greek life for two thousand years" (1976:237).

♦ Robert May, *Sex and Fantasy:* "In response to the question 'what happens in this story?' we might be tempted to focus on Persephone's abduction and release, and perhaps on Demeter's laying waste the earth. . . . But to seize on them would distort the myth. The important *event* here is Demeter's grieving. . . . The myth devotes itself to following the course of a complex emotion, grief. We are shown its vicissitudes, its ebbing and flowing, its alternation between self-laceration and angry attack on others, its precarious hunger for another child to make good the loss, its need for kindness and feeding from others, and its slow and demanding rhythms. Much respect is paid.

"Of the many morals implicit in this tale, one is that such emotions indeed deserve respect and attention. Another might be that we should not underestimate the strength of the tie between mother and daughter. And another still: 'Yet we mortals bear perforce what the gods send us, though we be grieved.' . . . But yet the lesson is not a pessimistic one. Two things are spoken of as being 'borne': grief and babies. But each holds promise as well as pain. The counsel of endurance is not merely aimed at a stoic bearing-up-under. Instead the bearing is to be creative; something will come out of it. A vital function of this endurance is to protect and keep alive inside us a fertile hope" (1980:12–13).

♦   Nor Hall, *The Moon & The Virgin:* ". . . The goddess's weary depression is a paradigm of psychological depression. Her sadness is punctuated by three stopping places at Eleusis. One is the *omphalos,* or navel—a belly button mound of earth at the spot where Persephone disappeared. This so-called world navel is what the sibyls used to sit on when the voices of gods would speak through them. . . . It is a point where two worlds meet and where one can be cut off—literally, the cord has been cut and the daughter is gone.

"Another spot where Demeter, in her ugly guise, rests 'vexed in her dear heart' is at the Maiden's Well. This well, where the girls of Eleusis came to draw water, was also called the 'well of flowers' (the flowering from the depths took place here). It is still visible at Eleusis today—and the excavators could see circles traced in the stone pavement around the well where initiates danced during the Mystery rites.

"The third spot where Demeter stops is called the *agelastos petra,* the Laughless Rock. Her sorrow halts nature in its path; nothing grows, life is dead. She has hardened her heart. A pallor has come over her. A dark cloak hides her shining hair. Nothing of her fruitfulness is revealed, for her creativity (represented by the maiden) has gone into hiding. In dreams, the maiden often represents the potential self, the *becoming* part of the person, a possibility that is not yet real. It is like being pregnant in a dream: something has been conceived—a new attitude or idea, the seeds of a poem, an unknown strength, the courage to resist or create or die" (1980:78).

♦   Patricia Berry, "The Rape of Demeter/Persephone and Neurosis": "A mourning Demeter who has lost the daughter, therefore hates the daughter, and all that underworld business the daughter represents. Neurotically, Demeter's consciousness clings all the more fervently (and destructively) to the upperworld, adamantly denying underworld attributes—such as, precision (the house becomes a mess), discrimination (one thing is as good as another—all feelings, all sensations of equal value, and thus of no value), sense of essence (things become of value for their superficial, rather than underworldly, attributes), sense of significance (the ordinary loses its link with the Gods, the archetypal, and is therefore 'nothing but').

"Demeter consciousness becomes depressed, and within this depression we can see many classically psychiatric attributes: she ceases to bathe, ceases to eat, disguises her beauty, denies the future (her possibilities of rejuvenation and productivity), regresses to menial tasks beneath her ability (or sees her tasks as menial), becomes narcissistic and self-concerned, sees (and actually engenders) world-wide catastrophe, and incessantly weeps" (1975:190).

◆ Phyllis Chesler, *Women & Madness:* "In our time, the stepmothers wander still—exiles, with no memory of what has gone before. Demeter has been known to curse at passing airplanes, to dress in shapeless mourning costumes, to talk to herself, to talk nonsense. . . . Often these days, when Demeter gives birth to a child, she abandons her then and there, turning her own face to the hospital wall. Sometimes, as in a trance, Demeter tries to keep her daughter at home with her again forever" (1972:xix).

◆ Carol Sheehan, "A Sketch for a Reading of the Homeric Hymn to Demeter": "Only on the tenth day does Hecate come to [Demeter]. . . . And Hecate asks the critical question: 'Who?' . . . For me, this brief scene is illuminated by the language of astrology. . . . The nine days of Demeter's blind search are like the nine years of human growth that pass between the Arian Fire of birth and the transformation of the Fire into creative, solar consciousness. . . . After nine years of life, then, one's Sun is born—one's solar will. So on the tenth day Hecate comes from her cave bringing a lunar light. The frenzied search becomes focused now, as the darkness is illuminated by this new light (the Moon, in astrology, is the subconscious, the repossessed soul) and the unfocused grief and despair are focused into solar consciousness and focused will by the specific question posed by Hecate. . . . Now the aid of Helios can be enlisted" (1978a:34–35; also see Sheehan 1978b).

◆ Adrienne Rich, *Of Woman Born:* "Jane Harrison considered the Mysteries to be founded on a much more ancient women's rite, from which men were excluded, a possibility which tells us how endangered and complex the mother-daughter cathexis was, even before recorded history. Each daughter, even in the millennia before Christ, must have longed for a mother whose love for her and whose power were so great as to undo rape and bring her back from death. And every mother must have longed for the power of Demeter, the efficacy of her anger, the reconciliation with her lost self" (1976:240).[5]

◆ C. G. Jung, "The Psychological Aspects of the Kore": "Demeter and Kore [Persephone], mother and daughter, extend the feminine consciousness both upwards and downwards. They add an 'older and younger,' 'stronger and weaker' dimension to it and widen out the narrowly limited conscious mind bound in space and time, giving it intimations of a greater and more comprehensive personality which has a share in the eternal course of things. . . . We could therefore say that every mother contains her daughter in herself and every daughter her mother, and that every woman extends backwards into her mother and forwards into her daughter. This participation and intermingling give rise to that peculiar uncertainty as regards *time:* a woman lives earlier as a mother, later as a daughter. The conscious experience of these ties produces the feeling that her life is spread out over generations—the first step towards the immediate experience and conviction of being outside time, which brings with it a feeling of *immortality.* The

Niobe, wife of Amphion, king of Thebes, trying to shelter her daughter from Artemis and Apollo, who avenged Niobe's insult to their mother Leto by killing her twelve children. Niobe had boasted about her much larger brood and so was bereft of children and turned into a weeping pillar of stone. The statue, preserved in Florence's Uffizi Gallery, is a fourth-century Roman copy of a Hellenistic original (Harter 1978b:48).

[5] Rich refers to Jane Harrison, *Prolegomena to the Study of Greek Religion,* 3d ed. (1922; reprint, New York: Meridian, 1955). Harrison also discusses the Thesmorphia, three-day agrarian rites celebrated solely by women at the time of autumn sowing. These too honored Demeter. See, e.g., Pomeroy 1975: 77–78. In his "Studies in Rituals of Women's Initiation," Bruce Lincoln contends that the Eleusinian Mysteries originated in women's puberty rites (1981:71–90).

individual's life is elevated into a type, indeed it becomes the archetype of woman's fate in general. This leads to a restoration or *apocatastasis* of the lives of her ancestors, who now, through the bridge of the momentary individual, pass down into the generations of the future. An experience of this kind gives the individual a place and a meaning in the life of the generations, so that all unnecessary obstacles are cleared out of the way of the life-stream that is to flow through her. At the same time the individual is rescued from her isolation and restored to wholeness. All ritual preoccupation with archetypes ultimately has this aim and this result" (1963:162).

♦ Erich Neumann, *Amor and Psyche: The Psychic Development of the Feminine:* "Seen from the standpoint of the matriarchal world, every marriage is a rape of Kore, the virginal bloom, by Hades, the ravishing, earthly aspect of the hostile male. From this point of view every marriage is an exposure on the mountain's summit in mortal loneliness, and a waiting for the male monster, to whom the bride is surrendered. The veiling of the bride is always the veiling of the mystery, and marriage as the marriage of death is a central archetype of the feminine mysteries. . . .

"The fundamental situation of the feminine . . . is the primordial relation of identity between daughter and mother. For this reason the approach of the male always and in every case means separation. Marriage is always a mystery, but also a mystery of death. For the male—and this is inherent in the essential opposition between the masculine and the feminine—marriage, as the matriarchate recognized, is primarily an abduction, an acquisition—a rape" (1956:62–63; also see chapter 5).

♦ Patricia Berry, "The Rape of Demeter/Persephone and Neurosis": "Much more fashionable nowadays is holding one's ground. . . . We forget that to be raped into consciousness is also a way.

"Even if the occasion of psychic rape is not foreign to us, we haven't known where to put it. And so we have had to fight off the experience all the more blindly. A working archetypal model for these overpowering, backward, downward movements is given by the Demeter/Persephone myth, in which rape was after all elevated to the status of a mystery in ancient Greece. Because we have lost these rites, rape is now even more threatening, and therefore we have a great deal of difficulty experiencing Demeter/Persephone consciousness in any but the most superficial, defensive, and neurotic ways" (1975:195–96).

♦ Phyllis Chesler, *Women & Madness:* "Persephone does not wish to be raped, nor do women today. Neither do they wish to recapitulate their mother's identity. But the modern Persephone still has no other place to go but into marriage and motherhood. Her father (men in general) still conforms to a rape-incest model of sexuality. And her mother has not taught her to be a warrior, i.e., to take difficult roads to unknown and unique destinations—gladly. Her mother and father neither prepare her for this task nor rejoice in her success. They do not mourn or comfort her in crucifixion, be it as a warrior (as Joan of Arc) or as a mother (as the Virgin Mary)" (1972:30).

♦ Erich Neumann, *The Great Mother:* "The one essential motif in the Eleusinian mysteries and hence in all matriarchal mysteries is the *heuresis* of the daughter by the mother, the 'finding again' of Kore by Demeter, the reunion of mother and daughter.

"Persephone (Proserpine) enthroned. (Gerhard, Archäolog. Zeit. tav. 11)" (Bayley 1912:i, 312, fig. 718). According to Bayley: *"Per,* the Fire or Light, was doubtless also the root of *Percides, Perseus,* and of *Persephone* or *Peroserpine,* who is here represented with the Fleur-de-lys-tipped sceptre of Light and is crowned with the tower of Truth" (ibid:311–12).

"Psychologically, this 'finding again' signifies the annulment of the male rape and incursion, the restoration after marriage of the matriarchal unity of mother and daughter. In other words, the nuclear situation of the matriarchal group, the primordial relation of daughter to mother . . . is renewed and secured in the mystery. And here Kore's sojourn in Hades signifies not only rape by the male—for originally Kore-Persephone was herself the Queen of the Underworld—but fascination by the male earth aspect, that is to say, by sexuality" (1963:308).

(Harter 1980a:16)

Psychologist David C. McClelland finds in Persephone's ambivalence toward Hades (e.g., eating the pomegranate and later protesting) evidence that "she feels some attraction to her dark lover though protesting like the good girl. . . ." Hades thus appears to her as he later appears in various European theatrical productions involving Harlequin (Arlecchino) and his Columbine— "both as a figure of terror who takes women away to their deaths and as a gay seducer" (1964a:102; also see, e.g., Willeford 1969:183, 187). After examining fantasies and dreams of terminally ill women, McClelland identifies what he calls "the Harlequin complex" in both "normal women" facing death and schizophrenic women "trapped into a terrifying death while . . . yet alive." He claims that many women experience "a thrill" about approaching death, "for death represents the demon lover—the symbol of a woman's own life urge, which is expressed paradoxically in the thought of yielding or dying" (1964a:119; also see McClelland 1964b:182–216). While it may differentiate the fantasies of terminally ill men (who more often envision death as Cronos with his sickle) and women, McClelland's analysis too easily can be read as an implicit justification for rape, since women can be said somehow to enjoy even the "ultimate," lethal rape. Unfortunately, neither his work nor the mythology he uses are unusual.

Fear of Men, Fear of Women:
Rape and the Vaginal Serpent/Vagina Dentata

In Western tradition myths involving rape abound. Persephone is by no means singular or exceptional. Zeus—who in the form of a snowy white bull abducted Europa and in the form of an eagle "ravished" her, and who in the form of a swan raped Leda—and Apollo—who successfully took Dryope after disguising himself first as a tortoise and then as a snake, but who was unsuccessful in his relentless pursuit of Daphne—are among the worst offenders. In Christianity, it is the Devil who forces his cold member and icy ejaculate into women.

In *Against Our Will: Men, Women and Rape,* Susan Brownmiller claims that the confusing and contradictory Greek and Roman stories abstracted from cultural context "actually . . . reveal very little about rape" (1975:313). Nevertheless, classicist Sarah B. Pomeroy suggests some psychological reasons why Greek women might have maintained such myths of rape:

The Devil seducing a witch. From Ulrich Molitor, *De lamiis et phitonicis mulieribus* ("Concerning Female Sorcerers and Soothsayers"), Constance, 1489 (Lehner 1971:58, fig. 82).[6]

[6]According to the *Malleus Maleficarum* ("The Witch Hammer"), the "handbook" by Heinrich Kramer and James Sprenger, famous inquisitors of witches in Northern Germany during the late 1400s: ". . . In times long past the incubus devils used to infest women against their wills, as is often shown by Nider in his *Formicarius,* and by Thomas of Brabant in his book on the *Universal Good,* or on *Bees.* But the theory that modern witches are tainted with this sort of diabolic filthiness is not substantiated only in our opinion, since the expert testimony of the witches themselves has made all these things credible; and that they do not now, as in times past, subject themselves unwillingly, but willingly embrace this most foul and miserable servitude" (Summers 1971:111). This influential book went through fourteen editions between 1487 and 1520, and some sixteen editions from 1574 to 1669 (pp. vii–viii). Wolfgang Lederer cites Jules Michelet's 1862 study, *Satanism and Witchcraft,* in which the latter suggests: "And at the Sabbath—the oft-described cold penis of the Devil, his icy ejaculate— could it not have been a prophylactic syringe?" (1968:203). In fact, much of the *Malleus Maleficarum* is devoted to associating witches with barrenness, birth control, and infant death.

We will never know whether Greek women dreamed of being Leda enfolded in the soft, warm caress of Zeus, or flattered themselves that they were as desirable as Europa, who was carried off by a most intriguing Zeus—masquerading as a bull. Perhaps they alleviated their anxieties by fantasizing that, like Danae, they avoided suffering penetration and were impregnated by a golden shower; or perhaps they freed themselves from the guilt attendant on an adultery fantasy by imagining that they were Alcmene, and innocently accepted Zeus as a lover because the king of the gods had disguised himself as their husband. (1975:12)

Pomeroy's suggestions are insidious, resembling those in William Butler Yeats's 1928 poem, "Leda and the Swan"[7]:

> A sudden blow: the great wings beating still
> Above the staggering girl, her thighs caressed
> By the dark webs, her nape caught in his bill,
> He holds her helpless breast upon his breast.
>
> How can those terrified vague fingers push
> The feathered glory from her loosening thighs?
> And how can body, laid in that white rush,
> But feel the strange heart beating where it lies?
>
> A shudder in the loins engenders there
> The broken wall, the burning roof and tower
> And Agamemnon dead.
>   Being so caught up,
> So mastered by the brute blood of the air,
> Did she put on his knowledge with his power
> Before the indifferent beak could let her drop?

Are we to accept that there is something to be gained in such submission, that it is somehow woman's "nature" to enjoy such ruthless assaults? At least from a male perspective, the ugly insinuation is that women cannot truly fear men; their fears and anxieties are actually pleasurable to them. They seek out and enjoy and gain from their attackers just as witches do devils.

But these are largely male terms and male-dominated mythologies. Women may never have thought or expressed their fears and hopes in such terms at all, but rather in private, unrecorded, informal systems of beliefs, narratives, rites and symbols of their own. Perhaps women realistically fear men and express their realism less often in narratives, especially within hearing of men, and more often in ongoing conversation with other women, both older and younger. Within this converse, it may be likely that rape is viewed frankly as a brutal fact of profane existence, *not* as a sacred rite of initiation.

The fear of rape, the fear of unwanted pregnancy, and the fear of monster children are all reflected in a slate carving collected by James G. Swan and a myth collected by Ensign Albert P. Niblack, U.S.N., from Haida Indians in

---

[7]Compare Yeats's version with Barbara Howe's 1954 poem, "The New Leda"—about the "goosegirl" who is about to become a "bride of Christ" (in Chester and Barba 1973:79–80).

British Columbia during the 1880s. (Both picture and text are reproduced from Col. Garrick Mallery's 1893 Bureau of Ethnology study, "Picture-Writing of the American Indians" [1972:478].)

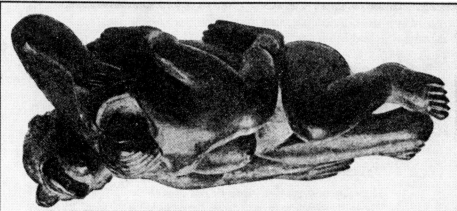

FIG. 665.—Bear-Mother. Haida.

The same author, Pl. XLIX, gives an explanation of Fig. 665, which is a copy of a Haida slate carving, representing the "Bear-Mother." The Haida version of the myth is as follows:

A number of Indian squaws were in the woods gathering berries when one of them, the daughter of a chief, spoke in terms of ridicule of the whole bear species. The bears descended on them and killed all but the chief's daughter, whom the king of the bears took to wife. She bore him a child half human and half bear. The carving represents the agony of the mother in suckling this rough and uncouth offspring. One day a party of Indian bear hunters discovered her up a tree and were about to kill her, thinking her a bear, but she made them understand that she was human. They took her home and she afterwards became the progenitor of all Indians belonging to the bear totem. They believe that the bear are men transformed for the time being. This carving was made by Skaows-ke′ay, a Haida. Cat. No. 73117, U. S. Nat. Museum. Skidegate village, Queen Charlotte Islands, British Columbia. Collected by James G. Swan.

◆   Madonna Kolbenschlag, *Kiss Sleeping Beauty Good-Bye:* "A considerable number of American popular novels and films in recent years have focused on a theme that can only be described as the 'demonic invasion of the womb.' Children, in various stages of development, and mothers in various stages of vulnerability or violation have been the principal figures in these parables of possession. One thinks of *Rosemary's Baby, Demon Seed, The Exorcist, Audrey Rose,* and *The Omen.*

"What is the significance of this wave of satanic fertility? The fact that the mothers are often divorced, estranged or abandoned certainly suggests the projection of parental impotence and the dissolution of family structures. But another motive, perhaps more subtle, is embedded in the popular theme—woman's rebellion against unwanted invasion by another life. In an age when women have begun to reclaim their autonomy, when the clouds of Victorian worship of motherhood have begun to dissipate, it should not be surprising that many women—*and* men—perceive pregnancy and childbearing, at least subconsciously, as demonic, as a threat to spiritual integrity" (1979:170).

Such fears are echoed in a belief common to Mexican and Mexican-American culture. Army officer and ethnologist John Gregory Bourke reported his observations along the Rio Grande borderlands while stationed at Fort Ringgold, Texas, during the late 1800s:

★ *Axolotl.*—The most curious and incomprehensible superstition of the Mexican people, and one which has the widest dissemination, concerns the curious lizard called the axolotl, a name by which it was known to the Aztecs, although I do not feel prepared to say that they had a superstition concerning it.

The axolotl frequents damp, slimy places, near pools or tanks of water, and all kinds of refuse ("basura").

It will enter the person of a woman, at certain times, and will remain just as long as would a human foetus.

Young girls, at their first change of life, are especially exposed, and will manifest all the symptoms of pregnancy.

It is within the limits of probability, although I am not sufficiently posted in medical matters to assert that such is the case, that a badly nourished girl would be susceptible to cold, rheumatism, and dropsy at such a critical moment in her life, and that imagination could supply any features that might be lacking to make the romance complete. There are several remedies; one calls for a liberal fomentation with hot goat's milk, and in the other, a young man appears to marry the girl. Often when women were bathing in the waters of the Rio Grande itself or in some of the great "acequias," mischievous boys would yell "Axolotl!" and cause a scampering of all the bathers. (1894:120–21)

Folklorist Rosan Jordan summarized her findings after fieldwork in West Texas during the late 1960s and early 1970s:

★ I found a lively tradition of related beliefs, legends, and memorates among Mexican-American women. This tradition . . . has to do with snakes and other reptiles in human bodies; . . . the animals enter the female reproductive system, where they may hatch a whole litter and mutilate or kill the woman, or (in one text) they may merely wriggle around in her vagina and drive her crazy. In memorates, the stories usually concern a snake known as a *chirrionero* that chases women (and in some instances is said to whistle at them); *chirrioneros* are particularly attracted by the smell of menstrual blood, and many Mexican-American women in West Texas have run home in fear of attempted assaults after sighting (or being chased by) a *chirrionero*. (Jordan de Caro 1973:64; also see Cardozo-Freeman 1978; Poulsen 1979)

A related popular belief about the so-called bosom serpent, a reptile which climbs into the mouth and invades the digestive tract, is found in both men's and women's folklore (Barnes 1972). Folklorist Richard M. Dorson collected such a legend in southwestern Michigan in 1952 from Mrs. E. L. (Leozie) Smith. Mrs. Smith, a black woman, had been born in Tupelo, Mississippi, some sixty years before, but moved first to Tennessee and then to Chicago in 1917.

A spring lizard he's kind of short, like a dark snake. This girl in Mississippi swallowed one drinking at the spring. And it growed inside of her and got so large till they thought she'd got "in the wrong path." And back in those days they mistreated you for anything like that. Well her brother was coming out through the yard from the field and happened to see her lying on the ground, just taking an evening nap, 'cause she didn't feel so good at times. And he seed what looked like a snake come out'n her mouth, like to choke her stiff. And he rushed in and told her mother and family, and they come out and took her to the hospital, they say in Memphis, Tennessee. They was so ashamed of having 'bused and dogged her.

I heard folks tell an old snake was in one person, and had prongs, about four feet long, and they had to hold it and it twisted and fit whiles they was pulling it out. (Dorson 1956:150–51)

♦   Rosan Jordan, "A Note about Folklore and Literature (The Bosom Serpent Revisited)": "These 'vaginal serpent' stories share certain motifs in common with the bosom serpent tradition. The same animals are involved, primarily snakes, lizards, water dogs; in some variants of both traditions we are told that the animal multiplied while inside the victim. . . . The motif of the victim's being mistreated because she appears to have gotten in trouble appears in several legends I collected in West Texas (about vaginal serpents), although . . . it is not 'typical' of the bosom serpent legend. It should be readily apparent that the two traditions function in quite different ways. The vaginal serpent legends are intimately tied up with the belief in and fear of snakes or lizards crawling into the vagina, and they thus reflect a specifically female viewpoint. It seems likely they may project feminine fears of penetration and annihilation. Or perhaps they may express some sort of anxiety related to the emphasis on virginity in young girls in a patriarchal culture. On the conscious level they certainly function, as one informant explained, to remind young women to watch out for snakes when they have to urinate 'behind a bush' " (1973:64–65).

♦   Karen Horney, "The Denial of the Vagina" [1933]: "In the first place there are the fantasies of rape that occur before coitus has taken place at all, and indeed long before puberty, and are frequent enough to merit wider interest. I can see no possible way of accounting for the origin and content of these fantasies if we are to assume the nonexistence of vaginal sexuality. For these fantasies do not in fact stop short at quite indefinite ideas of an act of violence, through which one gets a child. On the contrary, fantasies, dreams and anxiety of this type usually betray quite unmistakably an instinctive knowledge of the actual sexual processes. The guises they assume are so numerous that I need only indicate a few of them: criminals who break in through windows or doors; men with guns who threaten to shoot; animals that creep, fly, or run inside some place (e.g., snakes, mice, moths): animals or women stabbed with knives; or trains running into a station or tunnel" (1967:154).

♦   Karen Horney, "The Dread of Woman" [1932]: "The anatomical differences between the sexes lead to a totally different situation in girls and in boys, and really to understand both their anxiety and the diversity of their anxiety we must take into account first of all *the children's real situation* in the period of their early sexuality. The girl's nature as biologically conditioned gives her the desire to receive, to take into herself; she feels or knows that her genital is too small for her father's penis and this makes her react to her own genital wishes with direct anxiety; she dreads that if her wishes were fulfilled, she herself or her genital would be destroyed.

"The boy, on the other hand, feels or instinctively judges that his penis is much too small for his mother's genital and reacts with the dread of his own inadequacy, of being rejected and derided. Thus his anxiety is located in quite a different quarter from the girl's; his original dread of women is not castration anxiety at all, but a reaction to the menace to his self-respect" (1967:141–42).

Myths, tales and beliefs about the *vagina dentata* or toothed vagina are widespread (e.g., Thompson 1929:309; Lederer 1968:44–52; Leach 1972:1152). A strong male protagonist, usually a culture hero or trickster, must make heterosexual relations possible by destroying the teeth. Mrs. Judy Trejo remembers such a story involving Coyote. It was told by her Paiute grandfa-

"When the snake reached the palace, all the courtiers shook and trembled with fear down to the very scullion, and the King and Queen were in such a state of nervous collapse that they hid themselves in a far-away turret. Grannoia alone kept her presence of mind, and although both her father and mother implored her to fly for her life, she wouldn't move a step, saying 'I'm certainly not going to fly from the man you have chosen for my husband.'

"As soon as the snake saw Grannoia, it wound its tail round her and kissed her. Then, leading her into a room it shut the door, and throwing off its skin, it changed into a beautiful young man with golden locks, and flashing eyes, who embraced Grannoia tenderly, and said all sorts of pretty things to her."

—Illustration by H. J. Ford for "The Enchanted Snake," in Andrew Lang, ed., *The Green Fairy Book*, published in London ca. 1892 (1965:188–89).

ther during the winter, which "was reserved for grandfather's *(togo-o)* stories; if a family did not have a grandfather, the honor was given to the next oldest male in the family" (1974:66).

Once long ago when we were all the same, Coyote was trotting through a canyon on his long journey home when he saw a flash of light up above him. He sneaked up the canyon wall to investigate.

What he saw almost blinded him, so he squinted until his eyes got used to seeing the forbidden parts of the two females he saw squatting on the ground. This was back in the days when the female genital organs still had teeth. The flash of light Coyote saw came from the sun reflecting on those teeth. (It was forbidden to look upon the female genitalia, and besides the female organ was a threat to the male.) The two females that Coyote was watching were eating boiled rabbit. As

"Jack determined at once to attempt the adventure; so he advanced, and blew the horn which hung at the castle portal. The door was opened in a minute by a frightful giantess, with one great eye in the middle of her forehead.

"As soon as Jack saw her he turned to run away, but she caught him, and dragged him into her castle.

" 'Ho, ho!' she laughed terribly. 'You didn't expect to see *me* here, that is clear! No, I shan't let you go again. . . .' "

—Illustration by Lancelot Speed for "Jack and the Beanstalk," in Andrew Lang, ed., *The Red Fairy Book,* published in London, 1890 (1966:136, 137).

they stripped the meat off the rabbit bones, they would throw the bones underneath themselves, and the second set of teeth in their genitals devoured the bones hungrily (a sort of Paiute garbage disposal unit).

Coyote was just fascinated at what was going on. He decided to throw a piece of thorny rose bush under one of the females. The stick was quickly chewed up, thorns and all.

Horrified, Coyote next tossed pieces of shale under both women, breaking all their teeth and rendering their vaginas harmless to men ever after (Trejo 1974:69; also see Ramsey 1977a:236–39, 284).

♦   Bruce Jackson, *"Vagina Dentata* and Cystic Teratoma": "For obvious reasons the motif and the myths in which it appears have interest for psychoanalytically oriented students of verbal behavior—there would seem in that framework an ineluctable relationship between the myth and various kinds of castration anxiety. For the non-Freudian, the story complexes may have something to do with the human struggle against death itself, and the threat posed by the toothed vagina (which is described not simply as castrating, but as killing) that seeks to take away one's manhood can be seen as analogue for the threat of death that seeks to take away one's life" (1971:341).[8]

Psychoanalyst Wolfgang Lederer ends his introduction to *The Fear of Women* with this apologia:

If at times, the necessarily lopsided emphasis shows woman in a truly gruesome light, the kind reader may forgive: this book is not intended to give a complete or even a well-balanced panorama of the human scene. Even so, the very awe man feels for woman will picture her, in some chapters, radiant and sublime; so that at least to some extent the weaker (?) sex shall receive its due. (1968:viii)

The question remains: Is it possible to right the balance? To complete the panorama? Can a parallel book called "The Fear of Men" be written—one in which "at least to some extent the stronger (?) sex shall receive its due"? Should it be written, or should it continue to be told as heretofore—privately, and usually to other women?

Women Initiate Women

Lore about rape, pregnancy and marriage, about monster children and vaginal serpents, constitutes the informal learning and teaching of women. Sometimes such peer and intergenerational initiation is more formalized, and women—mothers, grandmothers or guides—ritually initiate younger women, as in the following selected accounts from Native America.

Beverly Hungry Wolf was born and raised on the Blood Indian Reserve in western Canada. Her mother, Ruth Little Bear, encouraged her to write about

---

[8]For an extensive Freudian analysis, see "13. Castration. I. Vagina Dentata," in Gershon Legman, *Rationale of the Dirty Joke: An Analysis of Sexual Humor,* Second Series (New York: Breaking Point, 1975), pp. 427–74. Legman claims, by the way, that judging from humor, "to most men, the fear of castration far transcends that of death" (p. 438). Also see Figes 1970, chap. 2, "A Man's God"; and Gulzow and Mitchell 1980.

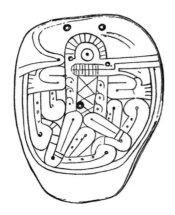

Shell gorget from prehistoric mounds in Tennessee and Missouri (Naylor 1975:32, fig. C).

Blackfoot women, a project which evolved into her book, *The Ways of My Grandmothers*. In it, she recalls that "the holy woman that I grew up knowing best is Mrs. Rides-at-the-Door."

A few years ago Mrs. Rides-at-the-Door camped with us in our tipi during a medicine lodge ceremony among our Blackfoot relatives in Montana. She went to assist the blind Mrs. Many-Guns, who had been asked to initiate a young woman who was sponsoring the ceremony. She said that it was very hard for old women such as herself to go through the four days of ceremonial work and fasting that precede the building of the medicine lodge, yet she hardly complained while she was doing it. Most of the holy work performed during those four days is private, but toward the end of it the holy woman's tipi is opened up so that the people can look in and see, while the sacred Natoas bonnet is fastened upon her head. Mrs. Rides-at-the-Door gave me a special blessing at that time by calling me in before her so that she could go through a brief ceremony during which I was initiated to wear a sacred necklace like those that holy women and their husbands wear. On it are beads, a shell, and a lock of hair, all with symbolic meanings. I thought how long back my ancestors have been passing on these meanings and blessings through the same ceremonial initiation, while the old holy woman painted my face, sang a song, and tied the necklace around me. (Hungry Wolf 1980:33)

While doing fieldwork in Oklahoma between 1967 and 1970, anthropologist David E. Jones was adopted by Comanche medicine woman Sanapia, the last surviving Comanche Eagle doctor. She told him how her mother began to initiate her into those powers.

The first stage in the actual power transmission from the mother was concerned with instilling power into Sanapia's mouth and hands, the areas of the body where an eagle doctor's powers are most strongly represented. The rituals involved with this first phase of transmission are very similar to the blessing ceremony, at least in the introductory stages. Sanapia's brother was told by the mother to lay a fire of pecan wood. After the wood burned to coals, the brother brought the coals to a secluded spot where Sanapia and her mother waited. The mother sat facing east, and Sanapia was instructed to sit facing her, while the mound of coals burned between them. Sanapia was cedared [*Note:* The dried leaves of the red cedar are sprinkled on live coals, and the rising smoke is wafted over the person who is being blessed.] and fanned by her mother with the standard blessings of long life and good health. This blessing also included the mother's singing of her Medicine song, an action which serves to call the *puhakut*'s power sources to his service. The mother, using her bare hand, then plucked a live coal from the mound of embers and handed it to Sanapia. At first, Sanapia reports, she balked at placing the burning coal in her hand, but at her mother's insistence she took it and was amazed that it did not burn her. She was then instructed to rub the coal over her hands. Once again the similarity in the concepts of "Medicine" and "courage" appear. Today, Sanapia interprets the handling of live coals as an act of faith in the doctor, a necessary first step in testing the potential doctor's resolve.

> I was sure scared then . . . almost got up and ran away. I was only a young girl at that time, you know. But, when I took them coals on my hand, inside and outside my hand I felt a chill, maybe. Oh, it was like chills in my hands. That has the meaning that power was in there . . . working in my hands. Felt like it would go up my arm even.

After Sanapia had taken the coal and covered her hands with the ashes, her mother began the transmission of supernatural powers to Sanapia's mouth. Two eagle feathers, manipulated by the mother, were drawn across Sanapia's opened mouth four times; however, in the course of the fourth movement of the feathers, one of the feathers disappeared. At this occurrence Sanapia's mother told her that the eagle feather had entered her mouth and would dwell there for the rest of her life. . . . Sanapia states that she does not believe that an eagle feather actually was inserted into her mouth but rather that the idea, the essence, or the Medicine which the eagle feather symbolized, was the entity which was placed in her mouth. She does not attempt to explain the disappearance of the second feather from her mother's hand except to suggest that her mother possessed certain powers which she did not transmit to Sanapia. This first phase was ended with the mother's application of red paint to Sanapia's face, forearms and legs, from the knees to, and including, the soles of the feet.

Two tabus, or "rules" as Sanapia calls them, were attached by the mother to the powers transmitted in this first phase of the actual transmission. Sanapia was forbidden to eat any kind of fowl. Her mother warned that if she broke that rule, the feather in her throat would kill her. The second tabu forbade Sanapia to allow people to pass behind her carrying food, especially meat, while she is eating.

> That eagle, when he eats, he don't like anybody to be behind him. When it's sitting on the ground, and it see anybody behind him, it twist all around and sit toward you. . . . (Jones 1972:32–33)

"Eagle-man mask" from a prehistoric vase of the Gulf Coast Group found at Jolly Bay, Florida (Naylor 1975:35, fig. C).

Anthropologist Lois Paul documented the lives and careers of midwives, who are both ritual and obstetrical specialists, in the Zutuhil (Mayan) community of San Pedro la Laguna in highland Guatemala. She characterizes Juana as a "prototypical midwife" who began her career when she was thirty-six years old.

Juana's mother, on her deathbed in 1958, a year before Juana herself fell ill, revealed to Juana her own divine destiny, unfulfilled because of *vergüenza* ["shame"] and fear of her husband's violent temper. She entrusted Juana's birth sign, the treasured piece of amniotic sac, to Juana's father, to be revealed at the proper time. Juana says her mother died prematurely young because of her failure to exercise her own mandate to be a midwife.

Juana had already lost six of her ten children when her mother died. For over a year she suffered weakness, shortness of breath, "heavy heart," a variety of aches and pains. . . . Finally she was "forced to stay in bed," a rare event for stoically trained Indian women. She was unable to eat or drink, grew weak, and slept only fitfully. She did not respond to pills, herbs, or prescription medicines. She lost weight, grew "thin" (wasted), and began having strange dreams.

In her dreams Juana was visited by big, fat women, all in radiant white, who told her that she was sick and that her children had died because she was not going to help the women in childbirth. These were the spirits of dead midwives. When she tried to sleep, the spirits would appear. They would grab her ears and scold her, tell her that she would die and her husband would die if she did not exercise her calling. They reminded her that she had already lost six children. You were punished, they said, because you did not pay attention to those who gave you the *virtud*. Now, if you continue to hesitate your other children will also die. Remember, they reminded her, that your mother died because you did not obey God's call.

Left: Prehistoric "long-necked bottle of eccentric form from Franklin County, Alabama." Right: "Painted design on the preceding, in red and white on gray" (Naylor 1975:8, figs. A, B).

When Juana protested that she was too ignorant and incompetent, that she knew nothing about the skills that a midwife must have, the spirits assured her they would instruct her. They showed her the signs of pregnancy, how to massage the pregnant woman, and to palpate the abdomen to feel if the fetus was in correct position for delivery. They demonstrated "external version" (turning the fetus). In her dreams she saw graphically a woman delivering a baby. The spirits showed her how to hold the white cloth with which to receive the fetus and how to clean the newborn infant. They showed her how to cut the umbilical cord before the placenta was presented. They showed her how the umbilical cord must be followed back up the placenta in case it does not come out, and the placenta removed manually if necessary. They showed her how to "smoke" a woman with embers from the fire in such cases. They told her they would always be present, though invisible, at deliveries to help her. The spirits instructed her how to bind the woman's abdomen after delivery to "hold the organs in place." "All these things I saw," Juana says, and in addition, they taught her prayers and ritual procedures.

When she related her disturbing dreams to her husband, he protested. He did not want her to go about the village as a midwife, neglecting the household and their children. Finally, he too fell ill and was visited in his dreams by the women in white. They scolded him, saying he must tell his wife to start practicing, or both would die. Juana's father, in his capacity as shaman, was finally consulted about their dreams. He lit candles in the house, burned incense, and performed divination rituals. He confirmed the warnings of the spirits and ceremoniously brought out the proof, the birth sign entrusted to him by her mother. Juana began to regain her strength.

Shortly thereafter, as Juana was returning from the lake, a curiously shaped white bone about nine inches long suddenly skipped down the road before her. She was frightened and dared not touch it. That night the women in white appeared again and instructed her to pick up the bone. They said, "This is your *virtud,* you must keep it always, never show it to anyone, guard it carefully." The next day the bone reappeared in her path. She obeyed the spirits, and picked it up. When she arrived home, the magic bone was no longer in her shawl but in her cabinet, already waiting for her. Soon afterward a small knife also appeared magically in her path. This time she did not hesitate, but picked it up and carried it home. This she uses to cut the umbilical cord.

Finding her objects was the final sign. Juana's father urged against further delay. He performed the nightlong *costumbres* this time, keeping Juana and her husband on their knees for many hours. (Paul 1978:134–35)

"An exceptionally fine example of a human effigy in pottery from the Middle Mississippi Valley Group; the body is painted, but the figure wears only a necklace" (Naylor 1975:1, fig. B).

Sophia: Woman as Wisdom

Wise women initiating younger, questing women are probably more common than available literature, usually researched and written by men, would indicate. However, most myths and accounts portray women, both young and old, offering wisdom to male heroes and creators of various kinds. In fact, in Western tradition, wisdom has come to be personified in female form as Sophia, who often appears as a flower or rose.

A Navajo example is typical of the situation where a male hero receives knowledge from female figures. Dr. Washington Matthews, a United States Army physician stationed at Fort Wingate, New Mexico, during the 1880s, frequently witnessed the Navajo Mountain Chant ceremony and recorded the events of its ritual as well as its origin myth for the Fifth Annual Report of the Bureau of Ethnology, 1883–84. In the latter part of the lengthy origin myth, the male hero Dsilyi'Neyáni and his wind god guide Niltci are on their journey back to the mortal's Navajo home, where the hero will reveal his new knowledge of healing rites to his people. During one of his many encounters with helpful deities he meets the Long Bodies, goddesses who teach him how to draw the second sandpainting of the Mountain-way ceremony.

56. From this place they journeyed on until they reached Acadsil (Leaf Mountain), and found the house that was made of dew-drops (Caco-behogan) and that had a door made of plants of many different kinds. This was the home of the Bitses-ninez (Long Bodies), who were goddesses. When they rose, as the strangers entered, the plumes of their heads seemed to touch the heavens, they were so very tall. The goddesses said to Dsilyi'Neyáni, "We give you no Kethawn [prayersticks], but look at us well and remember how we appear, for in your ceremonies you must draw our picture; yet draw us not, as we now stand, in the east, the south, the west, and the north; but draw us as if we all stood in the east." This is the origin of the second picture that is painted on the sand. (Matthews 1887:410)

Despite the myth text, which says this is the second of four major sandpaintings drawn during the ceremony, Matthews describes it as the third such:

172. Third Picture commemorates the visit of Dsilyi'Neyáni to Caco-behogan, or "Lodge of Dew" (paragraph 56). To indicate the great height of the Bitses-ninez the figures are twice the length of any in the other pictures, except the rainbows, and each is clothed in four garments, one above the other, for no one garment, they say, can be made long enough to cover such giant forms. Their heads all point to the east. . . . The Navajo relate . . . that this is in obedience to a divine mandate; but probably there is a more practical reason, which is this: if they had the cruciform arrangement there would not be room on the floor of the lodge for the figures and at the same time for the shaman, assistants, and spectators. Economy of space is essential; but, although drawn nearly parallel to one another, the proper order of the cardinal points is not lost sight of. The form immediately north of the center of the picture is done first, in white, and represents the east. That immediately next to it on the south comes second in order, is painted in blue, and represents the south. The one next below that is in yellow, and depicts the goddess who stood in the west of the House of Dew-Drops. The figure in the extreme north is drawn last of all, in black, and belongs to the north. As I have stated before, these bodies are first made naked and afterwards clothed. The exposed chests, arms, and thighs display the colors of which the entire bodies were originally composed. The gloi (weasel, *Putorius*) is sacred to these goddesses. Two of these creatures are shown in the east, guarding the entrance to the lodge. The appendages at the sides of the heads of the goddesses represent the gloi-bitca, or headdresses of gloi skins of different colors which these mystic personages are said to wear. Each one bears attached to her right hand a rattle and a charm, or plume stick, . . . we [also] see a conventional representation of a branch of choke cherry in blossom; this consists of five diverging stems in blue, five roots, and five cruciform blossoms in white. The choke cherry is a sacred tree, a mountain plant; its wood is used in making certain sacrificial plume sticks and certain implements of the dance; it is often mentioned in the songs of this particular rite. Some other adjuncts of this picture—the red robes embroidered with sunbeams, the arms and legs clothed with clouds and lightning, the pendants from the arms, the blue and red armlets, bracelets, and garters. . . . The object in the left hand is a wand of spruce.

173. The rainbow which incloses the picture on three sides is not the anthropomorphic rainbow. It has no head, neck, arms, or lower extremities. Five white eagle plumes adorn its southeastern extremity. Five tail plumes of some blue bird decorate the bend in the southwest. The plumes of the red shafted flicker (*Colaptes auratus* var. *mexicanus*) are near the bend in the northwest and the tail of the magpie terminates the northeastern extremity. Throughout the myth, it will

(Naylor 1975:210, from Matthews
1887:plate XVI)

be remembered, not only is the House of Dew-Drops spoken of as adorned with
hangings and festoons of rainbows, but many of the holy dwellings are thus
embellished. . . .

175. The ground of the picture is crossed with nebulous black streaks . . .
originally present in all the pictures. I have omitted them . . . lest they obscure
the details of the reduced copies. It has been explained to me . . . that all these
pictures were drawn by the gods upon the clouds and thus were shown to the
Navajo prophet. Men cannot paint on the clouds, but according to the divine
mandate they do the best they can on sand, and then sprinkle the sand with
charcoal, in the manner indicated, to represent the cloudy scrolls whereon the
primal designs of the celestial artists were painted. (Matthews 1887:450–51;
also see Wyman 1975:96–99)

"The Rose Maiden, the *Awakener,* the *rouse,* appears with three flowers springing from her forehead" (Bayley 1912:ii, 231, 232).

♦ Erich Neumann, *The Great Mother:* "The dual Great Goddess as mother and daughter can so far transform her original bond with the elementary character as to become a pure feminine spirit, a kind of Sophia, a spiritual whole in which all heaviness and materiality are transcended. Then she not only forms the earth and heaven of the retort that we call life, and is not only the whirling wheel revolving within it, but is also the supreme essence and distillation to which life in this world can be transformed.

"Sophia, who achieves her supreme visible form as a flower, does not vanish in the nirvanalike abstraction of a masculine spirit; like the scent of a blossom, her spirit always remains attached to the earthly foundation of reality. Vessel of transformation, blossom, the unity of Demeter united with Kore, Isis, Ceres, the moon goddesses, whose luminous aspect overcomes their own nocturnal darkness, are all expressions of this Sophia, the highest feminine wisdom" (1963:325–26).

> The Lord created me at the
>   beginning of his work,
>   the first of his acts of old.
> Ages ago I was set up,
>   at the first, before the beginning of
>   the earth.
> When there were no depths I was
>   brought forth,
>   when there were no springs
>   abounding with water.
> Before the mountains had been
>   shaped,
>   before the hills, I was brought
>   forth;
> before he had made the earth with its
>   fields,
>   or the first of the dust of the
>   world.
> When he established the heavens, I
>   was there,
>   when he drew a circle on the face
>   of the deep,
>   when he made firm the skies above,
>   when he established the fountains
>   of the deep,

when he assigned to the sea its limit,
   so that the waters might not
   transgress his command,
when he marked out the foundations
     of the earth,
   then I was beside him, like a
    master workman;
and I was daily his delight,
   rejoicing before him always,
rejoicing in his inhabited world
   and delighting in the sons of men.

    —Proverbs 8:22–31 (RSV).[9]

(Bayley 1912:ii, 243, fig. 1164)

Wisdom will praise herself,
   and will glory in the midst
    of her people.
In the assembly of the Most High
    she will open her mouth,
   and in the presence of his host
    she will glory:
"I came forth from the mouth of
    the Most High,
   and covered the earth like a mist.
I dwelt in high places,
   and my throne was in a pillar of
    cloud.
Alone I have made the circuit of
    the vault of heaven
   and have walked in the depths
    of the abyss.
In the waves of the sea, in the
    whole earth,
   and in every people and nation
    I have gotten a possession.

      . . .

"I grew tall like a cedar in Lebanon,
   and like a cypress on the heights
    of Hermon.
I grew tall like a palm tree in
    En-ge'di,
   and like rose plants in Jericho;
like a beautiful olive tree in the
    field,
   and like a plane tree I grew
    tall.

---

[9]*The Proverbs,* popularly associated with King Solomon but actually assembled and edited
by a teacher of the fourth or third century B.C., contains two poems in which Wisdom speaks
(1:20–33; 8:1–36), as well as numerous references to her nature and relationship with God.

Like cassia and camel's thorn I
gave forth the aroma of spices,
and like choice myrrh I spread
a pleasant odor,
like galbanum, onycha, and stacte,
and like the fragrance of
frankincense in the tabernacle.
Like a terebinth I spread out my
branches,
and my branches are glorious
and graceful.
Like a vine I caused loveliness to
bud,
and my blossoms became
glorious and abundant
fruit.

"Come to me, you who desire
me,
and eat your fill of my produce.
For the remembrance of me is
sweeter than honey,
and my inheritance sweeter than
the honeycomb. . . ."

—*Ecclesiasticus* 24:1–6,
13–20 (RSV).[10]

‡   "Beginning as a personified hypostasis [attribute] of God, Wisdom [Hebrew *hokhmah;* Greek *sophia}* grew in stature and importance for the Jews from the fourth to the first century B.C.E., until her power was virtually equivalent to that of any Hellenistic goddess. She combined in herself positive and some negative qualities, although she was often paired with another feminine figure called Folly, or the strange or foreign woman, who was entirely negative in character. By the beginning of the Christian era Sophia was portrayed as acting in history and assuming the roles of judge and savior of the Jewish people. At this point there can be no question that she rivaled the power of Yahweh himself. . . ." (Engelsman 1979:119; also see Patai 1978:255–56).

. . . Jesus began to speak to the crowds concerning John [the Baptist]: . . . "For John came neither eating nor drinking, and they say, 'He has a demon', the Son of man came eating and drinking, and they say, 'Behold, a glutton and a drunkard, a friend of tax collectors and sinners!' Yet wisdom is justified by her deeds."

—*Matthew* 11:7, 18–19 (RSV).

[10]The Apocryphal book *Ecclesiasticus* [meaning "The Church Book"], *or the Wisdom of Jesus the Son of Sirach* was written about 180 B.C. by a Jewish scribe named Joshua ben Sira, Hebrew for "Jesus the son of Sirach," who probably conducted an academy in Jerusalem. His book is a collection of teachings about ethics and religion which he doubtless used in his school. (Also see Collins 1977.) According to Bayley: "The Greek for honey is *meli* or *melissa,* and Melissa was one of the names of Isis. The beautiful half-mermaid Melusine who appears in European legend must be another form of the celestial Melissa who brings clusters of blossoms to the honey-drinkers" (1912:ii, 243–44).

‡   "Within a hundred years Sophia's power was broken and she was superseded by a masculine figure who took over her roles. In Hellenistic Judaism the personified Logos of Philo's philosophy became the firstborn image of God who was with God at creation, the principle of mind and rational order, and the intermediary between God and men. However, in deference to Jewish scripture, Sophia was not totally discarded, but was elevated to heaven, where she was relegated to a minor part in the divine/human drama. At the same time, the early Christians replaced her with Jesus and within a few decades of his crucifixion, all her powers and attributes had been ascribed to Christ. This was either done directly, as in Paul's letters and Matthew's Gospel, or indirectly, as in John which identified Christ with the Logos, a masculine figure similar to the one developed by Philo. Ultimately, Sophia's powers were so totally preempted by Christ that she herself completely disappeared from the Christian religion of that time" (Engelsman 1979:119–20; also see Bruns 1973:35–59; Ruether 1974).

During the ferment of the first Christian centuries, a number of sects developed which espoused doctrines considered heretical by the early Church Fathers, who collectively designated them "Gnosticism," from *gnosis,* the Greek word for "knowledge." Although widely divergent, most of these sectarian doctrines emphasized the liberation of the soul from matter through revealed knowledge rather than mere faith. In some forms of Gnosticism, possessing the occult knowledge itself constituted salvation. In writings like the following from *The Revelation of Marcus,* a second century Gnostic, the spiritual Christ is the saviour who liberates the "knowing one."

The Supreme Quaternion came down unto him from that region that cannot be seen or named, in a female shape, because the world would have been unable to bear them appearing in a masculine form; and revealed unto him the generations of the universe, untold before to either gods or man. When first the Father, the Inconceivable, Beingless, Sexless, began to be in labour, he desired that his Ineffable should be born, and his Invisible should be clothed with form; he therefore opened his mouth, and uttered the Word like unto Himself. This Word standing before Him showed what He was, manifesting himself as the Type or Form of the Invisible. . . .

The subsequent revelations of the Quaternion to Marcus, serve to explain the frequent occurrence of the naked female, the former Venus Anadyomene, on Gnostic monuments. "After having declared these things, the Quaternion added: I will show unto thee *Truth,* whom I have brought down from the celestial

"Venus standing under a canopy supported on twisted columns, arranging her hair before a mirror held up by a Cupid; two others hover, bearing up a wreath, above her head. In the field ΦΑΣΙΣ·ΑΡΙΩΡΙΦ, 'the manifestation of Arioriph.' Venus here stands for the personification of Gnostic *Sophia* or Achamoth; and as such is the undoubted source of our conventional representation of Truth" (King 1864:211, plate V).

mansions, that thou shouldst behold her naked, acknowledge her beauty, hear her speaking, and be astonished at her wisdom. Look up, therefore, at her head, A and Ω; at her neck, B and Ψ; at her shoulders, with her hands, Γ and X; at her breasts, Δ and Φ, at her chest, E and Y; at her back, Z and T; at her belly, H and Σ; at her thighs, Θ and P; and her knees, I and Π; at her legs, K and O; at her ancles [sic], Λ and Ξ; at her feet, M and N. This is the body of Truth: this is the form of the Letters; this is the character of the Writing. Whereupon Truth, looking upon Marcus, opened her mouth, and uttered a Word; and this Word became a Name—a Name which we know and speak—Christ Jesus; and having named him she held her peace. (King 1864:38–40)[11]

The Sophia of Jesus Christ is a Gnostic text found in 1945 among tractates from the Nag Hammadi Library in Egypt. It is a "heavily Christianized"

[11]King notes that the figure of Truth, "it will be perceived, is made by taking successive pairs of letters from each extremity of the alphabet; perhaps thus constituting them masculine and feminine" (1864:39). For more on Christian Gnosticism, see references in Joseph Campbell, *The Masks of God: Occidental Mythology* (New York: Viking Press, 1964), especially "The Illusory Christ" and "The Mission of Paul," pp. 362–82. Hans Jonas examines Christian, Jewish, Hellenistic and Eastern Gnosticism in *The Gnostic Religion: The Message of the Alien God and the Beginnings of Christianity*, 2d ed. rev. (Boston: Beacon Press, 1963). See especially Jonas' discussion of Sophia in "The Valentian Speculation," wherein he claims: "How this figure [Wisdom, or Sophia], or at least its name, came to be combined in gnostic thought with the moon-, mother-, and love-goddess of Near Eastern religion, to form the ambiguous figure encompassing the whole scale from the highest to the lowest, from the most spiritual to the utterly sensual (as expressed in the very combination 'Sophia-Prunikos,' 'Wisdom the Whore'), we do not know and, lacking evidence of any intermediate stages, cannot even hypothetically reconstruct. As early as Simon [the magus, B.C.] the figure is fully developed in its gnostic sense" (pp. 176–77). Also see the brief, useful chapter on gnosticism in Kurt Seligman, *Magic, Supernaturalism and Religion* (New York: Pantheon Books, 1948), pp. 60–66.

"In the emblem to the right Wisdom, the *Alma Mater,* is represented crowned 'like the Tower of David builded for an armoury' *{The Wedding Song of Wisdom}.*

" 'On the crown of her head the King throneth, Truth on her head doth repose.' [*Song of Solomon* iv. 4.]

"In one hand she holds the sunlight, in the other a chalice into which is distilling the dew of heaven. Representations of a fair and beautiful virgin clasping the symbolic chalice, set among evil spirits and beasts who try to drag her down, are common in mediaeval art. In the uncanonical *Books of the Saviour,* Christ is said to be He who 'bringeth a cup full of intuition and wisdom and also prudence and giveth it to the soul and casteth the soul into a body which will not be able to fall asleep and forget because of the cup of prudence which hath been given unto it; but will be ever pure in heart and seeking after the mysteries of light until it hath found them by order of the Virgin of Light in order (that the soul) may inherit the Light for ever' [*Fragments of a Faith Forgotten,* G. R. S. Mead, p. 518]" (Bayley 1912:i, 245–46, fig. 533).[12]

version of "a revelation discourse given by the risen Christ to his followers." The following excerpt is translated by Douglas M. Parrott:

Then Bartholomew said to him, "How (is it that) [he] was designated in the Gospel 'Man' and 'Son of man'? From which of them, then, is this son?" The Holy One said to him, "I desire that you understand that First Man is called 'Begetter, Mind who is complete in himself.' He reflected with the great Sophia, his consort, and revealed his first-begotten, androgynous son. His male name is called 'First-Begetter Son of God'; his female name is 'First Begettress Sophia, Mother of the Universe.' Some call her 'Love.' Now the First-begotten is called 'Christ.' Since he has authority from his Father, he created for himself a multitude of angels without number for retinue, from the spirit and the light." (Robinson 1977:206, 216–17)

◆   Erich Neumann, *The Great Mother:* ". . . We find later in alchemy a revival of the original matriarchal symbolism of the vessel that contains the whole. . . .
"The feminine vessel as vessel of rebirth and higher transformation becomes Sophia and the Holy Grail. It not only, like the Gnostic *krater,* receives that which is to be transformed, in order to spiritualize and deify it, but is also the power that nourishes what has been transformed and reborn.

---

[12]For an extensive discussion of the symbolism of milk coming from *Alma Mater*'s breasts and particularly its connection with representations of the Virgin Mary, see "The Milk of Paradise" in Warner 1976:192–205. Warner notes that the only two physical, human activities the Virgin was allowed were lactation and weeping. For good studies of the *Song of Solomon* in relation to mythology and women, see, e.g.: Samuel Noah Kramer, "The Sacred Marriage and Solomon's Song of Songs" in 1969:85–106; and Phyllis Trible, "Exegesis: Song of Songs" in 1976:228–34.

The four stages of the alchemical process. From Johann Daniel Mylius, *Philosophia reformata* (Frankfort on the Main, 1622). (Lehner 1969:71, figs. 328–31)[13]

"Just as in the elementary phase the nourishing stream of the earth flows into the animal and the phallic power of the breast flows into the receiving child, so on the level of spiritual transformation the adult human being receives the 'virgin's milk' of Sophia. This Sophia is also the 'spirit and the bride' of the Apocalypse, of whom is it written: 'And let him that is athirst come. And whosoever will, let him take the water of life freely' " (1963:328, 329).

On the other hand, it would seem that women who practiced alchemy and, in effect, took command of their own vessels, could not then be viewed as practitioners of "higher" and "spiritual" transformations. Too often, in the popular imagination at least, it is/was the lot of women who seek wisdom and practice their knowledge to be viewed as unwomanly and reprehensible, a subject explored further in chapter 4. Here, the painful paradox for women

[13]According to C. G. Jung, the four elements—earth, water, air, and fire (left to right)—are indicated on the balls. "Four stages are distinguished . . ., characterized by the original colors mentioned in Heraclitus: *melanosis* (blackening), *leukosis* (whitening), *xanthosis* (yellowing), and *iosis* (reddening). This division of the process into four was called . . . the quartering of the philosophy. Later, about the fifteenth or sixteenth century, the colours were reduced to three, and the xanthosis, otherwise called the *citrinitas,* gradually fell into disuse or was but seldom mentioned. . . . Whereas the original tetrameria corresponded exactly to the quaternity of elements, it was now frequently stressed that although there were four elements (earth, water, fire, and air) and four qualities (hot, cold, dry, and moist), there were only three colours: black, white and red" *(Psychology and Alchemy,* trans. R. F. C. Hull, Bollingen Series XX, 2d ed. [Princeton: Princeton University Press, 1968], p. 229). Fifty-eight of Mylius' engravings are reproduced in Stanislas Klossowski de Rola, *Alchemy: The Secret Art* (London: Thames and Hudson, 1973), pp. 98–107. (This plate appears on p. 99.)

may be illustrated by examining Jungian theorist Erich Neumann's conceptions of *The Origins and Development of Consciousness:*

. . . One thing, paradoxical though it may seem, can be established at once as a basic law: even in women, consciousness has a masculine character. The correlation "consciousness-light-day" and "unconsciousness-darkness-night" holds true regardless of sex, and is not altered by the fact that the spirit-instinct polarity is organized on a different basis in men and women. Consciousness, as such, is masculine even in women, just as the unconscious is feminine in men. (1954:42)

Two paragraphs from Neumann's discussion of "The Negative Elementary Character" of the Great Mother succinctly elaborate this basic proposition:

The phases in the development of consciousness appear then as embryonic containment in the mother, as childlike dependence on the mother, as the relation of the beloved son to the Great Mother, and finally as the heroic struggle of the male hero against the Great Mother. In other words, the dialectical relation of consciousness to the unconscious takes the symbolic, mythological form of a struggle between the Maternal-Feminine and the male child, and here the growing strength of the male corresponds to the increasing power of consciousness in human development.

Since the liberation of the male consciousness from the feminine-maternal unconscious is a hard and painful struggle for all mankind, it is clear that the negative elementary character of the Feminine does not spring from an anxiety complex of the "man," but expresses an archetypal experience of the whole species, male and female alike. For in so far as the woman participates in this development of consciousness, she too has a symbolically male consciousness and may experience the unconscious as "negatively feminine." (1963:148; also see Neumann 1959)

From Abraham Saur, "A Short, True Warning" (Frankfurt, 1582). (Lehner 1971:66), fig. 95) This also appears on the title page of the 1586 edition of Protestant physician Johan Weyer's questioning of witch hunts, *De Praestigiis Daemonum {On the Magic of Demons}*, first published in Basel in 1563 (Haining 1975:67).

Considered carefully and precisely, Neumann's formulations may be psychologically and analytically useful. However, the problem is obvious: the terms and polarities he establishes—between feminine-maternal unconscious and male consciousness, between Great Mother and male hero, between Maternal-Feminine and male child, etc.—are both stereotypical and clumsy. In ordinary usage, in contemporary society, and in individual thoughts and dreams, these designations tend subtly and blatantly to devalue, to overlook, and to debilitate women. Even the most cautious and well-meaning of such interpretations can polarize thoughts and feelings in ways that do violence to the complexity, richness and resilience of both individuals and mythic motifs and narratives.

Musings: Animus ≠ Anima, Yet

(Harter 1980b:77)

> Mnemosyne, queen of the Eleutherian hills,
>   bore them
> in Pieria, when she had lain
>   with the Kronian Father;
> they bring forgetfulness of sorrows,
>   and rest from anxieties.
> For nine nights Zeus of the counsels
>   lay with her, going
> up into her sacred bed, far away
>   from the other immortals.
> But when it was a year,
>   after the seasons' turning
> and the months had waned away, and many days
>   were accomplished,
> she bore her nine daughters, concordant
>   of heart, and singing
> is all the thought that is in them,
>   and no care troubles their spirits.
> She bore them a little way off
>   from the highest snowy summit
> of Olympos; there are their shining
>   dancing places, their handsome
> houses, and the Graces and Desire lived
>   beside them
> in festivity; lovely is the voice
>   that issues from their lips
> as they sing of all the laws and all
>   the gracious customs
> of the immortals, and glorify them
>   with their sweet voices.
> At that time, glorying in their power
>   of song, they went to Olympos
> in immortal music, and all the black earth
>   re-echoed to them
> as they sang, and the lovely beat
>   of their footsteps sprang beneath them
> as they hastened to their father, to him

who is King in the heaven,
who holds in his own hands the thunder
   and the flamy lightning,
who overpowered and put down
   his father Kronos, and ordained
to the immortals all rights that are theirs,
   and defined their stations.
      All these things the Muses who have
   their homes on Olympos
sang then, and they are nine daughters
   whose father is great Zeus:
Kleio and Euterpe, Thaleia and Melpomene,
Terpsichore and Erato, Polymnia and Ourania,
with Kalliope, who of all holds
   the highest position.

—Hesiod, *Theogony*, lines 53–79,
trans. Lattimore (1959:126–27).

♦   Bathusa Makin, *An Essay to Revive the Antient Education of Gentlewomen*, 1673: "We may infer from the Stories of the Muses, that this way of Education was very ancient. All conclude the *Heroes* were men famous in their Generation, therefore canonized after their Deaths. We may with like Reason conclude, *Minerva* and the nine Muses were Women famous for Learning whilst they lived, and therefore thus adored when dead" (quoted in Brink 1978:421).

‡   "The poetic personality of Sappho and the poetic phenomenon of Sappho have proven difficult for both ancients and moderns to understand. Later generations of ancients—Greeks of the fourth century B.C. and thereafter, Romans, and Byzantines—were unaccustomed to supreme lyric talent in a woman who wrote about seemingly private passions. Several ancient sources thus class the late seventh/early sixth century B.C. Sappho not among the leading male poets of her time, as the ninth great Greek lyric genius, but as tenth of the female Muses. In so doing, they may have suggested that she had not earned literary stature through toil and competition, as did the men of her field (and, according to some, as had the female poet Corinna). But by calling her a Muse they ranked her an inspired and immortal figure to whom poetic self-expression and success came naturally. Various works from the fourth century onward also represent Sappho as a mythic heroine, driven by her love for a younger man, Phaon, to a dramatic suicide" (Hallett 1979:447–48).

(Harter 1980b:59)

"Take back your *Corinne* [by Mme de Staël]," said Maggie. . . . "You were right in telling me she would do me no good; but you were wrong in thinking I should wish to be like her."
"Wouldn't you really like to be a tenth Muse, then, Maggie?" said Philip. . . .
"Not at all," said Maggie, laughing. "The Muses were uncomfortable goddesses, I think—obliged always to carry rolls and musical instruments about with them. . . ."
"You agree with me in not liking Corinne, then?"
"I didn't finish the book. . . ."

After quoting these lines from George Eliot's *The Mill on the Floss*, feminist literary critic Ellen Moers observes that the reader, like Philip Wakem in the novel, is surprised that "sensitive, misunderstood" Maggie Tulliver "is not to turn into a mature woman of intellectual distinction and wide ambition—a *femme supérieure*, like Mme de Staël or George Eliot herself—but instead into a merely pretty and dangerous flirt . . ." (1976:174).

> So it is from the Muses, and from Apollo
>   of the farcast,
> that there are men on earth who are poets,
>   and players on the lyre . . .
>
> Hail, then, children of Zeus:
>   grant me lovely singing.
>
>   —Hesiod, *Theogony,* lines 94–95, 104,
>   trans. Lattimore (1959:128, 129).

(Bowles & Carver 1970:86)

But who grants "lovely singing" to women? Must they remain others' muses only—rarely themselves be-mused, a-mused, guided, and inspired? In " 'Come Slowly—Eden': An Exploration of Women Poets and Their Muse," Joanne Feit Diehl addresses herself to revising Harold Bloom's theories in *The Anxiety of Influence: A Theory of Poetry* (1973), which she introduces as:

Bloom has turned to the rhetorical systems of Vico, Nietzsche, Freud, and the Kabbalah to illuminate his own vision. His use of these systems assumes the poet to be male, for the tropes these models offer convey a specific sexual identity. The oedipal struggle, the son's war with the father, the desire for and resentment of the seductive female muse echo through these philosophies of origins. Although Bloom keeps alluding to the sexual aspects of the poet's dilemma, he repeatedly avoids the question raised by his own speculations, "What if the poet be a women?" But how might the process of influence differ for women poets, and how do women poets perceive their relation to the male-dominated tradition? (1978a:572–73)

Diehl proposes that poets Emily Dickinson, Christina Rossetti and Elizabeth Barrett Browning proclaim a male Precursor/muse in their creative work,

(Harter 1978b:109)

an "antithetical force [who] is a male tempter, stranger, goblin, or Pan . . . dreaded despite his attractiveness, feared when he is confronted" (1978a: 586). [14] In answering her critics, who claim this model is too "heterosexual" (Faderman 1978) and too simplistic by assuming "that, in order to understand what the muse is for women, we simply switch genders" (Bernikow 1978:192), Diehl asks:

> Why should it be anathema to assert, on the basis of Dickinson's own words, that she perceives a mythic male as the chief source of her power, a composite figure who represents forces of father, God, and poet? This is the figure Dickinson called the Stranger, and her poems reveal a confrontation with this "other" which must be repeated to win the necessary fusion of powers to write poetry. If the "other" is not a muse, what should we call him? (1978b:195)

[14]Sandra M. Gilbert and Susan Gubar claim that Charlotte Brontë's *Shirley* (1849) contains an "allegorical narrative" which may be viewed superficially "as a woman's attempt to imagine a male muse with whom she can have a sexual interaction that will parallel the male poet's congress with his female muse" (1979:208).

(Harter 1978a:61)

In *The Madwoman in the Attic,* Sandra M. Gilbert and Susan Gubar suggest that the female poet's more basic problem is an " 'anxiety of authorship'—a radical fear that she cannot create, that because she can never become a 'precursor' the act of writing will isolate or destroy her" (1979:49). A later paper by Gubar on " 'The Blank Page' and the Issues of Female Creativity" shows how the "model of the pen-penis writing on the virgin page participates in a long tradition identifying the author as a male who is primary and the female as his passive creation. . . ." Gubar notes her earlier collaborative work on how, "especially in the nineteenth-century, women writers, who feared their attempts at the pen were presumptuous, castrating, or even monstrous, engaged in a variety of strategies to deal with their anxiety about authorship" (1981:247). Such anxiety is expressed in the myth of Athena's invention of the double flute, here reconstructed by Robert Graves from accounts by Diodorus Siculus, Hyginus, Apollodorus and Pliny:

> . . . One day, Athene made a double-flute from stag's bones, and played on it at a banquet of the gods. She could not understand, at first, why Hera and Aphrodite were laughing silently behind their hands, although her music seemed to delight the other deities; she therefore went away by herself into a Phrygian wood, took up the flute again beside a stream, and watched her image in the water, as she played. Realizing at once how ludicrous that bluish face and those swollen cheeks made her look, she threw down the flute, and laid a curse on anyone who picked it up. (1960:77)[15]

The nymph Echo's plight illustrates another aspect of this struggle. She "could no longer use her voice, except in foolish repetition of another's shout: a punishment for having kept Hera entertained with long stories while Zeus's concubines, the mountain nymphs, evaded her jealous eye and made good their escape" (Graves 1960:287).[16] Not only male but female precursors present obstacles.

(Harter 1980b:112)

---

[15]Graves recounts the remainder of the story as follows: "f. Marsyas was the innocent victim of this curse. He stumbled upon the flute, which he had no sooner put to his lips than it played of itself, inspired by the memory of Athene's music; and he went about Phrygia in Cybele's train, delighting the ignorant peasants. They cried out that Apollo himself could not have made better music, even on his lyre, and Marsyas was foolish enough not to contradict them. This, of course, provoked the anger of Apollo, who invited him to a contest, the winner of which should inflict whatever punishment he pleased on the loser. Marsyas consented, and Apollo impanelled the Muses as a jury. The contest proved an equal one, the Muses being charmed by both instruments, until Apollo cried out to Marsyas: 'I challenge you to do with your instrument as much as I can do with mine. Turn it upside down, and both play and sing at the same time.'

"g. This, with a flute, was manifestly impossible, and Marsyas failed to meet the challenge. But Apollo reversed his lyre, and sang such delightful hymns in honour of the Olympian gods that the Muses could not do less than give the verdict in his favour. Then, for all his pretended sweetness, Apollo took a most cruel revenge on Marsyas: flaying him alive and nailing his skin to a pine (or, some say, to a planetree), near the source of the river which now bears his name" (1960:77).

[16]In "Reading Reading: Echo's Abduction of Language" (1980), Caren Greenberg claims literary critics have too long accepted the Oedipus myth as paradigmatic and proposes various readings of Echo's myth to suggest feminist forms of reading which are "non-Oedipal."

(Harter 1980a:103)

Unlike her male counterpart, then, the female artist must first struggle against the effects of a socialization which makes conflict with the will of her (male) precursors seem inexpressibly absurd, futile, or even . . . self-annihilating. . . . Her battle . . . is not against her (male) precursor's reading of the world but against his reading of *her*. In order to define herself as an author she must redefine the terms of her socialization. . . . Frequently, moreover, she can begin such a struggle only by actively seeking a *female* precursor who, far from representing a threatening force to be denied or killed, proves by example that a revolt against patriarchal literary authority is possible. (Gilbert and Gubar 1979:49; also see Abel 1981)

The literary dilemma posed by muse and creator is mirrored in psychological terms. The notions of anima and animus in Jungian psychology, which are so important to ideas about creativity, growth and developing consciousness—at least in men, reflect the same ambivalence and differential evaluation which characterize discussions of men's and women's muses, as can readily be seen in comparing the following definitions of the two terms:

‡ "The anima is a personification of all feminine psychological tendencies in a man's psyche, such as vague feelings and moods, prophetic hunches, receptiveness to the irrational, capacity for personal love, feeling for nature, and—last if not least—his relation to the unconscious. It is no mere chance that in olden times priestesses (like the Greek Sibyl) were used to fathom the divine will and to make connection with the gods." (von Franz 1964:186)

‡ ". . . The number four is also connected with the anima because, as Jung noted, there are four stages in its development. The first stage is best symbolized by the figure of Eve, which represents purely instinctual and biological relations. The second can be seen in Faust's Helen: She personifies a romantic and aesthetic level that is, however, still characterized by sexual elements. The third is represented, for instance, by the Virgin Mary—a figure who raises love (*eros*) to the heights of spiritual devotion. The fourth type is symbolized by Sapienta, wisdom transcending even the most holy and the most pure. Of this another symbol is the Shulamite in the Song of Solomon. (In the psychic development of modern man this stage is rarely reached. The Mona Lisa comes nearest to such a wisdom anima.)" (von Franz 1964:195)

‡ "The male personification of the unconscious in woman—the animus—exhibits both good and bad aspects, as does the anima in man. But the animus does not so often appear in the form of an erotic fantasy or mood; it is more apt to take the form of a hidden 'sacred' conviction. When such a conviction is preached with a loud, insistent, masculine voice or imposed on others by means of brutal emotional scenes, the underlying masculinity in a woman is easily recognized. However, even

—Illustration by H. J. Ford for "Prince Darling," in Andrew Lang, ed., *The Blue Fairy Book,* published in London ca. 1889 (1965:288).

in a woman who is outwardly very feminine the animus can be an equally hard, inexorable power. One may suddenly find oneself up against something in a woman that is obstinate, cold, and completely inaccessible." (von Franz 1964:198)

‡ "The animus, just like the anima, exhibits four stages of development. He first appears as a personification of mere physical power—for instance, as an athletic champion or 'muscle man.' In the next stage he possesses initiative and the capacity for planned action. In the third phase, the animus becomes the 'word,' often appearing as a professor or clergyman. Finally, in his fourth manifestation, the animus is the incarnation of *meaning*. On this highest level he becomes (like the anima) a mediator of the religious experience whereby life acquires new meaning. He gives the woman spiritual firmness, an invisible inner support that compensates for her outer softness. The animus in his most developed form sometimes connects the woman's mind with the spiritual evolution of her age, and can thereby make her even more receptive than a man to new creative ideas. It is for this reason that in earlier times women were used by many nations as diviners and seers. The creative boldness of their positive animus at times expressed thoughts and ideas that stimulate men to new enterprises." (von Franz 1964:206–207)

Despite intimations of positive meaning in the animus, then, most discussion of it in relation to women's psychological development is discouragingly negative.

—Illustration by H. J. Ford for "East of the Sun and West of the Moon," in Andrew Lang, ed., *The Blue Fairy Book*, published in London ca. 1889 (1965:26–27).

"The North Wind woke her betimes next morning, and puffed himself up, and made himself so big and so strong that it was frightful to see him, and away they went, high up through the air, as if they would not stop until they had reached the very end of the world. Down below there was such a storm! It blew down woods and houses, and when they were above the sea the ships were wrecked by hundreds. And they tore on and on, and a long time went by, and then yet more time passed, and still they were above the sea, and the North Wind grew tired, and more tired, and at last so utterly weary that he was scarcely able to blow any longer, and he sank and sank, lower and lower, until at last he went so low that the crests of the waves dashed against the heels of the poor girl he was carrying. 'Art thou afraid?' said the North Wind. 'I have no fear,' said she; and it was true. But they were not very, very far from land, and there was just enough strength left in the North Wind to enable him to throw her on to the shore, immediately under the windows of a castle which lay east of the sun and west of the moon; but then he was so weary and worn out that he was forced to rest for several days before he could go to his own home again."

‡ "The ability to assume different forms seems to be a characteristic quality of spirit; like mobility, the power to traverse great distances in a short time, it is expressive of a quality which thought shares with light. . . . Therefore, the animus often appears as an aviator, chauffeur, skier, or dancer, when lightness and swiftness are to be emphasized. . . . Loki, the flaming one, and Mercury, with the winged heels, also represent this aspect of the logos, its living, moving, immaterial quality which, without fixed qualities, is to a certain extent only a dynamism expressing the possibility of form, the spirit, as it were, that 'bloweth where it listeth' "
(E. Jung 1974:215–16).

‡ "The most characteristic manifestation of the animus is not in a configured image (*Gestalt*) but rather in words. . . . It comes to us as a voice commenting on every situation in which we find ourselves, or imparting generally applicable rules of behavior. . . . First, we hear from it a critical, usually negative comment on every movement, an exact examination of all motives and intentions. . . . From time to time, this same voice may also dispense exaggerated praise, and the result of these extremes of judgment is that one oscillates to and fro between the consciousness of complete futility and a blown-up sense of one's own value and importance"
(E. Jung 1974:209).

◆ C. G. Jung, *Aion* [1951]: "As the animus is partial to argument, he can best be seen at work in disputes where both parties know they are right. Men can argue in a very womanish way, too, when they are anima-possessed and have thus been transformed into the animus of their own anima" (1970:112).

◆ Emma Jung, "On the Nature of the Animus" [1931]: "The anima figure . . . is characterized by the fact that all of its forms are at the same time forms of relationship. . . . But . . . the animus figure does not necessarily express a relationship. Corresponding to the factual orientation of man and characteristic of the logos principle, this figure can come on the scene in a purely objective, unrelated way, as sage, judge, artist, aviator, mechanic, and so on. Not infrequently it appears as a 'stranger.' Perhaps this form in particular is the most characteristic, because, to the

(Fox 1979:5)

purely feminine mind, the spirit stands for what is strange and unknown" (1974:215).

♦ C. G. Jung, "Study in the Process of Individuation, A" [1934]: "For a woman, the typical danger emanating from the unconscious comes from above, from the 'spiritual' sphere personified by the animus, whereas for a man it comes from the chthonic realm of the 'world and woman,' i.e., the anima projected on to the world" (1970:112).

In European traditions transplanted to the New World, women who themselves entered the "spiritual sphere" often were labelled witches, who even today are popularly depicted as riding on brooms. This is the result of a long developmental process; animals were first believed to have been witches' means of transportation with broomsticks less common than cleft sticks or even distaffs or shovels. Stephen of Bourbon, who died in 1261, reported evil *strigae* who rode wolves and "good women" on sticks who attended the mythical Dame Abundance. Other early "authorities" noted by literary historian Rossell H. Robbins reported various modes of transport:

"The earliest printed picture of witches in flight, from Ulrich Molitor's *De Lamiis* (1489). From Cornell University Library" (Lehner 1971:58, fig. 83; Robbins 1959:511).

> *Errores Gazariorum* (1450): stick (*baculum*) and flying ointment
> Molitor, *De Lamiis* (1489): wolf; forked stick
> Danean, *Les sorciers* (1564): staff or rod and ointment
> Bodin, *Demonomanie* (1580): black ram; broom
> Boguet (1602): white staff between her legs
> Guazzo (1608): goats; oxen; dogs

Robbins suggests that "the broomstick probably won out because of its tradition as the symbol of women (corresponding to the pitchfork for the male), and because it is easily identified as a phallic symbol" (1959:511–12). In time too, persons experiencing nightmares or nightmare-like states came to be identified as ridden by witches or by the Old Hag, or "hag-ridden" (e.g., Hufford 1976; Rickels 1979; Ross 1980).

♦ Marie-Louise von Franz, *An Introduction to the Psychology of Fairy Tales:* "Bluebeard is a murderer and nothing more; he cannot transform his wives or be transformed himself. He embodies the death-like, ferocious aspects of the animus in his most diabolical form; from him only flight is possible. . . .

"This throws into bold relief an important difference between the anima and the animus. Man in his primitive capacity as hunter and warrior is wont to kill, and it [is] as if the animus, being masculine, shares this propensity. Woman, on the other hand, serves life, and the anima entangles a man in life. . . .

"The animus in his negative form seems to be the opposite. He draws woman away from life and murders life for her. He has to do with ghost-lands and the land of death. Indeed, he may appear as the personification of death. . . ." (1973:125).

♦ Emma Jung, "On the Nature of the Animus": "It is well known that a really creative faculty of mind is a rare thing in woman. There are many women who have developed their powers of thinking, discrimination, and criticism to a high degree, but there are very few who are mentally creative in the way a man is. . . .

"The creativity of woman finds its expression in the sphere of living, not only in her biological functions as mother but in the shaping of life generally, be it in her

"Being come to the closet-door, she made a stop for some time, thinking upon her husband's orders, and considering what unhappiness might attend her if she was disobedient; but the temptation was so strong she could not overcome it. She then took the little key, and opened it, trembling, but could not at first see anything plainly, because the windows were shut. After some moments she began to perceive that the floor was all covered over with clotted blood, on which lay the bodies of several dead women, ranged against the walls. (These were all the wives whom Blue Beard had married and murdered, one after another.) She thought she should have died for fear, and the key, which she pulled out of the lock, fell out of her hand."

—Illustration by G. P. Jacomb Hood for "Blue Beard," in Andrew Lang, ed., *The Blue Fairy Book,* published in London ca. 1889 (1965:291–92; also see Opie 1974:103–109).

activity as educator, in her role as companion to man, as mother in the home, or in some other form. The development of relationships is of primary importance in the shaping of life, and this is the real field of feminine creative power" (1974:209–10).

♦   Naomi R. Goldenberg, *Changing of the Gods:* "The anima/animus model and its goal of unification works better for men than for women. The model supports stereotyped notions of what masculine and feminine are by adding mystification to guard against change in the social sphere, where women are at a huge disadvantage. In practice, men can keep control of all Logos activities and appropriate just whatever Eros they need from their women as a psychological hobby. Women, on the other hand, are not encouraged to develop Logos. Instead, they are thought of as handicapped by nature in all Logos areas—such as those found at the top of any important profession. Acceptance of the anima/animus theory does not support integration of the sexes, but rather leads to more separatism. Intrapsychically, the theory might do some good for people who have been afraid of experiences that

—Illustration by either H. J. Ford or Lancelot Speed for "Dapplegrim," in Andrew Lang, ed., *The Red Fairy Book,* published in London in 1890 (1966:250).

have been seen as appropriate for just one sex or the other. . . . However, the model is decidedly inadequate if a person is questioning the masculine and feminine stereotypes themselves" (1979:59).[17]

◆   C. G. Jung, commentary on *The Secret of the Golden Flower* [1929]: "The conscious side of woman corresponds to the emotional side of man, not to his 'mind.' Mind makes up the 'soul,' or better, the 'animus' of woman, and just as the anima of a man consists of inferior relatedness, full of affect, so the animus of woman consists of inferior judgments, or better, opinions" (1970:112).

◆   James Hillman, "On Psychological Femininity": "Hitherto we have always spoken of inferiority from a masculine, scientific, Apollonic view. The inferior was part of a polarity in which the male had the superior place. But how might it look from within itself? Perhaps this structure of conjoined consciousness is less hierarchical and without self-divisive polarities. Perhaps it may be conceived not mainly in terms of spatial levels and *Schichtentheorie* (this model of the psyche—usually in three layers—occurs repeatedly in this same line of thought from Plato and

[17]Goldenberg also observes rather caustically that: "Dr. Jolande Jacobi, one of the most successful female members of the second generation of Jungians, insisted that 'just as the male by his very nature is uncertain in the realm of Eros, so the woman will always be unsure in the realm of Logos.' The fact that Dr. Jacobi's very successful career as author and lecturer in the realm of Logos seemed to contradict this statement never bothered her at all. Jacobi was typical of many Jungians in that she did not let the facts of any individual's experience contradict an archetype that she wanted to believe was universal" (1979:59–60).

Aristotle, continuing without break to Freud and his id, ego, and superego). Hierarchical models require the inferiority of lower positions. But we can experience and conceive consciousness by means of other images. For example, rather than superimposed levels, we might speak of polycentricity, of circulation and rotation, of the comings and goings of flow. In this structure all positions are occasionally inferior, and no positions are ever finally inferior. In this kind of structure, inferiority in its old sense would come to an end" (1972:287).

◆   Barbara Charlesworth Gelpi, "The Androgyne": "So far in history, women as well as men (and not just Jungians) have associated consciousness-intellection, abstract thought—with the masculine principle. . . . But if something as bewilderingly mysterious as the appearance of consciousness was once possible, is the transmutation of that consciousness not also possible? As women grow in awareness, as, then, to

(Fox 1979:108)

use Neumann's vocabulary, the transformative aspect of the feminine principle becomes more pronounced, might we not be moving (how quickly or how slowly one cannot tell) to the point where someone—perhaps a man, perhaps a woman, perhaps a pair, or a group—breaks through and 'sees,' thereby creating a consciousness as different from ours as ours is different from that of the grazing warthogs on the Plain of Athi?

"If this new consciousness is so totally different from what we now think of as consciousness, it may be useless to speculate on its nature, but one can in a negative way see the evils identified with 'masculine' consciousness which it might help to overcome. Masculine consciousness separates its possessor from 'mother nature,' thereby setting him free on the one hand and binding him with guilt on the other. If Emma Jung is right when she says that 'the creativity of woman finds its expression in the sphere of living,' in 'the development of relationships,' then this new consciousness might not be divisive. It might 'see' the realm of intellection and the realm of matter as one in a way in which we cannot really see them now. It might also see the development of intellection and of personality as possible without the necessity of competition and so create a society based on relation, a community of knowledge and action, vision and pleasure" (1974:232–33; also see Griffin 1978).

◆   James Hillman, " 'Anima' ": "But I do doubt that woman's psychological development means animus development, for this is an erosion of the categories of the psyche and spirit. Animus refers to spirit, to logos, word, idea, intellect, principle, abstraction, meaning, *ratio, nous.* The discrimination of spirit is not at all of the same order as the cultivation of soul. If the first is active mind in its broadest sense, the second is the realm of the imaginal, equally embracing, but different.

"The assumption has been that because women are of the feminine gender they have soul—or rather are soul. As long as femininity and soul are an identity, then of course the soul problem of women is taken care of, again by definition, and by biology. But psyche, the sense of soul, is not given to woman just because she is born female. She is no more blessed with a congenitally saved soul than man who must pass his life in worry over its fate. She is no more exonerated from the tasks of anima cultivation than man; for her to neglect soul for the sake of spirit is no less psychologically reprehensible than it is in man who is ever being told by analytical psychology that he must sacrifice intellect, persona, and extraversion for the sake of soul, feeling, inwardness, i.e., anima" (1973:116).

Chapter 4
Moon, Menstruation, Menopause:
Myth and Ritual

Maidenly daughters of Cronian Zeus who are experts in music,
Muses, rehearse in sweet phrases a song of the long-wingéd Moon
  whose
Brightness embraces the earth when her light, as displayed in the
  heavens,
Shines from her immortal brow, whence in plenty embellishment rises
Under her splendid effulgence. The lustreless atmosphere lightens,
Taking the gold of her crown, and her beams are as lucid as daylight.
Thus, when the brilliant Selene, done bathing her beautiful body
Dipped in the Ocean, and donning her distantly-luminous garments,
Laying her yoke on the necks of her shining, high-spirited coursers,
Drives on her horses with beautiful manes in impetuous fashion,
Evening, at the full moon. Her magnificent orbit is filled, and
As she increases, her beams reach their brightest perfection in heaven,
Making the Moon a dependable token and sign unto mortals.
With her the scion of Cronus once mingled in friendship and slumber;
She, growing pregnant, gave birth unto Pandia, who is a maiden
With an exceptional beauty of form for an immortal goddess.
Hail to you, goddess and queen with white arms, brightly-shining
  Selene!
Favourable, beautifully coiffed. Having started with you I shall
  sing the
Praises of men who are semi-divine, whom the Muses' attendants
Celebrate—poets with admirable tongues—as they tell of their
  achievements.

> —Homeric Hymn XXXII "To Selene," trans. Daryl Hine
> (1972:83).

Luna Regia, the Moon Goddess, a Gnostic gem (Lehner 1969:89, fig. 464). This figure is identified as Selene, the Moon Goddess of Greece, in Jacob Bryant's 1774 volume, *A New System of Analysis of Ancient Mythology* (Harding 1973:116).

The moon serves as a ready measure, its phases commonly indicating "a month" and frequently symbolizing a lifetime, which may or may not, like the moon's, be renewed. The lunar cycle is also almost paradigmatic for a woman's life, even though she may menstruate for only part of that time. All these related measures—moons, months, and menses—have more usually been viewed as dark and dangerous to the solar, which is generally equated with the masculine, than as sources of fructifying power for either women or men.

Historian of religions Mircea Eliade notes that, while "the sun is always the same, always itself, never in any sense 'becoming,' the moon, on the other hand, is a body which waxes, wanes and disappears, a body whose existence

(Harter 1978a:54)

is subject to the universal law of becoming, of birth and death" (1958:154). He compares lunar symbolism in religions and mythologies worldwide:

> "Becoming" is the lunar order of things. Whether it is taken as the playing-out of a dream (the birth, fulness and disappearance of the moon), or given the sense of a "division" or "enumeration," or intuitively seen as the "hempen rope" of which the threads of fate are woven, depends, of course, on the myth-making and theorizing powers of individual tribes, and their level of culture. But the formulae used to express that "becoming" are heterogeneous on the surface only. The moon "divides," "spins," and "measures"; or feeds, makes fruitful, and blesses; or receives the souls of the dead, initiates and purifies—because it is living, and therefore in a perpetual state of rhythmic becoming. This rhythm always enters into lunar rituals. (Ibid:176—77)

Lunar deities with such attributes are both female and male, as illustrated below.

In Western tradition, on the whole, the lunar has come to be associated with the feminine and the unconscious, the solar with the masculine and the conscious. Many scholars claim this association results from an historical shift from matriarchal religions and societies to patriarchal ones. Jungian analyst M. Esther Harding may be taken as exemplary of such interpreters, among them Helen Diner, Robert Graves, Erich Neumann and Margaret Murray (see Rush 1976:16—20 for various citations).

In *Woman's Mysteries, Ancient and Modern: A Psychological Interpretation of the Feminine Principle as Portrayed in Myth, Story, and Dreams*, Harding speculates about "the rise of masculine power and of patriarchal society" and the relationship of sun and moon worship:

> . . . This change in secular power coincided with the rise of sun worship under a male priesthood, which began to supersede the much earlier moon cults, which, however, remained in the hands of women. Sun worship was usually introduced and established by an edict of a military dictator, as happened in Babylon and Egypt, and probably in other countries as well.
>
> The results of this change in emphasis between masculine and feminine were far-reaching. Perhaps one of the most important was that the concept of what constituted religious, or spiritual, values, which had been symbolized by the moon, was transferred to the sun and came under masculine control.
>
> In the days of moon worship, religion was concerned with the unseen powers of the spirit world, and even when the state religion was transferred to the sun, a god of war, of personal aggrandizement, and of the things of this world, the spiritual qualities remained with the moon deities. For the worship of the moon is the worship of the creative and fecund powers of nature and of the wisdom that lies inherent in instinct and in the at-one-ness with natural law. But the worship of the sun is the worship of that which overcomes nature, which orders her chaotic fullness and harnesses her powers to the fulfilling of man's ends. The masculine principle, or Logos, thus came to be revered in the person of the Sun God, and the godlike qualities inherent in man, his capacity to achieve and to order, to formulate, discriminate, and generalize, were venerated in a sun hero, who undertook his twelve labors and slew the dragons of ignorance and sloth, thus acquiring consciousness, a spiritual value of a different order. (1973:34—35)

(Crawhall 1974:16)

Harding claims that this dichotomizing has led to the devaluation of the lunar mode and its inspirations:

The moon, it was [once] thought, insinuates into man's mind ideas and intuitions which are not at all in accordance with intellectual standards but are strange and bizarre, and, because of the profound truth hidden beneath their unusual form, they may be creatively new. These ideas are filled with a peculiar emotion or with intoxicating delight, like the ecstasy of the soma drink. . . .

Thinking of this kind is despised among us, but it has been highly esteemed in many ages and many civilizations. It is thought to be due to a possession by a divine power. Even in extreme form, as in the case of lunacy (lune is moon), primitives and the ancients thought that a god spoke through the man's delirium. (1973:277)

Unfortunately, Harding contributes to this polarization by assigning Logos or "sun thinking" to the male and Eros or "moon thinking" to the female:

. . . Usually a man in whom "moon thinking" arises feels that there is something inferior about the whole process, something uncanny, something not quite clean, by which he is besmirched. He feels that such thinking is not a masculine but a "womanish" sort of thinking; and he may add that women think in that confused way most of the time. But certain women, if they were asked, would say that the thoughts and inspirations which come to them from the depths of their being are likely to be right, can be relied on, and can be acted on with confidence. When a woman thinks in her head as a man thinks, she is often wrong; she is very apt to be deceived by ready-made opinions, to spend her time on side issues; and her thinking, when of this kind, is usually unproductive and uncreative. Ideas formed under the moon, inferior though they may seem to be, yet have a power and compelling quality which ideas originating in the head rarely have. They are like the moon in that they grow of themselves. They demand an outlet; if a suitable one is not provided they may become obsessive and produce, as the primitives would say, "moon madness." For the children of the moon must come to birth just as surely as physical children. (1973:278–79)

Nevertheless, Harding also cautions that contemporary individuals of both sexes ignore lunar wisdom at their peril:

The ancient religions of the moon goddess represent the education of the emotional life as taking place, not through a course of study, not even as the result of a system of discipline, though both these things doubtless entered in, but through an initiation. [This] interpretation of the moon mysteries . . . links our modern life problems to those of the ancient peoples who recognized that in their day, as in ours, the world at times became sterile and was laid waste, not by war or

The Moon, Monday's Planet, as depicted in an old Hungarian "Gypsy Planet and Dream Book" (Lehner 1969:50, fig. 161).

pestilence, but because some essential fertilizing spirit had been withdrawn. . . .

Perhaps if more attention were directed to reinstating the goddess in the individual life, through psychological experiences, the modern equivalent to the initiations of the moon goddess, a way out of this impasse might open before us. (1973:xiv, xv)

Anne Kent Rush claims that "the position of the moon in a culture is the same as the position of women in that culture; our fates are inexorably shared" and that "awareness of the moon is part of the current cycle of re-balancing the female principle" (1976:16). She describes her own process of re-balancing thus:

When beginning to re-acquaint myself with the moon, i did much reading and also integrated her movements into mine. I paid attention to the relationship of my menstrual cycles with the moon's cycles, to the changes in my friends' moods as the moon changed, to the tides and the weather. The first revelations came by allowing myself to make place for the moon in my daily living. These moments have remained the strongest and most palpable knowing. I started with the recognition that because the moon was shining on me at night and pulling on me during the day, it probably had been 'speaking' to me for a long time, and i had not been listening. I had to learn its language. I decided to begin my research at night by standing and looking out an open window. (Ibid:21; also see Rush 1979)

This sort of inner exploration is also suggested by Esther Harding's observation:

For to women, life itself *is* cyclic. The life force ebbs and flows in her actual experience, not only in nightly and daily rhythms as it does for a man but also in moon cycles, quarter phase, half phase, full moon, decline, and so round to dark moon. These two changes together produce a rhythm which is like the moon's changes and also like the tides whose larger monthly cycle works itself out concurrently with the diurnal changes, sometimes increasing the swing of the tides and at other times working against the tidal movement, the whole producing a complex rhythm hard to understand. In the course of one complete cycle, which most strangely corresponds to the moon's revolution, the women's energy waxes, shines full and wanes again. These energy changes affect her, not only in her physical and sexual life but in her psychic life as well. Life in her ebbs and flows, so that she is dependent on her inner rhythms. (1973:82)[1]

(Crawhall 1974:48)

[1]Folklorist Kay Turner, citing this quotation in a discussion of the Mayan goddess Ix Chel (see "Lunar Deities" below), claims: "The moon goddess is the cosmic source for identifying this rhythm. . . . Women came to know themselves through reliance on her image as a model of behavior" (1976:46).

The exploration of lunar myths, rites and symbols has also led to the re-valuation of menstruation and menstrual rites, as well as to the institution of new ways to celebrate womanhood. Witchcraft too has been reexamined, and contemporary priestesses of the moon observe revitalized ancient rituals. This trend in interpretation and in practice has led to a general reconsideration of menopause and particularly the wise old woman, whose knowledge and power have so rarely been viewed as equivalent to those of the wise old man.

Lunar Deities

> I see the moon,
>   And the moon sees me;
> God bless the moon,
>   And God bless me.
>
> —Nursery rhyme
>   (Opie 1952:312).[2]

(Harter 1978a:19)

[2]The Opies cite a number of similar English children's sayings, the earliest from a 1784 collection, and an American version: "I see the moon, the moon sees me, The moon sees somebody I want to see" (1952:312).

O Lady Moon, your horns point toward the east:
    Shine, be increased.
O Lady Moon, your horns point toward the west:
    Wane, be at rest.

    —Christina Rossetti, "Lady Moon," 1872
    (Opie 1973:277).[3]

(Harter 1978b:101)

[3]Born in London of Italian parentage, Christina Georgina Rossetti (1830–94) grew up sickly, but managed to teach and write poetry, much of it religious. *Sing-Song,* "a nursery rhyme book," was published in 1872 (Opie 1973:379–80).

The Man in the Moon was caught in a trap
For stealing the thorns from another man's gap.
If he'd gone by, and let the thorns lie,
He'd never been Man in the Moon so high.

—Nursery rhyme (Opie 1952:296).[4]

"Man in the Moon." Its "Twin towers form an *aitch*, and the moon-face of Hermes surmounts an H" (Bayley 1912:ii, 138–49, fig. 1063).

In recent Western tradition it is the Man in the Moon more often than the Lady Who is the Moon who is invoked or alluded to in popular belief. Nevertheless, both classical and Christian mythologies portray the moon as a female deity.

Muse, sing a hymn about Artemis, sister of Phoebus the Archer,
Maidenly strewer of barbs who was nursed at the breast with Apollo.
When she has furnished her steeds at the deep reedy stream of the Meles
Swiftly through Smyrna she urges her chariot gilded all over
Unto the vineyards of Claros; the silvery bowman Apollo
Sits there, awaiting his sister, the accurate strewer of arrows.
This is my greeting to you and all goddesses, lyrical greetings!
Having begun with a hymn about you I shall turn to another.

—Homeric Hymn IX "To Artemis," trans. Daryl Hine (1972:59).

"Artemis (Diana), goddess of the Moon (Gorii, Mus. Flor., vol. 2, tav. 88)" (Bayley 1912:ii, 49, fig. 878).

‡ "Selene, daughter of Hyperion and Theia, is a goddess of the moon. Like her brother Helius, she drives a chariot, although hers usually has only two horses. . . .
"Many stories about the god of the sun, whether he be called Hyperion, Helius, or merely the Titan, were transferred to the great god Apollo, who, although in all probability not originally a sun-god, was considered as such in the classical period. . . . Apollo's twin sister, Artemis, became associated with the moon, although originally she probably was not a moon-goddess. Thus Selene and Artemis merge in identity, just as do Hyperion, Helius, and Apollo. Artemis, like Selene, as a moon-goddess is associated with magic, since the link between magic and the worship of the moon is close [Authors' note: "Hecate, goddess of the moon, ghosts, and black magic, is but another aspect of both Selene and Artemis."]. Apollo and Artemis themselves have a close link with the Titans. The Titan Coeus mates with his sister Phoebe, and their daughter Leto bore Artemis and Apollo to Zeus. Coeus and Phoebe are little more than names to us, but Phoebe is the feminine form of Phoebus, and she herself may very well be another moon-goddess. Phoebe became an epithet of Artemis, just as Phoebus is applied to Apollo. Again the identification of Apollo and Artemis with the sun and the moon is evident and confirmed by genealogy" (Morford and Lenardon 1977:29–30).

[4]According to the Opies: "This rhyme, heard by a contributor to *Folk-Lore* (1913) gives the traditional picture of the Man in the Moon who is identified by his lantern and bush of thorns (as in *A Midsummer Night's Dream*). The legend is that the man was banished to the moon for strewing a church path with thorns to hinder the people attending mass" (1952:296). They include two other "man in the moon" nursery rhymes (pp. 294–96), and an 1818 illustration (plate XII). Also note Grace Butcher's 1971 poem, "Wife of the Moon Man Who Never Came Back" (in Chester and Barba 1973:229).

Gnostic gem, "a large loadstone," depicting "Phoebus erect in his quadriga, holding in one hand the terrestrial globe, the other raised in the gesture of command. Under this ancient type, either Mithras, or the 'Sun of righteousness,' is indubitably understood . . ., as appears from the invocation about him . . . 'Thou art our Father!' to which the Hellenic sun-god had no claim according to the ancient system of mythology. . . . In the exergue [below figure, is] a frequent title of Mithras" (King 1864:233; facing title-page woodcut, no. 2; the gem's obverse is below).

Geraldine Thorsten, *God Herself: The Feminine Roots of Astrology:* "The egg, the serpent or dragon holding its tail in its mouth, and the circle all symbolized the Goddess as the original, ultimate One, without beginning or end, and Her law that life was an endless circle from birth to death to rebirth. And, since the Goddess was the ultimate One, it followed that all opposites such as night and day, female and male, heat and cold were born from Her and reconciled in Her. Gemini, originally symbolized by a woman and a man, is premised on this resolution of opposites. Interestingly enough, the Chinese zodiac begins with The Twin Women, their equivalent for our Virgo, which includes the idea that the Goddess sees the past and the future while presiding over the present. This attribute is a strongly realized feature of the Virgoan personality, and certainly deserves more attention in contemporary interpretation. Needless to say, Virgoan women do not have the scope of vision of the Goddess, but they do have an uncanny ability to relate past experience and to consider future consequences while dealing with the present" (1980:130–31).

> My dove, my perfect one, is only
>   one,
>   the darling of her mother,
>   flawless of her that bore her.
> The maidens saw her and called her
>   happy;
>   the queens and concubines also,
>   and they praised her.
> "Who is this that looks forth like
>   the dawn,
>   fair as the moon, bright as the sun,
>   terrible as an army with banners?"
>
> —*Song of Solomon* 6:9–10 (RSV).[5]

And a great portent appeared in heaven, a woman clothed with the sun, with the moon under her feet, and on her head a crown of twelve stars; she was with child and she cried out in her pangs of birth, in anguish for delivery. And another portent appeared in heaven; behold, a great red dragon, with seven heads and ten horns, and seven diadems upon his heads. His tail swept down a third of the stars of heaven, and cast them to the earth. And the dragon stood before the woman who was about to bear a child, that he might devour her child when she brought it forth; she brought forth a male child, one who is to rule all the nations with a rod of iron, but her child was caught up to God and to his throne, and the woman fled into the wilderness, where she has a place prepared by God, in which to be nourished for one thousand two hundred and sixty days.

—*Revelation* 12:1–6 (RSV).

Gnostic gem, "a large loadstone," depicting "Diana, or Luna, holding by the horns and guiding the bull, emblem of the Earth. Luna's car is properly drawn by a pair of silver bulls: an attribute translated from the silver antelopes harnessed to the wain of her prototype, the Hindoo *Chandra*" (King 1864:233; facing title-page woodcut, no. 2).

[5]For a discussion of "The Sacred Marriage and Solomon's Song of Songs" and its relationship to Mesopotamian mythology about Inanna/Ishtar and Dumuzi/Tammuz, see Kramer 1969:85–106. For a feminist exegesis see Trible 1976:228–34.

‡   "By the middle ages . . . the Church and the Virgin were closely identified, particularly with the symbol of the woman of the Apocalypse and the beloved of the Canticle [above]. The Virgin thereby acquired the lunar imagery previously applied to the Church; and as belief in her intercession with God became more profound, the idea crystallized that Mary, through her mediation, bent the beams of God's grace into the Christian soul, just as the Church stood before Christ, her bridegroom, irradiated by his grace, or as the moon is filled with sunlight and sheds it on the earth at night. Also through the Virgin, the sun was born at Christmas. Analogously, each Christian is reborn in the light of Christ, which she deflects on them" (Warner 1976:258).

‡   "As a lunar deity she was also closely associated with the sea. One interpretation of her name derives it from *mar,* Latin for sea. St. Jerome [ca. 341–420] glossed the Hebrew Miriam of the Gospel as *stilla maris,* a drop of the sea. The sway of astronomy over the medieval imagination was so strong, and the Virgin so closely identified with the heavens, that the slip of a scribe's hand introduced into Marian literature and art one of its most suggestive and beautiful metaphors. For an early copyist wrote *stella maris,* star of the sea, instead of *stilla maris,* a mistake that persisted until the most recent edition of Jerome's *On the Interpretation of Hebrew Names.* Thus the Virgin was associated not only with the moon, but also with other planets of the firmament" (Warner 1976:262).

‡   "As a sky goddess, Mary's colour is blue. Her starry mantle is a figure of the sky, as in Apuleius' vision of Isis; as late as 1649, Francisco Pacheco in his *Art of Painting* still laid down that she should wear a blue cloak. Blue is the colour of space and light and eternity, of the sea and the sky. The reason for the symbolism is also economic, however, for blue was an expensive pigment, obtainable only from crushed lapis lazuli imported from Afghanistan, and, after gold, it thus became the medieval painter's most fitting and fervent tribute to the Queen of Heaven" (ibid:266).

◆   Marina Warner, *Alone of All Her Sex:* "For all Western society's revival of astrology, for all our explorations and adventures in space, we look uncomprehendingly at the skies, if we look at them at all. Few people can distinguish a waxing moon from the sickle on the wane; and the unceasing rhythm of the heavenly bodies is barren of significance. . . .

"But this was not so in the hellenistic world that nurtured Christianity. In its symbolism and philosophy, no comparable disjunction between the tangible and visible world of nature and the intangible and invisible world of spirit existed;

(Crawhall 1974:48)

MOON, MENSTRUATION, MENOPAUSE   163

rather, they were fused in a rich and multilayered language soundly rooted in observation—sometimes scientific, sometimes not—of the planetary system in which the world moves.

"When the Virgin Mary, as the Immaculate Conception, hangs suspended in the heavens on the orb or on the crescent of the moon . . ., she recapitulates this language in a form that in some respects alters the original meaning, in others sustains it. For the moon at the Virgin's feet represents more than the 'great wonder' of Revelation 12:1 . . ., and the beloved of the Canticle . . . (Song of Solomon 6:10). The moon has been the most constant attribute of female divinities in the western world, and was taken over by the Virgin Mary because of ancient beliefs about its functions and role, which Christianity inherited" (1976:255–56).

Astrological sign for Virgo, the Virgin (Lehner 1969:61, fig. 252).

♦ Geraldine Thorsten, *God Herself: The Feminine Roots of Astrology:* "Virgo has always had a very special place in my heart, so it's been a particular joy to discover how very special a place Virgo holds, not only in the history of astrology, but in the history of our civilization. We can discard the dismal interpretations that traditional astrology routinely offers. A strong Virgo influence at work in your horoscope does *not* mean that you are destined to be a carping nag *or* sexually unresponsive *or* the drudge of the zodiac. As you'll see in the personal section of this chapter, the qualities and strengths that Virgo contributes are qualities that you can be proud of and grateful for.

"Buried under the dingy picture of Virgo that we're familiar with is the awesome portrait of the Mother of the Universe, worshipped as *the* Supreme Being in every portion of our planet from at least 15,000 B.C. onward. Her names changed and multiplied, Her figure varied from Rubenesque to reed-thin, She was sometimes portrayed mother-naked and sometimes resplendent in gold and brilliant gems, but certain facets of Her nature remained constant whatever the time or the place" (1980:129).

Native American traditions differ from classical and Judeo-Christian mythologies—sometimes portraying the moon as a female, sometimes as a male deity. The following entries from the *Funk & Wagnalls Standard Dictionary of Folklore, Mythology and Legend* identify some of these diverse beliefs:

Many American Indian languages lack specific words for moon and sun but have instead a noncommittal word meaning luminary, to which is prefixed "night" or "nighttime" and "day" or "daytime" for the moon and sun (compare, for example, the Delaware Indian . . .). Personification or deification of the sun and the moon is usual and the two appear as actors in several American Indian myths. The moon and the stars are the Night People or Fathers of Taos pueblo, and are more prominent in the pantheons of the northeastern Pueblo Indians than in the western ones. Moon-Old-Man is distinctly a personage at Taos, Isleta, Jemez, and Tewa. At Zuñi Moon's sex is reversed; she is Sun's younger sister or, in prayer, Moon Our Mother. Among the Apache of the Southwest, the Jicarilla are not consistent as to Moon's sex; they say that Moon is female, in connection with the menstrual cycle, but in a ceremonial race Moon is represented as a male, and Moon is also associated with Water, the father of one of the culture heroes. The Lipan Apache represent sun and moon as human beings who led the people after the emergence. . . . In the related mythology of the Navaho, Klehanoai, a male deity, is the Moon Carrier and husband of White-Shell Woman. Among the Cora Indians of northern Mexico the moon, like the sun, is a god, and is both man and woman.

The Chehalis of the Pacific Northwest have Moon as their Changer, a male Creator-Transformer; the Tillamook, however, while assigning to Moon the same role, make her a female changer. (Erminie W. Voegelin in Leach 1972:744)

(Crawhall 1974:16)

Probably all North American Indians, if the distribution of the item were known, have some explanation for the dark patches on the moon. That most frequently encountered among the western tribes is that the figures are those of Frog(s). Frog protects both Sun and Moon so that Bear will not swallow them. Or, Frog once swallowed Moon, but was in turn swallowed by her and is now in the center of Moon, weaving a basket. Or, two or more Frog sisters reject animal suitors; the latter weep; a flood ensues from the tears; the Frog sisters go to the house of Moon and jump on his face, where they may be seen at the present time; this latter tale is widespread in North America. Among the Caddo Indians of the Southeast a brother commits incest wtih his sister in the dark; she smears paint on his face and so later identifies him; he becomes the man in the moon. Some other tribes in the West say the figures are those of a giant, or of Coyote, or are the picture of a large oak tree from which the dead obtain their food, or that they are scars left on Moon after Bear bit her. The Shawnee of the Eastern Woodlands see their female creator's picture in the moon; she is bending over a cooking pot, with her little dog near her. The explanation of the figures in the moon is often added to tales, or inserted in them as an explanatory element. (Erminie W. Voegelin in Leach 1972:672)

In the cosmogony of the Taulipang (Guiana) and Ona Indians (Tierra del Fuego), the moon is personified and its phases are explained by the changes in his bodily appearance. The moon alternately loses and gains weight. According to the Bakairi (Central Brazil) the phases of the moon are caused by various animals which gnaw at it and finally swallow it.

The spots on the moon are often explained by the South American Indians as one of the consequences of incestuous relations between the Moon and his sister (generally identified with the Sun). The woman, not knowing who her mysterious lover was, marked him with genipa, ashes, or menstrual blood. The Moon, out of shame and fear, went to the sky (Taulipang, Cuna, Okaina, Conibo, Witoto, Zaparo, Shipaya, Guarani, Indians of the Yamunda and of Tumupasa).

According to the Yahgan and the Ona, the spots on the Moon are marks of the beating received by the Moon when the Sun discovered the secrets of the initiation rites. The Mataco and Chamacoco interpret the spots as the intestines of Moon which were bared when Moon was torn to pieces by ducks or rheas which he had tried to catch. To the Yuracare, the spots on the Moon are a four-eyed jaguar which escaped to the sky. (Alfred Métraux in Leach 1972:745)

◆ Kay Turner, "Ixchel: Biography of a Mayan Moon Goddess": "On May 21, 1974 Nancy Dean and I left New Jersey for Mexico and Guatemala. We packed up the swaying gray Volvo with pots, tent, and too many books and headed toward the moon. We went looking for Lady-Unique-Circular-Darkness, Lady-Unique-Splotch-of-Blood, Ix Hun Ahau. We had read of the ancient worship of a moon goddess in Central America. Unfortunately, each mention of her was tangential, undeveloped, essentially underplayed. The streaming brightness of conqueror sun filled page after page but it was the singular, erratic beams of moon which started our hearts turning to match her orbit. A deep desire was born. Discover, uncover, recover. Piece together the fragments of a reality so diminished by time and oppression as to seem lost forever. I speak of the reality of Ix Hun Ahau, the life of Lady-Unique-One, an American goddess worshipped in our hemisphere for centuries.

Ix Chel (*lady-unique-inclination-of-the-night,* cycle 5, autumn 1980, title-page).

She who is of us, we who are of her. . . . This goddess comes to us in our bodies. She enters through our eyes, our teeth, our nostrils. She resides within us but we do not know her. She was our land long before we lived here but we would not recognize her name. Diana, Isis, Aphrodite, Persephone, these are the classic goddesses whose stories we have inherited as one result of the dominance of western, white culture. We have never been taught the names of the goddesses of the Americas. And yet, goddess worship was a profoundly evident source of belief and power on this side of the world when the Spanish invaded in the 16th century. To the list of known goddesses we must add the names of Ix Hun Ahau, Ix Chel, Coatlicue, Tlazoteotl, and Xochiquetzal, those whose realm of being was destroyed by the advancement of the Europeans on this continent" (1976:42).

‡   "Ix Chel is Lady-Unique-Inclination-of-the-Night, moon goddess of the Americas. She is the Goddess, the Lady-Unique-All-Embracer whose domain extended through Southern Mexico, the Yucatan Peninsula, and Central America as far as El Salvador. It is difficult to assess the specific time period of her influence; she was still actively worshipped at the time of the Spanish Conquest of Mexico. The history of the period states that one of the *conquistadores . . .* landed on an island off the coast of Yucatan sometime around 1517 and found it overspread with female idols. . . . Other sources state that only women were found living there and, consequently, the island was named Isla de Mujeres (Island of Woman). The history of Ix Chel's reign before the Conquest probably extends back to the early beginning of Mayan culture especially in her function as Earth Mother and goddess of becoming (i.e. birth). . . . Her reign as the most prominent female deity in the Mayan world lasted approximately nine hundred years, spanning the classic and post-classic periods (600 A.D.–1500 A.D.). Contemporary Mayans still sense her presence in their world. They call her 'The Queen,' 'Our Grandmother,' 'Our Mother,' and 'The White Lady.' She is as she has been for centuries.

"Known most widely as Ix Chel, she had innumerable other names which designated her functions, aspects, and relations with the world. As creation goddess she was called Lady-Unique-Queen-of-the-Paint. She colors the things of the earth and by doing so brings them life.

"Because the moon goddess was the first person on earth to weave, she was deemed patroness of the art of weaving. (It is important to note that this goddess is always represented as a woman on earth. She is a personal being. Her story is the eternal story of each woman who identifies with her.) Her name as patroness of weaving is Ix Chebel Yax, the young goddess. In the ancient books, or codices as they are called, she is pictured with a spindle of spun cotton in her headdress. The present day Lacandon Indians of Chiapas, Mexico, picture her carrying loom sticks with her on the nightly journey across the sky. She crosses them in front of her to protect against savage cosmic jaguars lurking behind the stars. Weaving is her art alone, her primal creative self expressed. In the earliest myths, before the sun knew her, she weaved apart in solitude. She was represented as a beautiful spider, the web was the world and she was at its center. Weaving is the female metaphor for making the world just as 'making milpa' (designating a squared off area for corn to grow) is the male metaphor for the same act. Ix Chebel Yax incorporates the power of the spider. Only she can be called upon to heal the bites inflicted by spiders. Spider power is an ancient attribute of women's culture in North and South America. In our country Spiderwoman of the Navajos sits atop 800 foot Spider Rock in Canyon de Chelly, Arizona, managing the world as she sees fit from her isolated promontory. . . .

Mayan goddess statue from the Yucatan (Lehner 1969:26, fig. 62).

"Ancient Maya women knew Ix Chel most intimately as the Ix U Sihnal, Moon Patroness of Birth. Their deepest dreams and their most profound personal desires were answered through the mediation of the moon goddess. It was she who allowed conception, she who made birth of a living child possible. The moon is the place of generation. Most probably every Maya woman owned a figurine of Ix Chel or an even more elaborate altar to her honor. A woman in labor placed the figurine beneath her bed to ease the pain and insure the life of the child. A woman desiring to get pregnant did the same. The most famous shrine to Ix Chel on the Yucatan Peninsula of Mexico and Cozumel Island were visited by thousands of women yearly from all over the Mayan world. Some must have travelled hundreds of miles, over months of time, to reach the sacred places. It was the desire of every woman to make a pilgrimage, at least once in her lifetime, to one of the major shrines. Picture hundreds of women in dugout canoes, paddling across the 20 miles that separate Cosumel Island from the mainland, all intent on their devotion to the one who belongs to them, who makes them the bearers of life. . . . The moon goddess is the cosmic source for identifying this [inner female] rhythm; she is defined as owning the cycles of the universe. Women came to know themselves through reliance on her image as a model of behavior. In essence the ability to conceive and bear children happily was primarily a result of the relationship between an individual woman and Ix Chel. The role of the male, the need for intercourse, was not directly assumed to be influential. The belief that conception can most easily occur under the favor of the full moon is still a part of Maya folklore.

"Contemporary Maya refer to the moon goddess as wife of the sun. The progress of her history demonstrates the subjugations of her power and independence. In ancient days she was Ix Hun Ahau, translated Lady Number One, associated with the primordial emergence of meaning. She was called virgin, one-in-herself. Like all the great goddesses, she was a woman unto herself (Esther Harding's definition of the title Virgin). Her relationship with Itzamna (Iguana House, the major male creator god) could not be fixed in marriage. She was his consort as he was hers but each functioned primarily in their individual capacities as goddess and god. Ix Chel was known as the fickle one, attracted to various men but owned by none. Many of the myths about her indicate the attempt of the gods to harness her. But she refuses to be controlled. No sooner does she marry Sun, than she begins to have an affair with Venus, Sun's older brother. Upon discovering them, Sun plays a

Mayan goddess statue from the Yucatan (Lehner 1969:26, fig. 61).

vengeful trick on them which upsets Moon so much that she leaves Sun and goes to live with the king vulture. Sun eventually discovers the whereabouts of Moon through trickery and forces her to return with him. But she never willingly submits to him. In fact, one of the most significant aspects of the mythology about Ix Chel is that she does not have a vagina until Sun enlists a deer to trample her so that he can have intercourse with her. Clearly, she is forced to lose her virginity, her precious self apart, for the satisfaction of Sun (i.e. male society). Another legend tells of Sun decreasing the brightness of Moon's light by plucking one of her eyes out. These are the cruel images of suppression and subordination. It is for us to remember the time before her brightness was diminished, before the trampling of deer hoofs, the time in which she lived of herself, for herself. In the knowledge of her freedom is a source of our own deliverance" (Turner 1976:43–46; also see Anton 1973:64).

(Harter 1978a:28)

In Judeo-Christian tradition "the curse" is exactly that—a legacy from Eve's disobedience in the Garden of Eden. Roman Catholics came to believe that the Virgin Mary transcended that denunciation and vanquished the serpent, which had long since shed its lunar associations of wisdom and immortality and come to embody everything evil. "The penalty of eating the fruit of knowledge offered by the snake was partly the curse of menstruation; and the implication of the Immaculate Conception, whereby Mary conquers the serpent, is that she is spared it" (Warner 1976:268; also see Eliade 1958: 163–69).

At first glance the notion of a curse seems implicit in the following Tukano Indian myth about the origin of menstruation. However, it is the Sun father whose "wickedness" is remembered monthly, *not* an original sin of the Daughter of the Sun. Anthropologist Gerardo Reichel-Dolmatoff collected many narratives like this and extensively discussed their implications with Antonio Guzmán, a Desana Indian from the interior Amazon region close to the Colombian-Brazilian frontier who in 1966 was living in Bogotá. Guzmán apparently told the anthropologist that menstrual or "sun blood" serves as "a permanent reminder to humanity of the prohibition against incest," and "menstruation is then an occasion surrounded with shame and anxiety because the condition of the woman is a living memory of a criminal act that weighs continually on the conscience of humanity." Even the Moon's celestial cycle coincides with women's menstrual one to emphasize his brother's crime, for "he hides each month for three nights, and when he shows his full face the spots of blood of the Daughter of the Sun are on it" (Reichel-Dolmatoff 1971:60).

The daughter of the Sun had not yet reached puberty when her father made love to her. The Sun committed incest with her at Wainambi Rapids, and her blood flowed forth; since then, women must lose blood every month in remembrance of the incest of the Sun and so that this great wickedness will not be forgotten. But his daughter liked it and so she lived with her father as if she were his wife. She thought about sex so much that she became thin and ugly and lifeless. Newly married couples become pale and thin because they only think of the sexual act, and this is called *gamúri.* But when the Daughter of the Sun had her second menstruation, the sex act did harm to her and she did not want to eat anymore. She lay down on a rock, dying; her imprint there can still be seen on a large boulder at Wainambi Rapids. When the Sun saw this, he decided to make *gamú bayári,* the invocation that is made when the girls reach puberty. The Sun smoked tobacco and revived her. Thus, the Sun established customs and invocations that are still performed when young girls have their first menstruation. (Reichel-Dolmatoff 1971:28–29; for other such origin myths see, e.g., Leach 1972:707; Neithammer 1977:37–38.)

The Lord said to Moses and Aaron, . . . "When a woman has a discharge of blood which is her regular discharge from her body, she shall be in her impurity for seven days, and whoever touches her shall be unclean until the evening. And everything upon which she lies during her impurity shall be unclean; everything also upon which she sits shall be unclean. And whoever touches her bed shall wash his clothes, and bathe himself in water, and be unclean until the evening. And whoever touches anything upon which she sits shall wash his clothes, and bathe himself in water, and be unclean until the evening. And whoever touches anything upon which she sits shall wash his clothes, and bathe himself in water, and be unclean until the evening; whether it is the bed or anything upon which she sits, when he touches it he shall be unclean until the evening. And if any man lies with her, and her impurity is on him, he shall be unclean seven days; and every bed on which he lies shall be unclean.

—*Leviticus* 15:1, 19–24 (RSV).

If a man lies with a woman having her sickness, and uncovers his nakedness, he has made naked her fountain, and she has uncovered the fountain of her blood; both of them shall be cut off from among their people.

—*Leviticus* 20:18 (RSV).

★ "According to the rules laid down in *Leviticus,* all kinds of dire penalties ensue for the male who has congress with a menstruating female, including various forms of skin diseases. The rationale which lies behind these interdictions are protective—not for the man or woman, but for the child; it is thought that a child born of such a union may be scrofulous, feeble-minded, crippled, epileptic, or insane. Nevertheless, the menstruating female, who must avoid her husband, is not prohibited from baking the Sabbath bread, worshipping in the synagogue, blessing the candles, or preparing and serving food. Recent researches have uncovered the fact that menstruation as a special state is operative *only* for the matron and not for the girl. An unmarried Jewish girl does not have to observe the ceremonial purification in the *mikva* (ritual bath), which married women must take seven days after the cessation of the flow. This involves three total immersions of the body in a pool of 'living water.' After this has been done, the woman may then resume her conjugal duties" (Joffe in Leach 1972:706).

★ "According to the Talmud, if a woman at the beginning of her period passes between two men, she thereby kills one of them; if she passes between them toward the end of her period, she only causes them to quarrel violently" (Frazer 1913:83).

More often than not, in cultures throughout the world, "the menstruating woman is believed to emit a *mana,* or threatening supernatural power . . . [and] the taboos of menstruation are practices that help others to avoid her and her dangerous influence and that enable her to get through the menstrual period without succumbing to her own deadly power" (Delaney et al 1976:5). Examples of such beliefs, which almost always include prohibitions against sexual intercourse with a menstruating woman, abound—for example, in such diverse collections and studies as Sir James George Frazer's *The Golden Bough* (1911:145ff; 1913:22ff, esp. 76ff), H. R. Hays' *The Dangerous Sex* (1964), Janice Delaney, Mary Jane Lupton, and Emily Toth's *The Curse: A Cultural History of Menstruation* (1976), and Carolyn Neithammer's *Daughters of the Earth: The Lives and Legends of American Indian Women* (1977:49–52), among others.

Despite—or perhaps because of—the ambiguous powers attached to women's reproductive functions, in a significant number of societies world-wide, male initiation rites include symbolic and actual rituals of giving birth and even menstruation (see e.g., Eliade 1965). Delaney, Lupton and Toth bluntly state: "Not content to surround menstruation with images of filth and fear, man has tried for at least a few aeons to learn how to do it himself," and suggest that the term *saignade,* from *saigner* ("to bleed") be used to describe this equivalent to *"couvade,* the imagined motherhood of the male (from *couver,* 'to hatch')" (1976:205; also see Hand 1957). Their position about male initiation rites is similar to psychoanalyst Bruno Bettelheim's[6]:

Although classic anthropological explanations for the origin of circumcision claim that it is a hygienic practice, a preparation for sex life, a test of endurance, a tribal mark, a sacrifice to the goddess of fertility, or a sanctification of the generative faculties, such explanations tend to overlook that in causing himself to bleed from his genitals, man is *pretending to menstruate.* He is thereby recreating in himself the role that biology has assigned exclusively to women. *What actually happens* at adolescent circumcision is at least as important as the ceremony's sociological implications (ibid:208).

Nevertheless, anthropologist Mary Douglas points out that there are many important sociological meanings involving both couvade and menstruation. Surrounding the latter with elaborate rites and taboos can be used "(i) To assert male superiority"—females being unclean and thus inferior; "(ii) To assert separate male and female social spheres"—and to blame problems in the male one on trespassers from the female one; and "(iv) To lay claim to a special relationship"—basically proclaiming, e.g., a husband-wife relationship by observing avoidance customs (1975:62, 63). Interestingly, Douglas gives as her third functional category, "To attack a rival," claiming "women can fasten on these beliefs and use them against one another" by alleging transgression and thereby blaming the other for various misfortunes. This manipulation of a socially defined "dangerous" state points to the positive, creative aspects of menstruation and to a revaluation of it, intimations of which can be seen in the evolution of Ruth Underhill's work among the Arizona Papago Indians.

[6]Psychoanalyst Bruno Bettelheim rejects the orthodox Freudian position that initiation rites are a father's attempts to enforce the incest taboo and instill castration anxiety in the sons of whom he is jealous. Bettelheim proceeds instead on "the premise that *one sex feels envy in regard to the sexual organs and functions of the other"* (1962:19). Thus, males are led to simulate female organs through "symbolic wounds" during rites of subincision and circumcision, while females' rites involve manipulation to enlarge clitoris and labia. Although he maintains that penis envy is equally fundamental psychologically, Bettelheim concentrates on what he calls "male envy of female sex functions" because when men play more important, and by common consent desirable, social roles women's envy of them is openly admissible whereas men's envy of women's roles is considered "unnatural and immoral." He suggests that "one of the reasons why boys' initiation rites are usually much more complex than girls' is that in many societies women can express their envy of men openly, while men's comparable envy can be expressed only in ritual" (1962:56).

Papago basket design (Sides 1961: plate 43, fig. f).

Anthropologist Ruth Murray Underhill studied Papago Indian songs and ceremonies in 1931 and 1933, and described them in *Singing for Power* (1938). In a chapter entitled "Dangerous Woman," she contrasted women's "barren" monthly retreats with men's dream powers acquired during salt pilgrimages or through purificaiotn rites for scalping or eagle-killing:

Woman has, however, one direct contact with the supernatural denied to men. So mysterious do her female functions appear to the Papago that he places every woman, when under their magic influence, in the category of a man undergoing purification. No man would approach such a woman, any more than he would the scalper or the eagle-killer in his retreat. The awful power which fills her would disable him, destroy his weapons, and cripple his tools. Even a dish from which she had eaten would convey to him the contamination.

So he segregates her as he does the warrior, the salt pilgrim, and the eagle-killer. But her segregation is not for sixteen days which end in triumph. Once a month, the woman must leave her house and hide herself from the sun and fire. When her children are born, she must stay in retreat "until the moon comes back where it was" before she can be purified. She expects no dreams at this time, for she has performed no act of valor. Hers is a negative purification, ordained without her will and serving only to make her fit for human intercourse again. In preparation for this part of their lives, the women of the family build themselves a hut away from the main house. They do not regard their ostracism as a burden. From infancy they have expected it, as white girls might expect school and work. "It is not good when it is cold," they say. Otherwise, those monthly four days of peace and solitude are a sort of sabbath in their toilsome lives. So deeply do they feel their own dangerousness that they would not be happy in exposing their loved ones to it. There are Papago tales telling about lightning strokes which wiped out a whole family because one girl in it disobeyed the law. And a woman who visited a ceremony at this time would feel as guilty as a disease-carrier who distributed death among her unsuspecting kindred.

There are alleviations in this recurrent purification which the men do not have. The woman, who will have no visitors, need not fast. She is not forbidden the society of other women who know the mystery. So, for the only times in her life, she is away from the baby and the housework. She can sit at the door of her hut and chat with her friends, and her husband may not even call to her. No matter what she has left undone, and no matter what there is to do, she has a holiday. The villagers tell of women who always found themselves "dangerous" when their husbands grew quarrelsome. It has compensations. (Underhill 1973:125–27)

Papago basket design (Sides 1961:pl. 43, fig. e).

Interestingly, in her 1965 study of *Red Man's Religion: Beliefs and Practices of the Indians North of Mexico,* Underhill included some of this material in a chapter entitled "Woman Power." She quoted parts of her earlier interviews:

"Did some spirit make these rules?" I asked my Papago informants. They shook their heads.

"No spirit. Just got to do it. Like you come in when it rains."

"And if you do not come in? I mean, go to your special hut?"

"Maybe flood. Fire. People die."

The penalty, it appeared, might fall upon the whole village. . . .

This dread and exclusion seems not to have impressed the women of olden times with any sense of inferiority. "Do you mind being sent out of the house?" I once asked a Papago woman undergoing her days of separation. She laughed at me.

"Mind! Why, it's a holiday for us women. No work to do, no matter how the men may want it."

"You don't mind-er-people knowing?"

Now she was amazed. "Why should we? That is the time when we are powerful and the men are afraid. We like to see them slinking past with their backs turned." Then she chuckled. "No matter what my husband wants me to do in these days, he can't make me do it."

In fact, stories told by the women often deal with the way in which the men have been routed and frustrated by this power unattainable to them. Women did not mind letting the men conduct ceremonies and have visions while they, the females, attended to the essentials of propagating the race and providing it with food and shelter. (Underhill 1965:52)

Still another old woman decried the abandonment of these customs, claiming that "lots of trouble come because we Bean People forget that." According to Underhill: "She meant the ancient belief that woman, at her periods, is the vessel of a supernatural Power, the power that allows her to give birth . . . [which] is so different from the man's power to hunt and kill that the two must be kept apart" (ibid:51). Throughout this chapter, which includes customs from many tribes, Underhill makes explicit what was only implied in her 1938 chapter on "Dangerous Woman," namely, that women were *not,* as in *Leviticus,* considered unclean but rather viewed as full of sacred power for the propagation of the race.

Anthropologist Marla N. Powers focuses on this distinction in her analysis of Oglala myths and rituals associated with the girl's puberty ceremony, menstruation and sexual conduct. She suggests that the notion that menstruating women are somehow dirtied or defiled or degraded reflects a Western bias, giving as one example Sherry B. Ortner's interpretation of the Crow Indians' prohibition against menstruating women participating in ceremonies as symbolic defilement. According to Powers, "there is no empirical evidence that the Crow themselves share her interpretation" (1980:56). Among her countering examples is a statement from a personal interview with Philip Deere, a Muskogee from Oklahoma:

"Woman is the same as man—but at a certain age she changes into another stage of life. During this stage she *naturally* purifies herself each month. During their monthly time women *separate themselves* [my (Powers') emphasis] from men. Men must sweat [take a sweat bath] once a month while women are naturally purifying themselves to keep their medicine effective" (Powers 1980:57).

Certainly the creative power of a menstruating woman is suggested in a Southeastern Yuchi Indian creation myth collected by W. O. Tuggle in the late nineteenth century. Various animals have dived for and arranged the land, and both the stars and the moon have contributed some light, "but it was still dark":

T-cho, the Sun, said: "You are my children, I am your mother, I will make the light. I will shine for you."
She went to the east. Suddenly light spread over all the earth. As she passed over the earth a drop of blood fell from her to the ground, and from this blood and earth sprang the first people, the children of the Sun, the Uchees. (Swanton 1929:84)[7]

It should be noted, however, that such important mythological precedent did not mean that mortal, menstruating women were freed from taboo and seclusion (Speck 1909:96–97).

Although she recalls her mother referring to a menstruating woman as "unclean" (possibly a translation problem), the Winnebago Indian Mountain Wolf Woman clearly experienced an increment in power during her first menses:

Then I lived at home and the family went on a short hunting trip. After that they went off to find cranberries and on our return we stopped at the home of grandfather Náqi-Johnga. There it was that mother told me how it is with little girls when they become women. "Some time," she said, "that is going to happen to you. From about the age of thirteen years this happens to girls. When that happens to you, run to the woods and hide some place. You should not look at any one, not even a glance. If you look at a man you will contaminate his blood. Even a glance will cause you to be an evil person. When women are in that condition they are unclean." Once, after our return to grandfather's house, I was in that condition when I awoke in the morning.
Because mother had told me to do so, I ran quite far into the woods where there were some bushes. The snow was still on the ground and the trees were just beginning to bud. In the woods there was a broken tree and I sat down under this fallen tree. I bowed my head with my blanket wrapped over me and there I was, crying and crying. Since they had forbidden me to look around, I sat there with my blanket over my head. I cried. Then, suddenly I heard the sound of voices. My sister Hińakega and my sister-in-law found me. Because I had not come back in the house, they had looked for me. They saw my tracks in the snow, and by my tracks they saw that I ran. They trailed me and found me. "Stay here," they said.

---

[7] Anthropologist Frank G. Speck discusses three other variants of this myth. In one, the sun is male and later in the narrative "a woman in a vague way became the mother of a boy, who originated from a drop of her menstrual blood" (1909:105). The second is similar to Tuggle's, beginning with the line: "The Sun deity was in her menstrual course" (ibid:106). The third depicts the Moon "in her menstrual course." It is the Sun who picks up the drop of her blood, wraps it, and stores it for four days. "When the bundle was opened, he saw that it had turned into a human being. Then he said: 'You are my son. . . .' " (ibid:107).

"Frame of Ojibwa Wig-e-wam"
(Morgan 1881:117, fig. 7).

"We will go and make a shelter for you," and they went home again. Near the water's edge of a big creek, at the rapids of East Fork River, they built a little wigwam. They covered it with canvas. They built a fire and put straw there for me, and then they came to get me. There I sat in the little wigwam. I was crying. It was far, about a quarter of a mile from home. I was crying and I was frightened. Four times they made me sleep there. I never ate. There they made me fast. That is what they made me do. After the third time that I slept, I dreamed.

There was a big clearing. I came upon it, a big, wide open field, and I think there was a rise of land there. Somewhat below this rise was the big clearing. There, in the wide meadow, there were all kinds of horses, all colors. I must have been one who dreamed about horses. I believe that is why they always used to give me horses. (Lurie 1961:22–23)[8]

Menarche was particularly auspicious and dangerous. During the early 1900s, photographer, writer and explorer Edward S. Curtis collected a cau-

[8]Considering the possible spiritual gains during any menstrual period, folklorist Kay Turner reports how: "In northern California several women have constructed menstrual huts as ritual retreats where they can go during their monthly periods. Painting the red quarter moon on their foreheads as a symbol of their special condition, they use the time spent in the hut for experiencing and affirming the culmination of cyclic process. It is a time for meditation and separation, but separation without the patriarchal connotations of impurity, defilement and unworthiness. The menstrual flow is equated with the particular power of the feminine and time spent apart in the hut is for personally determining the course of that power" (1978:22, citing Mountaingrove and Culpepper 1976:64). Also see, e.g., Rush 1976; Budapest 1980; various articles in Spretnak 1982.

tionary tale about this powerful time from Jack Franco (Otíla), "a northwestern Maidu of the Valley division," in northern California. Similar stories were probably used in various tribes to insure and reinforce observance of menstrual taboos.

There was a girl who has having her first menses. Instead of going into the grass hut, she went into the mountains with her husband. She told him to climb a digger-pine and throw down some cones. He climbed up and threw down a cone. He said, "Try it; see if they are ripe."

She struck it with a stone and hurt her finger. She looked at it, and struck again, and again the stone struck her finger. She looked long at the finger.

The man in the tree was watching. He asked, "How is it?" He was wondering what she would do with the blood.

She answered, "It is all right." She licked off the blood. Again she struck her finger, and again licked off the blood. She kept licking at her blood, and then began to eat her flesh, singing, *"Dámiyâta péâ mísin* ['I-am-crazy eating myself']!" She devoured her whole body up to the chest. The man was still in the tree.

She said, "Come down, let us go home." But he feared to come down. He left his voice in the tree, and leaped down on the other side upon a rock, and ran away. The girl was rolling about on the ground. She hurled herself against the tree, and there was a crash like thunder. The tree shook, but the man did not fall down. Again and again she did this. Then she called out, "Come down!"

The voice in the tree answered, "I am coming."

At length she said, "He must be deceiving me." She went around the tree and saw where he had leaped upon the rock, and followed him, rolling along the ground. She would strike the rocks with the crash of thunder. Then she overtook the man and struck him. He was thrown high into the air, and when he fell he lay there a mere head with arms and chest. They went into the sky and became the thunder.

When mosquitoes get their stomachs full of blood, they take it to her, but they do not tell that they obtain it from people, lest she strike and kill people for their blood. They tell her it comes from oaks, so she strikes trees in hope of finding blood in them. (Curtis 1924:176)

"Maidu Lodge in the High Sierra"
(Morgan 1881:111, fig. 3).

The power of menstruation was also impressed upon the (unnamed by agreement) Fox woman whose autobiography, "written in the current syllabary," ethnologist Truman Michelson obtained in the summer of 1918. According to Michelson: "No attempt was made to influence the informant in any way; so that the contents are the things which seemed of importance to herself. It may be noted that at times the original autobiography was too naïve and frank for European taste; and so a few sentences have been deleted" (1925:295).

And then I was thirteen years old. "Now is the time when you must watch yourself; at last you are nearly a young woman. Do not forget this which I tell you. You might ruin your brothers if you are not careful. The state of being a young woman is evil. The manitous hate it. If any one is blessed by a manitou, if he eats with a young woman he is then hated by the one who blessed him and the (manitou) ceases to think of him. That is why it is told us, 'be careful' and why we are told about it beforehand. At the time when you are a young woman, whenever you become a young woman, you are to hide yourself. Do not come into your wickiup. That is what you are to do." She [mother] frightened me when she told me.

Lo, sure enough when I was thirteen and a half years old, I was told, "Go get some wood and carry it on your back." It was nearly noon when I started out. When I was walking along somewhere, I noticed something strange about myself. I was terribly frightened at being in that condition. I did not know how I became that way. "This must be the thing about which I was cautioned when I was told," I thought.

I went and laid down in the middle of the thick forest there. I was crying, as I was frightened. It was almost the middle of summer after we had done our hoeing. After a while my mother got tired of waiting for me. She came to seek me. Soon she found me. I was then crying hard.

"Come, stop crying. It's just the way with us women. We have been made to be that way. Nothing will happen to you. You will have gotten over this now in the warm weather. Had it happened to you in winter you would have had a hard time. You would be cold when you bathed as you would have to jump into the water four times. That is the way it is when we first have it. Now, to-day, as it is warm weather, you may swim as slowly as you like when you swim," I was told. "Lie covered up. Do not try to look around. I shall go and make (a wickiup) for you," I was told.

I was suffering very much there in the midst of the brush. And it was very hot.

It was in the evening when I was told, "At last I have come for you. I have built (a place) for you to live in. Cover your face. Do not think of looking any place." I was brought there to the small wickiup. And I was shut off by twigs all around. There was brush piled up so that I could not see through it. There was only a little space where I lived to cook outside. My grandmother must have made it a size so that there was only room for us to lie down in.

"I shall fetch your grandmother to be here with you," my mother told me. It was another old woman. As a matter of fact the reason she was brought there was for to give me instructions. I did not eat all day long. The next day I was told, "We shall fetch things for you to use in cooking." I was not hungry as I was frightened. The next day my grandmother went to eat. It was only as long as she (took) when she went to eat that I was alone, but I was afraid. In the evening I was brought little buckets to cook with, any little thing to eat, water and wood. Then for the first time I cooked.

And my grandmother would keep on giving me instructions there, telling me how to lead a good life. She really was a very old woman. Surely she must have spoken the truth in what she had been saying to me. "My grandchild," she would say to me, "soon I shall tell you how to live an upright life. To-day you see how old I am. I did exactly what I was told. I tried and thought how to live an upright life. Surely I have reached an old age," she told me. "That is the way you should do, if you listen to me as I instruct you. Now as for your mother, I began giving her instructions before she was grown up, every time I saw her. Because she was my relative is why I gave her instructions, although she was well treated by her father's sister by whom she was reared. That is why she knows how to make things which belong to the work of us women. If you observe the way your mother makes anything, you would do well, my grandchild. And this. As many of us as entered young womanhood, fasted. It was very many days: some fasted ten days, some four, five, every kind of way. To-day, to be sure, things are changing. When I was a young woman I fasted eight days. We always fasted until we were grown up," my grandmother told me.

My mother only came to fetch me water and little sticks of wood so that I might kindle a fire when I cooked. And we made strings. That is what we did.

"Do not touch your hair: it might all come off. And do not eat sweet things. And if what tastes sour is eaten, one's teeth will come out. It is owing to that saying that we are afraid to eat sweet things," my grandmother told me. She always gave me good advice from time to time. "Well, there is another thing. Now the men will think you are mature as you have become a young woman, and they will be desirous of courting you. If you do not go around bashfully, for a long time they will not have the audacity to court you. When there is a dance, when there are many boys saying all sorts of funny things, if you do not notice it, they will be afraid of you for a very long time. If you laugh over their words, they will consider you as naught. They will begin bothering you right away. If you are immoral your brothers will be ashamed, and your mother's brothers. If you live quietly they will be proud. They will love you. If you are only always making something in the same place where you live, they will always give you something whenever they get it. And your brothers will believe you when you say anything to them. When one lives quietly the men folks love one. And there is another thing. Some of the girls of our generations are immoral. If one goes around all the time with those who are immoral, they would get one in the habit of doing so, as long as one has not much intelligence. Do not go around with the immoral ones, my grandchild," my grandmother told me. "And this. You are to treat any aged person well. He(she) is thought of by the manitou; because he (she) has conducted his (her) life carefully is why he (she) has reached an old age. Do not talk about anyone. Do not lie. Do not steal. If you practice stealing, you will be wretched. Do not (be stingy) with a possession of which you are fond. (If you are stingy) you will not get anything. If you are generous you will (always) get something. Moreover, do not go around and speak crossly toward anyone. You must be equally kind to (every) old person. That, my grandchild, is a good way to do," my grandmother said to me. She was indeed always instructing me what to do.

Soon I had lived there ten days. "Well, at last you may go and take a bath," my mother said to me. We started to the river. "Take off your waist," I was told. After I had taken it off I leaped into the water. Then, "I am going to peck you with something sharp," I was told. "Only use your skirt as a breechcloth," is what I was told. I was also pecked on my thighs. "It will be that you will not menstruate much if the blood flows plentifully," I was told. I was made to suffer very much. I put on other garments. I threw away those which I had formerly been

(Harter 1978b:36)

wearing around. And then for the first time I looked around to see. And again I had to cook alone for myself outside for ten days. After ten days I again went to bathe. And then for the first time I began to eat indoors with (the others).

I told my mother, "My grandmother has been instructing me what I should do," I said to her. She laughed. "That is why I went after her, so she would instruct you thoroughly in what is right. 'She might listen to her,' is what I thought of you."

And I began to be told to make something more than ever. Moreover, when she made a basket, she said to me, "You (make one)." I would make a tiny basket. Later on the ones which I made were large ones. And then I was fifteen years old. (Michelson 1925:303–309)

Menarche is a joyful time among the Navajo Indians of the Southwest. The community joins in a four-night ceremony held at once or as soon as possible after the girl's first menstruation. Called the Kinaaldá, the ceremony includes songs, prayers, purification rites, races, the distribution of food and the "molding" or "straightening" of the girl's body. "Being part of the Blessing Way complex, the Kinaaldá is prophylactic, rather than curative; it ushers the girl into society, invokes positive blessings on her, insures her health, prosperity, and well-being, and protects her from potential misfortune" (Frisbie 1967:9; also see Lincoln 1981:17–33).

The mythological prototype for this ceremony is found in Changing Woman's Kinaaldá. According to anthropologists Clyde Kluckhohn and Dorothea Leighton, Changing Woman is "the favored figure among the Holy People." She played an important role in the creation of human beings and helped teach them to live in harmony with various malevolent and benevolent forces. Perhaps in all Navajo mythology, only she "is uniformly trustworthy and gratifying." Nowadays, "Changing Woman, ever young and ever radiant in beauty, lives in a marvelous dwelling on western waters," a residence she steadfastly refuses to change (Kluckhohn and Leighton 1962:181, 199).

In the following version of Changing Woman's birth and early life, she is called White Bead Woman.[9] The narrative is part of a long series of origin myths transcribed by Aileen O'Bryan for seventeen days during November 1928. These were told to her by a Navajo elder, Sandoval—Hastin Tlo'tsi (Old Man Buffalo Grass), who was told the stories "by his grandmother, Esdzan Hosh kige [whose] ancestor was Esdzan at a', the medicine woman who had the Calendar Stone in her keeping." They were "interpreted" by his nephew, Sam Ahkeah (O'Bryan 1956:vii, 1). O'Bryan's text is reproduced directly from the original Bureau of American Ethnology Bulletin 163 (1956: 71–75). Her bibliographic references will be found in the note.[10]

[9]Leland C. Wyman discusses various explanations offered for Changing Woman's name—"that she was born with the power of senescence and rejuvenation"; that she is the earth and its changing seasons; or that she changed her costume four times at her puberty ceremonial—and hence could appear as White Shell (or Bead) Woman, Turquoise Woman, Abalone Woman, or Jet Woman (1970:32). Also see a Jungian interpretation of Changing Woman in Moon (1970:166–83). The Navajo House Blessing Ceremony is also related to the myth of Changing Woman (McAllester and McAllester 1980; Frisbie 1980).

[10]O'Bryan's references (1956:185, 186):

Franciscan Fathers.
1910. An ethnologic dictionary of the Navajo language. 536 pp. Saint Michaels, Ariz.
1912. A vocabulary of the Navajo language . . . 2 vols. Saint Michaels, Ariz.
Matthews, Washington.
1886. Navajo names for plants. Amer. Naturalist, vol. 20, pp. 767–777.
1897. Navaho legends. Collected and translated . . . Mem. Amer. Folk-Lore Soc., vol. 5. Boston and New York.

A short interpretive (Jungian) summary of the ritual in Sandner (1979:122–32) is interesting. Notable studies of other girls' puberty rites include Driver 1941; Brown 1963; Farrer 1980; Lincoln 1981.

THE STORY OF THE COMING OF THE WHITE BEAD WOMAN [41]

All during this time First Man and First Woman lived on the top of Dzil na'odili, also called Chol'i'i.[42] This is the sacred mountain near Farmington, N. Mex. (See fig. 10.) The circle on top of this mountain is a cloud (fig. 11). Chol'i'i was completely hidden at first, then the bands or clouds rose and the mountain was seen. This is the sacred story which the old medicine men keep to themselves.

Figure 12 shows the cradle and how the baby in it lay. The cradleboard is the rainbow.[43]

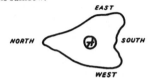

EAST

NORTH   SOUTH

WEST

THE POLES ARE IN THE CENTER

FIGURE 10.—The sacred mountain Dzil na'odili, also called Chol'i'i.

FIGURE 11.—The cloud circle on top of the mountain.

1. *THE RING OVER THE BABY'S HEAD.*
2. *THE BABY'S HEAD.*
3. *THE RAIN STRING.*
4. *THE FOOT BOARD IS THE SUN DOG.*
5. *THE LIGHTNING STRINGS.*
6. *THE CRADLE BOARD IS THE RAINBOW.*

FIGURE 12.—The cradle of the White Bead Baby.

---

[41] Matthews (1897, pp. 104–105).
Recorder's note: He says that two sisters were the mothers of the "Twins"; one, Estsanatlehi, was the Woman-Who-Changes (the turquoise image), and that Yol'kai estan is the White Bead Woman. The Sun and the Water Fall were the fathers of the boys. Lummis, in Pueblo Indian Folk Stories, associates the mother of the Twins with the moon. Whitman follows Matthews. But both the informant and the interpreter agreed that certain medicine men differ.
[42] Interpreter's note: The mountain on which the White Bead Baby was found is sometimes designated as Chol'i', and sometimes as the Mountain of the East, Sis'na'jin.
[43] Franciscan Fathers (1910, pp. 46–47, and 1912, p. 156: natsi'lid, rainbow.

◆   Penelope Washbourn, *Becoming Woman:* "In primitive cultures, the onset of menstruation is an ambiguous experience to be celebrated as well as feared. This explains why the rituals appear to fall into two categories, a cause of dancing and a cause for seclusion of the girl. In either case, the ritual marks an understanding that the girl needs a symbolic, interpretive framework as she negotiates her first life crisis and redefines herself as a mature female. These rituals also express an understanding that discovering our identity as women is not to be a solitary struggle but is to be worked out within the context of the community. In each primitive ritual a form of self-transformation is expressed through trials, symbolic acts, and words which promote healing and integrate the forces at play. The girls and the community move into a new identity *through* the crisis" (1977:9).

The baby was the White Bead Baby, the female baby, and her cradle is called natsi'lid eta cote, the rainbow cut short. The baby was wrapped in four clouds, black, blue, yellow, and white, and the four vapors, and all the flowers with all their pollens. The baby's head was to the west and her feet were to the east.

First comes the story of the White Bead Baby and of her growth. One day the mountain Chol'i'i was hidden by clouds and First Man said to his wife: "Now for the whole day we have seen clouds over the mountain. There must be some reason for this." That night when he saw a fire on the top of the mountain First Man said: "All day the clouds have covered the mountain and now there is a fire there. There must be someone there. I will go and find him." His wife said: "No, stay at home. There are many monsters on the earth who eat people. It is not safe for you to go." But First Man said: "I will go. It must be the will of the Most High Power." The next day he started out, chanting as he walked. He called himself the Dawn Boy in the chant. He climbed the mountain, but he found nothing, neither fire nor hogan. All that second day the clouds hung over the mountain, and when First Man returned home that night both he and his wife saw the fire burning on top of Chol'i'i. The next day First Man went again to the mountain but he found no fire or home or sign, so he returned to his home. That night when he saw the fire burning brightly he planted two forked sticks and sighted the fire, so that on the following day he could look and see at what point the fire had burned. In the morning, when he looked through the forked sticks, he knew just where to go. He started out as before and he chanted as he walked, naming the mountain toward which he was going, until he reached the top. On the top of the mountain there was a heavy mist. In the center of it he heard a baby crying. Lightning flashed from the baby and First Man saw her on her cradle-board.[44]

First Man picked the baby up and carried her home to his wife. But the baby was tied firmly on the cradleboard and First Woman did not know how to untie the strings. Just at this time they heard a noise: "ho'ho'ho'hooo." Then another noise: "A'ow, a'ow, ho'ho'ho' hooo." And two men entered the home. One said that his name was Ni'hada ho'nigi (he was Hasjelti), the other said he was Ni'ha ha nigi (Hasjohon). They were the two Yei. They told First Man and his wife that the baby had been their plan, and they showed them how to untie the cradle strings and told them what each string meant. Next they told First Man to go out and cut two slabs of wood from a tree, and to mark the tree, and to make from oak the bow for over the baby's head. They told him that he must make a cradle like this first

[44] Informant's note: There is a chant sung here.

one. He must gather the soft bark from awae'ts al, the baby bush or cliff rose,[45] and place that on the board before putting the baby on it. So First Man went out and made the cradle as the Yei had directed, for they took away the cradle on which the baby had been found. But before the two Yei left First Man said: "Now she will be my daughter." His wife took the baby and breathed on her four times. "Now," she said, "she will be my daughter." And so the Yei left First Man and his wife.

First Woman washed the baby in a white bead basket, then in a turquoise basket, and in a white shell basket, and in a black jet basket. At the end of the second day the baby laughed for the first time and there came a man, Atse'hashke, the First Coyote, who said: "I was told that my grandchild laughed for the first time." A woman came saying: "I was told that my grandchild laughed for the first time." She was the Salt Woman. First Woman took charcoal and gave it to the Coyote saying: "This is the only thing that lasts." So he painted his nose with it and said: "I shall know all things. I shall live long by it." And First Woman also gave the Coyote salt. He swallowed it and said: "This shall be my meat. It will make my meat taste good." And satisfied with his gifts he departed. It was the Salt Woman who first gave the gift of salt to First Woman. Then the two Yei returned for their gifts. One was given white bead moccasins, and the other decorated leggings. They took them and went away satisfied.

Now that is why all persons present receive a little gift when a baby laughs for the first time.[46] And later, when the White Bead Woman went West to her home she gave the gifts of beautiful flowers, the rain, and the plants bearing fruits and seeds for food.

The third day the baby sat up, the fourth day she walked. When the baby stood First Man put her on his knee and sang:

> The old woman standing,
> The old woman standing,
> The old woman standing.
> The White Bead Girl is standing.

The chant continues. It tells what developed on each day and how the White Bead Girl grew until the thirteenth day when she had her monthly period. (The same things happen to girls now, but the days of the White Bead Girl became our years.) On the thirteenth day she went to her foster-mother and said: "Something unusual has passed through me." First Woman spoke: "That is your 'first race.'"

[45] Recorder's note: Matthews (1886, vol. 20, pp. 767–777): Cliff rose, Cowania mexicana Don, a way tsal, baby's bed. The soft shredded bark of the cliff rose is used to line the baby basket. Franciscan Fathers (1910, p. 197): awaetsae, baby's bedding.
[46] Informant's note: Origin of the First Laugh Ceremony.

350675—56——6

♦   "The ability of a young woman to 'successfully' negotiate the life crisis of menstruation depends first on a recognition of it as a crisis by the girl and by the community. Ignoring its importance leaves the individual to struggle alone with her feelings and fears and provides no means for their expression. *Recognizing* does not necessarily imply *discussing* or providing information, although facts about menstruation are important as a preparation for the actual onset. *Recognizing* means marking the occasion so that the girl is supplied a symbolic framework within which to find resources for her questions of meaning. To ignore the event means that the girl's new framework will be casually formed by fears and rumors and by what the culture of school and society teach her about the nature of her identity as a woman. . . ." (ibid:12–13).

182   CHAPTER 4

First Woman told her husband that their foster daughter had kin nas ta, her first race (first menstruation), also called her first cake.

They laid different kinds of blankets inside the home. Under them were the white flowers,[47] coyote robes, and such things. The girl lay stretched on these, face down. First Man shaped her all over. He pulled her hair down and she had a quantity of hair. He shaped her face and it was beautiful, and he dressed her in all the beautiful goods, beads, bracelets, and earrings. They let her hair hang down and they tied it at the neck with the rain string which hung down with her hair.

Then First Man and First Woman stepped outside the hogan and told her to run her first race, to go around a cedar tree yonder, as the sun travels, and return home. When she came back she looked from the doorway into the home and said: "You hid the ground with the beautiful goods, you hid the ground with the mixed chips of stones." Now this is what First Man and First Woman had said.

First man commenced planning where they should have the first chant over her. It was decided that it would be in the home on the top of the eight rings of the mountain called Dzil na'odili, at the home which is called hoghan ho'tez sos, Changeable House. The Home that Stretches Out, hogan na' hat tson'e is its second name.[48]

A great crowd gathered the evening of the fourth day. All the different people filled the home and there were 11 rings, or 11 circles, of people around it. As the chant was about to begin some people put their heads inside the home and said: "Why were we not invited?" And everyone said: "Come in. There is room in front for you." These newcomers were the Beautiful Goods People, a whole group of them. They sat in front of the others.

Two hogan chants were sung by the people who planned how the White Bead Baby should be found. Then the White Bead Girl stood up and said that there was something missing. "You have not called upon Tse an no'hoi begay hojone, the Most High Power Whose Ways Are Beautiful," she said. "He should be put into your songs. No one knows his real name, but you must use the one I give you." So all the people sang their chants using the names of the Most High Power and that of the White Bead Girl.[49]

About dawn two men came in and asked why they had not been invited. Their moccasins and leggings were white; they were beau-

---

[47] Interpreter's note: The white flowers are the mariposa lily. Recorder's note: Mariposa lily, according to Franciscan Fathers (1910, p. 193), altsi'ni, *Calochortus luteus.*

[48] Informant's note: A chant should be sung here. Today, in the chant, "white flowers" is probably used to designate beautiful goods.

[49] Informant's note: Chants are sung here. They tell how the baby was found, about her growth, her first "race" or "cake," and when she went to the West and returned. No one man knows all the chants, only one group of them.

---

tifully dressed, each having 21 tail feathers for the headdress, and on the top of each feather there perched a beautiful singing bird. They were the two Yei, Hasjelti, the Dawn, and Hasjohon, the Twilight. They received gifts and they came in and sang their chant, and the dawn broke and it was day.

So now each girl at the time of her first and second "race" has this chant held over her. Her cake is made of the different colored corn flavored with a kind of yeast. This latter is made by soaking wheat in water and when it ferments it is dried and ground into powder. It makes the corn cake very sweet.

In the morning the men receive some of the maiden's cake as their gift for their chants.[50] Today the young girl sits in the back of the hogan and the goods or gifts are piled in front of her, symbolic of the Beautiful Goods People who filled the front circle in the "hogan" when the White Bead Girl had her first chant. The young girl, today, has her hair tied with a strip of buckskin from a deer not killed by a weapon.[51]

Now after the ceremony or Night Chant over the White Bead Girl the people went their ways and left First Man and First Woman and their foster daughter to live by themselves. It happened soon after this that this holy girl wished for a mate. Every morning when the sun rose she lay on her back until noon, her head to the west and her feet to the east. From noon on she went to the spring. She lay under the ledge and let spring water drip over her body. This took place each day for 4 days.

THE WHITE BEAD MAIDEN'S MARRIAGE WITH THE SUN

First Man said upon coming home one day: "Over to the east, at the foot of the mesa, there are two different kinds of grass. Their ripening seeds are plentiful." So First Woman and the girl went down to gather the seeds. But when they got there they began to think of the monsters who roamed about the country and became frightened.[52] Looking about them carefully they hurriedly gathered only one kind of seed before they ran back to their home. When they reached their hogan the girl said: "Mother, I want to go back and collect the seeds from the other grass." First Woman said: "No, daughter, you can not go there alone. Some monster might catch you." But the girl insisted. She promised to be careful and to look out for herself.

---

[50] Informant's note: Certain men know the chants of the different people gathered there. There are 8 or 10 groups of these songs.

[51] Informant's note: Today, the hide of a deer not killed by a weapon, for example, by a car, is used ceremonially.

[52] Franciscan Fathers (1910, pp. 189–191; 1912, p. 172). Informant's and interpreter's note: Two kinds of grasses with edible seeds. These are mountain grasses, tlo'tso and tlo'tsosi, tlo'dahikhali and ndid lidi. Tlo dei is Chenopodium, seeds-falling grass. This is what is called hard seed grass, also pigweed.

◆ "To emerge gracefully from the life crisis of menstruation would imply in our society that we are able to celebrate the value of our female body structure as potentially childbearing without identifying ourselves with it. . . .

"To emerge enriched from the life crisis of menstruation implies finally trusting and liking one's body. . . .

"To emerge enhanced from the crisis of menstruation is to receive an increased sense of value as an individual and the goodness of one's body structure. It heightens rather than diminishes personhood. It gives pride and status rather than shame and mistrust" (ibid:17–18; also see Grahn 1982).

Like menarche, the climacteric in women also constitutes a "life crisis," although one for which there is little public rite of passage. Although in many cultures the woman past childbearing age is allowed greater license and is sought after for counsel and healing, unfortunately, Western denigration of the old wise woman or the wise old woman
has obscured her image
as a guide . . .

(Harter 1978b:24)

trivializing . . .

(Harter 1978b:55)

and debasing her.

"Satan holding court for newly annointed witches," in Gerard d'Euphrates, *Livre de l'histoire & ancienne cronique,* printed in E. Groulleau, Paris, 1549 (Lehner 1971:67, fig. 96).

(Harter 1980a:44)

Gnostic gem depicting "Osiris, or the 'Old Man,' . . . at the foot the celestial globe and Masonic pentagon, or Solomon's Seal: the field occupied by symbols and letters seemingly Hebrew. The whole design is mediaeval . . . most evidently bespeaking a Rosicrucian origin. Deeply cut in a coarse-grained Green Jasper" (King 1864:213, plate VI, no. 1).

The witchcraft trials of the Inquisition and later profoundly influenced Western views of women's wisdom, especially older women's.[11] Widely disseminated witch-hunters' "manuals" such as the Dominican monks Heinrich Kramer and Jakob Sprenger's 1486 *Malleus Maleficarum* ("Hammer of Witches") basically denied women's knowledge, linking it to the Devil, and vilified the traditional healers and midwives (Summers 1971). In their germinal *Witches, Midwives and Nurses: A History of Women Healers,* Barbara Ehrenreich and Deirdre English suggest the deep-seated consequences of these persecutions, which were more often directed at women than at men. They explore how in Western tradition "for centuries women were doctors [and pharmacists] without degrees"—"called 'wise women' by the people, witches or charlatans by the authorities," and how today this "birthright" of medicine has been usurped by male professionals and women relegated to subordinate status in the medical world (1973:3; also see Ehrenreich and English 1979:33–98; Horsley 1979: 78–82; Glendinning 1982). These profound, ambivalent attitudes toward women's wisdom persist in folk, popular and elite Western traditions, and they are especially pernicious when applied to old women.

Consider the following quotations from analytical psychologist C. G. Jung's 1948 paper on "The Phenomenology of the Spirit in Fairytales":

♦ The frequency with which the spirit-type appears as an old man is about the same in fairytales as in dreams. The old man always appears when the hero is in a hopeless and desperate situation from which only profound reflection or a lucky idea—in other words, a spiritual function or an endopsychic automatism of some kind—can extricate him. But since, for internal and external reasons, the hero cannot accomplish this himself, the knowledge needed to compensate the deficiency comes in the form of a personified thought, i.e., in the shape of this sagacious and helpful old man (1968:217–18).

♦ The old man thus represents knowledge, reflection, insight, wisdom, cleverness, and intuition on the one hand, and on the other, moral qualities such as goodwill and readiness to help, which make his "spiritual" character sufficiently plain (ibid:222).

♦ Just as all archetypes have a positive, favourable, bright side that points upwards, so also they have one that points downwards, partly negative and unfavourable, partly chthonic, but for the rest merely neutral. To this the spirit archetype is no exception. Even his dwarf form implies a kind of limitation and suggests a naturalistic vegetation-numen sprung from the underworld (ibid:226).

♦ The old man, then, has an ambiguous elfin character—witness the extremely instructive figure of Merlin—seeming, in certain of his forms, to be good incarnate and in others an aspect of evil (ibid:227).

[11]Literature on witchcraft is both extensive and uneven. However, two reasonably authoritative "encyclopedias" provide ready, useful reference—Robbins 1959 and Newall 1974. In *Drawing Down the Moon* (1979), Margot Adler examines "Witches, Druids, Goddess-Worshippers, and Other Pagans in America Today." Notable among contemporary practitioners is feminist witch Z (Zsuzsanna Emese) Budapest, high priestess of the Susan B. Anthony Coven Number One in Los Angeles, who has publishd two volumes entitled *The Holy Book of Women's Mysteries* (1979, 1980). Also see, e.g., Rush 1976; Forfreedom and Julie Ann 1980; Jong 1981; Noel 1981; various articles in Spretnak 1982.

◆ The figure of the superior and helpful old man tempts one to connect him somehow or other with God (ibid:225).

From a male point of view at least, the equivalent female guide figure is *not* an old, but . . .

(Harter 1980b:81)

a *young* woman, perhaps an anima figure (see chapter 3 above).

(Harter 1978b:83)

Thus, Jung's (and others') virtual paean to the old man in magic tales could not be countered (until, perhaps, recently) with an equivalent paean to the old woman in such stories. "Frau Holle" provides a good illustration of why this is so. Folklorist MacEdward Leach briefly traces the evolution of this figure from wise goddess to ugly old woman "bogey" (also see Widdowson 1973; Garbáty 1968:345):

Holde, Holle, Hulda, Hulle, or *Holl.* A Germanic goddess, especially of the Suevi, Hessians, and Thuringians, appearing in many manifestations. Early she was a sky goddess, often to be seen riding on the wind. Snow was said to be feathers from her bed, detached as she was making it up. Often in her wild rides through the sky she is accompanied by a procession of witchlike creatures. Women suspected of witchcraft were said to "ride with Holde." To her realm in the sky went the souls of unbaptized babies. Holde is also associated with lake and stream. At noon she can often be seen, a beautiful white lady, bathing in the lake, and as she is observed she disappears under the water. To reach her dwelling one must dive down a well. Holde is also a maternal deity and goddess of the hearth. She presides over spinning and especially the cultivation of flax. In this manifestation she is helpful and kind. . . .

At present Holde has degenerated into a folk bogey, an ugly old woman with long nose and thick hair, sometimes seen in the forest leading a flock of sheep or goats. Peasant mothers frighten their children into good behavior by telling them Holde will "get" them if they are not good. (in Leach 1972:500; also see Hall 1980:207–15)

"Frau Holle," Grimm's no. 24 (Aarne-Thompson tale type 480), is, according to folktale scholar Stith Thompson: "one of the most popular of oral tales, being distributed over nearly the whole world. It is found in almost all collections from every part of Europe, from southern and eastern Asia, from northern and central Africa, and from North and South America. In the western hemisphere it occurs in three widely separated American Indian tribes; in the French folklore of Louisiana, Canada, the West Indies, and French Guiana; and in the Spanish tradition of Peru and the Portuguese of Brazil. A cursory examination of appropriate bibliographical works shows nearly six hundred versions" (1946:126). The following has been reproduced from *The Red Fairy Book* (1890), edited by Andrew Lang (1966) and illustrated by Lancelot Speed.

♦   Nor Hall, "The Goddess in the Consulting Room: A Jungian Perspective": "Frau Holle or Mother Hulda assists in times of crucial passage. She is the fateful door—the measure of wisdom and maturity. We don't really know how to talk of the passage from immaturity to maturity; it is not a time-specific passage like puberty but rather one that has to do with *attitude* and not knowing oneself. In terms of the fairy tale, maturity may mean recognizing that Golden Girl and Dirty Girl are sisters in one psyche—or two faces/facets of a single girl. The threshold goddesses grace the places of psychic conversion. Their presence signals moments of feminine emergence and transformation; in dreams they appear behind specially marked doors, on landings between floors or rising from the water, turning out of the shadows, carrying mirrors. Of all the attributes the mirror is most common—a mirror is a speculum, an instrument for seeing—for rendering hidden parts accessible to observation. It's a peculiarly feminine instrument that literally reflects

(Harter 1978b:57)

MOTHER HOLLE

ONCE upon a time there was a widow who had two daughters; one of them was pretty and clever, and the other ugly and lazy. But as the ugly one was her own daughter, she liked her far the best of the two, and the pretty one had to do all the work of the house, and was in fact the regular maid of all work. Every day she had to sit by a well on the high road, and spin till her fingers were so sore that they often bled. One day some drops of blood fell on her spindle, so she dipped it into the well meaning to wash it, but, as luck would have it, it dropped from her hand and fell right in. She ran weeping to her stepmother, and told her what had happened, but she scolded her harshly, and was so merciless in her anger that she said:

'Well, since you've dropped the spindle down, you must just go after it yourself, and don't let me see your face again until you bring it with you.'

Then the poor girl returned to the well, and not knowing what she was about, in the despair and misery of her heart she sprang into the well and sank to the bottom. For a time she lost all consciousness, and when she came to herself again she was lying in a lovely meadow, with the sun shining brightly overhead, and a thousand flowers blooming at her feet. She rose up and wandered through this enchanted place, till she came to a baker's oven full of bread, and the bread called out to her as she passed:

'Oh! take me out, take me out, or I shall be burnt to a cinder. I am quite done enough.'

So she stepped up quickly to the oven and took out all the loaves one after the other. Then she went on a little farther and came to a tree laden with beautiful rosy-cheeked apples, and as she passed by it called out:

'Oh! shake me, shake me, my apples are all quite ripe.'

She did as she was asked, and shook the tree till the apples fell

like rain and none were left hanging. When she had gathered them all up into a heap she went on her way again, and came at length to a little house, at the door of which sat an old woman. The old dame had such large teeth that the girl felt frightened and wanted to run away, but the old woman called after her:

'What are you afraid of, dear child? Stay with me and be my little maid, and if you do your work well I will reward you handsomely; but you must be very careful how you make my bed—you must shake it well till the feathers fly; then people in the world below say it snows, for I am Mother Holle.'

She spoke so kindly that the girl took heart and agreed readily to enter her service. She did her best to please the old woman, and shook her bed with such a will that the feathers flew about like snow-flakes; so she led a very easy life, was never scolded, and lived on the fat of the land. But after she had been some time with Mother Holle she grew sad and depressed, and at first she hardly knew herself what was the matter. At last she discovered that she was homesick, so she went to Mother Holle and said:

'I know I am a thousand times better off here than I ever was in my life before, but notwithstanding, I have a great longing to go home, in spite of all your kindness to me. I can remain with you no longer, but must return to my own people.'

'Your desire to go home pleases me,' said Mother Holle, 'and because you have served me so faithfully, I will show you the way back into the world myself.'

So she took her by the hand and led her to an open door, and as the girl passed through it there fell a heavy shower of gold all over her, till she was covered with it from top to toe.

'That's a reward for being such a good little maid,' said Mother Holle, and she gave her the spindle too that had fallen into the well. Then she shut the door, and the girl found herself back in the world again, not far from her own house; and when she came to the courtyard the old hen, who sat on the top of the wall, called out:

'Click, clock, clack,
Our golden maid's come back.'

Then she went in to her stepmother, and as she had returned covered with gold she was welcomed home.

She proceeded to tell all that had happened to her, and when the mother heard how she had come by her riches, she was most

the *inside* of woman. The kind of insight these goddesses grant frees a person to move out of "stuck" or ingrown situations; such movement is essential to the rites of maturity. Maturity is rooted in knowing the favorable moment for passage and is related to the words for morning (*māne*), goodness (*manis*) and familial-ancestral-spirits (*mānes*). To be mature then means not only to be ripe like the full red sun at dawn and ready to cross the world horizon, but to recognize your spiritual ancestry in yourself—and to move accordingly" (1979:16).

◆ Nor Hall, *The Moon & The Virgin:* "The sister who followed the way of her despairing heart found her 'huldmoder,' her spindle (feminine identity), and her way home. She knew when it was time to return to the upperworld. Her longing for home, even though it had been so disheartening a place, shows her willingness (psychologically) to integrate newfound contents into consciousness. Every hero

anxious to secure the same luck for her own idle, ugly daughter; so she told her to sit at the well and spin. In order to make her spindle bloody, she stuck her hand into a hedge of thorns and pricked her finger. Then she threw the spindle into the well, and jumped in herself after it. Like her sister she came to the beautiful meadow,

and followed the same path. When she reached the baker's oven the bread called out as before:

'Oh! take me out, take me out, or I shall be burnt to a cinder. I am quite done enough.'

But the good-for-nothing girl answered:

'A pretty joke, indeed; just as if I should dirty my hands for you!'

And on she went. Soon she came to the apple tree, which cried:

'Oh! shake me, shake me, my apples are all quite ripe.'

'I'll see myself farther,' she replied, 'one of them might fall on my head.'

And so she pursued her way. When she came to Mother Holle's house she wasn't the least afraid, for she had been warned about her big teeth, and she readily agreed to become her maid. The first day she worked very hard, and did all her mistress told her, for she thought of the gold she would give her; but on the second day she began to be lazy, and on the third she wouldn't even get up in the morning. She didn't make Mother Holle's bed as she ought to have done, and never shook it enough to make the feathers fly. So her mistress soon grew weary of her, and dismissed her, much to the lazy creature's delight.

'For now,' she thought, 'the shower of golden rain will come.'

Mother Holle led her to the same door as she had done her sister, but when she passed through it, instead of the gold rain a kettle full of pitch came showering over her.

'That's a reward for your service,' said Mother Holle, and she closed the door behind her.

So the lazy girl came home all covered with pitch, and when the old hen on the top of the wall saw her, it called out:

'Click, clock, clack,
Our dirty slut's come back.'

But the pitch remained sticking to her, and never as long as she lived could it be got off.[1]

[1] Grimm.

brings the treasure (or else the curse of failure) back to the world. The Mother who sends her manifestations into the world knows that the threshold needs to be crossed again and says, 'It pleases me well that you wish to return.'

"The old woman, who is regarded as the teacher of 'song, story, and spindle,' is Wisdom herself, spinning and weaving the thread of life. In Proverbs, where she is called 'honey for the soul,' her double nature as wise one and witch is described in the words of an old man talking to his son:

Say unto wisdom, Thou art my sister; and call understanding thy kinswoman: that they may keep thee from the strange woman, from the stranger which flattereth with her words.

The warning is that he be aware of the extremes to which his soul, the woman within, might pull. Seen from another perspective, it is a proverbial insight into the nature of the feminine at the medial pole. It is about the extremes to which a woman might herself be pulled (and about how close deception and truth are to each other) when perched on the brink of the unconscious. In fact, the golden girl and the dirty girl may be sisters in one psyche, or two faces of the same girl. One cannot draw near the nucleus—be it self or soul or spindle core—and the meaning of life, without also being on the edge of falling into greed, darkness, and the field of encircling shadows. Threshold gods and goddesses show human beings how to live on this particular edge without giving over completely to one side or the other" (1980:213–14).

‡ "Women's lives are defined in terms of their fertility. . . . While women are fertile they are of maximum interest to society and maximally restricted. . . . When fertility is over, women may be left alone, and then their chances enlarge. . . .

"In many primitive societies, old women are specialists in those critical moments when the designs of culture are threatened by a breakthrough of nature—birth, illness and death—moments when we are reminded of our animal origins and human limits. Women of advanced age are healers, midwives, dressers of corpses, and may be admitted to exclusively male realms which would be contaminated by association with young women; older ones have access to the objects and rituals of the hunt, spirits, warfare. Among the Saulteaux, Huichol, and Samoan people, for example, old women demonstrate their affinity with non-cultural forces as shamans, diviners, mediums, and magicians.

"Elderly females are often allowed to set aside behavior which demonstrates their sexual shame, and are given license and privilege allowed to no others. . . . Old Aztec women in Pre-Columbian society could drink fermented beverages. . . . In some societies old women are tricksters and clowns" (Myerhoff 1978:75, 1978a: 232–68; also see e.g. Griffen 1977).

(Bowles & Carver 1970:132)

Old Women walk, ſmoke and talk.

The good weef is both

weaver and wife, those old
words meant the-woman-as-a-maker,
not especially
bonded to one husband,
but to the Spider Woman of life
the one with ties that bind,
knitter of the sacred, magic knots,
who with her scissors or her knife,
is tie-breaking life-taker,
queen of what-is-not

Wife and weef and weaver,
she was the market-woman
of Europe. Ale-wife, she sold
the ale she brewed, oysterwife bawled
what from the mothersea she drew,
strawberrywife what she grew.

The fishwife brought her stinking
reputation with her to the modern ear,
reference, they say, to a certain smell,
said with a certain sneer. The smell is
of queens.
          The midwife stands midway
between the laboring weaver and her weaving
and the world, easily the way to life.
I am pleased to call myself a wife too,
a word-wyfe.

        —Judy Grahn, "The good weef is both"
        (November 1981), from
        The Queen of Wands.

Analyzing some sixty-four myths and tales he collected from Mrs. Victoria Howard, a Clackamas Chinook woman he had interviewed during the summer of 1930, anthropologist Melville Jacobs identified what he thought was a thoroughly ambivalent view of older women, as shown in the characters of Grizzly and Meadow Lark:

Grizzly was psychotic. She had intense maternal feeling, which Clackamas accepted as characteristic of females, even the worst of them. She was not merely a bundle of dangerous drives with constant need to kill; she lusted ravenously for human and other foods; she was so stupid, like many older women, that her drives sometimes got under way slowly; and her orgies of murder and voracity were supplemented by scheming and sadism to an extreme of madness. . . .

   . . . In my opinion, the Grizzly concept applied primarily or originally to somewhat older women, but unnumbered generations of discussants had allowed an extension of the stereotype to cover any married woman. Since women are nubile from the teens to the forties or later, one must not suppose that citation of a Grizzly with a baby necessarily meant a very young woman. . . .

   . . . [One] text offers visual imagery, especially of pendulous and unattractive breasts thrown over shoulders; Grizzly Women were also hairy and had long sharp claws because they were really grizzlies. The descriptive items again suggest feelings about older women (1959:160–61).

Meadow Lark . . . represented a spirit-power whose special ability was to know what was currently happening. Like most other supernaturals, she enunciated no values; she never spoke for society. She emitted only impeccable information and predictions in return for relationship with a human being. . . .

Why was a helper of this kind feminine among Clackamas and Sahaptins to their east? Lark stories do not reveal that she was married. Does that circumstance connect with a possible fact that unmarried older women were often shamans? Did an older and apparently unmarried woman grant especial security because she lacked kinship or community ties? Could she therefore give impartial assistance to all? Although answers to such questions await surveys of the region's shamanism . . . the Clackamas Lark bears the mark of having constituted or having been reinforced by a projection arising from the quest for definitive steps that could be taken in crises (ibid:162, 163; also see Jacobs 1958).

Drawing on her own background, folklorist Rayna Green attacks both the stereotype of women not having a (dirty or clean) wit of their own and that of demure Southern women in an article entitled "Magnolias Grow in Dirt: The Bawdy Lore of Southern Women":

One final group which participates in bawdry, however, is less bound on keeping up the image. I have to confess that many of the women who tell vile tales are gloriously and affirmatively old! They transcend the boundaries—not by their station and employment—but by aging beyond the strictures that censure would lay on the young. The South, like many traditional cultures, offers an increase in license to those who advance in age, and ladies I have known take the full advantage offered them in their tale-telling. They seem to delight in particular in presenting themselves as wicked old ladies. Once, when my grandmother stepped out of the bathtub, and my sister commented that the hair on her "privates" was getting rather sparse, Granny retorted that "grass don't grow on a race track."

A number of stories I've heard concern old women's fancy for young men. . . . As the Southern Black comedienne, Moms Mabley, used to say: "Ain't nothin' no old man can do for me 'cept bring me a message from a young man." I confess I look forward to old age if I can be as bad as Granny and Moms. (1977:30–31)

> They moved like rivers in their mended stockings,
> Their skirts, their buns, their bodies grown
> Round as trees. Over the kitchen fires
> They hoarded magics, and the heavy bowls
> Of Sunday bread rose up faithful as light.
> We smiled for them, although they never spoke.
> Silent as stones, they merely stared when birds
> Fell in the leaves, or brooms wore out, if children
> scraped their knees and cried. Within my village,
> We did not think it odd or ask for words;
> In their vast arms we knew that we were loved.
> I remember their happiness at the birth of children.
> I remember their hands, swollen and hard as wood:

And how sometimes in summer when the night
Was thick with stars, they gathered in the garden.
Near sleep, I watched them as they poured the wine,
Hung paper lanterns in the alien birches.
Then one would take a tiny concertina
And cradle it against her mammoth apron,
Till music hung like ribbons in the trees
And round my bed. Oh, still within my dreams,
Softly they gather under summer stars
And sing of the far Danube, of Vienna,
Clear as a flight of wild and slender girls!

—Mary Oliver, "The Grandmothers" (1965).

♦ Ursula Le Guin, "The Space Crone": "There are things the Old Woman can do, say, and think which the Woman cannot do, say or think. The Woman has to give up more than her menstrual periods before she can do, say, or think them. She has got to change her life. . . .

"The woman who is willing to make that change must become pregnant with herself, at last. She must bear herself, her third self, her old age, with travail and alone. Not many will help her with that birth. Certainly no male obstetrician will time her contractions, inject her with sedatives, stand ready with forceps, and neatly stitch up the torn membranes. It's hard even to find an old-fashioned midwife, these days. That pregnancy is long, that labor hard. Only one is harder, and that's the final one, the one which men also must suffer and perform.

"It may well be easier to die if you have already given birth to others or yourself, at least once before. This would be an argument for going through all the discomfort and embarrassment of becoming a Crone. Anyhow it seems a pity to have a built-in rite of passage and to dodge it, evade it, and pretend nothing has changed. That is to dodge and evade one's womanhood, to pretend one's like a man. Men, once initiated, never get the second chance. They never change again. That's their loss, not ours. Why borrow poverty?" (1976:110).

(Harter 1978b:9)

Chapter 5
Heroines:
Myth as Model

That lamp thou fill'st in Eros' name to-night,
O Hero, shall the Sestian augurs take
To-morrow, and for drowned Leander's sake
To Anteros its fireless lip shall plight.
Aye, Waft the unspoken vow: yet dawn's first light
On ebbing storm and life twice ebb'd must break;
While 'neath no sunrise, by the Avernian Lake,
Lo where Love walks, Death's pallid neophyte.
That lamp within Anteros' shadowy shrine
Shall stand unlit (for so the gods decree)
Till some one man the happy issue see
Of a life's love, and bid its flame to shine:
Which still may rest unfir'd; for, theirs or thine,
O brother, what brought love to them or thee?

—Dante Gabriel Rossetti, Sonnet LXXXVIII,
"Hero's Lamp," *House of Life*
(*Ballads and Sonnets,* 1881).

Dark Lanthorn

(Bowles & Carver 1970:100)

Hero, a priestess of Aphrodite who inhabited a tower at Sestos, on the European shore of the Hellespont or Dardanelles, can scarcely be called the hero-/ine of her own story. Rather, it is Leander, the young man from Abydus on the Asian side, whom she met and fell passionately in love with at a festival honoring Adonis, who performs the heroic feats of strength in swimming the mile or so of sea channel to rendezvous with his waiting beloved. Besides faithfully lighting the beacon for her lover's swim, Hero's only other action is to throw herself from crag (or tower) in order to join him in death.[1]

[1]The romance of Hero and Leander is a late Hellenistic addition to classical literature. Virgil mentions it in the *Georgics,* and two of Ovid's imaginary letters of mythical heroines in the *Heroides* use the theme. Musaeus, a Greek poet of the fifth century A.D. whose surname was the Grammarian, wrote an epic on Hero and Leander's romance. Renaissance scholars like J. C. Scaliger (1484–1558) and Aldus Manutius (1449–1515) mistakenly identified Musaeus with an ancient Musaeus, the legendary poet and teacher who preceded Homer and Hesiod and was said to be a son of the Muses. As a result, "Musaeus' work was soon translated into French, Spanish, and English; and by 1592 Abraham Fraunce was able to say that 'Leander and Heroes love is in every mans mouth' " (Mayerson 1971:203–204). Mayerson includes literary examples of this popular tragic theme from Marlowe and Chapman's "Hero and Leander" and Shakespeare's cynical reference to the tale in *As You Like It* through Byron's famous "Bride of Abydos" and "Written after Swimming from Sestos to Abydos" in May 1810, to twentieth-century poems by A. E. Housman and Malcolm Cowley (1971:204–208). Also see the discussion of Musaeus's 340-line poem and subsequent literary adaptations in Michael Grant, *Myths of the Greeks and Romans* (New York: World Publishing, 1962), pp. 374–78. Illustration no. 96 in Grant's book shows J. M. W. Turner's Hero and Leander painting, now in the Tate Gallery, London. Most of these works concentrate on Leander.

Ironically, in Western culture at least, *a* hero is generally thought to be male. Folklorist Roger D. Abrahams succinctly characterizes this long-standing tradition:

> The actions we consider heroic reflect a view of life which is based upon contest values and a social hierarchy built on the model of a male-centered family. A hero is a man whose deeds epitomize the masculine attributes most highly valued within such a society. Because there are various masculine traits which one group or another has found attractive, there are different kinds of heroes. (1966:341)

Indeed, notable early scholars like the Austrian J. G. von Hahn (*Sagwissenschaftliche Studien,* 1871–76), Freudian analyst Otto Rank (*The Myth of the Birth of the Hero,* 1909; English translation 1914), and English myth-ritualist Lord Raglan (*The Hero: A Study in Tradition, Myth and Drama,* 1936), who compared hero narratives to abstract typical biographical patterns (see, e.g., Taylor 1964), only considered male figures.

Although he claims that "the hero . . . is the man or woman who has been able to battle past his [sic] personal and local historical limitations to the generally valid, normally human forms," mythographer Joseph Campbell almost exclusively uses male exemplars of the "monomyth" (departure, initiation and return) of "the adventure of the hero" in *The Hero with a Thousand Faces* (1949, 1968). David Adams Leeming based his 1973 collection of readings entitled *Mythology: The Voyage of the Hero* on Campbell's monomyth. Most selections involve male heroes, but among the changes for the second edition is "the addition of several heroine myths" (Leeming 1981:xii). The new edition includes stories about the following figures:

Female (excluding heroes' mothers): Leda and Helen, Cybele, Virgin Mary, Joan of Arc, Pleiades (Australian Aboriginal), Penelope, Persephone and Demeter, Wanjiru (African), Inanna or Ishtar, and Hiiaka (Polynesian).

Male: Theseus, Buddha, Quetzalcoatl, Zoroaster, Siegfried, Karna, Maui, Moses, Attis, Water Jar Boy (Tewa), Kutoyis (Blackfoot), Huitzilopochtli, Lituolone (Bantu), Horus, Dionysos, Adonis, Jesus, Krishna, Heracles, Odysseus, King Arthur, Cuchulainn, David, Milarepa, Isaac Tens (Gitksan Indian), Wunzh (Ojibwa), Percival, Mohammed, Endymion, The Seven Sleepers (Christian), Achilles, Prometheus, Kyazimba (Tanzania), Gawain, Gilgamesh, Seth, Faust, Tammuz, Osiris, Orpheus, Odin, Lohiau (Polynesian), Hermodr (Icelandic), Izanagi (Japanese), Aeneas, Hyacinth, Telipinu, Bear Man (Cherokee), Abraham.

The imbalance is apparent, and it applies as well to other collections of hero tales (e.g., Coffin and Cohen 1978; Dorson 1973; Browne et al. 1972; Goodrich 1961). Unfortunately, because it lacks both an analytical stance/typology and an index, folklorist Tristram Potter Coffin's survey of *The Female Hero in Folklore and Legend* (1975) cannot be readily or usefully compared with similar surveys of male and/or female heroes.

Feminist Elizabeth Gould Davis contends that women are actually more heroic than men, being superior to them biologically and emotionally, and that "the word 'hero' was, after all, originally feminine—*hera,* as philology

Heracles
(Roman Hercules)
(Lehner 1969:23, fig. 44).

proves; and the original heroes of the ancient race were 'heras,' as the nomenclature of ancient places, even of continents, bears out" (1972:319).[2] She claims, at least of contemporary society that:

> "The heroic deeds of women are seldom recorded in books or periodicals," observes Dr. Georgio Lolli. Male editors, with their preconceived notions of female timidity, brush these stories aside as having some explanation other than courage. And male judges in granting heroism awards automatically eliminate the names of girls and consider only boys. . . .
>
> It all boils down to the fact that in the eyes and minds of the masculine judges, boys are heroes and girls are not. If a girl performs a heroic act it is an anomaly, a freak episode. One can only ask: how many times must an anomaly occur and recur before it ceases to be an anomaly? Odenwald, in his curiously antifeminist book, admits that "women in the past have taken their stand at the barricades and have carried, literally and figuratively, their men on their backs. But when they have done so, *everyone agreed they were exceptions* [author's italics]." How long must exceptions be repeated before they become the rule? The doctor goes on: "When they do so as a *regular* thing today, however, more and more people ask, 'Well, why not?' These people are saying *there should be no clear distinctions.*" In other words, says Odenwald, women have no right to be brave. Bravery is a man's province. And of course it is the acme, or nadir, of that most despicable thing, unfemininity, for women to invade man's province. Women must pretend to be cowards in order that men may appear more courageous by contrast. (Ibid:320–21)[3]

(Fox 1979:35)

Whatever one may think of Davis's arguments and rhetoric, she is not mistaken about the relative paucity of publically, collectively recognized female heroes, particularly in the world's epic song traditions and formalized hero cults, exemplified below by the Greek traditions, particularly the Homeric.

Magic tales or *Märchen* are a second powerful influence on Western hero traditions, particularly in providing ideal models for women's behavior. Although many, if not most, magic tales recount the adventures of male heroes who slay dragons, outwit giants, and perform all manner of marvelous feats to win their rightful rewards, at least in the Western literary *Märchen* tradition best exemplified by the Grimm brothers' collection, the stories' lessons usually

[2]For the philology of hera-hero, Davis cites Robert Eisler, *Man into Wolf* (London: Spring Books, 1949?), p. 177. Herodotus is her source for the "great women" etymologies of "Libya from 'a native woman of that place'; Europe from Europa, the ancestress of the Cretans; and Asia from the wife of the aboriginal Prometheus," all "probably great warrior-queens-heras of the time when women were engaged in leading the human race toward true civilization" (Davis 1972:319–20).

[3]Davis cites Lolli, *Social Drinking* (New York: World, 1960), p. 252; and Robert P. Odenwald, *The Disappearing Sexes* (New York: Norton, 1967), p. 23. She follows with the case of Dr. Mary Walker, a surgeon awarded the Congressional Medal of Honor for her heroism during the Civil War. Her medal was reconfirmed by Congress in 1907, but rescinded in 1917. According to Davis: "Dr. Walker, like Hypatia and Pope Joan before her, was reviled, ridiculed, and scorned by officialdom for her courage; and she, like them, was actually *stoned* in the streets of Washington, D.C., for her 'presumption' in protesting the unfair recall of her Medal of Honor. She died in 1917, a victim of the masculine myth of the incapacity of women to perform heroic deeds" (1972:322).

(Harter 1978a:29)

seem to be aimed at girls rather than boys. Female protagonists' passivity and docile endurance are more frequently rewarded in the tales chosen for translation and compilation. More often than not, in *Märchen* the reward for both men and women is marriage. For the male, however, this generally comes at the end of his trials, while for the woman it often marks the beginning of her tests. Her reward comes not through slaying the dragon but in transforming him, as discussed below in "Marriage—Consummation/Initiation."

Until recently, this deep-seated, longstanding dichotomy between male and female heroic figures has been bridged but seldom in either Native American or Western traditions. Three "Active Heroines"—Eskimo, contemporary Mexican-American, and classical—are presented below. Like the literary protagonists in Carol Pearson and Katherine Pope's *Who Am I This Time?: Female Portraits in British and American Literature,* such "female heroes refuse the supporting, dependent role and are seen by themselves and/or by others as the primary character in their own stories" (1976:3). Besides the Amazons further discussed in chapter 6, their most familiar Western prototype is undoubtedly Joan of Arc.

St. Joan (born ca. 1412 or 1413, burned at the stake May 30, 1431; canonized 1920; feast day May 30) is described by Marina Warner as "the image of female heroism"—"a universal figure who is female, but is neither a queen, nor a courtesan, nor a beauty, nor a mother, nor an artist of one kind or another, nor—until the extremely recent date of 1920 when she was canonized—a saint" (1981:6). Warner undertook to study both "The Life and Death of Jeanne la Pucelle" and "The Afterlife of Joan of Arc" since:

. . . Joan of Arc is a preeminent heroine because she belongs to the sphere of action, while so many feminine figures or models are assigned and confined to the sphere of contemplation. She is anomalous in our culture, a woman renowned for

(Harter 1980a:54)

"The martial ordeal par excellence was the single combat, conducted in such a way that it finally roused the candidate to the 'fury of the berserkers.' For not military prowess alone was involved. A youth did not become a berserker simply through courage, physical strength, endurance, but as the result of a magico-religious experience that radically changed his mode of being. The young warrior must transmute his humanity by a fit of aggressive and terror-striking fury, which assimilated him to the raging beast of prey. He became 'heated' to an extreme degree, flooded by a mysterious, nonhuman, and irresistible force that his fighting effort and vigor summoned from the utmost depths of his being. The ancient Germans called this sacred force *wut,* a term that Adam von Bremen translated by *furor;* it was a sort of demonic frenzy, which filled the warrior's adversary with terror and finally paralyzed him. The Irish *ferg* (literally 'anger'), the homeric *menos,* are almost exact equivalents of this same terrifying sacred experience peculiar to heroic combats. . . . As Miss Sjoestadt writes, 'The Hero is the man in fury, possessed by his own tumultuous and burning energy.' " (Eliade 1965:84)

doing something on her own, not by birthright. She has extended the taxonomy of female types; she makes evident the dimension of women's dynamism. It is urgent that this taxonomy be expanded further and that the multifarious duties that women have historically undertaken be recognised, researched and named. Like Eskimos, who enjoy a lexicon of many different words for snow, we must develop a richer vocabulary for female activity than we use at present, with our restrictions of wife, mother, mistress, muse. Joan of Arc, in all her brightness, illuminates the operation of our present classification system, its rigidity on the one hand, its potential on the other. (1981:9; also see Gies 1981; B. Fisher 1980)

Warner's study contributes significantly to the illumination of mythological/legendary models for herioc women (cf. e.g. Ellis 1978; Abernathy 1981; Blashfield 1981; Lichtenstein 1981; Raven and Weir 1981).[4]

The "Homeric" and Hero/ines

The adjective "Homeric" is defined as "of, like, or characteristic of the legendary Homer, his poems, or the Greek civilization that they describe (1200–1800 B.C.)," according to Webster's *New World Dictionary of the American Language.* It thus characterizes a poet (not usually thought to be female), a poetic form and content—the epic (not usually recounting the deeds and adventures of a female hero), and a specific age during which male warriors clashed in the name of petty *king*doms.

Although there are numerous epic traditions worldwide (cf. Oinas 1978; also see Coote 1977), those from ancient Greece are most familiar to Westerners. The Greek heroic age, the Mycenaean or Late Bronze Age, dates from ca. 1600 through ca. 1100 B.C. The fall of Troy has been variously dated as

(Harter 1978b:95)

[4]Nancy Shimmel has compiled a helpful list of "Active Heroines in Folktales for Children" (1978), distributed by Sisters' Choice, 2027 Parker Street, Berkeley, California 94704. Still other "active heroines" can be found in specially selected collections like Minard (1975) and Phelps (1978, 1981), in comicbook anthologies like Lee (1977), and in hagiography. Elizabeth Petroff, a scholar of comparative literature, undertook a "study of *Saints' Lives* about women who lived in Italy between 1200 and 1400," and claims that: "Having read more than fifty lives of Italian women saints from the 13th and 14th centuries, most of them available in Latin, I can testify to the fact that these official biographies chronicle a life-long process, mediated by visionary experience, which transformed these women from a passive, self-effacing ideal of female goodness into active, energetic, highly individualized women who were taking a forceful role in the world" (1977:72; also see Petroff 1978, 1981). Many European saints and their legends were transplanted to the New World, like the Pennsylvania Germans' Saint Genoveva of Brabant *(die heilige Genoveva),* while other female figures were native, like "Mountain Mary *(Die Berg-Maria),* a local Pennsylvania German hermitess who died in 1819 and about whom legends have arisen" (Don Yoder, "The Saint's Legend in the Pennsylvania German Folk-Culture," in *American Folk Legend: A Symposium,* ed. Wayland D. Hand [Berkeley: University of California Press, 1971], p. 173). Another legendary New World religious figure was Juana Ramírez, Sor Juana Inez de la Cruz (Phillips 1971–72; Ward 1978; Paz 1979). Finally, perhaps, the most powerful heroines will be sung privately, in family folklore told to daughters and granddaughters by mothers and grandmothers (e.g., Morgan 1966, 1980; Elsasser, MacKenzie and Tixier y Vigil 1980).

between 1250 B.C. and 1184 B.C. The Dorian invasions from north and east, which marked the Iron Age, are usually thought to have come around 1100 B.C., although some archeologists say 1200 B.C.

For a time, darkness descends upon the history of Greece, a darkness which is only gradually dispelled with the emergence of the two great Homeric epics, the *Iliad* and the *Odyssey*, in the ninth and eighth centuries B.C. The stories of the earlier period were kept alive by oral recitation, transmitted by bards like those described in the epics themselves. "Homer" almost certainly belongs to Asia Minor or one of the islands (e.g., Chios) off the coast. In the cities of this area in this period, we find that monarchy is the prevailing institution; significantly enough the social and political environment for the bard of this later age is not unlike that of his predecessors in the great days of Mycenae. (Morford and Lenardon 1977:16)

Greek cithara
(Harter 1980b:81).

Besides the *Iliad* and the *Odyssey*, there are records and/or fragments of other epics related to the Trojan War—*Cypria* (from the gods' decision to cause the war to Achilles and Agamemnon's quarrel), *Aithiopis* (from the Amazons' arrival to Aias' suicide), the *Little Iliad* (from Achilles' death to the Achaians' departure), and the *Sack of Ilion* (from the wooden horse through the Achians' departure)—and the various heroes' returns—*The Returns (Nostoi)*, as well as *Telegony* (ca. 568 B.C.), which follows Odysseus' return until his death (Lattimore 1951:26).

The question of Homer's identity remains provocative and insoluble (for a useful summary see Hansen 1978). In any case, whether one, two, or many, the composers are usually thought to have been male, if only because, as Roger Abrahams observes: "Traditionally, in many societies which exalt heroic action, the role of the storyteller commands great respect {and} the effective use of words is widely regarded as an exhibition of strength and manliness in itself" (1966:342). Thus, classicist Samuel Butler's 1897 study of *The Authoress of the Odyssey: Where and When She Wrote, Who She Was, the Use She Made of the* Iliad, *& How the Poem Grew Under Her Hands* comes as something of a surprise.

Citing Richard Bentley in R. C. Jebb, *Introduction to the Iliad and the Odyssey* (1888), Butler introduces his unusual work thus:

It was Bentley who . . . said that the "Iliad" was written for men, and the "Odyssey" for women. The history of literature furnishes us with no case in which a man has written a great masterpiece for women rather than men. If an anon-

Ancient harp
(Harter 1980b:81).

ymous book strikes so able a critic as having been written for women, a *primâ facie* case is established for thinking that it was probably written by a woman. I deny, however, that the "Odyssey" was written for women; it was written for any one who would listen to it. What Bentley meant was that in the "Odyssey" things were looked at from a woman's point of view rather than a man's, and in uttering this obvious truth, I repeat, he established once for all a strong *primâ facie* case for thinking that it was written by a woman. (Butler 1967:4)

He cautions potential critics:

It may be argued that it is extremely improbable that any woman in any age should write such a masterpiece as the "Odyssey." But so it also is that any man should do so. In all the many hundreds of years since the "Odyssey" was written, no man has been able to write another that will compare with it. It was extremely improbable that the son of a Stratford wool-stapler should write *Hamlet,* or that a Bedfordshire tinker should produce such a masterpiece as *Pilgrim's Progress.* Phenomenal works imply a phenomenal workman, but there are phenomenal women as well as phenomenal men, and though there is much in the "Iliad" which no woman, however phenomenal, can be supposed at all likely to have written, there is not a line in the "Odyssey" which a woman might not perfectly well write, and there is much beauty which a man would be almost certain to neglect. Moreover there are many mistakes in the "Odyssey" which a young woman might easily make, but which a man could hardly fall into—for example, making the wind whistle over the waves at the end of Book ii., thinking that a lamb could live on two pulls a day at a ewe that was already milked (ix. 244, 245, and 308, 309), believing a ship to have a rudder at both ends (ix. 483, 540), thinking that a dry and well-seasoned timber can be cut from a growing tree (v. 240), making a hawk while still on the wing tear its prey—a thing no hawk can do (xv. 527). (Ibid:9)

Butler marshals evidence like the following to bolster his contention that a Sicilian lady who portrays herself as Princess Nausicaa in the epic actually composed the *Odyssey:*

No great poet would compare his hero to a paunch full of blood and fat, cooking before the fire (xx. 24–28). The humour, for of course it is humorously intended, is not man's humour, unless he is writing burlesque. This the writer of the "Odyssey" is not doing here. . . .
The only other two points which suggest a female hand in Book xx.—I mean with especial force—are the sympathy which the writer betrays with the poor weakly woman who could not finish her task (105, &c), and the speech of Telemachus about his mother being too apt to make much of second rate people (129–133). (Ibid:153)

The instinctive house-wifely thrift of the writer is nowhere more marked than near the beginning of Book xxii., where amid the death-throes of Antinous and Eurymachus she cannot forget the good meat and wine that were spoiled by the upsetting of the tables at which the suitors had been sitting. (Ibid:154)

When Ulysses and Penelope are in bed (xxiii. 300–343) and are telling their stories to one another, Penelope tells hers first. I believe a male writer would have made Ulysses' story come first and Penelope's second. (Ibid:157)

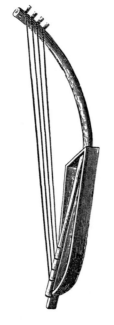

Ancient harp
(Harter 1980b:81).

(Harter 1980a:62). The so-called Mask of Agamemnon (eight inches high, of gold) from Mycenae, sixteenth century B.C.. Heinrich Schliemann, its discoverer, believed it depicted the great Homeric king and thus was a very early example of portraiture.

Even so, it is clear that within the poem itself Odysseus' story is sung, while Penelope bravely and in the end vainly spins and unravels her spinning to defend herself from the suitors' unwelcome advances. As she tells her disguised husband:

". . . But I waste my heart away in longing for Odysseus; so they speed on my marriage and I weave a web of wiles. First some god put it into my heart to set up a great web in the halls, and thereat to weave a robe fine of woof and very wide; and anon I spake among them saying: 'Ye princely youths, my wooers, now that goodly Odysseus is dead, do ye abide patiently, how eager soever to speed on this marriage of mine, till I finish the robe. I would not that the threads perish to no avail, even this shroud for the hero Laertes, against the day when the ruinous doom shall bring him low, of death that lays men at their length. So shall none of the Achaean women in the land count it blame in me, as well might be, were he to lie without a winding sheet, a man that had gotten great possessions.'

"So spake I, and their high hearts consented thereto. So then in the daytime I would weave the mighty web, and in the night unravel the same, when I had let place the torches by me. Thus for the space of three years I hid the thing by craft and beguiled the minds of the Achaeans. But when the fourth year arrived, and the seasons came round as the months waned, and many days were accomplished, then it was that by help of the handmaids, shameless things and reckless, the wooers came and trapped me, and chid me loudly. Thus did I finish the web by no will of mine, for so I must. And now I can neither escape the marriage nor devise any further counsel, and my parents are instant with me to marry, and my son chafes while these men devour his livelihood, as he takes note of all; for by this time he has come to man's estate, and is full able to care for a household, being such an one as Zeus vouchsafes to honor. . . ."

—*The Odyssey,* book 19, lines 137–64;
trans. Butcher (1882:347–48; also see Debrida 1982:139–41).

Women singers of epic tales, if they did exist in Greek tradition, are no less unusual than women heroes. Classicist Martin P. Nilsson traces the Greek hero-cult from the cult of the dead, claiming the former originated in the belief in powerful men's continued corporal existence after death. *Heros* originally meant a nobleman or lord. The horse, symbolic of the gentry, was regularly on nobles' tombstones and came to be considered a coat of arms emblematic of a hero. The hero's power was tied to his physical remains, and he "works from his grave and only in the place where his bones rest" (Nilsson 1964: 103–104). Nilsson summarizes hero worship in official Greek civic religion thus: "To them was sacrificed an animal, whose blood was caused to flow down a hole into the ground to moisten the dead man's ashes; games and races were held for them as formerly at the funeral of a nobleman; in some cases the funeral dirge was repeated for them, on a fixed day each year" (1964:250).

In *Greek Folk Religion,* Nilsson notes that in rural areas heroes were prayed to and invoked for protection and healing in much the same way the Christian saints were worshipped in later peasant communities. The countryside was dotted with numerous hero tombs and sanctuaries. Only a few heroes' names were well known, primarily through mythology; most were anonymous, known by the epithet "leader" or by the place of their cult. Heroes "were thought to appear in very concrete form"; they "were close to the people . . . [who] applied to them for help in all their needs," often to heal disease (Nilsson 1961:19–20). The physician Asclepius, for example, was a hero.

Pausanias, a Greek travel writer of the second century A.D., claims that the hero worshipped at Messenia in the southwestern Peloponnesus was a woman. Messenian ruler Glaukos reportedly "recognized Messene daughter of Triopas with all the religious offerings due to divine heroes" (IV.3.9., Levi 1971:111). According to Pausanias, when the city of Messenia was founded, sacrifices were made, "and then they called out together to the divine heroes to return and live with them, particularly to Triopas's daughter Messene . . ." (IV.27.6., Levi 1971:165). He also writes:

Messene's father was the grandest and most powerful figure in Greece at that time, so she had ideas, and felt it was below her husband [Polykaon] to live a private life. They collected forces from Argos and Lakonia, and arrived in this territory, and the whole country was named Messene after Polykaon's wife. Among the cities they founded was Andania, the royal capital. . . . So the first king and queen in this area were Lelex's son Polykaon and Polykaon's wife Messene. It was to this same Messene that Kaukon brought the mysteries of the Great goddess from Eleusis. Kaukon was the son of Kelainos and the grandson of Phylos; according to the Athenians Phylos was a son of Earth, and the hymn to Demeter that Mousaios wrote for the Lykonidai agrees with them. (IV.1.2ff, Levi 1971:103–104)

Whatever the veracity of Pausanias' reports, it is clear that most, if not all, Greek heroes were male, and it is unlikely that a significant number of the anonymous heroes worshipped locally were considered "dead" women. Both the "authoress" of the *Odyssey* and the hero Messene, if indeed either existed, were anomalous at best.

The Grimm's and Heroines

Although the 210 tales in Jacob and Wilhelm Grimm's *Kinder- und Haus-Märchen* (vol. I, 1812; vol. II, 1815; vol. III, 1822) contain stories other than those classified as numbers 300–749, "Tales of Magic," in *The Types of the Folktale* (Thompson 1973), the brothers' name is popularly considered virtually synonymous with fairy or magic tales. Folklorist Max Lüthi describes the situation in German-speaking countries of Europe:

If we are asked just which fairy-tale figures are generally best known, we immediately think of Sleeping Beauty, Cinderella, Snow White, Little Red Riding Hood, Rapunzel, The Princess in Disguise, and Goldmarie in "Mother Hulda"—all female figures. In "Hansel and Gretel" and in "Brother and Sister," the girl also plays the leading role. We find ourselves nearly at a loss when called upon for the names of male protagonists: Iron Hans and Tom Thumb, perhaps; the Brave Little Tailor, Strong Hans, and Lucky Hans—but here we are already in the realm of the folktale jest. How can one explain this peculiar predominance of women and girls? All the names mentioned are taken from the Grimm brothers' collection. Despite the existence of innumerable other collections, this one today is, in German-speaking countries, almost the sole surviving source for the public at large of real contact with the fairy tale. Now the Grimm brothers' informants were predominantly women. And today children learn fairy tales mainly from their mothers, grandmothers, aunts, and female kindergarten and school teachers. Thus, it is natural that the principal figures are mostly women. Moreover, the child—whether boy or girl—is basically closer to the feminine than the masculine, living in the domain of the mother and female teachers and not yet that of the father and male teachers. The fairy tales which grownups remember are those of their childhood. Furthermore, our era, whose character, despite everything, is still determined by men, feels the strong and clear need for a complementary antipole. The woman is

Jeanne A. Larousse, *The Studio* 73
(Grafton 1980: 125, fig. 549).

assigned a privileged position, not only by social custom; in art and literature, as well, she has occupied a central position since the time of the troubadours and the Mariology of the late Middle Ages. Thus, it comes as no surprise that she also plays a significant role in the fairy tale—which for centuries was one of the most vital and indirectly influential art forms in Europe—the feminine component, that part of man closer to nature, had to come to the forefront to compensate for the technological and economic system created by the masculine spirit, which dominated the external world of reality.

However, that was a peculiarity of the era. Tellers of fairy tales were not always predominantly women, and not always was existence influenced so strongly by the masculine spirit that the antipole asserted itself with such conspicuous force in art. (1970:135–36)[5]

In *The Classic Fairy Tales,* Iona and Peter Opie document and reprint "the texts of twenty-four of the best-known fairy tales as they were first printed in English" (1974:5; also see Dégh 1979). Although many of these are translations from French fairy tales (German versions of which also appear in the Grimm's), four—"Snow White and the Seven Dwarfs" ("Snow-drop"), "The Frog Prince," "The Twelve Dancing Princesses," and "Rumpel-Stilts-Kin"— first appeared in Edgar Taylor's 1823 *German Popular Stories, Translated from the Kinder and Haus-Märchen, collected by M. M. Grimm, from Oral Tradition* (Opie 1974:175–98). A fifth, "Hansel and Gretel," was first published in full in 1853, although parts of it had appeared in Taylor's second volume of 1826 (ibid:236–37). Margaret Hunt's two-volume translation of *Grimm's Household Tales with the Author's Notes* was published by Henry G. Bohn of London in 1884, and most subsequent English-language editions of all or some of these tales are based on this work.

In "Things Walt Disney Never Told Us," folklorist Kay Stone examines some of these editions:

What have the Grimm translations offered to North American children? Of the total of 210 stories in the complete edition, there are 40 heroines, not all of them passive and pretty. Very few translations offer more than twenty-five tales, and thus only a handful of heroines is usually included. Most of them run the gamut from mildly abused to severely persecuted. In fact, a dozen docile heroines are the

Ethel K. Burgess, *The Studio* 11 (Grafton 1980: 130, fig. 565).

[5]Folklorist Linda Dégh reports that such is *not* the case in Hungarian folk culture: "In Hungary, it is mostly the men who tell stories in public before a big audience, whereas the tales recorded by women show only that they know the stories and preserve them. By reason of their position in society and their work, women rarely become storytellers; Mrs. Palkó of Kakasd, who could vie with any man, is an exception to the rule. In general, the women remain within the family circle; they tell their stories to children or grandchildren or other adults in the family; the men, on the other hand, seek the big audiences, the publicity. . . . It is obvious that storytelling is mostly connected with male occupations and the places of work for men. Doubtless it is the men who are the storytellers among European peoples. There have been cases where men, when telling stories, excluded not only the children but the women. The storytelling of women is only a secondary matter in the estimation of folk society; it is limited to the family, to the entertainment of children, and to the communal work of the women" (1969:92–93).

"The Princess liked this knight still better than she had liked the other, and sat longing that he might be able to get up above . . ."

—Illustration by H. J. Ford for "The Princess on the Glass Hill," in Andrew Lang, ed., *The Blue Fairy Book*, published in London, ca. 1889 (1965:338).

overwhelming favorites, reappearing in book after book from the mid-nineteenth century to the present. . . .

The passivity of these heroines is magnified by the fact that their stories jump from twenty percent in the original Grimm collection to as much as seventy-five percent in many children's books. In this sense the fairy tale, a male-oriented genre in Europe (both by tale and teller), becomes a female-oriented genre in North American children's literature.

But if the Grimm heroines are, for the most part, uninspiring, those of Walt Disney seem barely alive. In fact, two of them hardly manage to stay awake. Disney produced three films based on *Märchen* ("Sleeping Beauty" and "Snow White" from the Grimms and "Cinderella" from Perrault). All three had passive, pretty heroines, and all three had female villains, thus strongly reinforcing the already popular stereotype of the innocent beauty victimized by the wicked villainess. In fact, only half of the Grimm heroine tales have female villains, and among the Anglo-American tales, only one-third. . . .

In brief, the popularized heroines of the Grimms and Disney are not only passive and pretty, but also unusually patient, obedient, industrious, and quiet. A woman who failed to be any of these could not become a heroine. Even Cinderella has to do no more than put on dirty rags to conceal herself completely. She is a heroine only when properly cleaned and dressed. (1975:43–44; also see Stone 1980, 1981)

Stone emphasizes how this is in direct contrast to male heroes in Grimm's, as well as 186 heroines in "five major Anglo-American folktale collections" from oral tradition by Katherine Briggs, Marie Campbell, Emelyn Gardner, Vance Randolph and Leonard Roberts. Stone also maintains, citing Lieberman (1972:385), that: "It does not seem an exaggeration to say, as one feminist writer does, that fairy tales may serve as 'training manuals' in passive behavior, and that 'Millions of women must surely have formed their ideas of what they could or could not accomplish, what sort of behavior would be rewarded, and of the nature of the reward itself, in part from their favorite fairy stories. These stories have been made the repositories of the dreams, hopes, and fantasies of generations of girls' " (1975:48; also see Dan 1977).

♦   Mircea Eliade, *Myth and Reality:* "Though in the West the tale has long since become a literature of diversion (for children and peasants) or of escape (for city dwellers), it still presents the structure of an infinitely serious and responsible adventure, for in the last analysis it is reducible to an initiatory scenario: again and again we find initiatory ordeals (battles with the monster, apparently insurmountable obstacles, riddles to be solved, impossible tasks, etc.), the descent to Hades or the ascent to Heaven (or—what amounts to the same thing—death and resurrection), marrying the princess. It is true, as Jan de Vries has very rightly stressed, that the tale always comes to a happy conclusion. But its content refers to a terrifyingly serious reality: initiation, that is, passing, by way of a symbolic death and resurrection, from ignorance and immaturity to the spiritual age of the adult. . . .

"We could almost say that the tale repeats, on another plane and by other means, the exemplary initiation scenario. The tale takes up and continues 'initiation' on the level of the imaginary." (1963:201–202)

♦   N. J. Girardot, "Initiation and Meaning in the Tale of Snow White and the Seven Dwarfs": "Snow White's period of 'death' involves a reiteration of the overall cycle of transformation. She is bathed ceremoniously, purifying baptismal waters being necessary for the final spiritual and physical union of marriage. The reference to the 'glass coffin' where Snow White remained unburied . . . is also interesting alchemically in that in various emblematic books concerning the 'great work' a crystal coffin is depicted as a prominent symbol of the vessel (retort, *aludel*, egg, gourd, etc.) of transformation. . . ." (1977:293)

♦   ". . . The owl in European folklore is often associated with the bringing of omens of death and darkness, or the onset of an eclipse. The black raven (or crow) is likewise an omen of death and the *nigredo* phase of the alchemical process. The dove, like the harbinger of new life for Noah in the Bible, signals the successful completion of the process. Finally, it is worth noting that these birds are said to 'weep over Snow White' which is analogous to another alchemical motif. . . .

"In many fairy tales and in some religious traditions birds are expressive of spiritualization or, in alchemy, symbolic of sublimation and volitilization as a final step in the refining work." (Ibid:295–96)

♦   Janice Delaney, Mary Jane Lupton, and Emily Toth, *The Curse:* "The unseemly haste with which nubile maidens were locked away in towers in the land of Grimm seems to be a direct narrative analogue to the customs of seclusion at menarche in most early societies. . . . The purpose of the seclusion was to protect the girl and her society from her mana at this dangerous time. Important during this seclusion were the instructions they received from the older women of the tribe in female matters. At the end of the seclusion, the girls were considered marriageable and were welcomed into the adult life of the tribe.

—Illustration by Lancelot Speed for "Snowdrop" (i.e., "Little Snow White," Grimm's no. 53, Aarne-Thompson tale type no. 709), in Andrew Lang, ed., *The Red Fairy Book,* published in London, 1890 (1966:337; also see Opie 1974:175–82).

"So they had a coffin made of transparent glass, and they laid her in it, and wrote on the lid in golden letters that she was a royal Princess. Then they put the coffin on the top of a mountain, and one of the Dwarfs always remained beside it and kept watch over it. And the very birds of the air came and bewailed Snowdrop's death, first an owl, and then a raven, and last of all a little dove."

   "Sleeping Beauty, Rapunzel, and Maid Maleen, to name a few, were kept from the eyes of the world during their adolescence and endured their seclusion at the behest of, or in the company of, a bad mother (a witch or other old person not their natural mother)." (1976:127; also see Lüthi 1970:109–19)

◆   N. J. Girardot, "Initiation and Meaning": ". . . Kay Stone's comments on what she considers to be the insipid and uninspiring 'passivity' of female characters in the Grimm tales, while not entirely unfounded, do seem to miss the point that ultimately initiation is the fortuitous work of the gods (however they are disguised). Heroes and heroines in fairy tales, more so than in epic or saga, do not ordinarily succeed because they act, but because they allow themselves to be acted upon—helped, protected, saved, or transformed—by the magic of the fairy world." (1977:284; also see Jones 1979, Girardot 1979)

Marriage—Consummation/Initiation

   Despite numerous proverbs, jokes and narratives about men's difficulties in marrying, it would seem to be the woman—the bride and wife—who faces (usually passively or with limited choices) the greater unknown. For her, mar-

—Illustration by H. J. Ford for "Beauty and the Beast" (Aarne-Thompson tale type no. 425C), in Andrew Lang, ed., *The Blue Fairy Book,* published in London ca. 1889 (1965:117; also see Opie 1974:137–50).[7]

riage is a mystery; for the groom-husband it is more likely a reward for initiatory ordeals successfully endured and knowledge already won.

The well-known Western magic tale of "Beauty and the Beast" has its counterpart in myths and tales worldwide. "Supernatural or Enchanted Husband (Wife) or Other Relatives" (Type nos. 400–59) comprise a major category of magic tales in Antti Aarne and Stith Thompson's *The Types of the Folktale: A Classification and Bibliography* (1973:128–56), and a number of these tales include *"beast marriage,* a common motif of folktale and ballad found all over the world, in which a human being is married to a beast, in very primitive tales to an actual animal, in later elaborations to a human being doomed to exist in beast form until some *woman* [italics added] will love him in the beast-shape" (Leach 1972:129). In his revised *Motif-Index of Folk-Literature* (1955–58), Thompson classifies numerous instances of this "narrative element" cross-culturally as B600 Marriage of person to animal, B610 Animal paramour, B620 Animal suitor, B630 Offspring of marriage to animal, B640 Marriage to person in animal form, and B650 Marriage to animal in human form. According to folklorists Iona and Peter Opie: "The most symbolic of the fairy tales after Cinderella, and the most intellectually satisfying, 'Beauty and the Beast' is the prime example of the world-wide beast-marriage story, of which the classic text is that of Madame Le prince de Beaumont [which] appeared in her *Magasin des enfans, ou dialogues entre une sage Gouvernante et plusieurs de ses élèves,* published in London in 1756, of which the English translation, *The Young Misses Magazine,* came out in 1761" (1974:137).[6]

[6]In *Breaking the Magic Spell: Radical Theories of Folk and Fairy Tales,* Jack Zipes traces the history of "Beauty and the Beast" in eighteenth-century France as "a good example of the drastic change of the folk tale for aristocratic and bourgeois audiences" (1979:8–11).

[7]Even more vivid imagery is found in the European tale "Prince Lindworm," in which a shepherd's daughter ritually transforms a loathsome, lethal serpent on their wedding night (in Joseph L. Henderson and Maud Oakes, *The Wisdom of the Serpent: The Myths of Death, Rebirth, and Resurrection* [New York: George Braziller, 1963], pp. 167–72). Also see Denise Levertov's "An Embroidery," her 1969 poem about Rose Red, Rose White, and the bear (in Chester and Barba 1973:108–10).

—Illustration by H. J. Ford for "Jack My Hedgehog" (Grimm's nö. 108, Aarne-Thompson tale type no. 441), in Andrew Lang, ed., *The Green Fairy Book*, published in London ca. 1892 (1965:309).

"Then Jack my Hedgehog rode on with his cock and bagpipes to the country of the second King to whom he had shown the way. Now this King had given orders that, in the event of Jack's coming the guards were to present arms, the people to cheer, and he was to be conducted in triumph to the royal palace.

"When the King's daughter saw Jack my Hedgehog, she was a good deal startled, for he certainly was very peculiar looking; but after all she considered that she had given her word and it couldn't be helped. So she made Jack welcome and they were betrothed to each other, and at dinner he sat next to her at the royal table, and they ate and drank together.

"When they retired to rest the Princess feared lest Jack should kiss her because of his prickles, but he told her not to be alarmed as no harm should befall her."

◆　Joseph L. Henderson, "Ancient Myths and Modern Man": "In this story, if we unravel the symbolism, we are likely to see that Beauty is any young girl or woman who has entered into an emotional bond with her father, no less binding because of its spiritual nature. Her goodness is symbolized by her request for a white rose, but in a significant twist of meaning her unconscious intention puts her father and then herself in the power of a principle that expresses not goodness alone, but cruelty and kindness combined. It is as if she wished to be rescued from a love holding her to an exclusively virtuous and unreal attitude.

"By learning to love Beast she awakens to the power of human love concealed in its animal (and therefore imperfect) but genuinely erotic form. Presumably this represents an awakening of her true function of relatedness, enabling her to accept the erotic component of her original wish, which had to be repressed because of a fear of incest. To leave her father she had, as it were, to accept the incest-fear, to allow herself to live in its presence in fantasy until she could get to know the animal man and discover her own true response to it as a woman.

"In this way she redeems herself and her image of the masculine from the forces of repression, bringing to consciousness her capacity to trust her love as something that combines spirit and nature in the best sense of the words" (1964:131; also see "Beauty Exorcises the Beast" in Kolbenschlag 1979:165–204).

♦   Bruno Bettelheim, *The Uses of Enchantment:* "Fairy tales speak to our unconscious mind and are experienced as telling us something important, irrespective of our sex and of the story's protagonist. Still it is worth remarking that in most Western fairy tales the beast is male and can be disenchanted only by the love of a female. The nature of the beast changes from place to place according to the local situation. For example, in a Bantu (Kaffir) story a crocodile is restored to its human form by a maiden who licks its face. In other tales the beast appears in the form of a pig, lion, bear, ass, frog, snake, etc., which is restored to human form by the love of a maiden. One must assume that the inventors of these tales believed that to achieve a happy union, it is the female who has to overcome her view of sex as loathesome and animal-like. There are also Western fairy tales in which the female has been bewitched into animal form, and then it is she who must be

(Fox 1979:97)

disenchanted by the love and determined courage of a male. But in practically all examples of animal brides there is nothing dangerous or repugnant in their animal form; on the contrary, they are lovely. "The Raven" has already been mentioned. In another Brothers Grimm tale, "The Drummer," the girl has been changed into a swan. Thus, it seems that while fairy tales suggest that sex without love and devotion is animal-like, at least in the Western tradition its animal aspects are nonthreatening or even charming, as far as the female is concerned; only the male aspects of sex are beastly" (1976:284–85).[8]

The first tale in Jacob and Wilhelm Grimm's collection is entitled "The Frog King or Iron Henry" (Aarne-Thompson tale type no. 440), in which: "A maiden princess promises herself to a frog in a spring. The frog comes to the door, the table, the bed. Turns into a prince" (Thompson 1973:149; Opie 1974:183–87). A similar, though clearly unrelated (except, perhaps, psychologically), Tlingit tale was recorded by anthropologist John R. Swanton at Wrangell, Alaska, between January and April 1904, from the mother of the local chief—a woman who "has lived for a considerable time among the whites at Victoria, but with one exception her stories appear to have been influenced little by the fact" (Swanton 1909:1).

There was a large town in the Yakutat country not very far back of which lay a big lake very full of frogs. In the middle of the lake was a swampy patch on which many frogs used to sit.

One day the town-chief's daughter talked badly to the frogs. She took one up and made fun of it, saying, "There are so many of these creatures, I wonder if they do things like human beings. I wonder if men and women cohabit among them."

When she went out of doors that night, a young man came to her and said, "May I marry you?" She had rejected very many men, but she wanted to marry this one right away. Pointing toward the lake he said, "My father's house is right up here," and the girl replied, "How fine it looks!" When they went up to it, it seemed as though a door was opened for them, but in reality the edge of the lake had been raised. They walked under. So many young people were there that she did not think of home again.

Meanwhile her friends missed her and hunted for her everywhere. Finally they gave her up, and her father had the drums beaten for a death feast. They cut their hair and blackened their faces.

Next spring a man who was about to go hunting came to the lake to bathe himself with urine. When he was done, he threw the urine among a number of

---

[8]Bettelheim notes: "The many stories of the animal-groom type from pre-literate cultures suggest that living in intimacy with nature fails to change the view that sex is something animal-like which only love can transform into a human relation. Nor does it alter the fact that more often than not the male is unconsciously experienced as the more animal-like partner because of his more aggressive role in sex" (1976:285). In European folk tradition, the male equivalent of "Beauty and the Beast" is the "Loathly Lady" motif found in folktales, ballads and romances about "the horrible hag or loathesome woman transformed (or disenchanted) into a beautiful woman by the act of love or a kiss" (Leach 1972:739). Heinrich Zimmer discusses this motif as it appears in the fifteenth-century romance about The Weddynge of Sir Gawen and Dame Ragnell in his The King and the Corpse: Tales of the Soul's Conquest of Evil, edited by Joseph Campbell, Bollingen Series XI (Princeton: Princeton University Press, 1971), pp. 88ff. Also see Ananda K. Coomaraswamy, "On the Loathly Bride," Speculum XX (October 1945):391–404; and Martha Heyneman, "Sir Gawain & Women's Liberation," A Journal of Our Time 1 (1977):15–20.

"Northwest Coast maskette made by the Tlingit Indians of Sitka. Carved of wood with pieces of shell glued on, the maskette represents an otter and frog, and belonged to a shaman" (Naylor 1975:75, fig. A).

frogs sitting there and they jumped into the water. When he was bathing next day he saw all the frogs sitting together in the middle of the lake with the missing woman among them. He dressed as quickly as possible, ran home to the girl's father and said, "I saw your daughter sitting in the middle of the pond in company with a lot of frogs." So her father and mother went up that evening with a number of other people, saw, and recognized her.

After that they took all kinds of things to make the frog tribe feel good so that they would let the woman return to her parents, but in vain. By and by her father determined upon a plan and called all of his friends together. Then he told them to dig trenches out from the lake in order to drain it. From the lake the frog chief could see how the people had determined, and he told his tribe all about it. The frog people call the mud around a lake their laid-up food.

After the people had worked away for some time, the trench was completed and the lake began draining away fast. The frogs asked the woman to tell her people to have pity on them and not destroy all, but the people killed none because they wanted only the girl. Then the water flowed out, carrying numbers of frogs which scattered in every direction. All the frog tribe then talked poorly about themselves, and the frog chief, who had talked of letting her go before, now had her dressed up and their own odor, which they called "sweet perfumery," was put upon her. After a while she came down the trench half out of water with her frog husband beside her. They pulled her out and let the frog go.

When anyone spoke to this woman, she made a popping noise "Hu," such as a frog makes, but after some time she came to her senses. She explained, "It was the Kîkca' (i.e., Kîksa'dì women) that floated down with me," meaning that all the frog women and men had drifted away. The woman did not eat at all, though they tried everything. After a while they hung her over a pole, and the black mud she had eaten when she was among the frogs came out of her, but, as soon as it was all out, she died. Because this woman was taken away by the frog tribe at that place, the frogs there can understand human beings very well when they talk to them. It was a Kîksa'dì woman who was taken off by the frogs, and so those people can almost understand them. They also have songs from the frogs, frog personal names, and the frog emblem. All the people know about them. (Swanton 1909:53–54)[9]

Swanton also collected tales from the last few members of various "Indian Tribes of the Lower Mississippi Valley and Adjacent Coast of the Gulf of Mexico." The following myth fragment ("The storyteller added that there were other parts to the myth, which he had forgotten.") was told to illustrate

[9]"Tales of beast marriages between men or women and animals are of frequent occurrence in North American Indian mythology. Some of the most widespread are the Fox-wife story of the Eskimo, the Piqued Buffalo Wife story of the Plains and Eastern Woodlands, Splinter-Foot-Girl of the Plains (in which the heroine marries a buffalo bull), Eagle and Whale Husband stories of the Eskimo, Snake Husband and Bear Husband tales of the plains, Dog Husband of the North Pacific Coast, and Deer Wife of the Plateau" (Leach 1972:129; also see McClellan 1970). The Navajo heroines in the Mountaintop Way and Beauty Way stories, among "the few chant myths having a woman rather than a man as the central character," also marry supernatural husbands (bear and snake, respectively) and thereby learn various helpful rites and lore (Katherine Spencer, *Mythology and Values: An Analysis of Navaho Chantway Myths*, Memoirs of the American Folklore Society, vol. 48, Philadelphia, 1957, p. 150). Also see Donald Sandner's Jungian analysis of these Navajo heroines in *Navaho Symbols of Healing* (1979:173–80).

the Tunica Indian belief that after the flood "animals, birds, and, in short, everybody and everything could change into human beings at night and talk, but not in the daytime" (Swanton 1911:323).

A very handsome youth once came to court a certain girl every evening, leaving before daybreak. By and by he asked her father and mother if he might marry her, but they refused because they did not know who he was. But the girl was foolishly in love with him, and one night, after her parents had again refused him, the youth asked her to run away. She consented and, after the old people were in bed she went off with him to his house. The house was a very nice one and the people there were the best-looking persons she had ever seen. After talking a long time she and her husband left the others sitting there and went to bed. She awoke at daybreak and, moving quickly, saw instead of a house the ugliest kind of a briar bush, in the midst of which she was lying. This was a rattlesnake nest, and the young man she had married was a rattlesnake. She tried to move, but every time she did so all the snakes rattled their tails, and she was obliged to lie where she was all day. She held her hands tightly clasped over her eyes so as not to see them. When night came again it was as it had been before, and everything looked pretty. Then she walked out and returned to her parents, glad to escape from that place. When she told what had happened all of her relatives gathered together to go out and kill the bad snakes. (Ibid)

During the summer of 1924, a Cochiti Pueblo Indian woman, a "well-known native narrator," told anthropologist Ruth Benedict about a girl who was successfully wooed by Coyote.

Long ago a girl would not marry. A boy came and brought her a manta, and a belt and moccasins, but she would not take them, for she did not want to marry. So the boy took his bundle and went out. A second boy came and brought her a manta, and a belt and moccasins, but she would not take them because she did not want to marry. So the second boy took his bundle and went out. A third boy came and brought her a manta, and a belt and moccasins, but she would not take them because she did not want to marry. So the third boy took his bundle and went out. Then the fourth boy came and brought her a bundle but she would not take it. And the fourth boy took his bundle and went out.

Coyote was living in White Mountain. He said to himself, "I will go and try to marry her." He dressed himself to dance. He put on his moccasins and his leggings, a dancer's skirt and a woman's belt, and a loose-sleeved manta. He tied wool yarn around his wrists, and put long parrot feathers in his hair and shorter ones on top of his head. He hung an abalone shell on his chest. He painted his face red and fastened a turtle-shell rattle on his leg, and took a gourd rattle in his hand. Then he looked at himself to see if he was handsome so that the girl would like him. "I am a handsome boy," he thought. "I shall get the girl; I look nice!" He went to the hill to get kapolin berries and he carried a branch of them in his left hand.

He went to the village, and he came in through the west street to the plaza. The girl called to her father and mother, "There is a beautiful boy ready to dance in the plaza. How I wish that I could get the bunch of kapolin berries which he is carrying. I wonder if he would give them to me. Father, shall I go down and ask him for his bunch of berries?" "Yes, perhaps he will give them to you." She went, the people were laughing at him. "She is running after Coyote," they said. When

Design from Cochiti pot
(Sides 1961:plate 33f).

she got near she said to him, "Boy, give me the kapolin berries!" "Yes." She took them. He said, "Now you are my sweetheart. Wait at your house for me and tell your father and mother that I am coming to-night to marry you."

She married him, and she had two children, and they were half coyote and half human. When they were grown they wanted to go with their father. So when they were big enough to walk to White Mountain he took his two children with him to his home, but their mother had to stay with her people. (Benedict 1931:83–84)[10]

The woman's experience of marriage—whether to man or "beast"—is profoundly ambivalent. The institution of marriage also establishes or endangers powerful human and/or human-to-animal social ties. In the following origin myth of the Omaha Indians, the woman's rebellion against custom precipitates far-reaching historical consequences, which ethnologists Alice Fletcher and Francis La Flesche attempt to detail in their historical commentary on the myth.[11] Both text and historical commentary are presented below:

. . . On Bow creek, Nebraska, near where the present town of St. James stands, a village of earth lodges was erected, and here the people remained until a tragedy occurred which caused a separation in the tribe and an abandonment of this village

[10]The Cochiti also tell of an even stranger lover: "A Navaho girl had no lover among her people. She went every day to the mountains. The people said, 'Where is it that she goes every day?' At last one of the men followed her. He tracked her to the mountains, and at last he came to the end of her foot prints. He hid himself near by. There was something covered up there. He heard talking. Pretty soon he heard an answer. They were making love to each other. Finally the girl got up and uncovered herself. She had been lying with her cactus lover (*yatapa,* a cactus). The man who had followed her came back and told the people what he had seen. That is why when we see yatapa, we call it 'the Navaho girl's lover' " (Benedict 1931: 119–20). Also see Leslie Silko's contemporary short story, "Yellow Woman," in Kenneth Rosen, ed., *The Man to Send Rain Clouds: Contemporary Stories by American Indians* (New York: Viking, 1974), pp. 33–45, and the commentary on it by A. LaVonne Ruoff, "Ritual and Renewal: Keres Traditions in the Short Fiction of Leslie Silko," *Melus* 5:4 (Winter 1978):2–17. Tales of Star Husbands are also widespread in many Native American traditions (Thompson 1965; Rich 1971; Young 1970, 1978).

[11]Alice Fletcher lived among and/or communicated extensively with the Omaha Indians for some twenty-nine years in the late nineteenth and early twentieth centuries. For over twenty-five years she collaborated with and legally adopted Francis La Flesche (1857–1932), son of Iron Eyes, the last "principal chief of the tribe." La Flesche, who joined the Smithsonian's Bureau of American Ethnology in 1910, had witnessed his tribe's rites, learned their significance from his father and tribal elders, and determined to learn English in order "to preserve in written form the history of his people as it was known to them, their music, the poetry of their rituals, and the meaning of their social and religious ceremonies . . . and to gather the rapidly vanishing lore of the tribe" (Fletcher and La Flesche 1911:30). For more on La Flesche, see Margot Liberty, "Francis La Flesche: The Osage Odyssey," *Proceedings of the American Ethnological Society,* Spring 1976, and Ronald Walcott, "Francis La Flesche: American Indian Scholar," *Folklife Center News,* American Folklife Center, Library of Congress, vol. IV, no. 1 (January 1981). Note too that Knud Rasmussen has recorded an Eskimo tale about the tribal consequences of a woman's marriage to an invisible man whose tribe seeks to avenge his death when, in a fit of curiosity similar to Psyche's in Apuleius's tale below, she murders him to see his form (1931: 245–46; Edward Field's reworking of this story appears in Jerome Rothenberg, ed., *Shaking the Pumpkin: Traditional Poetry of the Indian North Americas* [Garden City, New York: Doubleday, 1972], pp. 278–79).

by all the people. The site was known and pointed out in the last century as the place where stood the To^{n}wo^{n}pezhi, "Bad Village."

The following is the story of how this village came to be abandoned and received the name of "Bad Village." It is a story that used frequently to be told and is probably historical and suggests how separations may have come about in the more remote past.

In the Teci^n'de gens lived a man and his wife with their three sons and one daughter. Although the man was not a chief, he was respected and honored by the people because of his bravery and hospitality. His daughter was sought in marriage by many men in the tribe. There was one whom she preferred, and to whom she gave her word to be his wife. This fact was not known to her parents, who promised her to a warrior long past his youth. Against her will she was taken to the warrior's dwelling with the usual ceremonies in such marriages. The girl determined in her own mind never to be his wife. She did not cry or struggle when they took her, but acted well her part at the wedding feast, and none knew her purpose. When the feast was over and the sun had set, she slipped away in the dark and was gone. At once a search was started, which was kept up by the disappointed old warrior and his relatives for several days, but without success. The girl's mother grieved over the loss of her daughter, but the father was silent. It was noticed that a certain young man was also missing, and it was thought that the two were probably together. After the girl had been gone some time, a boy rushed to the father's house one morning, as the family were eating their meal, and said: "Your daughter is found! The old man has stripped her of her clothing and is flogging her to death. Hurry, if you would see her alive!" The father turned to his sons and said: "Go, see if there is truth in this." The eldest refused, the second son bowed his head and sat still. The youngest arose, seized his bow, put on his quiver, and went out. The village had gathered to the scene. As the brother approached, he heard his sister's cries of anguish. Pushing his way through the crowd he shouted words of indignation to those who had not tried to rescue the girl, and, drawing his bow, shot the angry old man. The relatives of the dead man and those who sympathized with his exercise of marital rights ran for their bows and fought those who sided with the young rescuer. A battle ensued; fathers fought sons and brothers contended with brothers. All day the two sides contested and many were slain before night put an end to the conflict. The next day those who had fought with the brother left the village with him and traveled eastward, while their opponents picked up their belongings, turned their back on their homes and moved toward the south. There was no wailing nor any outward sign of mourning. Silently the living separated, and the village was left with the unburied dead. * * *

"A new generation had grown up," this strange story continues, "when a war party traveling east beyond the Missouri river encountered a village where the people spoke the Omaha language. Abandoning their warlike intents, the Omaha warriors entered the village peaceably, persuaded their new-found relatives to return with them, and so the Omaha people were once more united." The village where the reunion took place was near one then occupied by the Iowa, not far from the site of the present town of Ponca City. (Fletcher and La Flesche 1911:85–86)

♦   Penelope Washbourn, *Becoming Woman:* "The emotional and spiritual danger in which a woman stands as she enters marriage is enormous. Too many inner voices are leading her to expect essential fulfillment as a woman in being a wife. The religious tradition, the psychological tradition of the West, a woman's parents,

(Harter 1978b:78)

and societal expectations and pressures teach her that marriage is essential to her fulfillment. In that marriage she gives up her individuality and her right to herself as she moves from being a virgin, either symbolically or literally, to becoming a wife and mother. To find herself enhanced through marriage and not destroyed and to discover the graceful possibilities within the institution of marriage in this society represents one of the most fundamental of all spiritual challenges facing women today. She and her partner will need an ultimate sense of trust in themselves and in each other to realize that possibility" (1977:84).

"Marriage"

Dearly beloved, you have come here to be united into this holy estate *We are the empty vessel* it behooveth you, then, to declare, in the presence of God and these witnesses *we are the body the flesh* the sincere intent you both have. *We are one with him* Who giveth this woman to be married to this man? *and he is the one.* Wilt thou have this man to be thy wedded husband *We bear his name* to live with him after God's ordinance in the holy estate of matrimony? *His knowledge is our knowledge, what he asks of us we give.* Matter impressed. *We are the background, the body, we receive.* Matter impressed with heat. The enlarging of the molecule. The polymerization of material. The desirable flexibility. The formation of plastic. *We*

(Harter 1978b:27)

have heard the story of the foolish virgins who were not always waiting for the bridegrooms. We wait. The making of plasticity. The material molded to desire. The synthesis of polyamide. The coupling of hexamethylene diamine with adipic acid. Nylon. *We have heard the story of Zeus's mother, of how she forbade marriage to Zeus, of how she feared the violence of his lust.* The material shaped. *Of how Zeus raped his mother.* Phenol mixed with formaldehyde. *We comply.* Bakelite. The material shaped at will. Ethylene reacting with chlorine. Polyvinyl chloride. Polystyrene. Plexiglass. Polythene. Polyethylene. *We know that after Zeus married Hera he angered her with infidelity. And we heard that after she rebelled against him he hung her from the sky, putting golden bracelets around her wrists and anvils about her ankles.* The material easily shaped. *We obey.* Artificial rubber. Artificial wood. Artificial leather. Easily used. Teflon. Silicone. Corfam. Malleable. Cellophane. Polyurethane foam. Mutable. Glass fiber resins. Bent to use. DDT 24-D. Ammonic detergent. *We have heard the story of Daphne. That she did not want to marry. That when Apollo pursued her, she fled. That when he seized her, she would not yield and she called out for help to her father, and that her father changed her to a laurel tree. And we heard that after this Apollo told her, "Your leaf shall know no decay. You shall always be as you are now, and I shall wear you for my crown."* Benzene. Hexachloride. *We yield.* Dichlorobenzene solvents. Polypropylene plastics. Design. The formation of the earth in strata. The convenient stratification of the elements. The utility of the complexities of the earth. The convenience of resources. The availability of treasure. *We were told that we exist for his needs, that we are a necessity.* Mineral salt. Coal. Metallic ores. *That it is in our nature to be needed.* The production of soil for agriculture. The general dispersal of metals useful to man. The disposition of certain animals for domestication. The provision of food and raiment by plants and animals. The size of animals in relation to man. The convenience of the size of goats for milking. The convenience of the size of ripened corn. The value of labor. The labor theory of value. Her labor married to his value. *We were told that Zeus swallowed Metis whole* Her labor *that from his belly* disappearing *she gave him advice.* Her labor not counted in his production. *We are the empty vessel, the background, the body.* His name given to her labor. The wife of the laborer called working class. The wife of the shopkeeper called petit bourgeois. The wife of the factory owner called bourgeois. *We were told that since it is in our nature to be needed* wilt thou love him, comfort him, honor him, obey him *that his need is our need* and keep him in sickness and in health *and that his happiness is our happiness* and forsaking all others, keep thee only to him *in all things.* so long as you both shall live? *And if we should suffer at his hands* In the presence of God and these witness, I take thee *we must have wished for this suffering* to be my wedded husband *that his sins are our sins* and plight thee my troth *that without him, we are not* till death do us part.

    —Susan Griffin, *Woman and Nature: The Roaring Inside Her* (1978: 100–102).

(Harter 1978b:64)

◆   Erich Neumann, *Amor and Psyche:* ". . . When we speak of 'marriage' we have in mind an archetype or archetypal experience, and not a merely physiological occurrence. The experience of the original situation of the marriage of death may coincide with the first real consummation of marriage, the defloration, but it need not, any more than the original situation of childbearing need coincide with actual childbearing. It is true that innumerable women consummate marriage or perform the act of childbearing without going through the corresponding 'experience'—as, to our surprise, we often observe in modern women—but this does not do away with the marriage situation as an archetype and central figure of feminine psychic reality" (1956:64–65).

Active Heroines

Among the Eskimo myths collected from Kodiak Island, Alaska, are ones which Margaret Lantis labels "Amazon Tales." According to her: "An interesting feature of Koniag folklore is the 'girl-heroine' theme. One such story, that of the girl who had remarkable adventures when she went in search of her lost lover, could very well be the story of a boy as far as her exploits are concerned. (This is the story of the girl who killed the cannibals.) The Huntress on the other hand focuses the attention on the abilities of a certain girl in comparison with her brothers" (1938:157). Lantis' outline of "The Huntress" shows the girl's "active" response to seclusion at menarche, as well as her acquisition of physical skills which help her do more than marry.

A. Girl in seclusion.
    1. Her first menses.
    2. Her parents were poor; they went away, leaving her no food.
    3. She ate only sea-weed from the beach, becoming weak.
B. Strength-giver.
    1. An old man came one night and told her to get up.
    2. Commanded her to drink from the river. Her strength partially returned.
    3. Second command to drink: she could place a tree trunk across the river.
    4. Third command: she could drink no more.
    5. The man disappeared.
C. Girl became a hunter.
    1. Made arrows for herself.
    2. Practised shooting until she could kill a seal.
    3. In hauling in a seal, she made four steps on a cape which can still be seen.
    4. Built a kayak.
D. Deceived her parents.
    1. When parents returned to see how she was, she pretended that she was barely alive.
    2. She was left alone again.
E. The girl and her three brothers.
    1. Went to her family's camping-place alone in her own kayak.
    2. Built a still better kayak.
    3. Killed sea-otters when her brothers could not.
    4. Brothers became jealous.
    5. Brothers attempted to trick her: took her arrows and left her.
    6. She circumvented the trick.
        a. Took hind flippers of a seal, gnawed them until only the nails were left.
        b. Tied a nail to her finger and somehow shot two otters.
        c. Overtook her brothers and accused them.
    7. Heavy sea, but the girl saved herself. (Brothers not mentioned again.)
F. Girl's marriage.
    1. Became handsome and was sought by many men.
    2. Married one man.
    3. They went hunting together.
        a. Big sea; she took her husband into her kayak.
        b. Made him close his eyes.

Sea otter (Rice 1979:75).

  c. She cut off her female parts and threw them on the sea.

  d. It grew calm and they returned home.

G. This woman continues to go many places. (Lantis 1938:157–58)

In April 1968, Joel Gómez collected a version of Aarne-Thompson tale type 425, "The Search for the Lost Husband," from seventy-four-year-old Mrs. P. E. of La Encantada, Texas. According to folklorist Américo Paredes: "La Encantada, formerly El Ranchito, is a village some eleven miles upriver from Brownsville, Texas, and Matamoros, Tamaulipas. The informant belongs to regional folk groups that have inhabited the area on both sides of the Rio Grande for some two centuries" (1970:211). Gómez "reports that his informant learned her folktale repertory from her mother, who not only was well known locally as a narrator, but also was celebrated for her singing and playing on the guitar. This may have some bearing on the fact that the heroine in this text sings and plays the guitar, carrying the instrument with her wherever she goes" (ibid:215–16).

There were three girls who were orphaned, and Luisa did much sewing. The other two said that they didn't like Luisa's kind of life. They would rather go to bars and such things. Well, that kind of women—gay women. So Luisa stayed home. She kept a jar of water on the window sill, and she sewed and sewed and sewed.

So then he came, the Greenish Bird that was an enchanted prince. And of course he liked Luisa a lot, so he would light there on the window sill and say, "Luisa, raise your eyes to mine, and your troubles will be over." But she wouldn't.

On another night he came and said, "Luisa, give me a drink of water from your little jar." But she wouldn't look to see if he was a bird or a man or anything. Except she didn't know whether he drank or not, but then she saw he was a man. She gave him some water. So then he came again and proposed to her, and they fell in love. And the bird would come inside; he would lie in her bed. There on the headboard. And he set up a garden for her, with many fruit trees and other things, and a messenger and a maid; so the girl was living in grand style.

What should happen but that her sisters found out. "Just look at Luisa, how high she has gone overnight. And us," she says, "just look at us the way we are. Let's spy on her and see who it is that goes in there." They went and spied on her and saw it was a bird, so they bought plenty of knives. And they put them on the window sill. When the bird came out, he was wounded all over.

He said, "Luisa, if you want to follow me, I live in crystal towers on the plains of Merlin. I'm badly wounded," he said.

So she bought a pair of iron shoes, Luisa did, and she took some clothes with her—what she could carry walking—and a guitar she had. And she went off after him. She came to the house where the Sun's mother lived. She was a blonde, blonde old woman. Very ugly. So she got there and knocked on the door and it opened. The old woman said, "What are you doing here? If my son the Sun sees you, he'll devour you," she said.

"I'm searching for the Greenish Bird," she said.

"He was here. Look, he's badly wounded. He left a pool of blood there, and he just left a moment ago."

She said, "All right, then, I'm going."

"No," she said, "hide and let's see if my son can tell you something. He shines on all the world," she said.

So he came in, very angry:

Whoo! Whoo!

I smell human flesh. Whoo-whoo!

If I can't have it, I'll eat you.

He said this to his mother.

"What do you want me to do, son? There's nobody here." Until she calmed him down and gave him food. Then she told him, little by little.

He said, "Where's the girl," he said. "Let her come out so I can see her." So Luisa came out and asked him about the Greenish Bird. He said, "Me, I don't know. I haven't heard of him. I don't know where to find him. I haven't seen anything like that, either. It could be that the Moon's mother, or the Moon herself, would know," he said.

Well then, "All right, I'm going now." Without tasting a bite of food. So then the Sun told her to eat first and then go. And so then they gave her something to eat, and she left.

All right, so she got to the house where the Moon's mother lived. And so, "What are you doing here? If my daughter the Moon sees you, she will devour you." And I don't know how many other things the old woman said to her.

"Well then, I'll go. I just wanted to ask her if she hadn't seen the Greenish Bird pass by here."

"He was here. Look, there's the blood; he's very badly wounded," she said.

All right, so she started to go away, but the Moon said, *"Hombre,* don't go. Come eat first, and then you can go." So they also gave her a bite to eat. As soon as they gave her something, she left. "Why don't you go where the mother of the Wind lives and wait for the Wind to come home? The Wind goes into every nook and cranny; there isn't a place he doesn't visit."

The mother of the Wind said, "All right," so she hid. She said, "But you'll have to hide, because if my son the Wind sees you, Heaven help us."

"All right," she said.

The Wind came home, all vapory and very angry, and his mother told him to behave, to take a seat, to sit down and have something to eat. So he quieted down. And then the girl told him that she was looking for the Greenish Bird.

But no. "I can't tell you anything about that. I've never seen anything," he said.

(Harter 1980b:113)

Well, so the girl went out again, but they gave her breakfast first and all that. The thing is that by the time she did find out, she had worn out the iron shoes she was wearing. It happened that there was an old hermit way out there, who tended to all the birds. He would call them by blowing on a whistle, and they would all come, and all kinds of animals, too. So she went there, too. And he asked her what she was doing out there, in those lonely wilds, and this and that. So she told the hermit, "I'm in search of the Greenish Bird. Don't you know where he lives?"

"No," he said. "What I do know is that he was here. And he's badly wounded. But let me call my birds, and it may be that they know or have heard where he is, or something."

Well, no. All the birds were called, but the old eagle was missing. The old eagle was right in the middle of it, eating tripe. The prince was to be married, but he had prayed to God that he would get leprosy, something like sores, and he was ill with sores. He was hoping Luisa would get there. But they were getting ready to marry him. The bride was a princess and very rich, but even so he didn't love her. He wanted to wait for his Luisa. Well then, so the old eagle was missing. The old man, the hermit, began blowing and blowing on his whistle until she came.

"What do you want, *hombre?* There I was, peacefully eating tripe, and you have to carry on like that, with all that blowing."

"Wait, don't be mean," he said. "There's a poor girl here looking for the Greenish Bird. She says she's his sweetheart and is going to marry him."

"She's looking for the Greenish Bird? The Greenish Bird is about to get married. The only reason he hasn't married yet is that he's very sick of some sores. Hmm, yes. But the wedding feast is going on, and the bride's mother is there and everything. But, anyway, if she wants to go, it's all right. I just came from there. I was there eating tripe and guts and all that stuff they throw away. If she wants to go, all she has to do is butcher me a cow, and we'll go."

The girl heard, and she was very happy, even if he was getting married and all that. The hermit called her, and she came out, and she saw all kinds of birds. And he said, "The old eagle says that if you butcher a cow, she will take you all the way to the very palace."

All right, she said she would. For she had plenty of money with her. The bird had made her well off from the beginning. He would have married her then and there, if it hadn't been for those bratty sisters of hers. So all right, so they did go. She slaughtered the cow, and the eagle took her and the cow on her back. She would fly high, high, high; and then she would start coming down.

"Give me a leg," she would say. And she would eat the meat. That's why we say a person is "an old eagle" when they ask for meat. She would give her meat. And, "What do you see?"

"Nothing," she would say. "You can't see anything yet. It's a very pretty palace made of nothing but glass. It will shine in the sun," the eagle would say. "I don't see anything yet." And she would keep on going, straight, straight ahead, who knows how far. And then she would fly up, and up, and up.

"What do you see?"

"Well, something like a peak that shines. But it's very far away."

"Yes, it's very far."

So the cow was all eaten up, and still they didn't get there. And she said she wanted more meat. Luisa said, "Here, take the knife." She told the eagle that. "Cut off one of my legs, or I'll cut it off myself," Luisa told the eagle. But she didn't say it wholeheartedly, of course. Not a chance.

Anyway the eagle said, "No, no. I only said it to test you. I'm going to leave you just outside because there are many cops around—or something like that—guarding the doors. You ask permission to go in from one of them. Tell them to let the ladies know you are coming in to cook. Don't ask for anything else," she said. "Get a job as a cook and then, well, we'll see how things go for you."

All right, so she left Luisa just outside the yard. It was a great big yard made of pure gold or God knows what. As beautiful as could be. She asked the guard to let her in. "And what is your reason for going in? What are you going to do?"

She said, "Well, I'm very poor, and I've come from a long way off. And I'm looking for work. Anything I can do to eat, no matter if it is working in the kitchen." And her carrying a golden comb, and all that the Greenish Bird had given her. And the guitar.

"Let me go ask the mistress," he said, "to see if they want to hire some kitchen help." So he went and told her, "A woman is looking for work." And who knows what else.

"What kind of woman is she?"

"Well, she is like this, and this way, and that way."

"All right, tell her to come in, and have her go around that way, so she won't come in through here in the palace," she said. She didn't want her to go through the house.

So she went over there. And everybody was very kind to her. Meanwhile the

(Harter 1980b:96)

Greenish Bird was a person now, but he was all leprous and very sick. There was a little old woman who had raised him. She was the one who took care of him. They had her there as a servant. First she had raised the boy, when she worked for his parents. Then she had moved over here, to the bride's house. She was no bride when the old woman first came there, but the girl had fallen in love with him. But he loved his Luisa.

And well, the wedding feast was in full swing, you might say, and he began to feel much better, for he heard a guitar being played, and he asked the old woman why they hadn't told him there were strangers in the house.

And when he heard the guitar, he told the woman who was taking care of him, who came to see him when he was sick, "Who is singing and playing the guitar?"

"Oh, I had forgotten to tell you. A lady came wearing a pair of worn-out iron shoes, and she also has a guitar and a comb.

"Is there anything on the comb?"

"Well, I don't know." She couldn't read any more than I can. "I don't know what's on it. They look like little wreaths or letters or I don't know what."

"Ask her to lend it to you and bring it here." And once he heard about the guitar, once he heard the guitar playing and all, he began to get well. He got much better. But neither the mother and father of the girl nor anybody else came to see him there.

He was all alone with the woman who took care of him. Because he looked very ugly. But then the woman went and told the princess who was going to be his mother-in-law, "You should see how much better the prince is, the Greenish Bird. He is quite well now."

So they all came to see him. And that made him angrier yet, because they came to see him now that he was well. The girl was very rich and a princess and all that, and Luisa was a poor little thing. But he said, "Go ask her to lend you her comb and bring it to me."

The old woman went and asked for the comb as if she wanted to comb her hair, and she went back where he was. He didn't say anything; he just looked at it.

"What do you say?"

"No, nothing," he said. "Tomorrow, or this afternoon, when they bring me food, have her bring it to me. She's working here, after all," he said.

So when it was time to take him his dinner, she said, "Listen, Luisa, go take the prince his dinner. I'm very tired now. I'm getting old." Luisa didn't want to go; she was putting on. She hung back and she hung back, but at last she went.

Well, they greeted each other and saw each other and everything. And she said, "Well, so you are already engaged and are going to get married," Luisa said. "And one cannot refuse anything to kings and princes."

"But I have an idea, ever since I heard the guitar," said the boy.

"What is it?"

"Everybody is going to make chocolate, and the cup I drink, I'll marry the one who made it."

And she says, "But I don't even know how to make chocolate!"

The old woman said she would make it for her, the woman who was taking care of him. Because Luisa went and told her about it. "Just imagine what the prince wants. For all of us to come in, cooks and no cooks and absolutely all the women here, princesses and all. And each one of us must make a cup of chocolate, and the cup he drinks, he'll marry the woman who made it." And she said, "I don't know how. . . ."

"Now, now," said the old woman, "don't worry about that. I'll make it for you. And you can take it to him."

Well, the first to come in were all the big shots, as is always the case. First the bride, then the mother-in-law, the father-in-law, sisters-in-law, and everybody. And all he said was, "I don't like it. I don't like it."

The mother-in-law said, "Now, I wonder who he wants to marry?" And, "I wonder who he wants to marry?"

Well . . . nobody. So then the old woman who took care of him came. Neither. Then the other cook came in. And Luisa was the last one. He told them that she was the one he wanted to marry. That she had come searching for him from very far away, and that he would marry her. And he drank all of Luisa's cup of chocolate. Bitter or not, he didn't care. And he married her. And *colorin* so red, the story is finished. (Paredes 1970:95–102)

This type of tale "apparently developed almost exclusively in a female milieu . . . [and] it is striking . . . to see to what extent this tale has been cherished by female storytellers" (Dégh 1969:93). The classical form of this narrative, Aarne-Thompson type 425A, "Cupid and Psyche" (also called Amor or Eros and Psyche), is a story (books 4–6) within a second-century A.D. Latin novel by Apuleius called *The Metamorphoses* or *The Golden Ass*. In the novel, an old woman in a thieves' den tells the tale, which is likely based on traditional Greek and Italian folktales (Thompson 1946:281–82, 97–100), to a young girl. Quotations in the following outline of the story are from the 1566 translation (Modern Library Edition) by William Adlington. (For a more contemporary translation and discussion of "Apuleius and his Work," see Lindsay 1932.)

Psyche was the youngest daughter of "a certain king." Her beauty rivaled that of Venus, whose worship was thus neglected. The enraged goddess summoned "her winged son Cupid" and ordered him to take revenge for her by causing Psyche to "fall in desperate love with the most miserable creature living, the most poor, the most crooked, and the most vile, that there may be none found in all the world of like wretchedness."

Although her two older sisters married kings, Psyche remained unmarried and "disquieted both in mind and body (Although she pleased all the world) yet hated she in herself her own beauty."

Her father suspected the gods were envious of his daughter. He consulted Apollo's oracle at Miletus and was told:

"Let Psyche's corpse be clad in mourning weed
    And set on rock of yonder hill aloft:
Her husband is no wight of human seed,
    But serpent dire and fierce as may be thought . . ."

The disheartened king returned home to lament with his wife their daughter's sad fate.

"But necessity compelled that poor Psyche should be brought to her appointed doom, according to the divine commandment; and when the solemnity of the wretched wedding was ended with great sorrow, all the people followed the living corpse, and they went to bring this sorrowful spouse, not to her marriage, but to her final end and burial." Although Psyche bravely chided them for their lamentations, she broke down after their departure. "Thus poor Psyche being left alone weeping and trembling on the highest top of the rock, there came a gentle air of softly breathing Zephyrus and carried her from the hill, with a meek wind,

(Harter 1978b:47)

which retained her garments up, and by little and little brought her down into a deep valley, where she was laid in a soft grassy bed of most sweet and fragrant flowers."

A veritable paradise awaited her, with invisible voices to attend her every whim. At night her husband would make love to her, departing before daybreak. One night, he "spake unto her (for she might not know him with her eyes, but only with her hands and ears)" and warned her not to heed her sisters' impending lamentations "for if thou do, thou shalt purchase to me a great sorrow, and to thyself utter destruction." Although she promised to obey her husband, Psyche yielded to her own loneliness and despair, finally persuading him to change his mind and order Zephyrus to carry the sisters to and from their paradise. He agreed, on the condition "that she should covet not (being moved by the pernicious counsel of her sisters) to see the shape of his person, lest by her wicked curiosity she should be deprived of so great and worthy estate and nevermore feel his embrace."

The sisters were duly impressed and soon consumed with envy. Despite renewed warnings about "those naughty hags, armed with wicked minds" and a final plea "to take pity on thyself, and on me, keep a seal on thy lips, and deliver thy husband, and thyself, and this infant within thy belly from so great and imminent a danger," Psyche demanded to see her sisters again. On this visit "they settled themselves to work their treason and snare against Psyche, demanding with guile who was her husband, and of what parentage or race he was" and receiving yet another fabricated response from their hapless sibling.

On their third visit, the sisters bluntly addressed Psyche: "Thou (ignorant of so great evil) thinkest thyself sure and happy, and sittest at home nothing regarding thy peril, whereas we go about thy affairs, and are exceeding sorry for the harm that shall happen unto thee: for we are credibly informed, neither can we but utter it unto thee, that are the companions of thy grief and mishap, that there is a great serpent of many coils, full of deadly poison, with a ravenous and gaping throat, that lieth with thee secretly every night. Remember the oracle of Apollo, who pronounced that thou shouldst be married to a dire and fierce beast; and many of the inhabitants hereby, and such as hunt about in the country, affirm that they have seen him towards evening returning from pasture and swimming over the river: whereby they do undoubtedly say that he will not pamper thee long with delicate meats, but when the time of delivery shall approach, he will devour both thee and thy child as a more tender morsel. Wherefore advise thyself, whether thou wilt agree unto us that are careful for thy safety, and so avoid the peril of death, and be contented to live with thy sisters, or whether thou wilt remain with the most cruel serpent, and in the end be swallowed into the gulf of his body. And if it be so that thy solitary life, thy conversation with voices, and this servile and dangerous pleasure, that is the secret and filthy love of the poisonous serpent, do more delight thee; say not but that we have played the parts of natural sisters in warning thee."

The distraught young wife begged her sisters to tell her what to do. Their advice: "Take a sharp razor, whetted upon the palm of your hand to its finest edge, and put it under the pillow of your bed, and see that you have ready a privy burning lamp with oil, hid under some part of the hanging of the chamber; and (finely dissimulating all the matter) when, according to his custom, he cometh to bed and stretcheth him fully out and sleepeth soundly, breathing deep, arise you secretly, and with your bare feet treading a-tiptoe, go and take your lamp, with the razor lifted high in your right hand, from the ward of its hiding-place that you may borrow from its light the occasion of a bold deed, and with valiant force cut off the head of the poisonous serpent at the knot of his neck."

Psyche followed her sisters' advice exactly, "so that by her audacity she changed herself to masculine kind." However, her light revealed not a serpent but the divine and "glorious" Cupid. She also marvelled at his bow and arrows, taking "one of the arrows out of the quiver, and trying the sharpness thereof with her finger, she pricked herself withal: wherewith she was so grievously wounded that some little drops of blood followed, and thereby of her own accord she fell in love with Love." Her passionate embraces caused "a drop of burning oil from the lamp [to fall] upon the right shoulder of the god." He awoke and flew away after chiding her infidelity.

A desperate Psyche tried to drown herself but the river, fearing Cupid, "threw her upon the bank amongst the herbs." There Pan comforted and counseled her to win back her husband. After first tricking each of her sisters into believing Cupid wanted to marry them next, thereby causing them to leap off the crag to their deaths, Psyche set out to find Cupid, "but he was gotten into his mother's chamber, and there bewailed the sorrowful wound which he caught by the oil of the burning lamp." There, Venus angrily confronted her son and vowed vengeance on both of them.

After storming out of her "golden chamber," Venus immediately came upon Juno and Ceres, neither of whom could check her wrath, and both of whom feared Cupid and "his dart and shafts of love." The desolate, wandering Psyche was then refused sanctuary, first at Ceres' temple and then at Juno's. Terrified, Psyche prepared to face Venus herself.

Meanwhile, that goddess had driven her chariot to "the royal palace of the god Jupiter," from whom she successfully demanded Mercury's services. "By and by Mercurius, obeying her commands, proclaimed throughout all the world that whatsoever he were that could bring back or tell any tidings of a king's fugitive daughter, the servant of Venus, named Psyche, let him bring word to Mercury, behind the Murtian temple, and for reward of his pains he should receive seven sweet kisses of Venus and one more sweetly honeyed from the touch of her loving tongue. After that Mercury had pronounced these things, every man was inflamed with desire of so great a guerdon to search her out, and this was the cause that put away all doubt from Psyche, who was all but come in sight of the house of Venus: but one of her servants called Custom came out, who, espying Psyche, cried with a loud voice: 'O wicked harlot as thou art, now at length thou shalt know that thou hast a mistress above thee; what, beside all thy other bold carriage, dost thou make thyself ignorant, as if thou didest not understand what travail we have taken in searching for thee? I am glad that thou art come into my hands, thou art now in the claws of Hell, and shalt abide the pain and punishment of thy great contumacy'; and therewithal she seized her by the hair, and brought her before the presence of Venus."

Venus "laughed loudly, as angry persons accustom to do" and "delivered Psyche to be cruelly tormented" by her handmaidens Sorrow and Sadness. "They fulfilled the commandment of their mistress, and after they had piteously scourged her with whips and had otherwise tormented her, they presented her again before Venus. Then she began to laugh again, saying: 'Behold, she thinketh that by reason of her great belly, which she hath gotten by playing the whore, to move me to pity, and to make me a happy grandmother to her noble child. . . .'

"When Venus had spoken these words, she leaped upon poor Psyche, and (tearing everywhere her apparel) took her violently by the hair, and dashed her head upon the ground. Then she took a great quantity of wheat, barley, millet, poppy-seed, pease, lentils, and beans, and mingled them all together on a heap,

(Harter 1978b:50)

Merino ram (Rice 1979:24).

saying: 'Thou art so evil-favoured, girl, that thou seemest unable to get the grace of thy lovers by no other means, but only by diligent and painful service: wherefore I will prove what thou canst do; see that thou separate all these grains one from another, disposing them orderly in their quality, and let it be done to my content before night.' " A tiny ant took pity on Psyche "and called to her all the ants of the country, saying: 'I pray you, my friends, ye quick daughters of the ground the mother of all things, take mercy on this poor maid espoused to Cupid, who is in great danger of her person; I pray you help her with all diligence.' Incontinently they came, the hosts of six-footed creatures one after another in waves, separating and dividing the grain, and after that they had put each kind of corn in order, they ran away again in all haste from her sight."

Venus returned, reviled her daughter-in-law for receiving help, and gave her "a morsel of brown bread." Early the next morning, "Venus called Psyche, and said: 'Seest thou yonder forest that extendeth out in length with the river-banks, the bushes whereof look close down upon the stream hard by? There be great sheep shining like gold, and kept by no manner of person; I command thee that thou go thither and bring me home some of the wool of their fleeces.' " Prepared to commit suicide in the river, Psyche was dissuaded by "a green reed, nurse of sweet music," and told to hide until after midday when the flocks rest by the river. Then, as "their great fury is past and their passion is stilled, thou mayest go among the thickets and bushes under the wood-side and gather the locks of their golden fleeces which thou shalt find hanging upon the briars."

A suspicious Venus immediately gave Psyche a third task, saying: " 'Seest thou the high rock that overhangs the top of yonder great hill, from whence there runneth down water of black and deadly colour which is gathered together in the valley hard by and thence nourisheth the marshes of Styx and the hoarse torrent of Cocytus? I charge thee to go thither and bring me a vessel of that freezing water from the middest flow of the top of that spring': wherewithal she gave her a bottle of carven crystal, menacing and threatening her more rigorously than before.

"Then poor Psyche went in all haste to the top of the mountain, rather to end her wretched life than to fetch any water, and when she was come up to the ridge of the hill, she perceived that it was very deadly and impossible to bring it to pass, for she saw a great rock, very high and not to be approached by reason that it was exceeding rugged and slippery, gushing out most horrible fountains of waters, which, bursting forth from a cavernous mouth that sloped downwards, ran below and fell through a close and covered watercourse which they had digged out, by many stops and passages, into the valley beneath. On each side she saw great dragons creeping upon the hollow rocks and stretching out their long and bloody necks, with eyes that never slept devoted to watchfulness, their pupils always awake to the unfailing light, which were appointed to keep the river there: the very waters protected themselves with voices, for they seemed to themselves likewise saying: 'Away, away, what wilt thou do? Fly, fly, or else thou wilt be slain.' " While she blankly surveyed this impossible task, "the royal bird of great Jupiter, the eagle," swooped down, snatched her bottle and flew quickly up to fill it.

An enfuriated Venus next demanded: "Take this box and go to Hell and the deadly house of Orcus, and desire Proserpina to send me a little of her beauty, as much as will serve me the space of one day, and say that such as I had is consumed away in tending my son that is sick: but return again quickly, for I must dress myself therewithal, and go to the theatre of the gods." A disconsolate Psyche prepared to hurl herself from "a high tower," but it spoke and instructed her as to where to find "the breathing-place of Hell" and what to bring with her—coins for Charon the ferryman and "two sops sodden in the flour of barley and honey" for the three-headed dog Cerebus. "And it shall come to pass as thou sittest in [Charon's] boat, thou shalt see an old man swimming on the top of the river holding up his deadly hands, and desiring thee to receive him into the bark; but have no regard to his piteous cry, for it is not lawful to do so. When thou art past over the flood thou shalt espy certain old women weaving who will desire thee to help them, but beware thou do not consent unto them in any case, for these and like baits and traps will Venus set, to make thee let fall but one of thy sops." Upon encountering Cerebus, "if thou cast one of thy sops, thou mayest have access to Proserpina without all danger: she will make thee good cheer, and bid thee sit soft, and entertain thee with delicate meat and drink, but sit thou upon the ground and desire brown bread and eat it, and then declare thy message unto her, and when thou hast received what she giveth, in thy return appease the rage of the dog with the other sop, and give thy other halfpenny to covetous Charon, and crossing his river come the same way again as thou wentest in to the upperworld of the heavenly stars: but above all things have a regard that thou look not in the box, neither be not too curious about the treasure of the divine beauty."

Psyche did as she had been instructed. "Then returning more nimbly than before from Hell, and worshipping the white light of day, though she was much in haste to come to the end of her task, she was ravished with great desire, saying: 'Am not I a fool, that knowing that I carry here the divine beauty, will not take a little thereof to garnish my face, to please my lover withal?' And by and by she opened the box, where she could perceive no beauty nor anything else, save only an infernal and deadly sleep, which immediately invaded all her members as soon as the box was uncovered, covering her with its dense cloud in such sort that she fell down on the ground, and lay there in her very steps on that same path as a sleeping corpse. But Cupid being now healed of his wound and malady, not able to endure the long absence of Psyche, got him secretly out at a high window of the chamber where he was enclosed, and (his wings refreshed by a little repose) took his flight towards his loving wife; whom when he had found, he wiped away the sleep from her face, and put it again into the box, and awaked her with an harmless prick of the tip of one of his arrows, saying: 'O wretched captive, behold thou wert well nigh perished again with thy overmuch curiosity; well, go thou, and do bravely thy message to my mother, and in the mean season I will provide all things accordingly'; wherewithal he took his flight into the air, and Psyche brought to Venus the present of Proserpina."

Cupid flew to Jupiter's palace and pleaded his cause before the highest god, who assembled all the gods and announced that Cupid had indeed found a worthy match. "Then he turned unto Venus, and said: 'And you, my daughter, take you no care, neither fear the dishonour of your progeny and estate, neither have regard in that it is a mortal marriage, for I will see to it that this marriage be no unequal, but just, lawful, and legitimate by the law civil.' Incontinently after, Jupiter commanded Mercury to bring up Psyche into the palace of heaven. And then he took a pot of immortality, and said: 'Hold, Psyche, and drink to the end thou mayest be immortal, and that Cupid may never depart from thee, but be thine everlasting husband.'

"By and by the great banquet and marriage feast was sumptuously prepared. Cupid sat down in the uppermost seat with his dear spouse between his arms: Juno likewise with Jupiter and all the other gods in order: Ganymede, the rustic boy, his own butler, filled the pot of Jupiter, and Bacchus served the rest: their drink was nectar, the wine of the gods. Vulcanus prepared supper, the Hours decked up the house with roses and other sweet flowers, the Graces threw about balm, the Muses sang with sweet harmony, fair Venus danced finely to the music, and the

(Harter 1980b:77)

entertainment was so ordained that while the Muses sang in quire, Satyrus and Paniscus played on their pipes: and thus Psyche was married to Cupid, and after in due time she was delivered of a child {a daughter}, whom we call Pleasure."

◆ Erich Neumann, *Amor and Psyche: The Psychic Development of the Feminine:* "Aphrodite's plan to destroy Psyche revolves around the four labors that she imposes upon her. In performing these four strange and difficult labors in the service of Aphrodite, Psyche becomes a feminine Heracles; her mother-in-law plays the same role as Heracles' step-mother. In both cases the Bad Mother plays the role of destiny, and in both cases this destiny leads to heroism and 'memorable deeds.' For us the essential is to note the heroism of the feminine differs from that of the masculine" (1956:93). [12]

◆ "As the tower teaches Psyche, 'pity is not lawful.' If . . . all Psyche's acts present a rite of initiation, this prohibition implies the insistence on 'ego stability' characteristic of every initiation. Among men this stability is manifested as endurance of pain, hunger, thirst, and so forth; but in the feminine sphere it characteristically takes the form of resistance to pity. This firmness of the strong-willed ego, concentrated on its goal, is expressed in countless other myths and fairy tales, with their injunctions not to turn around, not to answer, and the like. While ego stability is a very masculine virtue, it is more; for it is the presupposition of consciousness and of all conscious activity.
  "The feminine is threatened in its ego stability by the danger of distraction through 'relatedness,' through Eros. This is the difficult task that confronts every feminine psyche on its way to individuation: it must suspend the claim of what is close at hand for the sake of a distant abstract goal" (ibid:112).

◆ "With her first three acts Psyche sets in motion the knowledge-bringing masculine-positive forces of her nature. But, in addition, she converted the unconscious forces that had helped her into conscious activity and so liberated her own masculine aspect. Her way, consciously traveled by the ego in opposition to the Great Mother, is the typical career of the masculine hero, at the end of which Psyche would have been transformed into a Nike. A very questionable triumph, as feminine developments in this direction have sufficiently shown. For to achieve such a victorious masculine development at the price of her erotic attraction—that is, her attraction for Eros—would have been a catastrophe for a feminine Psyche, whose actions were undertaken for love, that is, under the sign of Eros. This outcome is prevented by what we have interpreted as 'Psyche's failure.'
  "After becoming conscious of her masculine components and realizing them, and having become whole through development of her masculine aspect, Psyche was in a position to confront the totality of the Great Mother in her twofold aspect as Aphrodite-Persephone. The end of this confrontation was the paradoxical victory-defeat of Psyche's failure, with which she regained not only an Eros transformed into a man, but also her contact with her own central feminine self" (ibid:135–36).

Nike (Roman Victoria) (Lehner 1969:136, fig. 808). Daughter of the underworld river Styx, she symbolizes "that mysterious moment when a game or battle turns into victory" (von Franz 1978:91; plate 11).

[12]For other psychological interpretations, see, e.g., von Franz 1970; Heuscher 1974:205–22; Johnson 1976; Durand 1981. Also see the novel by C. S. Lewis, *Till We Have Faces: A Myth Retold* (1956). Heracles' life and his twelve labors are discussed at length from a psychoanalytic perspective in Philip E. Slater, *The Glory of Hera* (1968).

◆ "The 'birth of the divine child' and its significance are known to us from mythology, but even more fully from what we have learned of the individuation process. While to a woman the birth of the divine son signifies a renewal and deification of her animus-spirit aspect, the birth of the divine daughter represents a still more central process, relevant to woman's self and wholeness.

"It is one of this myth's profoundest insights that makes it end with the birth of a daughter who is Pleasure-Joy-Bliss. This last sentence relating the transcendent birth of the daughter, which actually surpasses the myth itself, suggests a corner of inner feminine experience which defies description and almost defies understanding, although it is manifested time and time again as the determining borderline experience of the psyche and of psychic life" (ibid:140–41).

Psyche. . . . [a. Gr. ψυχή (in L. *p͞syche͞*) breath, f. ψύχειν to breathe, to blow, (later) to cool; hence, life (identified with or indicated by the breath); the animating principle in man and other living beings, the source of all vital activities, rational or irrational, the soul or spirit, in distinction from its material vehicle, the σῶμα or body; sometimes considered as capable of persisting in a disembodied state after separation from the body at death. . . .]

1. The soul, or spirit, as distinguished from the body; the mind. . . .

b. The animating principle of the universe as a whole, the soul of the world or *anima mundi.* . . .

c. In later *Greek Mythology,* personified as the beloved of Eros (Cupid or Love), and represented in works of art as having butterfly wings, or as a butterfly; known in literature as the heroine of the story related in the *Golden Ass* of Apuleius. Hence *attrib.* in sense 'like that of Psyche', as in *Psyche-knot* (of hair), *Psyche-mould, Psyche task.* . . .

2. a. (After Gr.) A butterfly. . . .

b. *Entom.* A genus of day-flying bombycid moths, typical of the family *Psychidae.* . . .

3. *Astron.* Name of one of the asteroids. . . .

4. A cheval-glass; also *psyche-glass.* . . .

Hence, *Psychean a. rare,* of or pertaining to Psyche; *Psycheism* (see quot. 1895). . . . *1895 Syd. Soc. Lex., Psycheism,* the somnolent condition induced by mesmerism; now most commonly termed the hypnotic state. *(The Oxford English Dictionary,* vol. VIII, pp. 1549–50; also see Miller 1973:14–20)

(Harter 1978a:34)

(Harter 1978a:34)

FAT AND LEAN.

(Bowles & Carver 1970:6)

Chapter 6
Origins and Matriarchy:
Myth as Charter

In the beginning the god made the female mind separately. One
he made from a long-bristled sow. In her house everything lies in
disorder, smeared with mud, and rolls about the floor; and she herself
unwashed, in clothes unlaundered, sits by the dungheap and grows
fat.

> —Semonides of Amorgos, "Poem on Women,"
> ca. seventh century B.C., lines 1–5, trans.
> Hugh Lloyd-Jones (1975:36).[1]

In respect of Character [in tragedy] . . .: First, and most important,
it must be good. Now any speech or action that manifests moral
purpose of any kind will be expressive of character: the character will
be good if the purpose is good. This rule is relative to each class. Even
a woman may be good, and also a slave; though the woman may be
said to be an inferior being, and the slave quite worthless. The second
thing to aim at is propriety. There is a type of manly valour; but
valour in a woman, or unscrupulous cleverness, is inappropriate.

> —Aristotle, *Poetics*, xv, 1–2, trans. S. H. Butcher (1951:53).

In the beginning is also the end, i.e., the *telos* or destiny. In recounting
origins—of the cosmos, humans, animals, plants, and customs—those who
tell or refer to such myths also validate the way things are today. These narratives serve as a charter for contemporary natural and social order.

British anthropologist Bronislaw Malinowski (1884–1942) is a primary
proponent of this interpretation for mythology. In 1922, drawing on extensive field experiences, he published *Argonauts of the Western Pacific: An Account
of Native Enterprise and Adventure in the Archipelagos of Melanesian New Guinea*,
in which he claimed that "the main social force governing all tribal life could
be described as the inertia of custom, the love of uniformity of behaviour."
Among the Trobrianders, "a strict adherence to custom, to that which is done

---

[1]Only 115 lines of this misogynist iambus survive. Semonides (usually spelled Simonides)
of Amorgos—a small island in the Sporades which lies northeast of Naxos—describes the origin of nine disagreeable women—from a sow, vixen, bitch, earth, sea, ass, ferret, mare, and
monkey—and one good one, from the bee. Nevertheless, he condemns them all as "the worst
plague Zeus has made." For an excellent discussion of the genre, comparison with Hesiod and
others, history of the text, translation and exegesis, see Hugh Lloyd-Jones, *Females of the Species: Semonides on Women* (1975), with photographs by Don Honeyman of sculptures by
Marcelle Quinton.

(Crawhall 1974:88)

by everyone else, is the main rule of conduct . . . [and] an important corollary to this rule declares that the past is more important than the present." Trobrianders "instinctively" look to mythical, not immediate ancestors for guidance. Thus, "the stories of important past events are hallowed because they belong to the great mythical generations and because they are generally accepted as truth, for everybody knows and tells them." According to Malinowski, such myths "bear the sanction of righteousness and propriety in virtue of these two qualities of pretarity and universality" (chap. xii, sect. vi; 1961:326–27; also see Malinowski 1939).

During November 1925 lectures delivered in honor of Sir James George Frazer at the University of Liverpool, Malinowski re-emphasized the living context of true mythology, contending that "myth as it exists . . . in its living primitive form, is not merely a story told but a reality lived" (1948: 100). Indeed, throughout his work Malinowski insisted that myths were not "idle tales" but served important non-symbolic, pragmatic functions. He maintained such "charter" myth "expresses, enhances, and codifies belief; it safeguards and enforces morality; it vouches for the efficiency of ritual and contains practical rules for the guidance of man" (1948:101).

Although soundly criticized for a narrow and simplistic view of mythology (e.g., Kluckhohn 1943), Malinowski's notions of myth as charter are useful when comparing myths about the origin of women and men and when considering the "real-life" consequences of living in societies which espouse one or another origin story. Are women viewed as inferior, equal or superior? Important or insignificant? In what sense is anatomy destiny?

Each of the following sections—"The Origin of Women," "The Origin of Men (and Women)," and "The Origin of Women/Men"—begins with a Native American origin myth, then examines major Western ones—Pandora, the Garden of Eden, and *Genesis* I, respectively. (A discussion of "Lilith— Adam's First Wife—and Her Legendary Kinswomen" follows the Garden of Eden section.) The final sections on "Amazons" and "Myths of Matriarchy" look at Amazons such as Wonder Woman, various evolutionist's schemes like those of Johan Jakob Bachofen, and South American myths of earlier women's rule to illustrate another kind of charter: In early or mythic times, women proved themselves unfit to rule and thus do not/should not rule today.

The Origin of Women—Pandora's "Box"

The Netsilik Eskimo woman Nâlungiaq (see chapter 7) told anthropologist Knud Rasmussen several accounts of the origin of women, and their part in nurturing early human beings.

Woman was made by man. It is an old, old story, difficult to understand. They say that the world collapsed, the earth was destroyed that great showers of rain flooded the land. All the animals died, and there were only two men left. They lived together. They married, as there was nobody else, and at last one of them became with child. They were great shamans, and when the one was going to bear a child they made his penis over again so that he became a woman, and she had a child. They say it is from that shaman that woman came.

(Crawhall 1974:23)

That is all I know about people. I have also heard that the earth was here before the people, and that the very first people came out of the ground from tussocks. But these are hard things to understand, difficult things to talk about, all this about where something began, where the first people came from. It is sufficient for us to see that they are here and that we ourselves are here.

And there are those who say that the children of the earth were not the first people, and that they only came to make people many. Women who happened to be out wandering found them sprawling in the tussocks and took them and nursed them; in that way people became numerous. (Rasmussen 1931:209)

The misogynous Hesiod recounts two versions of the origin of women. The more familiar tale of Pandora and her jar is part of his poem *Works and Days*. Zeus speaks to Iapetos' son Prometheus:

> "Son of Iapetos, deviser of crafts beyond all others,
> you are happy that you stole the fire,
>   and outwitted my thinking;
> but it will be a great sorrow to you,
>   and to men who come after.
> As the price of fire I will give them an evil,
>   and all men shall fondle
> this, their evil, close to their hearts,
>   and take delight in it."
>   So spoke the father of gods and mortals;
>   and laughed out loud.
> He told glorious Hephaistos to make haste, and plaster
> earth with water, and to infuse it with a human voice
> and vigor, and make the face
>   like the immortal goddesses,
> the bewitching features of a young girl;
>   meanwhile Athene
> was to teach her her skills, and how
>   to do the intricate weaving,
> while Aphrodite was to mist her head
>   in golden endearment
> and the cruelty of desire and longings
>   that wear out the body,
> but to Hermes, the guide, the slayer of Argos,
>   he gave instructions
> to put in her the mind of a hussy,
>   and a treacherous nature.
>   So Zeus spoke. And all obeyed Lord Zeus,
> the son of Kronos.
> The renowned strong smith modeled her figure of earth,
>   in the likeness

Hermes (Roman Mercury)
(Lehner 1969:23, fig. 46).

of a decorous young girl, as the son of Kronos
   had wished it.
The goddess gray-eyed Athene dressed and arrayed her;
   the Graces,
who are goddesses, and hallowed Persuasion
   put necklaces
of gold upon her body, while the Seasons,
   with glorious tresses,
put upon her head a coronal of spring flowers,
[and Pallas Athene put all decor upon her body].
But into her heart Hermes, the guide,
   the slayer of Argos,
put lies, and wheedling words
   of falsehood, and a treacherous nature,
made her as Zeus of the deep thunder wished,
   and he, the gods' herald,
put a voice inside her, and gave her
   the name of woman,
Pandora, because all the gods
   who have their homes on Olympos
had given her each a gift, to be a sorrow to men
who eat bread. Now when he had done
   with this sheer, impossible
deception, the Father sent the gods' fleet messenger,
   Hermes,
to Epimetheus, bringing her, a gift,
   nor did Epimetheus
remember to think how Prometheus had told him never
to accept a gift from Olympian Zeus,
   but always to send it
back, for fear it might prove
   to be an evil for mankind.
He took the evil, and only perceived it
when he possessed her.
   Since before this time the races of men
had been living on earth
free from all evils, free from laborious work,
   and free from
all wearing sicknesses that bring
   their fates down on men
[for men grow old suddenly
in the midst of misfortune];
but the woman, with her hands lifting away the lid
   from the great jar,
scattered its contents, and her design
   was sad troubles for mankind.
Hope was the only spirit that stayed there
   in the unbreakable
closure of the jar, under its rim,
   and could not fly forth
abroad, for the lid of the great jar
   closed down first and contained her;

Pot from Coclé, central Panama
(Lothrop 1976:60).

this was by the will of cloud-gathering Zeus
    of the aegis;
but there are other troubles by thousands
    that hover about men,
for the earth is full of evil things,
    and the sea is full of them;
there are sicknesses that come to men by day,
    while in the night
moving of themselves they haunt us,
    bringing sorrow to mortals,
and silently, for Zeus of the counsels
    took the voice out of them.

So there is no way to avoid what Zeus has intended.

    (lines 54–105, trans. Lattimore 1959: 25–31)[2]

(Harter 1979–80:78)

‡   "Her name is ambiguous. It can mean 'giver of all gifts,' making her a
benevolent fertility figure, or 'recipient of all gifts.' Hesiod chooses the latter
interpretation in order to attribute to the first woman the woes of mankind."
(Pomeroy 1975:2)

◆   Jane Harrison, *Prolegomena to the Study of Greek Religion:* "Pandora is in ritual and
matriarchal theology the earth as Kore, but in the patriarchal mythology of Hesiod
her great figure is strangely changed and minished. She is no longer Earth-born,
but the creature, the handiwork of Olympian Zeus. . . . Zeus the Father will have
no great Earthgoddess, Mother and Maid in one, in his man-fashioned Olympus,
but her figure *is* from the beginning, so he remakes it; woman, who was the
inspirer, becomes the temptress; she who made all things, gods and mortals alike,
is become their plaything, their slave, dowered only with physical beauty, and
with a slave's tricks and blandishments. To Zeus, the arch-patriarchal *bourgeois,* the
birth of the first woman is but a huge Olympian jest." (1903; quoted in Spretnak
1978:38–39)[3]

◆   Sarah B. Pomeroy, *Goddesses, Whores, Wives, and Slaves:* "Pandora is comparable to the temptress Eve, and the box she opened may be a metaphor for carnal
knowledge of women, which was a source of evil to men." (1975:4)

‡   "In time, the jar changed shape, but not meaning: after many centuries of
latency—the Romans for some reason failed to propagate the myth—Pandora and
her vessel reappear in the 16th century, the large jar now transformed into a box,

---

[2]The other version is in Hesiod's *Theogony,* lines 565–612, in which the farmer poet contends: "For from her originates the breed of female women, and they live with mortal men,
and are a great sorrow to them . . ." (lines 590–92, Lattimore 1959:158). Also see Arthur
1973, 1976.

[3]Spretnak's reworking of the myth has Pandora opening her jar to release fruit trees, medicinal plants, minerals, virtues of all kinds, and "the seeds of peace" (1978:41–42). She cites
the Harrison quotation as being on pp. 280–81 of the 1922 Cambridge University edition.

(Harter 1979–80:79)

(Harter 1979–80:78)

a small vase or a covered cup. Thus she is shown in a 17th century engraving, naked, and holding the little vessel over her pubic triangle; to which the publisher comments:

> " 'The artist has represented his subject as she is holding the box with her right hand down over the area it is covering—whence has sprung so much misery and anxiety for men—as if he wanted to say that from the midst of the fountain of delights there rises always some bitterness, and from amid the flowers some thorn.' " (Lederer 1968:73; also see Panofsky 1962:75, 76)

‡ "In eighteenth-century New England the term 'Pandora's Box' seems to have been applied to a receptacle containing several medical instruments, perhaps not unlike the proverbial 'little black bag' of the country doctor." (Panofsky 1962:139)

‡ "In the twentieth century two prominent postimpressionist artists have tried to recapture the pessimistic implications of the Hesiodian tale and to restate them with reference to the more lurid aspects of our own civilization: Paul Klee and Max Beckmann. Both, characteristically, obliterated the heroine and employed Pandora's box as a kind of independent hieroglyph. Paul Klee, ironically inscribing his little drawing (dated 1920) *Die Büchse der Pandora als Stilleben . . .* represented the ominous receptacle as a kind of goblet rather than a box and converted it into a psychoanalytical symbol: it is rendered as a kantharos-shaped vase containing some flowers but emitting evil vapors from an opening clearly suggestive of the female genitals. . . . Max Beckmann's gouache, begun in 1936 but thoroughly repainted in 1947, first anticipated and then recorded the horrors of the atomic bomb: his 'Pandora's box' is a small, square object charged with an incalculable amount of energy and exploding into a chaos of shattered form and color. . . ." (Panofsky 1962:112–13)

♦ Wolfgang Lederer, *The Fear of Women:* "Thus Pandora, whom Voltaire called 'the original sin,' has also served to symbolize the sin which may turn out to be our last" (1968:73).

The Origin of Men (and Women)—The Garden of Eden

Anthropologist Curt Nimuendajú collected the following text from the Sherente Indians of eastern Brazil. It has been translated from his manuscript by anthropologist Robert H. Lowie:

In the beginning there were no women, only men. These practiced homosexual intercourse. One of them became pregnant as a result, but was unable to give birth and died.

Once several men reaching a spring saw in it the reflection of a woman who was sitting high up in the branches of a tree that was standing beside the water. They mistook the reflection for reality and for two days vainly tried to grasp it. At last one of them looked up and espied the woman at the top of the tree. They brought her down and since each wanted to have her, they cut her into little pieces, each wrapping one of them up in a leaf and sticking it into the grass wall of his house. Then all went hunting.

When they got home they sent a messenger ahead, who entered and found that the pieces of flesh had all turned into women. The suaçurana (Felis concolor, puma), who had taken a piece from the chest, thereby got a very pretty wife. The sariema, on the other hand, who had twisted his slice too tight, got a very lean woman. But each man now had a wife, and the very next time they went hunting they took their wives along. (Lowie 1944:186)

Hunters

Hunters with game bags

Indian designs on spindle whorls and decorated beads from the central coast of Ecuador, 500–1500 A.D. (Shaffer 1979:1,2, figs. 2, 4)

Our Grandmother, the Shawnee female creator deity (see chapter 2), figures in a conversation-cum-narrative between Charles Bluejacket and J. Spencer. According to the latter: "In the autumn of 1858 I was appointed to the Shawnee Indian Methodist Mission, where I remained for two years. During this time, Charles Bluejacket, my interpreter, a man of consistent piety and of a fine and well-cultivated intellect, frequently talked to me of the ancient customs and manners of his people, and of their former rites and ceremonies." Spencer notes: "Charles Bluejacket was born on the Huron River, Michigan, in 1816. He was the son of Jim Bluejacket, a war-chief and grandson of Wey-zah-pih-ehr-senh-wah, the Bluejacket who had been stolen in his young boyhood from a Virginia family. At the time of his capture he wore a blue jacket or blouse, hence the name of the family." In Bluejacket's Flood account, a white family and an old Indian woman were spared.

After the Flood she lived in a valley, with a hill intervening between her and her white brother and his family, over which she could see the smoke rise from the white man's wigwam. When the sense of her loneliness and destitution came over her, she began to weep very bitterly. There then appeared a heavenly messenger, and asked her why she was so sorrowful. She told him that the Great Spirit had left her white brother his family, but she was just a poor old woman alone, and that there was to be an end of her people. Then said the visitor, "Remember how the first man was made," and then he left her. From this she knew that a new creation was meant; so she made small images of children from the earth, as directed, as the Great Spirit had made the first man. When, however, she saw that they had no life, she again wept. Again the messenger appeared, and inquired the cause of her grief. She said she had made children from clay, but that they were only dirt. Then said the visitor, "Remember how the Great Spirit did when the first man was made." At once she understood, and breathed into their nostrils, and they all became alive. This was the beginning of the red men. The Shawnees to this day venerate the memory of the one they call their Grandmother as the origin of their race. (Spencer 1909:319)

A strong Roman Catholic influence is evident in Miguel Mendes' version of "how the first people were made." According to collector Elsie Clews Parsons: "These tales I heard in Mitla [Oaxaca, Mexico], in 1930 and 1931, while engaged in a general study of the town. . . . Miguel Mendes narrated in Zapoteca with Eligio Santiago translating into Spanish." The following narrative was told "when I asked him for a story about the first people in the world."

The true God took up one ounce of earth and began to work it. "What are you doing?" asked God's sister [Maria Santissima]. God answered, "Something that you may not know more about than I know." He made an image (*mono*) in the shape of a man and set it to dry. He blessed it (with the sign of the cross) and it changed into a man. God gave him a pick and a *pala* and took him to a spring and told him to make a ditch to the garden he (God) had which was dry from lack of water. The man dug the ditch and the water flowed in it into the garden. . . . [God built an oven in which he made clay images of oxen and cows come to life. These were put under the patronage of San Lucas.] . . . The man began to cultivate his field. San Havier would go to the field to take him a breakfast of *tortillas* and one day the man did not want to eat. God asked San Lucas and San Havier why the man was not eating. San Havier said he did not want to eat because he wanted a wife. God said, "I will give him a wife, but today I will not send him any food." San Miguel went to the man and said that God agreed to give him a wife but that today he would not send him any food. The man said that would be all right. The man went to sleep in his field and as he was sleeping God came and opened his left side and took out a rib and put it alongside the man and when the man awoke his arm was around the woman. (Parsons 1932:287–88)

Perhaps the most familiar myth in the Old Testament is the narrative about the origin of man and woman and their misadventures in the Garden of Eden. The source document for this influential story— known as the Yahwist text after the writer's use of the Hebrew YHWH (Yahweh, such a sacred name for God that it could not be pronounced, and one which was traditionally but erroneously rendered in English as Jehovah)—dates from about 950 B.C., and comes from Judah in the south of Israel. It thus predates by some five hundred years the Priestly writings which include *Genesis* 1 and which use Elohim to designate the creator. However, here and in only one other place in the Pentateuch *(Exodus* 9:30) is God referred to as Yahweh-Elohim (usually translated as Lord God), possibly to assure that the two names were known to belong to the same deity.

In the day that the Lord God made the earth and the heavens, when no plant of the field was yet in the earth and no herb of the field had yet sprung up—for the Lord God had not caused it to rain upon the earth, and there was no man to till the ground; but a mist went up from the earth and watered the whole face of the ground—then the Lord God formed man of dust from the ground, and breathed into his nostrils the breath of life; and man became a living being. And the Lord God planted a garden in Eden, in the east; and there he put the man whom he had formed. And out of the ground the Lord God made to grow every tree that is pleasant to the sight and good for food, the tree of life also in the midst of the garden, and the tree of the knowledge of good and evil.
A river flowed out of Eden to water the garden, and there it divided and became four rivers. The name of the first is Pishon; it is the one which flows around the whole land of Havilah, where there is gold; and the gold of that land is good;

(Bowles & Carver 1970:125)

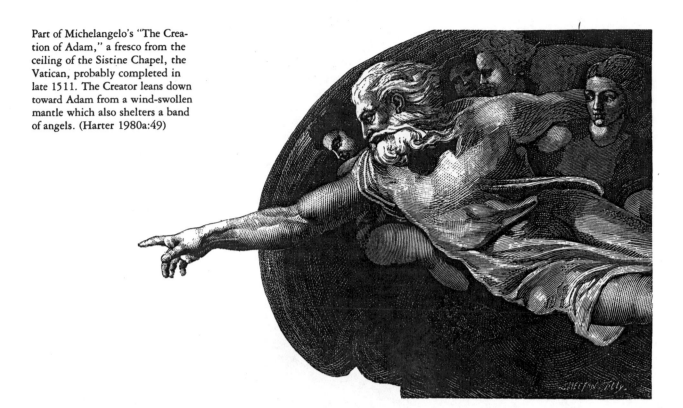

Part of Michelangelo's "The Creation of Adam," a fresco from the ceiling of the Sistine Chapel, the Vatican, probably completed in late 1511. The Creator leans down toward Adam from a wind-swollen mantle which also shelters a band of angels. (Harter 1980a:49)

bdellium and onyx stone are there. The name of the second river is Gihon; it is the one which flows around the whole land of Cush. And the name of the third river is Tigris, which flows east of Assyria. And the fourth river is the Euphrates.

The Lord God took the man and put him in the garden of Eden to till it and keep it. And the Lord God commanded the man, saying, "You may freely eat of every tree of the garden; but of the tree of the knowledge of good and evil you shall not eat, for in the day that you eat of it you shall die."

Then the Lord God said, "It is not good that the man should be alone; I will make him a helper fit for him." So out of the ground the Lord God formed every beast of the field and every bird of the air, and brought them to the man to see what he would call them; and whatever the man called every living creature, that was its name. The man gave names to all cattle, and to the birds of the air, and to every beast of the field; but for the man there was not found a helper fit for him. So the Lord God caused a deep sleep to fall upon the man, and while he slept took one of his ribs and closed up its place with flesh; and the rib which the Lord God had taken from the man he made into a woman and brought her to the man. Then the man said,

> "This at last is bone of my bones
>   and flesh of my flesh;
> she shall be called Woman,
>   because she was taken out of Man."

Therefore a man leaves his father and his mother and cleaves to his wife, and they become one flesh. And the man and his wife were both naked, and were not ashamed.

Now the serpent was more subtle than any other wild creature that the Lord God had made. He said to the woman, "Did God say, 'You shall not eat of any tree of the garden'?" And the woman said to the serpent, "We may eat of the fruit of the trees of the garden; but God said, 'You shall not eat of the fruit of the tree which is in the midst of the garden, neither shall you touch it, lest you die.' " But the serpent said to the woman, "You will not die. For God knows that when you eat of it your eyes will be opened, and you will be like God, knowing good and evil." So when the woman saw that the tree was good for food, and that it was a delight to the eyes, and that the tree was to be desired to make one wise, she took of its fruit and ate; and she also gave some to her husband, and he ate. Then the eyes of both were opened, and they knew that they were naked; and they sewed fig leaves together and made themselves aprons.

And they heard the sound of the Lord God walking in the garden in the cool of the day, and the man and his wife hid themselves from the presence of the Lord God among the trees of the garden. But the Lord God called to the man, and said to him, "Where are you?" And he said, "I heard the sound of thee in the garden, and I was afraid, because I was naked; and I hid myself." He said, "Who told you

The Tree of the Knowledge of Good and Evil. Woodcut by Jost Amman, from Jacob Rueff, *De conceptu et generatione hominis,* printed by Peter Fabricius, Frankfurt, 1587. (Lehner 1971:132, fig. 192)

that you were naked? Have you eaten of the tree of which I commanded you not to eat?" The man said, "The woman whom thou gavest to be with me, she gave me the fruit of the tree, and I ate." Then the Lord God said to the woman, "What is this that you have done?" The woman said, "The serpent beguiled me, and I ate." The Lord God said to the serpent,

> "Because you have done this,
>   cursed are you above all cattle,
>   and above all wild animals;
> upon your belly you shall go,
>   and dust you shall eat
>   all the days of your life.
> I will put enmity between you and the woman,
>   and between your seed and her seed;
> he shall bruise your head,
>   and you shall bruise his heel."
> To the woman he said,
> "I will greatly multiply your pain in childbearing;
>   in pain you shall bring forth children,
> yet your desire shall be for your husband,
>   and he shall rule over you."
> And to Adam he said,
> "Because you have listened to the voice of your wife,
>   and have eaten of the tree
> of which I commanded you,
>   'You shall not eat of it,'
> cursed is the ground because of you;
>   ` in toil you shall eat of it all the days of your life;
> thorns and thistles it shall bring forth to you;
>   and you shall eat bread
> till you return to the ground,
>   for out of it you were taken;
> you are dust,
>   and to dust you shall return."

The man called his wife's name Eve, because she was the mother of all living. And the Lord God made for Adam and for his wife garments of skins, and clothed them.

Then the Lord God said, "Behold, the man has become like one of us, knowing good and evil; and now, lest he put forth his hand and take also of the tree of life, and eat, and live for ever"—therefore the Lord God sent him forth from the garden of Eden, to till the ground from which he was taken. He drove out the man; and at the east of the garden of Eden he placed the cherubim, and a flaming sword which turned every way, to guard the way to the tree of life.

—*Genesis* 2:4–3:24 (RSV).

The Woman's Bible of 1895 contains "comments" on *Genesis, Exodus, Leviticus, Numbers,* and *Deuteronomy* by Elizabeth Cady Stanton, Lillie Devereux Blake, Rev. Phebe Hanaford, Clara Benwick Colby, Ellen Battelle Dietrick, Ursula N. Gestefeld, Mrs. Louisa Southworth, and Frances Ellen Burr. They were part of a larger revising committee proposed and guided by Stanton after the publication of the Revised Version of the Bible (New Testament in 1881,

Old Testament in 1885). No women were among the scholars either on the British Committee or the American one which corresponded with it. As Stanton laments in her introduction: "They have never yet invited a woman to join one of their Revising Committees, nor tried to mitigate the sentence pronounced on her by changing one count in the indictment served on her in Paradise" (Stanton and Revising Committee 1974:9; also see Coalition Task Force on Women and Religion 1975). Stanton concludes her introduction with a personal credo: "The only points in which I differ from all ecclesiastical teaching is that I do not believe that any man ever saw or talked with God, I do not believe that God inspired the Mosaic code, or told the historians what they say he did about women, for all the religions on the face of the earth degrade her, and so long as woman accepts the position that they assign her, her emancipation is impossible. Whatever the Bible may be made to do in Hebrew or Greek, in plain English it does not exalt and dignify woman" (ibid:12). Excerpts from her comments and those of Lillie Devereux Blake on the 1888 Revised Version edition of *Genesis* 2 and 3 follow:

♦ In v. 23 Adam proclaims the eternal oneness of the happy pair, "This is now bone of my bone and flesh of my flesh;" no hint of her subordination. How could men, admitting these words to be divine revelation, ever have preached the subjection of woman!

Next comes the naming of the mother of the race. "She shall be called Woman," in the ancient form of the word Womb-man. She was man and more than man because of her maternity.

The assertion of the supremacy of the woman in the marriage relation is contained in v. 24: "Therefore shall a man leave his father and his mother and cleave unto his wife." Nothing is said of the headship of man, but he is commanded to make her the head of the household, the home, a rule followed for centuries under the Matriarchate. L.D.B. (Ibid:21–22)

♦ In this prolonged interview [with the serpent], the reader must be impressed with the courage, the dignity, and the lofty ambition of the Woman. The tempter evidently had a profound knowledge of human nature, and saw at a glance the high character of the person he met by chance in his walks in the garden. He did not try to tempt her from the path of duty by brilliant jewels, rich dresses, worldly luxuries or pleasures, but with the promise of knowledge, with the wisdom of the Gods. Like Socrates and Plato, his powers of conversation and asking puzzling questions were no doubt marvellous, and he roused in the woman that intense thirst for knowledge, that the simple pleasures of picking flowers and talking with Adam did not satisfy. Compared with Adam she appears to great advantage through the entire drama.

The curse pronounced on woman is inserted in an unfriendly spirit to justify her degradation and subjection to man. With obedience to the laws of health, diet, dress, and exercise, the period of maternity should be one of added vigor in both body and mind, a perfectly natural operation should not be attended with suffering. By the observance of physical and psychical laws the supposed curse can be easily transformed into a blessing. Some churchmen speak of maternity as a disability, and then chant the Magnificat in all their cathedrals round the globe. Through all life's shifting scenes, the mother of the race has been the greatest factor in civilization. E.C.S. (Ibid:24–25)

◆ Note the significant fact that we always hear of the "fall of man," not the fall of woman, showing that the consensus of human thought has been more unerring than masculine interpretation. Reading this narrative carefully, it is amazing that any set of men ever claimed that the dogma of the inferiority of woman is here set forth. The conduct of Eve from the Beginning to the end is so superior to that of Adam. The command not to eat of the fruit of the tree of Knowledge was given to the man alone before the woman was formed. Genesis ii, 17. Therefore the injunction was not brought to Eve with the impressive solemnity of a Divine Voice, but whispered to her by her husband and equal. It was a serpent supernaturally endowed, a seraphim . . . who talked with Eve, and whose words might reasonably seem superior to the second-hand story of her companion—nor does the woman yield at once. She quotes the command not to eat of the fruit to which the serpent replies "Dying ye shall not die," v. 4, literal translation. In other words telling her that if the mortal body does perish, the immortal part shall live forever, and offering as the reward of her act the attainment of Knowledge.

(Bowles & Carver 1970:50)

Then the woman fearless of death if she can gain wisdom takes of the fruit; and all this time Adam standing beside her interposes no word of objection. "Her husband with her" are the words of v. 6. Had he been the representative of the divinely appointed head in married life, he assuredly would have taken upon himself the burden of the discussion with the serpent, but no, he is silent in this crisis of their fate. Having had the command from God himself he interposes no word of warning or remonstrance, but takes the fruit from the hand of his wife without a protest. It takes six verses to describe the "fall" of woman, the fall of man is contemptuously dismissed in a line and a half.

The subsequent conduct of Adam was to the last degree dastardly. When the awful time of reckoning comes, and the Jehovah God appears to demand why his command has been disobeyed, Adam endeavors to shield himself behind the gentle being he has declared to be so dear. "The woman thou gavest to be with me, she gave me and I did eat," he whines—trying to shield himself at his wife's expense! Again we are amazed that upon such a story men have built up a theory of their superiority!

Then follows what has been called the curse. Is it not rather a prediction? First is the future fate of the serpent described, the enmity of the whole human race. . . .

(Bowles & Carver 1970:139)

Next the subjection of the woman is foretold, thy husband "shall rule over thee," v. 16. Lastly the long struggle of man with the forces of nature is portrayed. . . . With the evolution of humanity an ever increasing number of men have ceased to toil for their bread with their hands, and with the introduction of improved machinery, and the uplifting of the race there will come a time when there shall be no severities of labor, and when women shall be freed from all oppressions.

"And Adam called his wife's name Life for she was the mother of all living" (v. 20, literal translation).

It is a pity that all versions of the Bible do not give this word instead of the Hebrew Eve. She was life, the eternal mother, the first representative of the more valuable and important half of the human race L.D.B. (Ibid:26–27)

A contemporary exegesis by Phyllis Trible, "Depatriarchalizing in Biblical Interpretation" (1976; a slightly different version in Christ and Plaskow 1979:74–83), makes a number of similar points, among them: (a) 'adham is basically androgynous and can be used as a generic term for all humankind; (b) the words for "a helper fit for him" imply equality, a counterpart, not an inferior; and (c) Adam *calls* the newly-created being *woman*—a common, not a proper noun; he does not *name* her, thereby exercising power and authority over her.

♦ Concern for sexuality, specifically for the creation of woman, comes last in the story, after the making of the garden, the trees, and the animals. Some commentators allege female subordination based on this order of events. . . . But the last may be first, as both the Biblical theologian and the literary critic know. Thus the Yahwist account moves to its climax, not its decline, in the creation of woman. She is not an afterthought, she is the culmination. Genesis 1 itself supports this interpretation, for there male and female are indeed the last and truly the crown of all creatures. The last is also first where beginnings and endings are parallel. In Hebrew literature the central concerns of a unit often appear at the beginning and the end as an *inclusio* device. Genesis 2 evinces this structure. The creation of man first and of woman last constitutes a ring composition whereby the two creatures are parallel. In no way does the order disparage woman. Content and context augment this reading. (Trible 1976:222)

♦ Why does the serpent speak to the woman and not to the man? Let a female speculate. If the serpent is "more subtle" than its fellow creatures, the woman is more appealing than her husband. Throughout the myth she is the more intelligent one, the more aggressive one, and the one with greater sensibilities. Perhaps the woman elevates the animal world by conversing theologically with the serpent. At any rate, she understands the hermeneutical task. In quoting God she interprets the prohibition ("neither shall you touch it"). The woman is both theologian and translator. She contemplates the tree, taking into account all the possibilities. . . . Thus the woman is fully aware when she acts. . . . The initiative and the decision are hers alone. There is no consultation with her husband. . . . She acts independently. By contrast the man is a silent, passive, and bland recipient. . . . The narrator makes no attempt to depict the husband as reluctant or hesitating. The man does not theologize; he does not contemplate; he does not envision the full possibilities of the occasion. His one act is belly-oriented, and it is an act of quiescence, not of initiative. . . . These character portrayals are truly extraordinary in a culture dominated by men. I stress their contrast not to promote female chauvinism but to undercut patriarchal interpretations alien to the text. (Ibid:226, 227)

God considered from which part of man to create woman. He said, I will not create her from his head, lest she hold up her own head too proudly; nor from his eye, lest she be too curious; nor from his ear, lest she be an eavesdropper; nor from his mouth lest she be a chatterer; nor from his heart, lest she be too jealous; nor from his hand, lest she be too acquisitive; nor from his foot, lest she be a gadabout; but from his rib, a hidden and modest part of his body, so that she may be modest, not fond of show, but rather of seclusion. But woman baffles God's design. She is haughty and walks with outstretched neck *(Isa.* iii, 16) and wanton eyes *(Isa.* iii, 16). She is given to eavesdropping *(Gen* xviii, 10). She chatters slander *(Numb.,* xii, 1), and is of a jealous disposition *(Gen.,* xxx, 1). She is afflicted with kleptomania *(Gen.,* xxxi, 19), and is fond of running about *(Gen.,* xxiv, 1). In addition to these vices, she is gluttonous *(Gen.,* iii, 6), lazy *(Gen.* xviii, 6), and bad tempered *(Gen.,* xvi, 6).

   —*Midrash: Genesis Rabbah,* xviii, 2 (ca. 550; in Stevenson 1948:2575).

Sumerologist Samuel Noah Kramer asks: "Why a rib?" He proposes that the answer lies in Dilmun, the Sumerian Garden of Eden sacred to the goddess Ninhursag, who curses the water-god Enki for eating her eight precious plants. Enki languishes until at last the fox persuades Ninhursag to return and heal him. She asks which organ hurts and then brings to life a healing deity from each afflicted part. Enki's rib was among them, and Nin-ti, "the lady of the rib," was thus created to heal it. In Sumerian, *ti,* or "rib," also

(Harter 1979–80:14)

means "to make live," and so Nin-ti, "the lady of the rib," by word play also signifies "the lady who makes live." Kramer claims that "it was this, one of the most ancient literary puns, which was carried over and perpetuated in the Biblical paradise story, although here, of course, it loses its validity, since the Hebrew word for 'rib' and that for 'who makes live' have nothing in common" (1959:146).

In *The Creation of Woman,* psychoanalyst Theodor Reik proposes instead that the myth describes an initiation rite. Adam could only acquire a wife through circumcision, and Eve is "bone of my bones, and flesh of my flesh" in the same way Moses is a "bloody [i.e., circumcised] husband" for Zipporah (1960:11). Reik claims Freud was interested in his interpretation, proudly announcing: "We have undertaken a lonely job of research and our study in depth has led to the insight that the Biblical story does not tell of the creation of woman but of the recreation of man, or the reaching of manhood of the primeval hero who became united with a woman" (1960:114).

> The woman she was taken
> From under Adam's arm,
> So she must be protected
> From injuries and harm.
>
> —Abraham Lincoln,
> "Adam and Eve's
> Wedding Song,"
> written for Sarah
> Haggard on her
> marriage to Aaron
> Grigsby, August 2,
> 1826 (in Stevenson
> 1948:2575; also see
> Utley 1957).

◆ Kate Millett, *Sexual Politics:* "But at the moment when the pair eat of the forbidden tree they awake to their nakedness and feel shame. Sexuality is clearly involved, though the fable insists it is only tangential to a higher prohibition against disobeying orders in the matter of another and less controversial appetite—one for food. Róheim points out that the Hebrew word for 'eat' can also mean coitus. Everywhere in the Bible 'knowing' is synonymous with sexuality, and clearly a product of contact with the phallus, here in the fable objectified as a snake. To blame the evils and sorrows of life—loss of Eden and the rest—on sexuality, would all too logically implicate the male, and such implication is hardly the purpose of the story, designed as it is expressly in order to blame all this world's discomfort on the female. Therefore it is the female who is tempted first and 'beguiled' by the penis, transformed into something else, a snake. Thus Adam has 'beaten the rap' of sexual guilt, which appears to be why the sexual motive is so repressed in the Biblical account. Yet the very transparency of the serpent's universal phallic value shows how uneasy the mythic mind can be about its shifts. Accordingly, in her inferiority and vulnerability the woman takes and eats, simple carnal thing that she is, affected by flattery even in a reptile. Only after this does the male fall, and with him, humanity—for the fable has made him the racial type, whereas Eve is a mere sexual type and, according to tradition, either expendable or replaceable. And as the myth records the original sexual adventure, Adam was seduced by woman, who was seduced by a penis. 'The woman whom thou gavest to be with me, she gave me the fruit and I did eat' is the first man's defense. Seduced by the phallic snake, Eve is convicted for Adam's participation in sex" (1971:53).

(Harter 1979–80:91)

★ "[In the Ozarks] . . . is the notion that a 'bad woman can't make good applesauce'—it will always be mushy, and not sufficiently tart. This is so generally accepted in some sections as to have passed into the language, and the mere statement that a certain woman's applesauce is no good is generally understood as a slighting reference to her morals" (Randolph 1947:65).

★ "*Adam's apple* The prominence made by the thyroid cartilage in the front of the human throat, conspicuous in men: the morsel of forbidden fruit which stuck in Adam's throat. . . ." (Leach 1972:9).

‡ "Rabbi Joshua was asked: 'Why does a man come forth at birth with his face downward, while a woman comes forth with her face turned upward?' 'The man,' he replied, 'looks toward the place of his creation (the earth), while the woman looks upward toward the place of her creation (the rib).'

". . . We similarly learn that 'the voice of women is shrill, not so the voice of men; when soft foods are cooked, no sound is heard; but put a bone in a pot and at once it crackles. A man is more easily placated than a woman because a few drops of water suffice to soften a clod of earth, while a bone stays hard after days of soaking.'

"Differences between the sexes in dress, social forms, sexual dynamics, and moral obligations similarly derive from their reputed origins: ' "Why does the man make demands upon the woman, while the woman does not make demands upon the man?" "The man . . . seeks what he has lost (his rib), but the lost article does not seek him." "Why does a man deposit sperm within a woman while a woman does not deposit sperm within a man?" "This is like a man who has an article in his hand and seeks a trustworthy person with whom he may deposit it." ' Woman covers her hair in token of Eve's having brought sin into the world; she tries to hide her shame. Women precede men in funeral cortege because it was woman who brought death into the world. The precept of menstruation was given her because she shed the blood of Adam. Those religious commands addressed to women alone are connected with the history of Eve. Adam was the heave-offering of the world, and Eve defiled it. As expiation, all women are commanded to separate a heave offering from the dough. And because woman extinguished the light of man's soul, she is bidden to kindle the Sabbath light." (Lacks 1980:33, 34)

(Crawhall 1974:1)

◆ Rosyln Lacks, *Women and Judaism:* "Whether so bumbling and ill conceived a rationale for so virulent an etiology of these few forms of worship permitted woman—the lighting of Sabbath candles—can bolster the spirits of those women who remain faithful to Judaic percepts is more than dubious. More often than not, the pious mother of the family who welcomes each Sabbath by lighting candles and blessing them each Friday evening is blissfully unaware of Rabbi Joshua's dissertation on the reasons for her sacred task; such learned inquiries remain the province of male domains of scholarship and spiritual authority from which she is—by virtue of her 'inviolate sex'—excluded" (1980:35–36).

♦ Judith Hauptman, "Images of Women in the Talmud": "It would be impossible to ignore . . . one of the blessings that an adult male Jew recites every morning, not because the prayer is so significant but because it, more than any other passage, has generated so much anger and scorn. The blessing reads: 'Blessed be God, King of the universe, for not making me a woman.' Women in general, and the women's liberation movement in particular, are incensed by these words, because they seem to imply that women are inferior, and that discrimination against them is in order.

"The earliest written record of this blessing dates back to the second century. In the Tosefta, Rabbi Judah comments that this blessing expresses a man's gratitude for being created male, and therefore for having more opportunities to fulfill divine commandments than do women, who are exempted from a good many. Given this interpretation, the words lose most of their sting. They merely reiterate the social facts of life, namely, that's a woman's primary concern was with husband and children, and that she was instructed to give familial obligations priority over religious ones" (1974:196).

♦ Mary Daly, *Beyond God the Father*: ". . . I am tearing the image of 'the Fall' from its context in patriarchal religion. I have suggested that the original myth revealed the essential defect or 'sin' of patriarchal religion—its justifying of sexual caste. I am now suggesting that there were intimations in the original myth—not consciously intended—of a dreaded future. That is, one could see the myth as prophetic of the real Fall that was yet on its way, dimly glimpsed. In that dreaded event, women reach for knowledge and, finding it, share with men, so that together we can leave the delusory paradise of false consciousness and alienation. In ripping the image of the Fall from its old context we are also transvaluating it. That is, its meaning is divested of its negativity and becomes positive and healing.

"Rather than a Fall *from* the sacred, the Fall now initiated by women becomes a Fall *into* the sacred and therefore into freedom. . . . If the symbols and myths of patriarchal religion are dying, this is hardly a total tragedy, since they have perpetuated oppression. To the extent that they have done this, they have represented a pseudosense of the sacred. The Fall beyond the false dichotomy between good and evil has the potential to bring us away not only from the false paradise of the pseudo-sacred symbols of patriarchy but also from the banal nonreligious consciousness. . . . It can bring us into a new meeting with the sacred" (1973:67–68). (*Note:* Since publication of *Beyond God the Father* the author's thinking has changed in regard to the terms "God" and "androgyny." For an explanation of her more recent thinking see the Prefact to *Gyn/Ecology: The Metaethics of Radical Feminism,* Beacon Press, 1978.)

Lilith—Adam's First Wife—and Her Legendary Kinswomen

The Thompson Indians of what is now British Columbia told anthropologist James A. Teit a seemingly familiar biblical tale with a twist that highlights Lilith, traditionally Adam's first wife.

When this earth was very young, only two people lived on it,—a man called A'tām and a woman called Īm. The Chief (or God) lived in the upper world, and the Outcast (or Devil) lived in the lower world. They were enemies to each other, and tried to do each other harm, but God was the more powerful. He frequently visited the earth and talked with A'tām and Īm.

One day the Devil created an animal like a horse, and made it appear before the man and woman. When the latter saw it, she said, "That is God come to visit us"; but A'tām said it was not. At last, however, he believed it must be God, and they went and spoke with it. Soon afterwards God appeared, and then they recognized the difference. He was angry and said, "Why do you mistake the Devil for me and converse with him? Have I not told you he is evil, and will do you harm?" Then, looking at the animal, he said to the couple, "Well, since this beast is here, I will so transform him that he will be useful to you." He wetted both his thumbs, pressed them on the animal's front legs, and thus marked him, saying, "Henceforth you will be a horse and a servant and plaything of the people, who will ride you, and use you for many purposes. You will be a valuable slave of man."

Now the mosquitoes were tormenting the horse very much, so God plucked some long grass which grew near by, and threw it at the animal's backside, and it became a long tail. He also threw some on the horse's neck, and it became a mane. He said, "Henceforth you will be able to protect yourself from the mosquitoes." Then he plucked out more grass, and threw it ahead of the horse, saying, "That will be your food." It turned into bunch grass, which soon spread over the whole country.

Now God departed, telling the man and woman he would soon return and show them which trees bore the proper kinds of food to eat. Hitherto they had eaten no fruit, for they did not know the edible varieties. At that time all trees bore fruit, and the pines and firs in particular had large sweet fruit. Now the Devil appeared, and, pretending to be God, he took the large long fruit of the white pines, and gave it to Īm. She thought he was God, ate the fruit as directed, and gave some to A'tām. Then the Devil disappeared; and all the fruit on the trees withered up, and became transformed into cones. Some kinds shrivelled up to a small size, and became berries. When God came and saw what had happened, he sent the woman to live with the Devil, and, taking A'tām, he broke off his lower rib, and made a woman out of it. This rib-woman became A'tām's wife, and bore many children to him. (Teit 1912, as reprinted with comparative notes in Thompson 1929:261–62; also see Ramsey 1977)

Lilith has a long history in the ancient Near East, first appearing on a king list (ca. 2400 B.C.) as Lillu, a male demon who begat the hero Gilgamesh. A Sumerian epic from about 2000 B.C. has been pieced together and translated by Sumerologist Samuel Noah Kramer. He summarizes the poem's story as follows:

Once upon a time there was a *huluppu*-tree, perhaps a willow; it was planted on the banks of the Euphrates; it was nurtured by the waters of the Euphrates. But the South Wind tore at it, root and crown, while the Euphrates flooded it with its waters. Inanna, queen of heaven, walking by, took the tree in her hand and brought it to Erech, the seat of her main sanctuary, and planted it in her holy garden. There she tended it most carefully. For when the tree grew big, she planned to make of its wood a chair for herself and a couch.

Years passed, the tree matured and grew big. But Inanna found herself unable to cut down the tree. For at its base the snake "who knows no charm" had built its nest. In its crown, the Zu-bird—a mythological creature which at times wrought mischief—had placed its young. In the middle Lilith, the maid of desolation, had built her house. And so poor Inanna, the light-hearted and ever joyful maid, shed bitter tears. And as the dawn broke and her brother, the sun-god Utu, arose from his sleeping chamber, she repeated to him tearfully all that had befallen her *huluppu*-tree.

Now Gilgamesh, the great Sumerian hero, the forerunner of the Greek Heracles, who lived in Erech, overheard Inanna's weeping complaint and chivalrously came to her rescue. He donned his armour weighing fifty minas—about fifty pounds— with his "ax of the road," seven talents and seven minas in weight—over four hundred pounds—he slew the snake "who knows no charm" at the base of the tree. Seeing which, the Zu-bird fled with his young to the mountain, and Lilith tore down her house and fled to the desolate places which she was accustomed to haunt. The men of Erech who had accompanied Gilgamesh now cut down the tree and presented it to Inanna for her chair and couch. . . . (Kramer 1944:33–34)

A dubious Biblical reference to Lilith occurs in Isaiah's imprecations against Edom:

> And wild beasts shall meet with
> hyenas,
>   the satyr shall cry to his fellow;
> yea, there shall the night hag alight
>   and find for herself a resting place.
>
> —*Isaiah* 34:14 (RSV).

In the Talmudic period (second to fifth centuries A.D.), Lilith became known as a devourer of children and a succuba. Babies were protected by amulets on which Senoy, Sansenoy and Samangelof, the angels' names, were written. Men, however, could only heed the warning of Rabbi Hanina (first century A.D.): "It is forbidden for a man to sleep alone in a house, lest Lilith get hold of him." Raphael Patai synthesizes the legends upon which these beliefs were based:

> . . . However, Adam and Lilith could find no happiness together, not even understanding. When Adam wished to lie with her, Lilith demurred: "Why should I lie beneath you," she asked, "when I am your equal, since both of us were created from dust?" When Lilith saw that Adam was determined to overpower her, she uttered the magic name of God, rose into the air, and flew away to the Red Sea, a place of ill-repute, full of lascivious demons. There, Lilith engaged in unbridled promiscuity and bore a demonic brood of more than one hundred a day. God, however, sent after her three angels, Senoy, Sansenoy, and Semangelof by name, who soon located her in the same wild waters in which the Egyptians were to drown in the days of the Exodus. The angels gave her God's message, but she refused to return. When they threatened drowning her in the sea, she argued: "Let me be, for I was created in order to weaken the babes: if it is a male, I have power over him from the moment of his birth until the eighth day of his life [when he is circumcised and thereby protected], and if a girl, until the twentieth day." The angels insisted however, and in order to make them desist, she swore to them in the name of God: "Whenever I shall see you or your names or your images on an

(Bowles & Carver 1970:24)

amulet, I shall do no harm to the child." Moreover, she gave her consent to the death of one hundred of her own children day after day—which is the reason why that many demons die every day. This agreement between the three angels and Lilith is the basis for writing the names Senoy, Sansenoy, and Semangelof on amulets hung around the necks of newborn babes: when Lilith sees the names, she remembers her oath and leaves the child alone.

However, in spite of her determined refusal to return to Adam, Lilith soon became attracted to him again, and managed to sleep with him against his will. In the meantime Adam had received Eve as his wife, was persuaded by her to eat from the fruit of the Tree of Knowledge, and was expelled from the Garden of Eden with the curse of death hanging over his head. When Adam became aware that because of his sin God decreed mortality upon him and all his future descendants, he embarked upon a period of penitence which lasted for 130 years. He fasted, refrained from intercourse with Eve, and, in order to mortify his flesh, wore a belt of rough fig twigs around his naked body. He could not, however, control his involuntary nocturnal emissions, which were brought about by female spirits who came and coupled with him and bore him spirits, demons, and Lilin. At the same time, male spirits came and impregnated Eve, who thus became the mother of innumerable demon children. The spirits thus procreated are the plagues of mankind. (Patai 1978:183–84; also see Patai 1964; Graves and Patai 1966:65–69; Lacks 1980:38–61)

Writer-journalist Lilly Rivlin interprets Lilith in Jewish tradition as a convenient scapegoat for both men and women who feared their instinctual drives. Thus, men could blame her for their nocturnal emissions, women for their frustrations, and both for infant deaths which might otherwise have been attributed to parental negligence or abuse. Her figure was also invoked by men to keep women in line lest they be denounced as "Lilith's." Rivlin deplores these uses of such a "deformed and evil archetype," but she considers "most damaging" to women the fact that Lilith's myth prevented them from joining together fruitfully. "Vital female qualities—sensuality, passion, independence—were associated with a feared, hated, and perhaps secretly envied, female symbol," and women with such attributes were suspect and shunned (1972:97).

The Judaic Lilith harmful to men and to children is echoed in Hispanic American and certain Native American folk traditions. Among the best known "bogey" figures is *La Llorona,* "The Weeping Woman." Various New World legends about this and similar "kinswomen" of Lilith follow:

★ "Luis González Obregón tells us that the Weeping Woman was first heard in Mexico City about 1550, especially on moonlit nights. She was dressed in white, went through the streets wailing in great anguish, and disappeared into a lake. Among the various explanations offered was the suggestion that she was the infamous Doña Marina, who had repented of her Quisling coöperation with Cortés and who, as La Llorona, now wept for her sin.

"An interesting account is given by Thomas A. Janvier: The Wailing Woman had drowned all her children in the canales of Mexico City. Finally repentant, she began to haunt the streets at night, 'weeping and wailing,' clad in white. Meeting a watchman or a lonely traveler, she would cry out for her children, then disappear. He would lose consciousness or go mad. An officer who coaxed her to cast aside her *rebozo* was rewarded by the sight of a skeleton; he felt 'an icy breath' and fell, unconscious. Later, having reported the incident, he died. To hear her is frightening; to see, to stop, to speak to her is very dangerous" (Leddy 1948:273).

(Harter 1980b:75)

"Tsimshian skin apron with painted decoration and quilled embroidery. The painted animal forms are realistic, while the embroidery designs are geometric" (Naylor 1975:79, fig. A).

★ "Not always is the lady a pitiful figure. According to some [Mexican] sources, she is La Sirena, the siren. She appears in this form in villages of the highlands of Chiapas just after dusk when the men are returning from the fields. She tries to lure them to their doom by leading them to high cliffs, often calling in the familiar voices of their wives or sweethearts. Or, at times, she tries to throw her victims into one of the gigantic cacti common to that region. In other sections of the country, she haunts lakes and canals where she lures children to their deaths.

"The lady is also sometimes regarded as Matlachiuatl, an Aztec goddess. According to this account, she is 'The Woman with the Net,' a vampire-like creature who feeds on men. She walks the lonely places of the countryside, always armed with a big net with which she hopes to capture her victims" (Leddy 1950:364–65; also see Barakat 1969).

★ "[The Aztec goddess] Cihuacoatl possessed, among other qualities, these attributes: she was believed to roar out at night as an omen; she was sometimes represented as a toad; she was, in one aspect that equated her at least partially with Coatlicue [see chapter 2], depicted as carrying a child in her arms. As an earth goddess she may have been associated with earthquakes and volcanoes, though at present the evidence to confirm this supposition is lacking" (Kirtley 1960:164; also see Barakat 1965, 1969).

★ "Dzelarkhons, according to Kanhade, head-chief of the [Northwest coast] Tsimsyan, was a mythical being whose very name, in Haida, means Frog. She was also called Weeping Woman, because of the dirges or traditional laments attributed to her after the destruction of the village by the volcano. . . . Some of the Haida carvings in wood or in argillite, show small frogs under the eyelids or long teardrops running down her desolate face, the drips broadening into small frogs" (Barbeau 1953:25–26).[4]

[4]Bacil F. Kirtley cites Marius Barbeau (Totem Poles, National Museum of Canada Bulletin No. 119, Anthropological Series No. 32, n.d., vol. 1, p. 79) for a description of "the Dzelarkhons pole at Tanu, [on which] Weeping Woman is depicted clutching her dead child, which hangs down, on her breast" (1960:164).

★ "The Quinault, a Salishan tribe of the Northwest Coast, have stories of a creature called *cao' mcao'm,* which is thought of as being something like a large, hairless wildcat with a human face. It cries out in a voice which simulates that of a friend or relative of the hearer. In the story given by Olson, the being wails repeatedly 'Oh, my children!' Its call is an omen of death" (Kirtley 1960:165).

★ "The Penobscot Indian Pskégdemus [see chapter 2] is a swamp spirit who wails near camps to entice men and children. A man who shows any sympathy for her, even in thought, is lost, for he will never be satisfied to marry a human woman. Another such demon of the Penobscot, dressed in moss and cedar bark, likes children and pets them. But good-willed though she be, children have a way of going to sleep forever when she fondles them" (Leach 1972:622).

★ "There was a myth of *La Llorona,* the weeping woman [in Hispanic northern New Mexico]. She was believed to be the soul of a woman who went from house to house weeping at night to atone for her sins. Each village seemed to have a different version. . . . Nurse told me that the weeping woman lived in a big, black rock that stood in the meadow in back of our house. At night she came out wrapped in a white mist. She grew taller and taller, finally vanishing from sight, and only her moans and cries were heard throughout the village. Whenever we passed by the black rock I hung closely to Nurse's side, until we were at a safe distance" (Jaramillo 1972:104).[5]

★ "The first story I heard about La Llorona in Tucson told of a widow whose only son was lost playing near a flooded river. Insane from grief, she seeks to kidnap any small child she sees. Often her fingerprints are found on windows, or screens are torn where she tried to enter homes. . . . I have been told, with emphatic nods, 'She gets 'em, often'. . . ." (Leddy 1948:274).

★ ". . . In Canoga Park [Los Angeles] by the wash just north of Vanowen on Canoga Avenue, La Llorona was following a path to Calabasas. A man driving down the street saw her, and his car plunged into the drainage ditch. Neighbors who witnessed the incident wouldn't go near the scene for some time. The bodies of a man and wife were encountered and the clothes of a baby, but there was no [infant's] body to be found. She is constantly searching for her children, and she believes all children to be hers" (Hawes 1968:160).

★ ". . . [In a] *New Yorker* article—'Fly Trans-Love Airways' by Renata Adler . . . the author interviewed a number of the teen-age habituees of Los Angeles' Sunset Strip. Two of them, identified by the pseudonyms 'Dot' and 'Meg,' 'began to reminisce about how they had become acquainted—in a juvenile home where Meg had been sent as a "habitual runaway," and Dot for the vaguer offense of what she described as being "in danger of leading an idle and desolate life." They spoke of the ghost story the Mexican inmates used to tell—about La Harona [sic], a woman who, crazed by syphilis, killed her children.

[5]Speaking of her childhood in Arroyo Hondo, New Mexico, before the turn of the century, Jaramillo comments that: "I believe now that this fear of the *abuelos* [disguised "grandfathers" who chased and sometimes whipped bad children at Christmas], and Lupe's ghost and witch stories, and the sore example put before us of bad children like the *mal hijo* ["bad son," who raised his hand to knife his father and it froze with the knife in his own wrist] made our lives exceedingly timid" (1972:30).

(Harter 1978b:60)

" ' "They said if you shouted 'La Harona!' five times, she would come to you,"
Meg said, "and a lot of kids in my unit wanted to test it."
" ' "I was so terrified I cried all night," Dot said.
" ' "They said she came through mirrors." Both girls still seemed terrified at
this thought' " (Hawes 1968:160–61).

★   "Juanita H.: 'This girl was busted and put in [the isolation unit at Juvenile
Hall]. It was visiting Sunday, and she was waiting for her mother to come down
from Fresno to see her. The mother was in an accident on the way down. The girl
kept asking for her. Finally, she threw a fit. That night she started screaming, and
when a counsellor opened the door, she was gone. There was a note on the wall:
See, I told you my mother was coming for me' ' " (Hawes 1968:170).

♦   Wolfgang Lederer, *The Fear of Women:* "It would seem then that, in all such
stories, we are caught with our defense in disarray; some uncomfortable and
embarrassing truth is showing: we do think that women can be dangerous. We do
think that mothers can reject, disown, harm, kill, even eat their children. In all of
this, incidentally, whether we consider myth or anthropological reality, baby girls
tend to fare worse than boys; and so the paranoia of women, which Freud
attributed to their fear of being killed by their mothers, may have some historical
validity" (1968:66).

♦   Dorothy Bloch, *"So the Witch Won't Eat Me":* "When we consider both the
child's physical and psychological vulnerability and the inevitably threatening
character of his outer world, we may well marvel how he manages to survive. That,
despite his terror, he does survive, except in rare instances, is a tribute to the
psyche's resourcefulness as well as to the predominantly positive character of
parental care. It is a rare parent whose wish for the child to die is not balanced or
outweighed by the wish for him to live. The child may respond to the varying
intensity of the hostile wish and its expression, however, by developing a system of
defenses that we call emotional illness. In all the instances I have encountered, his
refuge from his fear of infantcide appeared to be his parents' love. The hope of
eventually winning it, therefore, became the foundation of the psychic structure he
designed from his earliest years and, judging from its continuing role with
considerably older patients, might frequently maintain until death. . . .

"In almost all my patients, the primary instrument for maintaining the self-deception and defense against the fear of infanticide was fantasy. Although at first I was struck by what appeared to be the antithetical character of child and adult fantasies, it soon became apparent that they served an identical function. Children's fantasies appeared to concentrate on the fear of being killed, but the displacement of terror onto monsters and imaginary creatures was obviously designed to preserve an idealized image of their parents, from whom it was therefore possible to receive the love so essential for survival. The tenacity of my adult patients' dedication to a fantasy that appeared to focus on winning their parents' love, on the other hand, repeatedly concealed an unconscious fear of being killed by them" (1978:11, 12).

The Origin of Women/Men—Notes on Genesis I and Androgyny

The first part of a Yana (California) Indian myth told to linguist Edward Sapir by Sam Bat'wī tells about a radical transformation which suggests some of the myths of matriarchy discussed below.

Women (were formerly men and) used to go hunting deer but came back home without having killed anything. The women, (now men), stayed at home, making acorn meal and acorn bread. Again the men went out to hunt deer, but did not succeed in killing any. The women were finished with their acorn pounding when the sun came up in the east. They killed only one deer. There were thirty men, and similarly there were thirty women. The people had no fresh meat to eat, for no deer were killed by the men. (Said Gray Squirrel and Cottontail Rabbit to one another,) "It is bad. What shall we do?" said the women. "The men have not killed any deer." "Let us make men out of these women. Yes!" The men arrived home. The men were angry, and whipped their wives. "It is bad. Let us make women out of the men, and let us make men out of the women."

At daybreak they went off to hunt deer. In the east a certain person (Cottontail Rabbit) was building a fire on the ground. Now the men came, hunting deer. The one that was building a fire sat there. He took smooth round stones and put them into the fire. Those who were hunting deer sat around the fire in a circle. That one person also sat there, but the men did not see the fire, did not see the stones. Suddenly the stones burst off from the fire. They popped about in very direction. "S·!" said those who had till then been men, who were there in great numbers. Their private parts were cleft by bursting stones.

"Let us make men of those there." So it was, and they now became men, while

The Wife turns Soldier, & the Husband spinning

(Bowles & Carver 1970:107)

those who had formerly been men had now become women. Now they stayed at home, pounding acorns and making acorn bread. Now the men went out hunting deer and killed many deer. Cottontail Rabbit was standing there and said: "Hehehê! Yes! Now it is good. It is good," said he, looking while they killed deer. The women made acorn bread and pounded acorns. Hehe^e! The people did not die, the people were very numerous. Coyote said, "I do not wish the people to be numerous. There are too many women and too many men in every direction, there are too many children in every direction. The people do not die, they grow old. There is no poisoning by magic, there is nobody to cry in winter," thus he spoke. There was nobody that knew about death. . . . (Sapir 1910–11:88–89)

The first chapter of *Genesis,* the Priestly story of creation, probably fashioned around 500–450 B.C., refers to God as Elohim, possibly a bisexual and certainly a plural divinity. Her/his/their creation was an "equal" human couple. Some traditions identify the woman as Lilith, while others, like the Gnostics and certain mystics, view the two as the perfect androgynous being.

> Then God said, "Let us make men in our image, after our likeness; and let them have dominion over the fish of the sea, and over the birds of the air, and over the cattle, and over all the earth, and over every creeping thing that creeps upon the earth." So God created man in his own image, in the image of God he created him; male and female he created them. And God blessed them, and God said to them, "Be fruitful and multiply, and fill the earth and subdue it; and have dominion over the fish of the sea and over the birds of the air and over every living thing that moves upon the earth."

—*Genesis* 1:26–28 (RSV).

The passive female element; what has been there from the beginning of all things. "And God divided the waters which were under the firmament from the waters which were above the firmament."

The active male element; what comes from on high; the effective element in time. "And God divided the light from the darkness."

As the male element pervades the female, so creation takes place, since everything belonging to the living world is compounded of the confluence of male and female. In remote ages in the East, and also in early Northern mythology, this sign of the wheel-cross was a symbol of the Sun.

From *The Book of Signs,* collected, drawn, and explained by Rudolf Koch (1955:2–3).

♦ *Woman's Bible:* "In the great work of creation the crowning glory was realized, when man and woman were evolved on the sixth day, the masculine and feminine forces in the image of God, that must have existed eternally, in all forms of matter and mind. All the persons in the Godhead are represented in the Elohim the divine plurality taking counsel in regard to this last and highest form of life. Who were the members of this high council, and were they a duality or a trinity? Verse 27 declares the image of God male and female. How then is it possible to make woman an afterthought? We find in verses 5–16 the pronoun 'he' used. Should it not in harmony with verse 26 be 'they,' a dual pronoun? . . .

"The above texts plainly show the simultaneous creation of man and woman, and their equal importance in the development of the race. All those theories based on the assumption that man was prior in the creation, have no foundation in Scripture. E.C.S." (Stanton and Revising Committee 1974:15).

> This is the book of the generations of Adam. When God created man, he made him in the likeness of God. Male and female he created them, and he blessed them and named them Man when they were created.
>
> —*Genesis* 5:1–2 (RSV).

♦ *Woman's Bible:* "The dual relation, both in the Godhead and humanity, is here again declared, though contradicted in the intervening chapters. In this and the following chapters we have a prolix statement of the births, deaths, and ages in the male line. They all take wives, beget sons, but nothing is said of the origin or destiny of the wives and daughters; they are incidentally mentioned merely as necessary factors in the propagation of the male line. E.C.S." (Stanton and Revising Committee 1974:34).

In Plato's dialogue *Symposium,* written about 385 B.C., friends at a supper party deliver speeches on the nature of love. Aristophanes narrates an allegorical origin myth which purports to explain why both males and females are "always trying to reintegrate our former nature, to make two into one, and to bridge the gulf between one human being and another," whether woman to man, woman to woman, or man to man (line 191d, trans. Joyce 1961:544).

"You ought first to know the nature of man, and the adventures he has gone through; for his nature was anciently far different from that which it is at present. First, then, human beings were formerly not divided into two sexes, male and female; there was also a third, common to both the others, the name of which remains, though the sex itself has disappeared. The androgynous sex [hermaphrodite], both in appearance and in name, was common both to male and female; its name alone remains, which labours under a reproach.

"At the period to which I refer, the form of every human being was round, the back and the sides being circularly joined, and each had four arms and as many legs; two faces fixed upon a round neck, exactly like each other; one head between the two faces; four ears, and everything else as from such proportions it is easy to conjecture. Man walked upright as now, in whatever direction he pleased; but when he wished to go fast he made use of all his eight limbs, and proceeded in a rapid motion by rolling circularly round,—like tumblers, who, with their legs in

Roman representation of Janus, "The Beginning and the End," on a Gnostic gem illustrated in Jacob Bryant's 1774 *A New System of Analysis of Ancient Mythology* (Lehner 1969: 88, fig. 458).

the air, tumble round and round. We account for the production of three sexes by supposing that, at the beginning, the male was produced from the sun, the female from the earth; and that sex which participated in both sexes, from the moon, by reason of the androgynous nature of the moon. They were round, and their mode of proceeding was round, from the similarity which must needs subsist between them and their parent.

"They were strong also, and had aspiring thoughts. They it was who levied war against the Gods; and what Homer writes concerning Ephialtus and Otus, that they sought to ascend to heaven, and dethrone the Gods, in reality relates to this primitive people. . . ."

[In order to end this "emergency" without destroying the people, Zeus cut the extraordinary beings "in half, as people cut eggs before they salt them, or as I have seen eggs cut with hairs." He had Apollo sew them up and put their sex organs in front, so that they might find their "other half."]

"From this period, mutual love has naturally existed between human beings; that reconciler and bond of union of their original nature, which seeks to make two one, and to heal the divided nature of man. Every one of us is thus the half of what may be properly termed a man, and like a pselta [flatfish] cut in two, is the imperfect portion of an entire whole, perpetually necessitated to seek the half belonging to him." (lines 189d–190b, 191d, trans. Shelley 1895:52–54, 56)

‡ "For anyone trying to understand the strange sequence of the first two chapters of Genesis without the aid of modern source criticism, it would have been very plausible to read such a myth [of a bisexual progenitor] into the text—expecially if one lived in a culture where Plato's version . . . was widely known. Small wonder, then, that . . . a midrashic tradition, extant in several variants . . . clearly betrays the influence of Plato: 'R. Samuel bar Nahman said, When the Holy One, blessed be he, created the first man, he created him *diprosōpon*. Then he split him and made two bodies, one on each side, and turned them about. Thus it is written, "He took one of his sides.' " But even the simpler versions betray by their interchangeable use of the Greek loan-words *androgynos* and *diprosōpos* (or, more often, *du'prosōpa*) their Platonic paternity. Though the Palestinian adaptation of the myth cannot be precisely dated, Philo attests the familiarity of this reading of the Genesis story in first-century Alexandria. Of course the use to which the Jews put the androgyne myth is quite different from its meaning in Aristophanes' tale in the *Symposium*. Only those elements which could be adjusted to the midrashic problems of Genesis 1–2—and to a thoroughly heterosexual ethos—were retained. In Judaism the myth serves only to solve an exegetical dilemma and to support monogamy" (Meeks 1974:185–86).

‡ "Some Jewish teachers (perhaps influenced by the story in Plato's *Symposium*) had suggested that Genesis 1:26–27 narrates an androgynous creation—an idea that gnostics adopted and developed. Marcus . . . not only concludes from this account that God is dyadic ('Let *us* make mankind'), but also that 'mankind, which was formed according to the image and likeness of God/[Father and Mother] was masculo-feminine.' And his contemporary, Theodotus, explains: 'the saying that Adam was created "male and female" means that the male and female elements together constitute the finest production of the Mother, Wisdom.' We can see, then, that the gnostic sources which describe God in both masculine and feminine terms often give a similar description of human nature as a dyadic entity, consisting of two equal male and female components" (Pagels 1976:298; also see Buckley 1980).

Gnostic gem showing "Athor seated with her legs extended and raised (a posture adopted in the original figure to display as distinctly as possible the androgynous nature of this divinity). In one hand she grasps a lion, in the other a serpent, and rests upon a base supported by four diminutive human figures in various attitudes: a rough imitation of the bas-relief adorning the base of the actual idol" (King 1864:220; plate IX, fig. 2).

The Gnostic tractate *Trimorphic Protennoia* was finalized about 200 A.D., with its Christian elements secondary introductions. "As the tractate proclaims, Protennoia is the Thought of the Father, the one born first of all beings, the one who has three names and yet exists alone, as one. She dwells at all levels of the universe; she is the revealer who awakens those that sleep, sho utters a call to remember, who saves. In three descents from the realm of Life and Light, the divine Protennoia brings to the fallen world of mortality a salvation through knowledge and the 'Five Seals' " (Turner 1977:461).

I am the Voice that appeared through my Thought, for I am "He who is syzygetic," since I am called "the Thought of the Invisible One." Since I am called "the unchanging Sound," I am called "She who is syzygetic."
I am a single one (fem.) since I am undefiled. I am the Mother [of] the Voice, speaking in many ways, completing the All. . . .
. . . I am androgynous. [I am both Mother and] Father since [I copulate] with myself. I [copulate] with myself [and with those who love] me, [and] it is through me alone that the All [stands firm]. I am the Womb [that gives shape] to the All by giving birth to the Light that [shines in] splendor. I am the Aeon to [come. I am] the fulfillment of the All, that is, Me[iroth]ea, the glory of the Mother. I cast a Sound [of the Voice] into the ears of those who know me. (Turner 1977:465–66, 467)

Religion scholar Elaine Pagels defines three ways in which the androgyne appears in gnostic works: "first, to indicate a state of human autonomy; second, to describe the original unity of humankind, or its state of ultimate perfection; third, to represent the 'fullness' of the divine" (1978:9). She notes that all such secret gospels, revelations and mystical teachings were never canonized. Instead, orthodox Christians labelled them heretical, and "by the time the process of sorting the various writings ended—probably as late as the year 200—virtually all the feminine imagery for God had disappeared from orthodox Christian tradition" (Pagels 1979:57).

> . . . There is neither Jew nor Greek, there is neither slave nor free, there is neither male nor female; for you are all one in Christ Jesus.
>
> —*Galatians* 3:28 (RSV).

In *Life Against Death,* philosopher Norman O. Brown notes that cabalistic mysticism viewed *Genesis* 1:27 as indicating God's androgynous nature. This was carried into Boehme's Christian mysticism, and he fused it with the Pauline notion in *Galatians* 3:28. According to Brown, "in neglecting Boehme, or this side of Boehme, later Protestantism only keeps its head in the sand." He cites Berdyaev's claim that the myth of the androgyne is the only one on which to base "an anthropological metaphysic." Berdyaev believes God's conception of man is of "a complete, masculinely feminine being, solar and telluric, logoic and cosmic at the same time." Thus original sin is the "division into two sexes and the Fall of the androgyne, i.e., of man as a complete being" (Brown 1959:133).

♦ Mary Daly, "Feminist Postchristian Introduction" to *The Church and The Second Sex* ("A critical review of [her 1968 A.D. work] . . ., written from the perspective of 1975 A.F. *(Anno Feminarum)"): "Daly does a competent analysis of Pauline texts. . . . However, I must suppress my feelings of impatience when I read her desperate straw-grasping attempt to propose one Pauline text (Galatians 3:27–28) as an instance where 'the dichotomy of fixed classes as dominant-subservient is transcended' (p. 84). The question that comes to my mind is: 'What sense does it make to assert that *in Christ* "there is neither male nor female"?' Wasn't 'Christ' an exclusively male symbol, even though somewhat 'feminized'? What on earth, then, could the text mean? But that is the point: it could not mean anything on earth, where there definitely were and are females and males and where that distinction has been overemphasized and distorted, especially in the church. If 'in Christ' meant some unearthly place, then certainly Daly could never have been there since the symbol *says* 'for men only' " (1975:22–23).

Hermaphroditism and androgyny also played important roles in classical myth and ritual.

‡ "Aphrodite's son Hermaphroditus was a youth with womanish breasts and long hair. Like the *androgyne,* or bearded woman, the hermaphrodite had, of course, its freakish physical counterpart, but as religious concepts both originated in the transition from matriarchy to patriarchy. Hermaphroditus is the sacred king deputizing for the Queen . . ., wearing artificial breasts. Androgyne is the mother of a preHellenic clan which has avoided being patriarchalized; in order to keep her magistratal powers or to ennoble children born to her from a slave-father, she assumes a false beard, as was the custom at Argos. Bearded goddesses like the Cyprian Aphrodite, and womanish gods like Dionysus, correspond with these transitional stages" (Graves 1960:73; also see Delcourt 1961).

◆ Mircea Eliade, *The Two and the One:* "The androgyne is understood by decadent writers simply as a hermaphrodite in whom both sexes exist anatomically and physiologically. They are concerned not with a wholeness resulting from the fusion of the sexes but with a superabundance of erotic possibilities. . . .

"This idea of the hermaphrodite has probably been encouraged by the study of certain ancient sculptures. But the decadent writers did not know that the hermaphrodite represented in antiquity an ideal condition which men endeavoured to achieve spiritually by means of imitative rites; but that if a child showed at birth any signs of hermaphroditism, it was killed by its own parents. In other words, the actual, anatomical hermaphrodite was considered an aberration of Nature or a sign of the gods' anger and consequently destroyed out of hand. Only the ritual androgyne provided a model, because it implied not an augmentation of anatomical organs but, symbolically, the union of the magico-religious powers belonging to both sexes" (1965a:100).

◆ June Singer, *Androgyny: Toward a New Theory of Sexuality:* "The Adam from whose rib Eve is taken is the hermaphroditic Adam. He fulfills the definition of the hermaphrodite as one who is imperfectly formed as to sexuality, with the characteristics of the opposite sex anatomically present but in a distorted, incomplete and inferior form. From here comes the tradition that the hermaphrodite is a distortion of the natural man. Like Dionysus, the Edenic Adam is a man-woman, and as hermaphrodite he is basically asexual. This is because the feminine is present within him but he is unconscious of her being there; hence he cannot relate to her, nor, by the same token, can she relate to him. This asymmetrical relationship, which is also unconscious, is necessarily impotent and passive. Nothing dynamic can come of it until the male is first separated from the female" (1976:98–99; also see Heilbrun 1973).

A. W. Dodd, *The Studio* 34
(Grafton 1980:82, fig. 255).

In his *Metamorphoses* the Roman poet Ovid recounts one reason why the Greek seer Tiresias was blind:

> While thus on earth things took their destined way,
> And twice-born Bacchus cradle-guarded lay,
> Once, when the nectar flowed, and Jove at ease
> In mellow mood was passing pleasantries
> With Juno, letting cares for once repose,
> An argument, at first in jest, arose.
> The woman's pleasure—Jove would have it so—
> Is greater than the man's. His wife said no.
> Tiresias (they concurred), who knew by test
> Both sides of love, would judge the issue best.
> Once in the woods at mating-time he broke
> On two huge serpents with his stick's rude stroke;
> And, changed from man to woman at the blow,
> (A thing most strange) he passed seven seasons so.
> The eighth, he saw the selfsame pair, and cried:
> "If in your contact such strong spells reside,
> That whoso strikes, from sex to sex must go,
> I'll try the charm again," and, striking so,
> He felt the power, was changed again, and wore
> This time for good, the shape his mother bore.
> So, called to judge the playful suit that day,
> He found for Jove, and Juno, so they say,
> Was vexed so deeply that, forgetting all
> Justice and reason in a thing so small,
> She made her chosen umpire feel her spite,
> Dooming his eyes to everlasting night.
> Almighty Jove (since no god can undo
> Another's work) gave him a vision new,
> The power to see events before they came,
> And soothed his sufferings with a prophet's fame.
> Through all the land his answers won repute,
> And, when he spoke, the critic's voice was mute.
>
> —Book III, lines 316–38,
> trans. Watts (1980:58–59).

‡ "Ritual transformation into a woman . . . though rare, . . . is not confined to northeastern Asia; transvestitism and ritual change of sex are found, for example, in Indonesia . . ., in South America (Patagonians and Araucanians), and among certain North American tribes (Arapaho, Cheyenne, Ute, etc.). Ritual and symbolic transformation into a woman is probably explained by an ideology derived from the archaic matriarchy; but . . . it does not appear to indicate any priority of women in the earliest shamanism. In any case, the presence of this special class of men 'similar to woman' . . . cannot be laid to the 'decadence of the shaman' . . ." (Eliade 1964:258).

‡ "As for the bisexuality and impotence . . ., they arise from the fact that these priest-shamans are regarded as the intermediaries between the two cosmological planes—earth and sky—and also from the fact that they combine in their own

A. W. Dodd, *The Studio* 34
(Grafton 1980:82, fig. 256).

person the feminine element (earth) and the masculine element (sky). We here have a ritual androgyny, a well-known archaic formula for the divine biunity and the *coincidentia oppositorum*" (Eliade 1964:352).

♦　Mircea Eliade, *Patterns in Comparative Religion:* "In short, from time to time man feels the need to return—if only for an instant—to the state of perfect humanity in which the sexes exist side by side as they coexist with all other qualities, and all other attributes, in the Divinity. The man dressed in woman's clothes is not trying to make himself a woman, as a first glance might suggest, but for a moment he is effecting the unity of the sexes, and thus facilitating his total understanding of the cosmos. The need man feels to cancel periodically his differentiated and determined condition so as to return to primeval 'totalization' is the same need which spurs him to periodic orgies in which all forms dissolve, to end by recovering that 'oneness' that was before the creation. . . . And all these rituals have as their exemplar model the myth of divine androgyny" (1958:424–25).

The Aztecs also inherited a tradition of divine androgyny. The anonymous *Historia Tolteca-Chichimeca* was compiled around 1545. Some of the poems in it date from an earlier period than the Aztec. According to scholar Miguel León-Portilla, one song "tells something of the original Toltec concept of the Deity. . . . The significance of this poem lies in its reference to the same supreme god of duality whose discovery subsequent texts attribute to Toltec sages. This would suggest that 'a very ancient philosophical school (one dating from at least Toltec times) held that the origin of all things is one single principle—masculine and feminine—which has begotten the gods, the world and men' " (León-Portilla 1963:80, citing Alfonso Caso, *La Religión de los Aztecas,* Mexico City, 1936, p.8; also see Nash 1978).

> Lines 5–6: *The celestial god is called the Lord of Duality. And his consort is called the Lady of Duality, the celestial Lady.*

Contained in these lines is the key to understanding the idea of "one true god and his consort": "The celestial god [Ilhuicateotl] is called the Lord of Duality [Ometecuhtli]." Although he is one, at the same time he possesses a dual nature. Therefore, his metaphysical abode is named *Omeyocan,* place of duality, and he is also given the more abstract name Ometéotl (god of duality). Correspondingly, the name of his consort, "his equal," is, as the text says, "Dual Lady (Omecíhuatl)."
. . . The powers of generation and of conception—requisites for the appearance of life in our world—were thus combined in a single being. The affirmation is made, first implicitly and later, in other terms, explicitly, that the *nelli téotl* or Ometéotl is the cosmic principle by which all that exists is conceived and begotten. (León-Portilla 1963:83)

♦　Mary Ritchie Key, *Male/Female Language:* "The Aztec language is a good example, because we know something of their ancient beliefs and it is a language which does not have masculine and feminine gender in the grammatical system. . . . [The third person singular pronoun] cannot be translated into English. It may refer to 'he, she or it.' . . . They believed that the origin of the world and all human beings was *one single principle* with a dual nature. This supreme being had a male and female countenance. . . . This god had the regenerating ability of both male and female. This dual deity, *Ometeotl,* had two different aspects of a single supreme being. Ome = 'two' and teotl = 'god.'

a   b

Ancient Mexican flat stamps representing the sun emblem: *a*, Veracruz; *b*, Oaxaca; *c*, Mexico City
(Enciso 1953:152).

c

". . . There is a plural form in Aztec, if the ancients had wanted to use it, but
they referred to this god in the singular. . . .

"Besides the gender difficulty in rendering these ideas into English, there is the
difficulty of the multitudes of gods being *one god*. Do we use 'is' or 'are'? Note that
I have not used either pronoun referent 'he' or 'she' so far, in reference to this Aztec
god. There is nothing in the Aztec language to indicate which gender should be
used, and there is simply no way to translate this into English. Nevertheless it is
significant that the eminent authorities who discuss Aztec religion all use the
pronoun 'he' in the discussions. There is no more reason to use the male referent
than to use 'she' " (1975:20–21; also see Miller and Swift 1976:64–74).

♦   Phyllis Trible, "Depatriarchalizing in Biblical Interpretation": "To summarize:
Although the Old Testament often pictures Yahweh as a man, it also uses gyn-
omorphic language for the Deity. At the same time, Israel repudiated the idea
of sexuality in God. Unlike fertility gods, Yahweh is neither male nor female;
neither he nor she. Consequently, modern assertions that God is masculine, even
when they are qualified, are misleading and detrimental, if not altogether
inaccurate. Cultural and grammatical limitations (the use of masculine pronouns
for God) need not limit theological understanding. As Creator and Lord, Yahweh
embraces and transcends both sexes. To translate . . .: the nature of the God of
Israel defies sexism" (1976:220–21).

♦   Mircea Eliade, *Patterns in Comparative Religion:* "Divine bisexuality is an element found in a great many religions and—a point worth noting—even the most supremely masculine or feminine divinities are androgynous. Under whatever form the divinity manifests itself, he or she is ultimate reality, absolute power, and this reality, this power, will not let itself be limited by any attributes whatsoever (good, evil, male, female, or anything else)" (1958:421).

♦   Carol Ochs, *Behind the Sex of God:* "What Einstein did with regard to matter and energy, Spinoza with mind and body, and Aristotle with knowledge and change, is precisely what I feel must be done with the apparent opposition of matriarchy and patriarchy. I reject dualism. I reject dualism, be it the duality of knowledge and change, mind and body or matriarchy and patriarchy. While methodologically we may define things in opposition we know that what truly is other cannot be part of a shared reality" (1977:133).

♦   "My position is that God is not apart from, separate from, or other than this reality. We, all together, are part of the whole, the All in All. God is not father, nor mother, nor even parents, because God is not other than, distinct from, or opposed to creation" (ibid:137).

♦   Mary Daly, *Gyn/Ecology:* "Spinsters spinning out the Self's own integrity can break the spell of the fathers' clocks, spanning the tears and splits in consciousness. Spanning splits, however, involves something totally Other than attempting to fasten together two apparently opposite parts, on the mistaken assumption that these 'halves' will make a whole. We have seen, for example, that attempts to combine masculinity and femininity, which are patriarchal constructs, will result only in pseudointegrity. Feminist theorists have gone through frustrating attempts to describe our integrity by such terms as *androgyny.* Experience proved that this word, which we now recognize as expressing pseudowholeness in its combination of distorted gender descriptions, failed and betrayed our thought. The deceptive word was a trap, hard to avoid on an earlier stage of the Journey. When we heard the word echoed back by those who misinterpreted our thought we realized that combining the 'halves' offered to consciousness by patriarchal language usually results in portraying something more like a hole than a whole. Thus *androgyny* is a vacuous term which not only fails to represent richness of be-ing. It also functions as a vacuum that sucks its spellbound victims into itself. Such pseudowholeness, which characterizes all false universalisms (e.g., humanism, people's liberation) is the deep hole—the chasm—which Spinsters must leap over, which we must span" (1978:387–88).

Amazons

The *Iliad* contains the earliest Greek references to Amazons as women warriors (book 2, lines 189ff; book 6, lines 179ff), and they figure in various stories about Heracles (Merck 1978:97–101). Amazons are also described in *The Histories* by Herodotus of Halicarnassus (484–?, sometime after 430 B.C.). In book four on the Scythians, Herodotus recounts a story from the Sauromatae—how during a war between the Greeks and Amazons at the Thermodon River, the victorious Greeks captured a boatload of Amazons, known to the Sythians as *Oeorpata* or "mankillers." At sea, the women slaughtered their

(Harter 1978b:33)

captors but did not know how to sail and so were blown to Cremni, the Cliffs, in Scythian territory. There they seized horses and began looting.

When the Scythians realized the invaders they fought were women they determined to beget children by the Amazons and sent out a detachment of young men with orders to tantalize and not harm them. Eventually the two bands got together. The Amazons learned the Scythians' language but the men did not learn the women's language. The women refused to marry the men and live in Scythia because they could not get along with the Scythian women; the latter knew only "women's work" and "feminine tasks" at home while the former were "riders" whose business was with bow and spear. The men agreed to move away with their wives, and they travelled across the Tanais eastward and then northward to a new home in an area between what is now the Black Sea and the Caspian Sea.

Thus the Sauromatae speak a corrupt form of Scythian. The women keep their old ways, wear men's clothing, and often hunt and make war with or without their men. No woman can marry before killing an enemy in battle, and thus "some of their women, unable to fulfill this condition, grow old and die in spinsterhood" (Herodotus, rev. trans. Burn 1972:309).

The Athenians also maintained a myth about the Amazons whom Theseus defeated. The Athenian treasury at Delphi, built around 505 B.C., depicts the labors of Heracles, the labors of Theseus, and the battles of Greeks against Amazons—the Amazonomachy, the warring Amazons. The Parthenon on the Acropolis in Athens, begun in 447 B.C., also shows the Greeks repelling the Amazons. By the fifth century B.C., the Athenian festival of the Theseia, which celebrated Theseus's rescue from the Minotaur, was coupled with a commemoration of his defeating the Amazons. A fourth-century history by Cleidemus records actual logistics and locales of the Amazons' attack on Athens (Merck 1978:101–107).

‡   "We have seen how the myth of Athens' triumph over the Amazons was used to historicise the claims of that state. In his 'Funeral Oration' the Athenian orator Lysias (c. 459–380) joins that patriotic theme to another:

> They (the Amazons) would not return home and report their own misfortune and our ancestors' valour: for they perished on the spot, and were punished for their folly, making our city's memory imperishable in its valour; while

Amazon (Harter 1978b:46).

owing to their disaster in this region, they rendered their own country nameless. And so these woman, by their unjust greed for others' land, justly lost their own.

"As victory thrust the Athenian state into immortality, so defeat removed the Amazons from history altogether, effectively expunging them from the record" (Merck 1978:107).

♦   Mandy Merck, "The City's Achievements": "The Amazon myth resolved this tension [between the private and the public, the family and the state] by representing such a rebellion as already concluded in deserved defeat. Lysias suggests that greed for land was the source of the tribeswomen's downfall. The association of their image with primitive, chaotic or alien forces . . . produces similar justifications. So, interestingly, do the folk etymologies invented by the Greeks in explanation of a name whose derivation was already lost.

"Perhaps the most famous of these is 'a-mastos', variously translatable as 'breastless,' 'not brought up by the breast', 'beings with strong breasts', and 'with one breast'. This has been suggested as the source of the tradition that the Amazons excised one breast to further their military prowess (a tradition notably absent from both Greek art and myth . . .).

"Other retrospective etymologies include 'a-maza', 'without barley bread'; 'azona', 'chastity belt'; and 'amazosas', 'opposed to man'. What is significant in these inventions is their characterisation of the warrior women as anti-feminine, self-mutilating, man-hating and technically under-developed. . . .

"Where the Greeks could not christen their enemies, they invented etymologies; where they could—in the individual Amazon names inscribed on vases or in the myths—the choices are again significant. Several of these names link the women with their traditional animal, the horse. . . . Did such bestial, murderous beings deserve better than annihilation at the hands of civilisation?" (1978:110; also see Phyllis Chesler, "The Amazon Legacy," in Steinem et al. 1972; Sobol 1972; Sanday 1981:86–87; Sojourner 1982:59–60).

Anthropologists Orlando and Claudio Villas Boas devoted some thirty years to protecting the Xingu Indians of central Brazil from the depredations of colonialists "opening" the interior for development. The following myth, which portrays (literally) Amazon women without breasts, is taken from the brothers' extensive journals. It is identified as told among the Kamaiurá, a Tupi tribe of the Alto-Xingu.

The Iamuricumá women held a great festival for the ear-piercing of the boys. After the festival, one part of the village went fishing. The fishermen took along a lot of beijus to eat. The fishing area was far from the village. When they got there, they pounded some *timbó* [poisonous liana] into the water and began to catch fish. The days went by and the fishermen did not go home. It was taking them a long time. The boys whose ears had been pierced were in confinement, waiting for the fish that their fathers had gone to catch for them. More than a moon passed, and still the fishermen were gone. In the village, a man who had not gone fishing, the son of the morerequát, decided to go after the fishing party and see what had happened. He had some beijus made for the trip and went off. When he arrived at their camp, the fishermen hid their fish. They did not want him to see them. His people were making a frightful racket. They were all turning into wild pigs and other forest animals. The son of the morerequát did not like it and went home.

Back at the village he said the fishermen would be a few more days fishing. But he told his mother the truth and said his father and the other people were turning into things, animals of the forest.

The chief's wife then ordered the women to prepare beijus for the festival and to cut their sons' hair, the boys whose ears had been pierced. When the beijus were ready, the women set up stools in the center of the village, where their sons would sit while their hair was cut in the ceremony. After it was over, the chief's wife told the other women that they could not stay there any longer. They had to leave that place because their husbands were not people any more, they were turning into animals. All night long, the women talked about it, repeating over and over that they could not stay there any longer. The chief's wife spoke endlessly; day and night she carried on about the need for leaving at once and for abandoning the village forever. Then they all began preparing to leave. They spent two days getting ready, gathering their things, preparing everything: ornaments, necklaces, cotton yarn to wrap around their arms, all things that their men wore.

The morerequát's wife, before anyone else, began to adorn herself with feathers, armbands, necklaces, and to paint herself with urucu and genipap. After adorning herself exactly like the men, she began to sing. By herself, she sang and sang continuously. Singing, she climbed on top of a house and there went on singing. The men who were left in the village started to complain and curse, but the singing went on. Another woman, adorned the same way, climbed on top of another house and began to sing too. After a while, still chanting their songs, the two women came down to the center of the village, where the other women, by now also adorned and painted like men, joined in the song. Then they started to spread poison over their bodies, to turn themselves into *mamaés* [spirits]. That is why today, in the place where the lamuricumá lived, no one is allowed to remove lianas, roots, or anything else from the forest. Whoever does goes mad and gets lost, never to be seen again. They also drank the poison they rubbed on their bodies.

The songs and dances in the village lasted for two whole days. Then the lamuricumá women, without interrupting their song, slowly began to move away. But before this, they grabbed an old man and dressed him in the shell of a *tatu-açu*. They put beiju spatulas in his hand and told him to lead the way. As he set off, the old man said, "Now I'm not a person any more, I'm an armadillo." Saying this, he took the lead. After taking a few turns around the village, the lamuricumá women, still singing, followed behind the tata-açu, who went ahead, burrowing. He kept taking dives into the ground. He would plunge down at one spot, only to bob up ahead of them. Farther on, the women went past their husbands, who were still fishing. The small children were being carried. The fishermen asked their wives to stop, so the boys could eat some fish. The women would not listen and went on their way. Singing, adorned with feathers, and painted with urucu and genipap, each day they traveled farther, following the armadillo, who went along opening tunnels in the earth. Farther on, they passed the Macão-acáp village. It was midday. The local chief asked his people not to look, so as not to be taken away by the lamuricumá women. The women did not obey and looked, and the lamuricumá women carried them all off. Their husbands, who went after them, were also captured. Farther ahead, they passed another village called Etapemetáp. The chief gave his people the same warning, but they would not obey either, and they too were captured.

The lamuricumá women went on with their journey, traveling forever. They walked day and night without stopping. The small children were thrown into the lagoons, and they turned into fish. The lamuricumá women are walking still

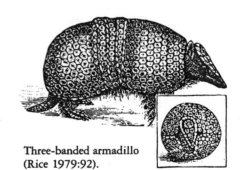

Three-banded armadillo (Rice 1979:92).

today, ever adorned and singing. They use bows and arrows and do not have a right breast, so they can pull back their bowstrings more easily. (Villas Boas and Villas Boas 1973:123–25; also see Fox 1978:251–54)

◆   J. J. Bachofen, *Mother Right:* "Everywhere it is an assault on woman's rights which provokes her resistance, which inspires self-defense followed by bloody vengeance. In accordance with this law grounded in human and particularly in feminine nature, hetaerism must necessarily lead to Amazonism. Degraded by man's abuse, it is woman who first yearns for a more secure and a purer life. The sense of degradation and fury of despair spur her on to armed resistance, exalting her to that warlike grandeur which, though it seems to exceed the bounds of womanhood, is rooted simply in her need for a higher life. . . .

". . . Amazonism, despite its savage degeneration, signifies an appreciable rise in human culture. A regression and perversion at later cultural stages, it is, in its first appearance, a step forward toward a purer form of life, and not only a necessary stage of human development, but one that is beneficial in its consequences" (1967:104–05; also see Diner 1973).

◆   Mandy Merck, "The City's Achievements": "Is the idea of 'autonomous warrior women' invariably paradoxical in patriarchal culture? Can it resolve itself only in the reversal of the sexes, making the heroines into their opponents, men?" (1978:111).

Like so many such designations, the term Amazon in English came to be applied not just to a female soldier but to "a strong, tall, or masculine woman" (*Oxford English Dictionary*) or "a large, strong, masculine woman" (*Webster's New World Dictionary of the American Language*), often with derogatory intent. Thus, when journalist-anthropologist Peter Nabokov refers to the woman runner Part-Sky-Woman as a "Chippewa amazon" (1981:85–87),[6] it is difficult to view the term with positive or even neutral connotations. Hence, feminist historians and artists have attempted strongly affirmative revaluations of what psychologist Phyllis Chesler calls "The Amazon Legacy" (e.g., Steinem et al. 1972; Merck 1978; various contributions to Spretnak 1982).

Wonder Woman, created in 1941 by psychologist William Moulton Marston under the pen name Charles Moulton, is certainly within this revisionist tradition. Lovely as Aphrodite, wise as Athena, possessing Mercury's speed and Hercules' strength, Wonder Woman was able to avenge injustice and right wrongs while viewing men's problems and prowess as "mere child's play." No one outside her Paradise Island home knew her identity—that she was Princess Diana, daughter of Amazon Queen Hippolyte, who had once let Hercules take her magic girdle and so subjected herself and her people to an insupportable male domination. Aphrodite finally decreed that the enslaved women be freed, that they leave to make a better world elsewhere, always wearing the bracelets of their former captors as reminders of a dark past. She promised them eternal life as long as they never again were beguiled by men.

Only in the comicbook's inaugural issue did Wonder Woman (mild, bespectacled Diana Prince in her everyday United States life) wear skirts. Thereafter, she dressed in star spangled shorts for better "action pictures" (Steinem et al. 1972, no pagination). Among Moulton's early creations was the "strange and thrilling case of 'The Ice-Bound Maidens'," in which Wonder Woman must confront the Seal Men of Prince Pagli and Count Frigid to save herself, Eve Electress, and several "maidens" of Eveland from being frozen (Steinem et al. 1972). Later recreations show Wonder Woman confronting other villains stereotypically hostile to women, e.g., "The Fiend with the Face of Glass," who tries to steal Wonder Woman's beautiful face to replace her own cracked one and who tries to crush her helpless victim in a plastic wrap coccoon! (*Wonder Woman*, vol. 34, no. 221, December–January 1975/1976, written by Martin Pasko and drawn by Curt Swan and Vince Colletta). Yet another 1970s version presents an interesting twist on patriarchal religions overthrowing matriarchal ones. The sky gods, mounted on kangaroos, invade Paradise Island and are conquered by the youthful Wonder Woman riding a rabbit. Fortunately, they turn out to be masked women and so Aphrodite's law banning men from Paradise Island has not been broken ("Attack of the

[6]Nabokov refers to Ruth Landes's account of the athletic Part-Sky-Woman, in *The Ojibwa Woman* (1971:23–26). According to Landes: "Athletic games offer women the same recognition as men, the only sphere in which this is allowed. In racing, the standard of accomplishment is the same for both sexes" (1971:22). Successful women runners and hockey players behave the same way successful male athletes do. In *Indian Running*, Nabokov also documents cases of women runners who equal or outstrip men in various Native American cultures, notably the Tarahumara of northern Mexico (1981: 164–65, 167, 171).

Sky Demons," *Wonder Woman,* vol. 32, no. 209, December–January 1973/ 1974, pencils by Ric Estrada, inks by Vince Colletta)—until, of course, Army Intelligence Captain Steve Trevor's plane crashes there later.

♦   Jules Feiffer, *The Great Comic Book Heroes:* "Well, I can't comment on the image girls had of Wonder Woman. I never knew they read her—or any comic book. That *girls* had a preference for my brand of literature would have been more of a frightening image to me than any number of men being beaten up by Wonder Woman. . . .

"My problem with Wonder Woman was that I could never get myself to believe she was that good. For if she was as strong as they said, why wasn't she tougher looking? Why wasn't she bigger? Why was she so flat-chested? And why did I always feel that, whatever her vaunted Amazon power, she wouldn't have lasted a round with Sheena, Queen of the Jungle?

"No, Wonder Woman seemed like too much of a put-up job, a fixed comic strip—a product of group thinking rather than the individual inspiration that created Superman. It was obvious from the start that a bunch of men got together in a smoke-filled room and brain-stormed themselves a Super Lady. But nobody's heart was in it. It was choppily written and dully drawn. . . . Her violence was too immaculate, never once boiling over into a little fantasmal sadism. Had they given us a Wonder Woman with balls—that would have been something for . . . us to wrestle with!" (1965:44–45).

♦   Gloria Steinem, "Wonder Woman: An Introduction": "The trouble is that the comic book performers of such superhuman feats—and even of only dimly competent ones—are almost always heroes. Literally. The female child is left to believe that, even when her body is as grown-up as her spirit, she will still be in the childlike role of helping with minor tasks, appreciating men's accomplishments, and being so incompetent and passive that she can only hope some man can come to her rescue. Of course, rescue and protection are comforting, even exhilarating experiences that should be and often are shared by men and boys. Even in comic books, the hero is frequently called on to protect his own kind in addition to helpless women. But dependency and zero accomplishments get very dull as a steady diet. The only option for a girl reader is to identify with the male characters—pretty difficult, even in the androgynous years of childhood. If she can't do that, she faces limited prospects: an 'ideal' life of sitting around like a technicolor clothes horse, getting into jams with villains, and saying things like 'Oh, Superman! I'll always be grateful to you,' even as her hero goes off to bigger and better adventures. It hardly seems worth learning to tie our shoes.

"I'm happy to say that I was rescued from this plight at about the age of seven or eight; rescued (Great Hera!) by a woman. Not only was she as wise as Athena and as lovely as Aphrodite, she had the speed of Mercury and the strength of Hercules. Of course, being an Amazon, she had a head start on such accomplishments, but she had earned them in a human way by training in Greek-style contests of dexterity and speed with her Amazon sisters. (Somehow it always seemed boring to me that Superman was a creature from another planet, and therefore had bullet-proof skin, x-ray vision, and the power to fly. Where was the contest?) This beautiful Amazon did have some fantastic gadgets to help her: an invisible plane that carried her through dimensions of time and space, a golden magic lasso, and bullet-proof bracelets. But she still had to get to the plane, throw the lasso with accuracy, and be agile enough to catch bullets on the steel-enclosed wrists" (1972:n.p.).

About that time there arose no little stir concerning the Way. For a man named Demetrius, a silversmith, who made silver shrines of Artemis, brought no little business to the craftsmen. These he gathered together, with the workmen of like occupation, and said, "Men, you know that from this business we have our wealth. And you see and hear that not only at Ephesus but almost throughout all Asia this Paul has persuaded and turned away a considerable company of people, saying that gods made with hands are not gods. And there is danger not only that this trade of ours may come into disrepute but also that the temple of the great goddess Artemis may count for nothing, and that she may even be deposed from her magnificence, she whom all Asia and the world worship."

When they heard this they were enraged, and cried out, "Great is Artemis of the Ephesians!" So the city was filled with the confusion; and they rushed together into the theater, dragging with them Gaius and Aristarchus, Macedonians who were Paul's companions in travel.

—*Acts* 19:23–29 (RSV).

‡ "In the western sections of Anatolia [now Turkey], matrilineal descent and Goddess worhsip continued into classical times. Strabo, shortly before the birth of Christ, wrote of northern Anatolian towns, as far east as Armenia, where children who were born to unmarried women were legitimate and respectable. They simply took the name of their mothers, who, according to Strabo's reports, were some of the most noble and aristocratic of citizens.

"It is possible that at the time of the Hittite invasions many of the Goddess-worshipping peoples may have fled west. The renowned temple of the Goddess in the city of Ephesus was the target of the apostle Paul's zealous missionary efforts.. . . . This temple, which legend and classical reports claim was founded by 'Amazons,' was not completely closed down until A.D. 380. All along this western section, which included the areas known as Lycia, Lydia and Caria, there were accounts in classical Greek and Roman literature of the widespread veneration of 'The Mother of all Deities,' along with reports of women warriors, the Amazons. . . . It was in the land of Lydia that the legendary Indo-European Greek Hercules was said to have been kept as a servile lover to Queen Omphale. We may at this point question whether the numerous tales of 'Amazon' women may not actually have been the later Indo-European Greek accounts of the women who tried to defend the ancient Goddess shrines and repel the patriarchal northern invaders" (Stone 1976:45–46; for the Aztec case, see Nash 1978).

◆ Merlin Stone, *When God Was a Woman:* "Many questions come to mind. How influenced by contemporary religions were many of the scholars who wrote the texts available today? How many scholars have simply assumed that males have always played the dominant role in leadership and creative invention and projected this assumption into their analysis of ancient cultures? Why do so many people educated in this century think of classical Greece as the first major culture when written language was in use and great cities built at least twenty-five centuries before that time? And perhaps most important, why is it continually inferred that the age of the 'pagan' religions, the time of the worship of female deities (if mentioned at all), was dark and chaotic, mysterious and evil, without the light of order and reason that supposedly accompanied the later male religions, when it has been archaeologically confirmed that the earliest law, government, medicine,

Diana of Ephesus
(Lehner 1969:17, fig. 5).
Alabaster and bronze statue, Rome, 2d century A.D. According to Erich Neumann: "This unquestionably is a representation of the Great Many-Breasted Mother, as ruler and nourisher of the animal world. She finds her classical form in the Diana of Ephesus, but in Mexico there is also a representative of this Great Goddess, Mayauel, goddess of the Agave, surnamed 'the woman with four hundred breasts' " (1963:126, and plate 35).

agriculture, architecture, metallurgy, wheeled vehicles, ceramics, textiles and written language were initially developed in societies that worshipped the Goddess? We may find ourselves wondering about the reasons for the lack of easily available information on societies who, for thousands of years, worshipped the ancient Creatress of the Universe" (1976:xxiv).

Johann Jakob Bachofen was a nineteenth-century exception to Stone's challenge. In 1861, Henry Sumner Maine's *Ancient Law* was published in London, while Bachofen's *Das Mutterrecht; eine Untersuchung über die Gynaikokratie der alten Welt nach ihrer religiösen und rechtlichen Natur* ("Matriarchy; an Investigation of the Gynocracy of Antiquity according to its Religious and Legal Nature") appeared in Germany. The Englishman proposed an evolutionary scheme which proclaimed the primacy of patriliny and patriarchy, while the Swiss Bachofen pronounced the reverse, that: "[Demetrian] matriarchy is followed by patriarchy and preceded by unregulated hetaerism" (1967:93). His fanciful descriptions of these stages may be viewed as themselves allegorical-philosophical myths.

> . . . At the lowest, darkest stages of human existence, the love between the mother and her offspring is the bright spot in life, the only light in the moral darkness, the only joy amid profound misery. . . . The close relation between child and father, the son's self-sacrifice for his begetter, require a far higher degree of moral development than mother love, that mysterious power which equally permeates all earthly creatures. Paternal love appears later. . . . Raising her young, the woman learns earlier than the man to extend her loving care beyond the limits of the ego to another creature, and to direct whatever gifts of invention she possesses to the preservation and improvement of this other's existence. Woman at this stage is the repository of all culture, of all benevolence, of all devotion, of all concern for the living and grief for the dead. (Ibid:79)

> . . . There is no doubt that matriarchy everywhere grew out of woman's conscious, continued resistance to the debasing state of hetaerism. Defenseless against abuse by men, and according to an Arabian tradition preserved by Strabo, exhausted by their lusts, woman was first to feel the need for regulated conditions and a purer ethic, while men, conscious of their superior physical strength, accepted the new constraint only unwillingly. This context alone enables us to understand the full historical significance of the strict discipline which is one of the distinguishing features of matriarchal life, and to accord conjugal chastity, the highest principle of every mystery, its proper place in the history of human manners. (Ibid:94)

The matriarchal period is indeed the poetry of history by virtue of the sublimity, the heroic grandeur, even the beauty to which woman rose by inspiring bravery and chivalry in men, by virtue of the meaning she imparted to feminine love and the chastity and restraint that she exacted of young men. To the ancients all this appeared in very much the same light as the chivalric nobility of the Germanic world to our own eyes. Like us, the ancients asked: What has become of the heroines whose praises were sung by Hesiod, poet of the matriarchy? . . . All warlike peoples, Aristotle remarks, serve the woman, and the study of later epochs teaches the same lesson: to defy danger, to seek out adventure, and to serve beauty—these virtues betoken the fullness of a nation's youth. (Ibid:83–84)

Evolutionary schemes such as Bachofen's (e.g., Briffault 1927; Graves 1948; Davis 1972; Diner 1973) have been much criticized (e.g., Hultkrantz 1961; Hackett and Pomeroy 1972; Cothran 1974). More recent schemata, no less vulnerable to criticism, such as writer Elizabeth Fisher's *Woman's Creation: Sexual Evolution and the Shaping of Society*, rely in part on the archeological record to reinterpret dominant "theories of evolution in which only men evolve"[7]:

"Thompson basket with 'fish net' (or 'deer net') design" (Naylor 1975:110, fig. E).

The carrier bag and women's gathering activities could have been the master pattern in human evolution. An extension of this idea involves the invention of many kinds of household equipment, from containers to baskets and pottery, from digging sticks to stone pounding tools and scrapers and cutters, all used primarily by women in the recent past.

The use of the carrier bag facilitated the accumulation of botanical information. Hominid females would communicate the whereabouts of a rich stand of fruiting bushes, when seeds or nuts could be picked from grass or trees and where they grew, so that a whole store of knowledge of different kinds of plants enlarged the human brain, which in turn enabled the developing hominids to classify and investigate the natural world about them, in the classic model of the feedback mechanisms that shaped the evolution of humanity. Experimentation with the

[7]Fisher claims: "Popularizers like Robert Ardrey went even further, calling the animal bones weapons pure and simple, claiming that '*man* is a predator whose natural instinct is to kill with a weapon' and that when archaeologists discuss 'tools' they really mean weapons. He described our predecessors as killer apes and gave a more extreme version of the aggression theory of evolution. His ideas are graphically enacted in the Clarke-Kubrick film *2001: A Space Odyssey*, which opens on an arid desert with piles of bones here and there and several hairy creatures crouch-hopping about. Suddenly one of the apelike individuals picks up a bone hesitantly, swings it idly, and, in a flash of genius, brings it down on a fellow creature's head. From this first scene of unmotivated violence, the film leaps to others depicting group hunts and skirmishes against neighboring bands. In four scenes with a total of twenty-odd males, only one female appears: a nighttime shot shows a group huddled on the ground sleeping as one member holds a baby to her breast. . . . The almost total disappearance of woman in *2001* typified the high misogyny which characterized the nineteen fifties and sixties. If the ratio of females to males presented above—the section in the film titled 'Dawn of *Man* Four Million B.C.'—had actually obtained, there would have been no proliferation, no evolutionary success, and no human race" (1979:50, 51).

materials necessary for containers and carriers led to the exploration of the raw materials in the world around so that the developing hominids came to penetrate the resources of their environment and to develop technology.

Food was shared first with infants but also with older siblings and with compatible females who went out to gather, thus increasing both socializing and planning capacities of the new species. . . .

. . . The earliest remaining tools—natural stones, called manuports by the archaeologists, and very simple flaked stones—are two to five million years old. As recently as ten years ago, their use was credited to men, and they were interpreted as weapons or implements for big-game hunting. Today they are being re-examined in the light of the greater importance now assigned to women, as well as to plants, in human evolution, and they look more like household equipment. Tools which used to be called choppers were probably used for pointing digging sticks (today used chiefly by the women of foraging as well as of horticultural peoples), and for cutting by means of a sawing action. Others of heavier stone were used for hammering and bashing, for example, breaking open nuts and preparing parts of plants inedible in their natural state but palatable and digestible after pounding. . . .

The digging stick was probably the second hominid invention, after the container. . . . (Fisher 1979:62–64)

◆ M. Z. Rosaldo, "The Use and Abuse of Anthropology: Reflections on Feminism and Cross-cultural Understanding": "But at the same time that Woman the Gatherer has, in fact, begun to set the record straight, it seems to me that this revised account is far from adequate, if what we seek is not simply an appreciation of the contribution women make but instead an understanding of how these women organized their lives and claims in any actual society. The account insists, with reason, that our gathering sisters did important things; but it cannot explain why hunting people never celebrated women's deeds so necessary to human survival. Indeed, if we appeal to the contemporary evidence for what it might say about the past, hunting peoples celebrate—both in all male and in collective rites—not gathering or childbirth but rather the transcendent role of hunters. Man the Hunter boasts about his catch, and women choose as lovers able hunters; but in

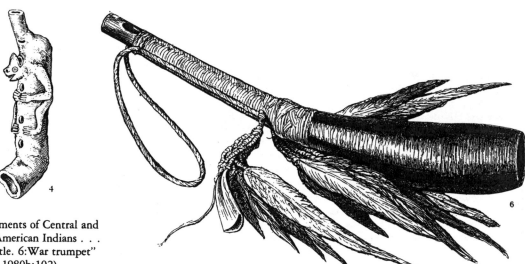

"Instruments of Central and South American Indians . . . 4: Whistle. 6: War trumpet" (Harter 1980b: 102).

no report are we informed of women celebrated for their gathering skill or granted special recognition because of their success as mothers.

"Yet more serious, perhaps, Woman the Gatherer as presently portrayed is overwhelmingly a biological being whose concerns are dictated by her reproductive role. She seeks a male who will impregnate and, perhaps, provide; but she has no cause to forge—or to resist—ongoing adult bonds, or to create and use a jural order made of regular expectations, norms, and rules. If anything, Woman the Gatherer seems a being who is content unto herself; absorbed in what in fact appear as relatively domestic chores, she frees her male associates to engage in risky hunts, forge wider bonds, and so, again, she allows Man the upper hand, permitting him to make the social whole" (1980:411–12).

Anthropologist Joan Bamberger summarizes a widespread South American myth of matriarchy (e.g., Reichel-Dolmatoff 1971:169–70; Villas Boas and Villas Boas 1973:119–21; Lévi-Strauss 1973:271ff; Murphy and Murphy 1974:88–89)[8]:

. . . The Juruparí myths [from the northern Amazon] and those of the [Tierra del] Fuegian Hain and Kina lodges share a common set of themes that are their hallmark. First, the secret objects belonging to men (masks, trumpets, ritual lodges, songs, and the like) originally were invented by women and owned by them; or, if they originated with the men, their secrets were discovered by women, who contaminated their sacredness by viewing or touching them. . . . Spying on the sacred instruments was a death warrant for all violators of the prohibition. An obvious relationship is established in these myths between viewing, touching, and forbidden sex, although the association is a symbolic one and should perhaps be seen as part of a complex set of cultural laws establishing the proper set of behaviors expected between the sexes.

A second theme running through these myths is that a position of authority adheres to the possessors of tribal secrets, and that those who sit in authority, whether females or males, may also enjoy a life of relative leisure. The trumpets and lodges are the badge of this authority, permitting one sex to dominate the other. However begun, the myths invariably conclude with the men in power. Either the men have taken from the women the symbols of authority and have installed themselves as the rightful owners of the ceremony and its paraphernalia, or they invoke violent sanctions against the women who have dared to challenge male authority. In no versions do women win the battle for power. Instead, they remain forever the subjects of male terrorism, hidden in their huts, fearing to look out on masked spirits and trumpeting ancestors. (Bamberger 1974:274–75)

◆ Joan Bamberger, "The Myth of Matriarchy": "Certainly the mythical message used to bind women to their household duties in aboriginal South America stresses moral laxity and an abuse of power rather than any physical weakness or disability

[8]Compare Mircea Eliade's contention that: "According to the myths of certain primitive peoples, the aged women of the tribe 'naturally' possessed fire in their genital organs and made use of it to do their cooking but kept it hidden from men, who were able to get possession of it only by trickery. These myths reflect the ideology of a matriarchal society and remind us, also, of the fact that fire, being produced by the friction of two pieces of wood (that is, by their 'sexual union'), was regarded as existing naturally in the piece which represented the female" (1971:80). Among Eliade's sources is Sir James George Frazer, *Myths of the Origin of Fire* (London: Macmillan, 1930). A slightly different version of the myth outlined by Bamberger was collected by a Czech traveller from the Chamacoco Indians of Paraguay in 1928 (Métraux 1943:116–18).

3

"Instruments of Central and South American Indians: . . . 3: Bone flute" (Harter 1980b:102).

on the part of women. If the dictates of biology were carefully adhered to, women might well find themselves still in the seat of power, for it is obvious that the biological functions of females are necessary for the continuity of any human group. No male occupation, however exalted, can compensate for the unique ability of the female to conceive, bear, and nurse the young of the species. This important contribution of women to group survival is celebrated in female puberty ritual but overlooked in myth. . . .

"Whether or not women actually behaved in the manner of the charges recorded in the myth is not an issue in understanding the insistent message of the myth. What is at issue is the ideological thrust of the argument made in the myth of the Rule of Women, and the justification it offers for male dominance through the evocation of a vision of a catastrophic alternative—a society dominated by women. The myth, in its reiteration that women did not know how to handle power when in possession of it, reaffirms dogmatically the inferiority of their present position" (1974:279).

◆ "The final version of woman that emerges from these myths is that she represents chaos and misrule through trickery and unbridled sexuality. This is the inverse of Bachofen's view of pre-Hellenic womanhood. . . . The elevation of woman to deity on the one hand, and the downgrading of her to child or chattel on the other, produce the same result. Such visions will not bring her any closer to attaining male socioeconomic and political status, for as long as she is content to remain either goddess or child, she cannot be expected to shoulder her share of community burdens as the coequal of man. The myth of matriarchy is but the tool used to keep woman bound to her place. To free her, we need to destroy the myth" (ibid:280; also see Davis 1978).

In "Myths & Matriarchies," anthropologist Sally Binford maintains that there is absolutely no "valid reason" to proclaim a "golden age of matriarchy," claiming that "if we did once live in matriarchal societies, we blew it by letting the patriarchs take over." She blasts "the true believer in the fundamentalist faith of the Fall from Matriarchy and the Overthrow of the Mother Goddess" (1979:66; also see Hackett and Pomeroy 1972; Cothran 1974; and especially the debate—"Are Goddesses and Matriarchies Merely Figments of Feminist Imagination?"—between Binford, Merlin Stone and Charlene Spretnak in Spretnak 1982:541–61, where this quote appears on p. 547).

◆ Margot Adler, *Drawing Down the Moon:* "The idea of matriarchy has ramifications that go beyond the question of whether or not the matriarchy ever existed in reality. When a feminist reads Strabo's description of an island of women at the mouth of the Loire, or when she reads an account of an ancient college of priestesses or Sappho's academy on Lesbos, or the legends of the Amazons, a rich and possibly transforming event takes place" (1979:184).

◆ Paula Webster, "Matriarchy: A Vision of Power": "Though the matriarchy debate revolves around the past, its real value lies in the future: not as a model for a future society, for ultimately it doesn't resolve the problems of hierarchy, sex oppression, or class relations, and not in its mythic evocation of past glories, but in its rejection of power in the hands of men, regardless of the form of social organization. It pushes women (and men) to imagine a society that is not patriarchal, one in which women might for the first time have power over their lives. Women have been powerless, and have had their reality defined for them, for so long that imagining such a society is politically important. Because the matriarchy discussion uncovers the inadequacies of old paradigms, it encourages women to create new ones" (1975:155; also see Newton and Webster 1973).

> It is that dream world Anaïs speaks of
> that dark watery place
> where everything is female
> where you open the door of the house
> and she waits upstairs
> the way you knew she would
> and her hair floats over the world

Every woman has a history
mother and grandmother and the ones before that
the faces she sees in dreams or visions
and wonders *Who?* A childless woman
waking at night to the hard pull, the old
contractions, the birth cry of her mothers.
Or the heaviness in her back from stooping,
her hips from iron belts, the lines in
her face from mountain women.

Or, longer ago than that, the spears
and battleaxes, that ache in the thighs
from straining tight on the horses.
And the old queens, before history began,
when it was her story they told,
did they wrap their heads in bright cloth,
wear bracelets? or were they nude
and savage, their breasts large and
firm, their feet solid on their solid earth?

Each one is queen, mother, huntress
though each remembers little of it
and some remember nothing at all,
resting in crazy houses
from the long spin of history
drinking the grief of their sex
eating it in bitter pills
muttering in kitchens,
telling their daughters
the story of a sleeping princess
but knowing it takes more than a man's kiss
to wake one so bent on sleeping her life away:

someone who should be kept in an ice-box
until she is ready; then wake her up, as now,
into a cave or a field,
using perhaps the kiss of a sister.
Let her go from there, start over,
live it again, until she knows who she is.

(Harter 1978a:79)

Until she rises as though from the sea
not on the half-shell this time
nothing to laugh at
and not as delicate as he imagined her:
a woman big-hipped, beautiful, and fierce.

  —Sharon Barba, "A Cycle of Women"
  (n.d., in Chester and Barba 1973:356–57).[9]

[9]Also see Diane DiPrima's undated poem, "Prayer to the Mothers" (in Chester and Barba 1973:236–37) and Charlotte Perkins Gilman's utopian novel *Herland*, serialized in 1915 (1979).

Chapter 7
Appreciating the Mundane:
Women and Mythology

"I am just an ordinary woman, knowing nothing from myself. I have never been ill and seldom dream. So I have never seen visions. When I sometimes go up country to gather fuel I am only happy in feeling the heat of the sun, and many are the memories that rush over me from the parts I see again and where I have wandered ever since I was a little girl. I experience nothing but that when I am alone, I have to be content to listen when others tell. So all that I know I have from an old uncle, Unarâluk the shaman. His helping spirits were his dead father and mother, the sun, a dog, and a sea scorpion. These spirits enabled him to know everything about what was on the earth and under the earth, in the sea and in the sky.

"But what you have asked me about, and what I am going to tell you about, is something that is known to every child that has been hushed to sleep with a story by its mother. Children are full of life, they never want to sleep. Only a song or monotonous words can make them quieten down so that at last they fall asleep. That is why mothers and grandmothers always put little children to sleep with tales. It is from them we all have our knowledge, for children never forget. And now my story begins:"

—Nâlungiaq, a Netsilik Eskimo woman (Rasmussen 1931:207).

(Harter 1978b:74)

Women *in* mythology have been fairly well documented and discussed, although generally from male perspectives. Women *and* mythology is another matter. Mythographers and researchers of all persuasions simply do not know very much about women's mythology. Very little can be said with certainty about what verbal, visual and ritual expressions women themselves hold and have held sacred and deeply meaningful, let alone whether such forms differ significantly or not from those verbal, visual, and ritual expressions which have been designated "myth," "mythic" and "mythology," at least as far as men are concerned.

Folklorist Stith Thompson, for example, has suggested a minimal, practical definition of myth as a narrative which "has to do with the gods [sic] and their actions, with creation, and with the general nature of the universe and the earth" (1958:173). Anthropologist Anthony F. C. Wallace classifies mythology as an instance of "reciting the code," one of thirteen "minimal categories of religious behavior." This code is a sacred literature, oral or written, asserting "what is truth in religion." It includes statements about cosmology and pantheon, moral injunctions of prophets and gods [sic], and myths chronicling "the activities of divine beings, particularly at the time of the origin of things" (1966:57). According to Wallace, origin myths, culture hero [sic] myths and trickster myths "describe the supernatural community with which man [sic] must interact" (1966:58).

Philosopher-theologian Alan W. Watts notes that "myth is quite different from philosophy in the sense of abstract concepts, for the form of myth is always concrete—consisting of vivid, sensually intelligible, narratives, images, rites, ceremonies, and symbols" (1963:7). In his discussion of the Christian myth as it had flowered in Europe by the late thirteenth century, Watts claims that "myth is to be defined as a complex of stories—some no doubt fact, and some fantasy—which, for various reasons, human beings regard as demonstrations of the inner meaning of the universe and of human life" (ibid). He emphasizes that such narratives recount events which "have a miraculous or 'numinous' quality which marks them as special, queer, out of the ordinary, and therefore representative of the powers or Power behind the world" (ibid:8). This stance is echoed in historian of religions Mircea Eliade's basic definition of myth:

> . . . Myth tells how, through the deeds of Supernatural Beings, a reality came into existence, be it the whole of reality, the Cosmos, or only a fragment of reality—an island, a species of plant, a particular kind of human behavior, an institution. . . . In short, myths describe the various and sometimes dramatic breakthroughs of the sacred (or the "supernatural") into the World. It is this sudden breakthrough of the sacred that really *establishes* the World and makes it what it is today. Furthermore, it is as a result of the intervention of Supernatural Beings that man himself is what he is today, a mortal, sexed, and cultural being. (1963:3–6)

Both Watts and Eliade are indebted to Rudolf Otto's description of the religious experience in his 1917 study, *Das Heilige* ("The Sacred"). The sacred "breaks through" and confronts mortals as a phenomenon "wholly other" (*ganz andere*), totally different from humans and their world. Faced with the numinous (the word is derived from the Latin *numen* or god), one is as nothing, experiencing "the *feeling of terror* before the sacred, before the awe-inspiring mystery (*mysterium tremendum*), the majesty (*majestas*) that emanates an overwhelming superiority of power . . . [and] *religious fear* before the fascinating mystery (*mysterium fascinans*) in which perfect fullness of being flowers" (Eliade 1961:9–10).

Now Moses was keeping the flock of his father-in-law, Jethro, the priest of Midian; and he led his flock to the west side of the wilderness, and came to Horeb, the mountain of God. And the angel of the Lord appeared to him in a flame of fire out of the midst of a bush; and he looked, and lo, the bush was burning, yet it was not consumed. And Moses said, "I will turn aside and see this great sight, why the bush is not burnt." When the Lord saw that he turned aside to see, God called to him out of the bush, "Moses, Moses!" And he said, "Here am I." Then he said, "Do not come near; put off your shoes from your feet, for the place on which you are standing is holy ground." And he said, "I am the God of your father, the God of Abraham, the God of Isaac, and the God of Jacob." And Moses hid his face, for he was afraid to look at God. *(Exodus 3:1–6, RSV)*

Moses' response to his encounter with God recalls that, in Latin, another meaning of the word *numen* is "a nod"—a bending of the head to avert the eyes

286　　CHAPTER 7

from the *mysterium tremendum,* the *majestas,* and the *mysterium fascinans.*

According to such views, language is ordinarily inadequate to express the *ganz andere,* and telling myths is a primary means of communicating numinous experiences. People *want* to proclaim such events, which they believe to be true and truly significant. Thus, they attempt to convey them to others as forcefully as possible—through richly symbolic story, song and ceremony.

The problems with such definitions are obvious: What if women's stories, songs and ceremonies were entirely different from men's? What if numinous experiences were expressed differently by women, perhaps using "ordinary" language and narration? Indeed, what if the *ganz andere* had no meaning for women at all? What if women deeply believe in other experiences, other truths, other beings? What if they *want* to tell other stories, sing other songs, participate in other ceremonies and rituals? Finally, what if their different expressions and experiences are neither antithetical nor complementary to men's sacred and expressive domains?

(Harter 1980a:51)

The case of the Mundurucú Indians of Amazonian Brazil is both instructive and heuristic. Anthropologists Yolanda Murphy and Robert F. Murphy report:

. . . It must be remembered that the women have no mythology or rites of their own whatever. This is due in part, of course, to the fact that they are either wholly excluded from the religious life or play only restricted roles in it. But are they kept out of something to which they avidly want access? Not at all—the women look on religious rites as something the men do, which only partially concerns them and which is not of great interest to them. Rituals are social affairs to both sexes, yet to the women they are mainly social affairs. They like to listen to myths, although they are far less absorbed in their content than are the men and usually keep up a subdued conversation among themselves during the narration. And they never tell myths themselves. They are, however, deeply afraid of sorcery, the Yuruparí and similar supernatural threats, and are constant visitors to the shaman—their primary religious concern is with threat, evil, and personal affliction, whereas they are apathetic to the positive and reaffirmative aspects of religion.

The women are secular and pragmatic in their orientation to life. There is a matter-of-factness and straightforward earthiness in their manner and world view. . . . They believe the myths, they credit the efficacy of the ritual, they are sure that there are spirits—they believe all these things, but they do not think too much about them. . . . As for the men's house, they seemed largely indifferent to it except as a living arrangement. They knew all about its ritual paraphernalia, though none would admit peeking, and they were neither mystified nor cowed. It is as if they had investigated the secret sources of men's power—and had found absolutely nothing. (1974:140–41)

(Harter 1978b:96)

What the Mundurucú women *want* to tell, listen to and participate in, what they believe and enjoy, is gossiping together in work and dwelling-house groups apart from the men. Then, they collaboratively create an absorbing, ongoing narrative through the "exchange of valuable information about people" of this world (ibid:133).

Winnebago woman's moccasins
(Naylor 1975:41, figs. D,F).

Gossip is also mentioned by anthropologist Ruth Landes in comparing Ojibwa women's and men's religious lives and socioeconomic pursuits:

. . . Women "dream" beadwork patterns, songs, decorations for a dress, complicated dance patterns; men dream traditional tales, or tales about culture heroes, or have visions of the architecture of the after-world. . . .

Just as boys are carefully coached to secure power by a special technique of fasting, so they are carefully coached in special economic and honorific pursuits. Just as girls pick up power by the way, adopting suggestions which fall about their ears but which they are not pressed to adopt, so they may pick up the economic and honorific pursuits of men and those of women. Men occupy themselves outside of the home: they hunt, trap, fish, hold religious performances, and engage in war. Women are supposed to stay at home and convert the fruits of hunting and fishing into edibles and clothing, they make the lodge furnishings, do bead-work and porcupine-quill work, make twine, fish-nets and bark matting, pick berries, cure sugar and rice with the help of the men, collect medicinal herbs, cook, mend, and bear children. Whenever men fulfill their duties creditably, they are lauded. In company they tell endless stories about their adventures, for their duties are always "adventures"; they hold stag feasts of religious importance after a successful hunt. Even the mythology occupies itself with the pursuits and rewards of men. The important visions, which men have been driven all their youth to pursue, bestow power for the masculine occupations. A successful hunter can parade this fact in ways licensed by his visions: songs that he sings publicly, amulets that are conspicuous and worn in public, charms that he can sell. He has also sumptuary privileges, such as polygyny. Women's work on the contrary "is spoken of neither for good nor for evil"—at least in a gathering of men. Conventionally it is not judged in any way, it is simply not given any thought. Privately, a man may be proud of his wife's handiwork in tanning or bead-weaving; in an unguarded moment he may even explain that these excellences had led him to walk many miles to claim the woman as his wife. The women themselves live in a world of values all their own, a world closed to the men. Mother and daughters discuss the merits of their work just as men do the merits of theirs, and when the village quarter of the year comes about, the various families visit, and wider groups of women discuss their own interests. But these discussions and boasts are not formal, as the men's are; they belong to the level of gossip. (Landes 1971:9, 10–11)

This usage of gossip betrays a Western, sexist bias not unlike that of Charles Francis Potter in his definition of folklore:

There is also, beside the juvenile, a strong feminine element in folklore, because its origin antedates the emergence of reason and belongs in the instinctive and intuitional areas. It is irrational and highly imaginative: much of it truly is termed "old wives' tales." Women have always been the savers and conservators of beliefs, rites, superstitions, rituals, and customs. (in Leach 1972:401)

The development of such social attitudes toward gossip is encapsulated in the first four definitions given in the *Oxford English Dictionary:*

1. A godfather or godmother; a sponsor. Now only *arch.* and *dial.*
2. A familiar acquaintance, friend, chum. Now only (somewhat *arch.*) of women. ME.
3. A person, mostly a woman, who delights in idle talk; a tattler 1566.
4. The tattle of such a person; idle talk; trifling or groundless rumour 1811.

Although men certainly gossip—by any definition of the term—it is women's talk which has become virtually synonymous with the term and which consequently has been devalued. Thus, although gossiping requires various narrative and performance skills, and although participants consider it tremendously important, it is not recognized by outsiders and so not investigated thoroughly and compared with, e.g., mythology and the occasions during which myths are recited, enacted and/or elaborated through exegesis and discussion. As folklorist Claire R. Farrer points out, "women's expressive vehicles are the nonlegitimate forms, even though they are as ordered and as rule-governed as the male forms" (1975:xiv). In short, myths have served as the measure of narration while gossip and so-called old wives' tales have been relegated to insignificant status or ignored altogether. In fact, it may turn out, after more and better fieldwork is conducted, that "myth narration and gossip may simply be two kinds of meaningful storytelling, each with its own style, both equally valuable to two different groups of people within the same culture" (Weigle 1978:3; also see, e.g., Yerkovich 1976; Kodish 1980).

While considering verbal interaction between members of two women's "rap groups," for example, folklorist Susan Kalčik had difficulty identifying "stories" or personal narratives," a problem she attributed to the discovery that "some women's stories are not structured in ways that have been commonly studied." Instead, she found recurrent "collaborative" narratives which

(Harter 1978b:51)

she called "kernel stories," ones "structured in part by the conversational context from which [they] emerge" and in the narration of which everyone's "conversation can become part of the story," the women in a sense narrating "together" rather than singly and serially (Kalčik 1975:8; also see Bromberg-Ross 1975). Speculating in terms of contemporary American society, Kalčik suggests:

> Further investigation may show that the kernel story as described . . . is uniquely a woman's genre. One might conjecture that the structure of such stories parallels the rhythm of many women's lives, filled as they are with small tasks and constant interruptions from children, husbands, telephones, repairmen. It is common in our culture that men and women do not value women's speech or stories; they are labeled "just gossip" or, significantly, "women's talk." That women have thus learned to be brief and apologetic in their speech unless encouraged seems to be reflected in the story structure I have described. The fact that the stories I found were a group product may have its roots in women's sense of powerlessness and their realization that they need to work together. (1975:11)[1]

Anthropologist Susan Harding describes both the form and content of the stories women in the Spanish village she calls Oroel tell each other—stories

---

[1] A different sort of woman's group also developed their own story out of an "attempt to do theology communally." According to theologian Judith Plaskow: "We considered what it would mean to write a systematic theology that affirmed the experiences we had been discussing. . . . But we were worried about the disappearance of the four of us sitting there, our coming together, behind the framework we would create. We clearly needed a form that would grow out of the content and process of our time together" (1979: 205). Eventually, ". . . we arrived back at the story form. We recognized the difficulties of 'inventing' a myth, however, and so we wanted to tell a story that seemed to grow naturally out of our present history. We also felt the need for using older materials that would carry their own reverberations and significance, even if we departed freely from them. We chose, therefore, to begin with the story of Lilith. . . . Through her story, we could express not only our new image of ourselves, but our relation to certain of the elements of our religious traditions. Since stories are the heart of tradition, we could question and create tradition by telling a new story within the framework of an old one" (ibid). Also see Phyllis Chesler's brief commentary on "The Conversation," sculptor unknown (1972:pl. 11).

which are "not unlike" their woman-to-woman gossip, which "as a genre of speech . . . is also personal and intimate, and it develops plots . . . [with, however] real, known, and present characters":

> . . . The stories women tell each other are about personal, intimate situations, very often about a man, a woman, and a marital problem or anomaly, but the characters are anonymous, unknown, and unnamed, so their affairs may be told in relatively public situations. One story is about a woman who gets separated from her husband on the streets of a strange city on their wedding night. . . . Each one presents a personal complication or crisis which is the real focus of the story. Its resolution is not very important, and many of the stories end without one: they are simply statements of the problem.
>
> These stories are the myths of women. Like myths in primitive societies, they are repetitious and are repeated often. The characters, situations, and actual events change, but the stories are always the same in the sense that the underlying structures animated and transmitted by them are the same. Like myths, the stories instruct as they entertain. They focus, and they represent a focus of, attention on cultural and social reality, and they structure and interpret that reality. Their tendency not to resolve their complication, just to raise it, suggests that the contradictions which they treat, like the contradictions embedded in the lives of women, are not solved. In any case, these stories belong to women in Oroel; men do not tell them among themselves. . . . (1975:296–97; also see Harding 1978)

(Harter 1978b:18)

Sometime between 1931 and 1933, the old Arizona Papago Indian woman Chona talked about her life with anthropologist Ruth M. Underhill, who recorded her words verbatim and translated them "as best I could, with her help and that of companions spieling Papago, Spanish, and English" (1979:x). Although she added a part on "Chona: Her Land and Time" from memory for the new edition, Underhill did not alter the material from her 1936 Memoir (No. 46) of the American Anthropological Association. Chona recalled the joys of summertime and nineteenth-century Papago life:

We women did not have to fetch water. We could sit in the house and make baskets. Or else we could go off over the land to pick the fine fresh green things. At sunset all the village was full of laughing people, eating around their home fires.

Then we heard the crier call, "Come hither! Bring your cigarettes. We will smoke and talk of what we shall do!"

That call was for the men, not for the women. They got up from the fires and we saw them passing in the starlight against the gray desert that looks almost white on summer nights. I know what my father used to say to them in that meeting, for he has often told me how they spoke after the cigarette went round.

"Well! will you be ready? Take care, for often I have warned you. You must make arrows and your bow you must have in readiness, for when the enemy will arrive, you do not know. At night he may come; at night or in the morning or when the sun stands anywhere in the sky. Then you will arise, your bow you will snatch and therewith will fight the enemy.

"Close by you must keep your bow, your quiver, your hardwood arrows, and your reed arrows with the stone tip. Early in the morning must you have your food that you may be able to fight the enemy. Your girls very early must cook and must give food to the youths that they may be strong to fight no matter where the sun stands in the sky. Your girls shall pour water and shall search for wood and shall cook food. Early in the morning your girls shall run that when the enemy shall come, they can run swiftly and can save their lives.

"This I feel and this I say. Listen and my words shall enter your ears and enter your heads."

So he talked to them, and then they spoke of whether they would widen the ditches and if the boys were practicing well for the races, and maybe a man from some other village was there to tell them the news. There was not a man among us who would miss that meeting.

We women sat in the dark, under the shelter, and told about the strange things we had heard. We told how there is a root which men carry to make the deer come to them and it makes women come, too. It smells strong and sweet, and you can smell it on the sweaty hands of a man beside you in the dance. If it is very strong and has been used in many love matches, sometimes it turns into a man. It walks up beside a woman while she is sleeping and makes her dream.

We told how, in our village, a girl was struck by lightning. Someone must have been menstruating and not have confessed it, said the medicine man. So he called all the girls, took out his crystals and looked at them. "It was the girl herself," he said. "She has killed herself."

We told how, when a woman does not seem to care for any man or a man for any woman, that person is really married to a snake. There was a man in our village who used to go out alone into the desert and disappear in a wash. His parents followed him and found there a little red snake with her baby snakes on her back. They said to their son, "What! have you a family of snakes?" He said, "No, she is a beautiful woman." That is how snakes fool you. The older women used to tell us, too, that if we thought too much about any boy before we married, that boy would seem to come to make love to us. But it would not be he, it would only be a snake. So girls must not think too much about boys. That was what the old women told us. We must not think about boys and we must not talk to boys. When we were married it would be time enough to speak to a man. Now it was better to work and be industrious.

So I worked. But I used to think while I was sitting under the shelter with my basketry, about whether I would get a good man and whether I would like being married. (1979:53–54)

Papago basket design
(Sides 1961:plate 43, fig. a).

The Papago women in this example are absorbed in one kind of verbal interaction, the men in another. The women expect to celebrate publicly neither their eagerly attended evening talks nor their menstrual seclusions (see chapter 4 above), but that should not mean that such private occasions are not "mythic" in their importance as vivid symbol systems which create meaning in human lives. Heretofore, however, mythology has usually been defined and studied as a public, collective, male-dominated means of communication which pertains to cyclic time and metaphysical or supernatural reality (the numinous). In order to appreciate the full picture of myth in the sense of mouth, speech, story and so on, we must *also* look at the mundane, the everyday, the private, the informal, the conversational, and all that has previously been dismissed as trivial, ordinary, prattle, idle chatter, gossip, old wives' tales, and the like—those forms too often disregarded because they are of women's domain.

When it comes to that domain researchers of both sexes, but particularly male ones, have been all too ready to ignore or overlook most women whom they consult. Farrer notes this with respect to folklore: "Nonetheless, the general trend throughout the history of the *Journal {of American Folklore}* has been to rely on data from women for information about health, charms, some games, and various beliefs and customs but in other areas to use women as informants only when men informants were unavailable" (1975:vi).[2] Anthropologist Edwin Ardener frames the problem in terms of anthropology:

We have here, then, what looked like a technical problem: the difficulty of dealing ethnographically with women. We have, rather, an analytical problem of this sort: if the models of a society made by most ethnographers tend to be models derived from the male portion of that society, how does the symbolic weight of

[2]Farrer also suggests a remedy in terms of folklore, one which is equally applicable to mythology: "Consider, for example, the early work in the *Journal*. Men knew the beliefs women had, or were said to have, just as men today know many women believe it will make them sick to wash their hair during menstruation. But we have no data concerning what beliefs men of that time had or how men or women actually utilized their beliefs. I am not suggesting we stop collecting beliefs from women; I *am* suggesting we collect also from men and consider the attitudes of both men and women toward our collectanea. Further, I am suggesting that we no longer base our theories, hypothetical constructs, and models on half of the available data. Because the other half of the data is more difficult to reach is no reason to ignore it" (1975:ix). Also see Jessie Bernard, *The Female World* (1981).

Illustration by H. J. Ford for "The Nettle Spinner," in Andrew Lang, ed., *The Red Fairy Book*, published in London, 1890 (1966:290).

that other mass of persons—half or more of a normal human population, as we have accepted—express itself? Some will maintain that the problem as it is stated here is exaggerated, although only an extremist will deny its existence completely. It may be that individual ethnographers have received from women a picture of society very similar to the picture given by men. This possibility is conceded, but the female evidence provides in such cases confirmation of a male model which requires no confirmation of this type. The fact is that no one could come back from an ethnographic study of 'the X', having talked only *to* women, and *about* men, without professional comment and some self-doubt. The reverse can and does happen constantly. It is not enough to see this merely as another example of 'injustice to women'. I prefer to suggest that the models of society that women can provide are not the kind acceptable at first sight to men or to ethnographers, and specifically that, unlike either of these sets of professionals, they do not so readily see society bounded from nature. They lack the metalanguage for its discussion. To put it more simply: these will not necessarily provide a model for society as a unit that will contain both men and themselves. They may indeed provide a model in which women and nature are outside men and society. (1975:3)[3]

[3]The complicated conceptualization of nature/woman vs. culture or society/men referred to by Ardener has received recent treatment in an anthropological collection, *Nature, Culture and Gender*, edited by Carol P. MacCormack and Marilyn Strathorn (1980). Also related is poet Susan Griffin's *Woman and Nature: The Roaring Inside Her* (1978) and historian of science Carolyn Merchant's *The Death of Nature: Women, Ecology, and the Scientific Revolution* (1980). For a discussion of this in the work and lives of Simone de Beauvoir and Jean-Paul Sartre, see McCall 1979; Benton 1981.

Anthropologist Knud Rasmussen spent six months living with the Netsilik Eskimo couple Nâlungiaq and Inûtuk, "and all that we had gone through in the time we lived together had made them most trustful towards me." Nevertheless, he, like so many other fieldworkers, both male and female, found that "our talks on religious subjects were always split up on account of all the questions I had to put in order to learn anything at all. This applies to both men and women."

However, an evening came when Nâlungiaq suddenly, and quite without any solicitation on my part, began to tell me everything about the very things in their lives that she knew I took such a passionate interest in. The whole thing started so casually. A sunset revived memories of her childhood, and, once her recollections began to stream over her, she became chatty and, without fear of interrupting her, I was then able to interject various questions, with the result that all unconsciously she gave me a connected account of the views they hold of life. I admit that this had scarcely been possible if an intimate knowledge of her temperament had not enabled me to put my questions in the right way, psychologically. While she talked I could make no notes, for then she would quickly have discovered my intention and her free, almost pert delivery would have stiffened. Therefore it has been necessary to reconstruct our conversation as well as I could immediately after it took place. . . . (1931:206)

Nâlungiaq responded to Rasmussen's zeal for religious questions with myths like the ones in chapter 6 (above) and with a modest but ironic disclaimer (quoted in the epigraph to this chapter). Although she says she does not know the powerful sorts of things shamans and men know, she tries to show Rasmussen that it is from mothers and grandmothers that "we all have our knowledge, for children never forget." Only anthropologists do.

The talk between women, no less than that between women and children, has been equally neglected. Many times this is due to the sex of the fieldworker; men simply may not be able to talk with or even observe women and children. In mixed company, in public, or in situations involving outsiders—whether male or female, women may be expected to remain silent or at least circumspect. In his 1918 study of *Folklore in the Old Testament,* for example, Sir James George Frazer devotes a chapter (No. 22) to "The Silent Widow," including among his numerous examples the following from Native America:

In describing the Nishinam tribe of California Indians, a writer who knew these Indians well, as they were in the third quarter of the nineteenth century, mentions that "around Auburn, a devoted widow never speaks, on any occasion or upon any pretext, for several months, sometimes a year or more, after the death of her husband. Of this singular fact I had ocular demonstration." (1975:344; also see Key 1975:127–32; Stannard 1977:53–54, 61–62; Weigle 1978:4–5)

If *mythos* is derived from Greek words relating to the mouth, speech, and oral storytelling, then such restrictions on women's verbal expressions clearly challenge our ability as outsiders either to construct or reconstruct a sense of women and mythology and of women's mythology.

(Harter 1978b:93)

A gathering of women. *"Witches Bringing a Shower of Rain.* Woodcut from Ulrich Molitor's *De Lamiis et Phitonicis Mulieribus* ["Concerning Female Sorcerers and Soothsayers"] (Cologne, 1489). The notion that it is wrong or vulgar for a woman to whistle is a relic of the ancient belief that witches can raise a tempest: a noise which sounds like a wind will start a gale" (Newall 1974:178; illustration from Lehner 1971:59, fig. 84).[4]

[4]According to Archer Taylor *(The Proverb* [Cambridge, Massachusetts: Harvard University Press, 1931], p. 72): "The belief that *A whistling girl and a crowing hen will come to no good end,* which also occurs in the form

> Whistling girls and crowing hens
> Will all *(var.* surely) come to some bad ends,

as well as in the more cheerful, contradictory version:

> Girls that whistle and hens that crow
> Will always have fun, wherever they go,

involves a superstition of international currency." Vance Randolph reports in *Ozark Superstitions* that: "If a hen makes any sound suggestive of crowing near the door, it is a sure sign of death, and I have been told of cases in which somebody died within ten minutes" (1947:306). Also see Dundes 1976:132–33.

A gathering of men
(Harter 1980a:94).

Yet another ethnocentric attitude militates against such attempts. Much of mythology as presently defined deals with time-out-of-time, with the upper worlds and the underworlds, with the extraordinary, but not with the present, flux, the everyday, the ordinary. *Mundus* has been devalued, and *mythos* exalted as the cherished expression and object of study. Now, a revaluation of the mundane is taking place—in the ethnography of communication, in sociolinguistic studies of conversation and narration, in microsociology, and in the study of legends, rumor, gossip, anecdote and the like in folklore and mythology.

(Harter 1979–80:16)

This revaluation should contribute to a deeper awareness of the powerful worlds created by gossip and legend, by women considering their own and the lives of those around them, by women telling each other, often privately, about the strange and not-so-strange, the actual, the plausible and the incredible in their physical, interpersonal and intrapersonal lives. As a result, we may come to know, not just the special cases—Enheduanna (high priestess daughter of Sargon the Great of Akkad, c. 2300–2230 B.C., and the first named author in world literature), Sappho, "the authoress of the *Odyssey*," and so on—but also the sacred beliefs, practices, verbal and visual arts of such as Socrates' wife Xantippe, who, although denied the Agora and a scribe like Plato, is certainly no less significant in human terms. And those women who—like Joan of Arc, the "manly-hearted" North Piegan Blackfoot Indian women (Lewis 1941), the *máien*—female leaders among the Coast Miwok Indians of northern California (Parkman 1981), and Wonder Woman—excell in what seem basically male terms will be joined by the likes of Mary Daly's Spinsters/Hags/Crones, as well as particular, known female friends and family members from personal networks.

Journalist Stan Steiner was a friend of artist and feminist Bonita Wa Wa Calachaw Nuñez (1888–1972) in New York City. "Years before, when we had first met, she had showed me an old, battered trunk full of letters, notebooks, drawings, photographs, and the lost memories of decades. In that aged chamber she had stored not only the story of her life, but the history of the Indian people who came to the cities like vision seekers in the dark, white world" (1980:xvi–xvii; the concluding quotation below is on pp. xvii–xviii). Years later, after her death, he sought that trunk. A Puerto Rican woman, a neighbor from across the hall, showed him into the apartment.

On the way downstairs, she thanked me for coming. If I had not come, she said, the welfare people would have come to nail shut the apartment, and the housing people would have come to throw all her painting, all her writing, into the street, into the gutter, "like garbage."

"Now she is not garbage," she said.

"She is a spirit now," I said.

Design from Zia Pueblo pot
(Sides 1961:plate 20, fig. b).

Bibliography

Abel, Elizabeth
 1981   (E)Merging Identities: The Dynamics of Fe-
        male Friendship in Contemporary Fiction by
        Women. Signs 6:413–35.
 1981a (Ed.) Writing and Sexual Difference. Critical
        Inquiry 8, 2.

Abernathy, Francis Edward, ed.
 1981   Legendary Ladies of Texas. Publications of
        the Texas Folklore Society No. 43. Dallas:
        E-Heart Press.

Abraham, Karl
 1927   Selected Papers of Karl Abraham, M.D. Doug-
        las Bryan and Alix Strachey, trans. New York:
        Brunner/Mazel.

Abrahams, Roger D.
 1966   Some Varieties of Heroes in America. Jour-
        nal of the Folklore Institute 3:341–62.

Adler, Margot
 1979   Drawing Down the Moon: Witches, Druids,
        Goddess-Worshippers, and Other Pagans in
        America Today. New York: Viking Press.

Allen, Sally G., and Joanna Hubbs
 1980   Outrunning Atalanta: Feminine Destiny in
        Alchemical Transmutation. Signs 6:210–29.

Angus, Samuel
 1925   The Mystery Religions and Christianity. Lon-
        don.

Anonymous
 1973   Women in Antiquity. Arethusa 6, 1.
 1974   Feminism and Religion. Radical Religion 1,
        2.
 1975   Women and Spirituality. Quest: a feminist
        quarterly 1, 4.
 1978   Androgyny. Parabola: Myth and the Quest
        for Meaning 3, 4.
 1980   Woman. Parabola: Myth and the Quest for
        Meaning 5, 4.

Anton, Ferdinand
 1973   Woman in Pre-Columbian Art. New York:
        Abner Schram.

Ardener, Edwin
 1975   Belief and the Problem of Women. In Per-
        ceiving Women. Shirley Ardener, ed. Pp.
        1–17. New York: John Wiley & Sons. (First
        pub. 1972.)
 1975a The 'Problem' Revisited. In Perceiving
        Women. Shirley Ardener, ed. Pp. 19–27.
        New York: John Wiley & Sons.

Argüelles, Miriam & José
 1977   The Feminine: Spacious as the Sky. Boulder,
        Colorado: Shambala.

Arnold, Marigene
 1978   Célibes, Mothers, and Church Cockroaches:
        Religious Participation of Women in a Mex-

ican Village. *In* Women in Ritual and Symbolic Roles. Judith Hoch-Smith and Anita Spring, eds. Pp. 45–53. New York: Plenum Press.

Arthur, Marylin B.
1973 Early Greece: The Origins of the Western Attitude Toward Women. Arethusa 6, 1.
1976 Review Essay: Classics. Signs 2:382–403.

Ashe, Geoffrey
1976 The Virgin. London: Routledge & Kegan Paul.

Auerbach, Nina
1981 Magi and Maidens: The Romance of the Victorian Freud. Critical Inquiry 8:281–300.

Babb, Jewel, as told to Pat Ellis Taylor
1981 Border Healing Woman: The Story of Jewel Babb. Austin: University of Texas Press.

Bachofen, J. J.
1967 Myth, Religion, and Mother Right: Selected Writings of J. J. Bachofen. Ralph Manheim, trans. Bollingen Series 84. Princeton: Princeton University Press.

Bade, Patrick
1979 Femme Fatale: Images of Evil and Fascinating Women. New York: Mayflower Books.

Balfe, Judith H.
1978 Comment on Clarke Garrett's "Women and Witches." Signs 4:201–2.

Bamberger, Joan
1974 The Myth of Matriarchy: Why Men Rule in Primitive Society. *In* Woman, Culture, and Society. Michelle Zimbalist Rosaldo and Louise Lamphere, eds. Pp. 263–80. Stanford, California: Stanford University Press.

Bannan, Helen M.
1980 Spider Woman's Web: Mothers and Daughters in Southwestern Native American Literature. *In* The Lost Tradition: Mothers and Daughters in Literature. E. M. Broner and Cathy N. Davidson, eds. Pp. 268–79. New York: Frederick Ungar.

Barakat, Robert A.
1965 Aztec Motifs in 'La Llorona.' Southern Folklore Quarterly 39:288–96.
1969 Wailing Women of Folklore. Journal of American Folklore 82:270–72.

Barbeau, Marius
1945 Bear Mother. Journal of American Folklore 59:1–12.
1953 Haida Myths Illustrated in Argillite Carvings. National Museum of Canada Bulletin No. 127, Anthropological Series No. 32. Ottawa.

Barnes, Daniel R.
1972 The Bosom Serpent: A Legend in American Literature and Culture. Journal of American Folklore 85:111–22.

Bayley, Harold
1912 The Lost Language of Symbolism: An Inquiry into the Origin of Certain Letters, Words, Names, Fairy-Tales, Folklore, and Mythologies. 2 vols. London: Williams and Norgate.

Benedict, Ruth
1931 Tales of the Cochiti Indians. Bureau of American Ethnology Bulletin 98. Washington: GPO.

Benton, J. F.
1981 Comment on McCall's "Simone de Beauvoir, *The Second Sex,* and Jean-Paul Sartre." Signs 6:546–47.

Benwell, Gwen, and Arthur Waugh
1961 Sea Enchantress: The Tale of the Mermaid and Her Kind. London.

Bercholz, Hazel Silber, Micheline Stuart, and Vincent Stuart, eds.
1973 Woman: Maitreya 4. Berkeley, California: Shambala.

Bernard, Jessie
1981 The Female World. New York: The Free Press.

Bernikow, Louise
1978 Comment on Joanne Feit Diehl's " 'Come Slowly—Eden': An Exploration of Women Poets and Their Muse." Signs 4:191–95.
1980 Among Women. New York: Crown Publishers.

Berry, Patricia
1975 The Rape of Demeter/Persephone and Neurosis. Spring, pp. 186–98.
1980 Echo and Beauty. Spring, pp. 49–59.

Bettelheim, Bruno
1962 Symbolic Wounds: Puberty Rites and the Envious Male. Rev. ed. Glencoe, Illinois: The Free Press of Glencoe. (First pub. 1954.)
1976 The Uses of Enchantment: The Meaning and Importance of Fairy Tales. New York: Alfred A. Knopf.

Bierhorst, John, ed.
1976 The Red Swan: Myths and Tales of the American Indians. New York: Farrar, Straus and Giroux.

Binford, Sally R.
1979 Myths & Matriarchies. Human Behavior, May, pp. 63–66.

Blashfield, Jean F.
1981 Hellraisers, Heroines, and Holy Women:

Women's Most Remarkable Contributions to History. New York: St. Martin's Press.

Bloch, Dorothy
1978   "So the Witch Won't Eat Me": Fantasy and the Child's Fear of Infanticide. Boston: Houghton Mifflin.

Boas, Franz
1888   The Central Eskimo. *In* Sixth Annual Report of the Bureau of Ethnology to the Secretary of the Smithsonian Institution, 1884–1885. J. W. Powell, Director. Pp. 399–669. Washington: GPO.
1917   (Ed.) Folk-Tales of Salishan and Sahaptin Tribes. Memoirs of the American Folk-Lore Society, vol. 11. Lancaster, Pennsylvania: American Folk-Lore Society.

Boetti, Anne-Marie Sauzeau
n.d.   Arachnee the Spider. H. Martin, trans. Chrysalis 10:87–89.

Bogan, Meg
1976   The Women Troubadours. New York: Paddington Press Ltd.

Boulding, Elise
1976   The Underside of History: A View of Women through Time. Boulder, Colorado: Westview Press.

Bourke, John Gregory
1894   Popular Medicine, Customs, and Superstitions of the Rio Grande. Journal of American Folk-Lore 7:119–46.

Bowles & Carver
1970   Catchpenny Prints: 163 Popular Engravings from the Eighteenth Century. New York: Dover Publications.

Boyer, L. Bryce
1979   Childhood and Folklore: A Psychoanalytic Study of Apache Personality. New York: Library of Psychological Anthropology.

Brandon, Elizabeth
1976   Folk Medicine in French Louisiana. *In* American Folk Medicine: A Symposium. Wayland D. Hand, ed. Pp. 215–34. Berkeley: University of California Press. (Originally presented at a UCLA conference in 1973.)

Brantl, George, ed.
1961   Catholicism. Great Religions of Modern Man. New York: George Braziller.

Briffault, Robert
1927   The Mothers: A Study of the Origins of Sentiments and Institutions. 3 vols. New York: Macmillan.

Brindel, June Rachey
1980   Ariadne. New York: St. Martin's Press.

Brink, J. R.
1978   Bathusa Makin: Scholar and Educator of the Seventeenth Century. International Journal of Women's Studies 1:417–26.

Briscoe, Virginia Wolf
1979   Ruth Benedict: Anthropological Folklorist. Journal of American Folklore 92:445–76.

Bromberg-Ross, JoAnn
1975   Storying and Changing: An Examination of the Consciousness-Raising Process. Folklore Feminists Communication 6:9–11.

Brown, Joseph Epes, ed.
1953   The Sacred Pipe: Black Elk's Account of the Seven Rites of the Oglala Sioux. Norman: University of Oklahoma Press.

Brown, Judith K.
1963   A Cross-Cultural Study of Female Initiation Rites. American Anthropologist 65:837–53.

Brown, Karen McCarthy
1980   Women and Goddesses in Haitian Voodoo. Lady-Unique-Inclination-of-the-Night, Cycle 5, pp. 56–67.

Brown, Mrs. W. Wallace
1890   Wa-Ba-Ba-Nal, or Northern Lights. Journal of American Folk-Lore 3:213–14.

Brown, Norman O.
1959   Life Against Death: The Psychoanalytical Meaning of History. New York: Vintage Books.

Browne, Ray B., Marshall Fishwick, and Michael T. Marsden, eds.
1972   Heroes of Popular Culture. Bowling Green, Ohio: Bowling Green University Popular Press.

Brownmiller, Susan
1975   Against Our Will: Men, Women, and Rape. New York: Simon and Schuster.

Bruns, J. Edgar
1973   God as Woman, Woman as God. New York: Paulist Press.

Buckley, Jorunn Jacobsen
1980   Two Female Gnostic Revealers. History of Religions 19:259–69.

Budapest, Z(suzsanna Emese)
1979   The Holy Book of Women's Mysteries: Part One. Los Angeles, California: Susan B. Anthony Coven No. 1.
1980   The Holy Book of Women's Mysteries: Part Two. Los Angeles, California: Susan B. Anthony Coven No. 1.

Bullough, Vern L., with the assistance of Bonnie Bullough
1973   The Subordinate Sex: A History of Attitudes toward Women. Urbana: University of Illinois Press.

Burn, A. R., rev, trans. and ed.
1972   Herodotus, The Histories. Aubrey de Sélincourt, trans. New York: Penguin Books.

Burnside, Madeline
1978   Weaving. Heresies 1, 4:27.

Buss, Fran Leeper
1980   La Partera: Story of a Midwife. Ann Arbor: University of Michigan Press.

Butcher, S. H., trans.
1951   Aristotle's Theory of Poetry and Fine Art. New York: Dover Publications. (First pub. 1894.)

Butcher, S. H., and A. Lang, trans.
1882   The Odyssey of Homer: Done into English Prose. Boston: D. Lothrop.

Butler, Samuel
1967   The Authoress of the Odyssey. David Grene, ed. Chicago: University of Chicago Press. (First pub. 1897.)

Campbell, Joseph
1968   The Hero with a Thousand Faces. 2d ed. Bollingen Series 17. Princeton: Princeton University Press. (First pub. 1949.)
1980   Joseph Campbell on the Great Goddess. Parabola 5, 4:74–85.

Cardozo-Freeman, Inez
1978   Serpent Fears and Religious Motifs Among Mexican Women. Frontiers: a journal of women studies 3, 3:10–13.

Castillejo, Irene Claremont de
1973   Knowing Woman: A Feminine Psychology. New York: G. P. Putnam's Sons for the C. G. Jung Foundation for Analytical Psychology.

Chervin, Ronda, Mary Neill & You
1980   The Woman's Tale: A Journal of Inner Exploration. New York: Seabury Press.

Chesler, Phyllis
1972   Women & Madness. New York: Avon Books.

Chesser, Barbara E.
1978   Comment on Naomi Goldenberg's "A Feminist Critique of Jung" (vol. 2, no. 2). Signs 3:721–24.

Chester, Laura, and Sharon Barba, eds.
1973   Rising Tides: 20th Century American Women Poets. New York: Pocket Books.

Chicago, Judy
1979   The Dinner Party: A Symbol of Our Heritage. Garden City, New York: Anchor Press/Doubleday.

Chicago, Judy, with Susan Hill
1980   Embroidering Our Heritage: The Dinner Party Needlework. Garden City, New York: Anchor Press/Doubleday.

Christ, Carol P.
1978   Why Women Need the Goddess. Heresies, Spring, pp. 8–13. (Reprinted in Christ and Plaskow 1979:273–87.)
1980   Diving Deep and Surfacing: Women Writers on Spiritual Quest. Boston: Beacon Press.

Christ, Carol P., and Judith Plaskow, eds.
1979   Womanspirit Rising: A Feminist Reader in Religion. San Francisco: Harper & Row.

Clark, Elizabeth, and Herbert Richardson, eds.
1976   Women and Religion: A Feminist Interpretation of Christian Thought. New York: Harper & Row.

Coalition Task Force on Women and Religion
1975   Study Guide to The Woman's Bible. Seattle: Coalition Task Force on Women and Religion.

Coffin, Tristram Potter
1975   The Female Hero in Folklore and Legend. New York: Seabury Press.

Coffin, Tristram Potter, and Hennig Cohen, eds.
1966   Folklore in America. Garden City, New York: Doubleday.
1978   The Parade of Heroes: Legendary Figures in American Lore. Garden City, New York: Anchor Press/Doubleday.

Cohen, Anne B.
1973   Poor Pearl, Poor Girl!: The Murdered-Girl Stereotype in Ballad and Newspaper. Publications of the American Folklore Society, Memoir Series, vol. 58. Austin: University of Texas Press.

Collins, John J.
1977   Cosmos and Salvation: Jewish Wisdom and Apocalyptic in the Hellenistic Age. History of Religions 17:121–42.

Collins, Sheila D.
1974   A Different Heaven and Earth: A Feminist Perspective on Religion. Valley Forge, Pennsylvania: Judson Press.

Converse, Mrs. Harriet Maxwell Clarke
1908   Myths and Legends of the New York State Iroquois. New York State Museum Bulletin 125. Arthur C. Parker, ed. Pp. 5–195. Albany.

Cooper, Patricia, and Norma Bradley Buford
1978   The Quilters: Women and Domestic Art. Garden City, New York: Anchor Press/Doubleday.

Coote, Mary P.

1977   Women's Songs in Serbo-Croatian. Journal of American Folklore 90:331–38.

Costello, Peter
     1979   The Magic Zoo: The Natural History of Fabulous Animals. New York: St. Martin's Press.

Cothran, Kay L.
     1974   Review Essay: *The First Sex,* by Elizabeth Gould Davis. Journal of American Folklore 87:89–93.

Courtot, Martha
     1976   Herstory vs. History: Memories of a Catholic Girlhood. Lady-Unique-Inclination-of-the-Night, Cycle 1, pp. 66–72.

Crawhall, Joseph
     1974   Pictorial Archive of Quaint Woodcuts in the Chap Book Style. Theodore Menten, ed. New York: Dover Publications.

Culin, Stewart
     1975   Games of the North American Indians. New York: Dover Publications. (First pub. 1907.)

Curtin, Jeremiah
     1899   Creation Myths of Primitive America in Relation to The Religious History and Mental Development of Mankind. London: Williams and Norgate.

Curtis, Edward S.
     1924   The North American Indian. Vol. 14. Norwood, Massachusetts.

Daly, Mary
     1973   Beyond God the Father: Toward a Philosophy of Women's Liberation. Boston: Beacon Press.
     1975   The Church and the Second Sex: With a New Feminist Postchristian Introduction by the Author. New York: Harper & Row. (First pub. 1968.)
     1978   Gyn/Ecology: The Metaethics of Radical Feminism. Boston: Beacon Press.

Dan, Ilana
     1977   The Innocent Persecuted Heroine: An Attempt at a Model for the Surface Level of the Narrative Structure of the Female Fairy Tale. *In* Patterns in Oral Literature. Heda Jason and Dimitri Segal, eds. Pp. 13–30. The Hague: Mouton.

Davis, Elizabeth Gould
     1972   The First Sex. Baltimore, Maryland: Penguin Books. (First pub. 1971.)

Davis, Natalie Zemon
     1978   Women on Top: Symbolic Sexual Inversion and Political Disorder in Early Modern Europe. *In* The Reversible World: Symbolic Inversion in Art and Society. Barbara A. Babcock, ed. Pp. 147–90. Ithaca, New York: Cornell University Press. (First pub. 1975.)

Dean, Nancy
     1978   A Bibliography and Selected Review of Goddess-Related Materials. Lady-Unique-Inclination-of-the-Night, Cycle 3, pp. 73–80.

de Beauvoir, Simone
     1961   The Second Sex. H. M. Parshley, trans. and ed. New York: Bantam Books. (First pub. 1949; trans. 1953.)

Debrida, Bella
     1982   Drawing from Mythology in Women's Quest for Selfhood. *In* The Politics of Women's Spirituality: Essays on the Rise of Spiritual Power within the Feminist Movement. Charlene Spretnak, ed. Pp. 138–51. Garden City, New York: Anchor Press/Doubleday.

Dégh, Linda
     1969   Folktales and Society: Story-Telling in a Hungarian Peasant Community. Emily M. Schossberger, trans. Bloomington: Indiana University Press. (First pub. 1962.)
     1979   Grimm's *Household Tales* and Its Place in the Household: The Social Relevance of a Controversial Classic. Western Folklore 38: 83–103.

Delaney, Janice, Mary Jane Lupton, and Emily Toth
     1976   The Curse: A Cultural History of Menstruation. New York: E. P. Dutton.

Delcourt, Marie
     1961   Hermaphrodite: Myths and Rites of the Bisexual Figure in Classical Antiquity. Jennifer Nicholson, trans. London: Studio Books. (First pub. 1956.)

Demetracopoulou, D.
     1933   The Loon Woman Myth: A Study in Synthesis. Journal of American Folk-Lore 46: 101–28.

Demetrakopoulos, Stephanie A.
     1979   Hestia, Goddess of the Hearth: Notes on an Oppressed Archetype. Spring, pp. 55–75.

Densmore, Frances
     1910   Chippewa Music. Bureau of American Ethnology Bulletin 45. Washington: GPO.
     1918   Teton Sioux Music. Bureau of American Ethnology Bulletin 61. Washington: GPO.

Deutsch, Helene
     1944   The Psychology of Women: A Psychoanalytic Interpretation. Vol. 1. New York: Grune & Stratton.

Dewhurst, C. Kurt, Betty MacDowell, and Marsha MacDowell
     1979   Artists in Aprons: Folk Art by American

Women. New York: E. P. Dutton with the Museum of American Folk Art.

Diehl, Joanne Feit
1978a   "Come Slowly—Eden": An Exploration of Women Poets and Their Muse. Signs 3: 572–87.
1978b   Reply to Faderman and Bernikow. Signs 4: 195–96.

Diner, Helen
1973   Mothers and Amazons: The First Feminine History of Culture. John Philip Lundin, ed. and trans. Garden City, New York: Anchor Press/Doubleday. (First pub. 1930s under pseudonym "Sir Galahad"; trans. 1965.)

Dinnerstein, Dorothy
1976   The Mermaid and The Minotaur: Sexual Arrangements and Human Malaise. New York: Harper & Row.

Dobie, J. Frank
1923   Weather Wisdom of the Texas-Mexican Border. In Coffee in the Gourd. J. Frank Dobie, ed. Publications of the Texas Folk-Lore Society, No. 2. Pp. 87–99. Austin: Texas Folk-Lore Society.

Dorsey, J. Owen
1889   Teton Folk-Lore Notes. Journal of American Folk-Lore 2:133–39.

Dorson, Richard M.
1956   Negro Folktales in Michigan. Cambridge: Harvard University Press.
1971   How Shall We Rewrite Charles M. Skinner Today? In American Folk Legend: A Symposium. Wayland D. Hand, ed. Pp. 69–95. Berkeley: University of California Press.
1973   America in Legend: Folklore from the Colonial Period to the Present. New York: Pantheon Books.

Douglas, Mary
1975   Couvade and Menstruation: The Relevance of Tribal Studies. In Implicit Meanings: Essays in Anthropology. Pp. 60–72. London: Routledge & Kegan Paul. (First pub. 1968.)

Downing, Christine
n.d.   Persephone in Hades. Anima 4, 1:22–29.
1978   Ariadne, Mistress of the Labyrinth. Lady-Unique-Inclination-of-the-Night, Cycle 3, pp. 6–16.
1979   Coming to Terms with Hera. Quadrant, Winter, pp. 26–49.
1980   Ariadne, Mistress of the Labyrinth. In Facing the Gods. James Hillman, ed. Pp. 135–49. Irving, Texas: Spring Publications.

1980a   Beginning with Gaea. Lady-Unique-Inclination-of-the-Night, Cycle 5, pp. 22–38.
1981   "Dear Grey Eyes": A Revaluation of Pallas Athene. Archē: Notes and Papers on Archaic Studies 6:9–39.
1981a   The Goddess: Mythological Representations of the Feminine. New York: Crossroad.

Driver, Anne Barstow
1976   Review Essay: Religion. Signs 2:434–42.
1977   Reply to Kraemer. Signs 3:518.

Driver, Harold E.
1941   Girls' Puberty Rites in Western North America. University of California Publications in Anthropological Records 6:21–90.
1969   Girls' Puberty Rites and Matrilocal Residence. American Anthropologist 71:905–908.

Dundes, Alan
1962   Earth-Diver: Creation of the Mythopoeic Male. American Anthropologist 64:1032–51.
1976   The Crowing Hen and the Easter Bunny: Male Chauvinism in American Folklore. In Folklore Today: A Festschrift for Richard M. Dorson. Linda Dégh, Henry Glassie, and Felix J. Oinas, eds. Pp. 123–38. Bloomington: Indiana University.

Durand, Gilbert
1981   Psyche's View. Jane A. Pratt, trans. Spring, pp. 1–19.

Economou, George D.
1972   The Goddess Natura in Medieval Literature. Cambridge: Harvard University Press.

Ehrenrich, Barbara, and Deirdre English
1973a   Complaints and Disorders: The Sexual Politics of Sickness. Glass Mountain Pamphlet No. 2. Old Westbury, New York: Feminist Press.
1973   Witches, Midwives and Nurses: A History of Women Healers. Glass Mountain Pamphlet No. 1. Old Westbury, New York: Feminist Press.
1979   For Her Own Good: 150 Years of the Experts' Advice to Women. Garden City, New York: Anchor Press/Doubleday. (First pub. 1978.)

Eliade, Mircea
1958   Patterns in Comparative Religion. Rosemary Sheed, trans. Cleveland, Ohio: World Publishing. (First pub. 1949.)
1960   Myths, Dreams and Mysteries: The Encounter between Contemporary Faiths and Archaic Realities. Philip Mairet, trans. New York: Harper & Row. (First pub. 1957.)

1961   The Sacred and the Profane: The Nature of Religion. Willard R. Trask, trans. New York: Harper & Row. (First pub. 1957.)

1963   Myth and Reality. Willard R. Trask, trans. New York: Harper & Row.

1964   Shamanism: Archaic Techniques of Ecstasy. Willard R. Trask, trans. Bollingen Series 76. Princeton: Princeton University Press. (First pub. 1951.)

1965   Rites and Symbols of Initiation: The Mysteries of Birth and Rebirth. Willard R. Trask, trans. New York: Harper & Row. (First pub. 1958.)

1965a The Two and the One. J. M. Cohen, trans. Chicago: University of Chicago Press. (First pub. 1962.)

1967   From Primitives to Zen. New York: Harper & Row.

1969   The Quest: History and Meaning in Religion. Chicago: Univeristy of Chicago Press.

1971   The Forge and the Crucible. Stephen Corrin, trans. New York: Harper & Row. (First pub. 1956.)

1975   Some Observations on European Witchcraft. History of Religions 14:149–72.

1978   A History of Religious Ideas. Vol. 1: From the Stone Age to the Eleusinian Mysteries. Willard R. Trask, trans. Chicago: University of Chicago Press.

Ellis, Bill
1978   "The 'Blind' Girl" and the Rhetoric of Sentimental Heroism. Journal of American Folklore 91:657–74.

Elms, Alan C.
1977   "The Three Bears": Four Interpretations. Journal of American Folklore 90:257–73.

Elsasser, Nan, Kyle MacKenzie, and Yvonne Tixier y Vigil
1980   Las Mujeres: Conversations from a Hispanic Community. Old Westbury, New York: Feminist Press.

Enciso, Jorge
1953   Design Motifs of Ancient Mexico. New York: Dover Publications. (First pub. 1947.)

Engelsman, Joan Chamberlain
1979   The Feminine Dimension of the Divine. Philadelphia: Westminster Press.

Ernster, Virginia L.
1975   American Menstrual Expressions. Sex Roles 1:3–13.

Estrada, Alvaro
1981   Maria Sabina: Her Life and Chants. Henry Munn, trans. and ed. Santa Barbara, California: Ross-Erikson.

Faderman, Lillian
1978   Comment on Joanne Feit Diehl's " 'Come Slowly—Eden': An Exploration of Women Poets and Their Muse." Signs 4:188–91.

Falk, Nancy Auer, and Rita M. Gross, eds.
1980   Unspoken Worlds: Women's Religious Lives in Non-Western Cultures. San Francisco: Harper & Row.

Farrer, Claire R.
1975   Introduction, Women and Folklore: Images and Genres. Journal of American Folklore 88:v–xv.

1975a (Ed.) Women and Folklore. Austin: University of Texas Press. (First published as a special issue of the Journal of American Folklore, vol. 88, no. 347, January–March 1975.)

1980   Singing for Life: The Mescalero Apache Girl's Puberty Ceremony. In Southwestern Indian Ritual Drama. Charlotte J. Frisbie, ed. Pp. 125–59. School of American Research Advanced Seminar Series. Albuquerque: University of New Mexico Press.

Fee, Elizabeth
1973   The Sexual Politics of Victorian Social Anthropology. Feminist Studies 1, 3–4:23–39.

Feiffer, Jules, ed. and comp.
1965   The Great Comic Book Heroes. New York: Bonanza Books.

Feinberg, Jean, Lenore Goldberg, Julie Gross, Bella Lieberman, and Elizabeth Sacre
1978   Political Fabrications: Women's Textiles in 5 Cultures. Heresies 1, 4:28–37.

Fewkes, Jesse Walter
1973   Designs on Prehistoric Hopi Pottery. New York: Dover Publications. (First pub. 1919.)

Field, Frederick V.
1974   Pre-Hispanic Mexican Stamp Designs. New York: Dover Publications.

Figes, Eva
1970   Patriarchal Attitudes. New York: Stein & Day Publishers.

Fiorenza, Elisabeth Schüssler
1979   Feminist Spiritualism, Christian Identity, and Catholic Vision. In Womanspirit Rising: A Feminist Reader in Religion. Carol P. Christ and Judith Plaskow, eds. Pp. 136–48. San Francisco: Harper & Row. (First pub. in National Institute for Campus Ministries Journal, fall 1978, vol. 1, no. 4.)

Fischer, Clare B., Betsy Brenneman, and Anne McGrew Bennett, eds.

1975 Women in a Strange Land: Search for a New Image. Philadelphia: Fortress Press.

Fishbane, Michael
1981 Israel and the "Mothers." *In* The Other Side of God: A Polarity in World Religions. Peter L. Berger, ed. Pp. 28–47. Garden City, New York: Anchor Press/Doubleday.

Fisher, Berenice
1980 Who Needs Women Heroes? Heresies 3, 1: 10–13.

Fisher, Dexter
1980 The Third Woman: Minority Women Writers of the United States. Boston: Houghton Mifflin.

Fisher, Elizabeth
1979 Women's Creation: Sexual Evolution and the Shaping of Society. Garden City, New York: Doubleday.

Fisher, Elizabeth, et al., eds.
1973 Matriarchy. Aphra: The Feminist Literary Magazine 4, 3.

Fletcher, Alice C., and Francis La Flesche
1911 The Omaha Tribe. *In* Twenty-seventh Annual Report of the Bureau of American Ethnology to the Secretary of the Smithsonian Institution, 1905–1906. W. H. Holmes, Chief. Pp. 16–672. Washington: GPO.

Foote, Audrey C.
1977 Notes on the Distaff Side. Atlantic, January, pp. 89–91.

Forfreedom, Ann
1979 Diana Triumphant. Lady-Unique-Inclination-of-the-Night, Cycle 4, pp. 36–45.

Forfredom, Ann, and Julie Ann, eds.
1980 Book of the Goddess. Sacramento, California: The Temple of the Goddess Within.

Fox, Charles Philip
1979 Old-Time Circus Cuts: A Pictorial Archive of 202 Illustrations. New York: Dover Publications.

Fox, Hugh, ed.
1978 First Fire: Central and South American Indian Poetry. Garden City, New York: Anchor Press/Doubleday.

Frank, Hardy Long
1978 Virginal Politics. Frontiers: a journal of women studies 3, 1:46–50. (Errata in *Frontiers* 3, 2 [1978]:21.)

Frazer, James George
1911 Taboo and the Perils of the Soul. The Golden Bough: A Study in Magic and Religion, part 2. London: Macmillan.

1913 Balder the Beautiful: The Fire-Festivals of Europe and the Doctrine of the External Soul. The Golden Bough: A Study in Magic and Religion, part 6, vol. 1. London: Macmillan.

1975 Folklore in the Old Testament: Studies in Comparative Religion, Legend, and Law. New York: Hart Publishing. (First pub. 1918.)

Friedrich, Paul
1978 The Meaning of Aphrodite. Chicago: University of Chicago Press.

Frisbie, Charlotte Johnson
1967 Kinaaldá: A Study of the Navaho Girl's Puberty Ceremony. Middletown, Connecticut: Wesleyan University Press.

1980 Ritual Drama in the Navajo House Blessing Ceremony. *In* Southwestern Indian Ritual Drama. Charlotte J. Frisbie, ed. Pp. 161–98. School of American Research Advanced Seminar Series. Albuquerque: University of New Mexico Press.

Gage, Matilda Joslyn
1980 Woman, Church & State: The Original Exposé of Male Collaboration Against the Female Sex. Sally Roesch Wagner, ed. Watertown, Massachusetts:Persephone Press. (First pub. 1893.)

Garbáty, Thomas J.
1968 Chaucer's Weaving Wife. Journal of American Folklore 81:342–46.

Garrett, Clarke
1977 Women and Witches: Patterns of Analysis. Signs 3:461–70.

1979 Reply to Honegger and Moia. Signs 4:802–4.

Garrison, Dee
1981 Karen Horney and Feminism. Signs 6:672–91.

Gelpi, Barbara Charlesworth
1974 The Androgyne. *In* Women & Analysis: Dialogues on Psychoanalytic Views of Femininity. Jean Strouse, ed. Pp. 227–38. New York: Grossman Publishing.

Ghanananda, Swami, and Sir John Stewart-Wallace, ed. advisers
1955 Women Saints East and West. Hollywood, California: Vedanta Press.

Geis, Frances
1981 Joan of Arc: The Legend and the Reality. New York: Harper & Row.

Gies, Frances and Joseph
1978 Women in the Middle Ages. New York: Thomas Y. Crowell.

Gilbert, Sandra M., and Susan Gubar
1979 The Madwoman in the Attic: The Woman

Writer and the Nineteenth-Century Literary Imagination. New Haven: Yale University Press.

Gilman, Charlotte Perkins
  1979   Herland. Ann J. Lane, intro. New York: Pantheon Books. (First pub. 1915.)

Gimbutas, Marija
  1974   The Gods and Goddesses of Old Europe, 7000 to 3500 B.C. Berkeley: University of California Press.

Girardot, N. J.
  1977   Initiation and Meaning in the Tale of Snow White and the Seven Dwarfs. Journal of American Folklore 90:274–300.
  1979   Response to Jones: "Scholarship is Never Just the Sum of All Its Variants." Journal of American Folklore 92:73–76.

Glazer-Malbin, Nona
  1976   Review Essay: Housework. Signs 1:905–22.

Glendinning, Chellis
  1982   The Healing Powers of Women. In The Politics of Women's Spirituality: Essays on the Rise of Spiritual Power within the Feminist Movement. Charlene Spretnak, ed. Pp. 280–93. Garden City, New York: Anchor Press/Doubleday.

Goldenberg, Judith Plaskow, ed.
  1973   Women and Religion: 1972. Waterloo, Ontario: American Academy of Religion, for the C.S.R. Executive Office, Waterloo Lutheran University.

Goldenberg, Naomi R.
  1976   A Feminist Critique of Jung. Signs 2:443–49.
  1978   Reply to Barbara Chesser's Comment on "A Feminist Critique of Jung." Signs 3:724–26.
  1978a Woman and the Image of God: A Psychological Perspective on the Feminist Movement in Religion. International Journal of Women's Studies 1:468–74.
  1979   Changing of the Gods: Feminism and the End of Traditional Religions. Boston: Beacon Press.

Goodrich, Norma Lorre
  1961   Medieval Myths. New York: New American Library.

Grafton, Carol Belanger
  1980a Pictorial Archives of Printer's Ornaments from the Renaissance to the 20th Century. New York: Dover Publications.
  1980   Treasury of Art Nouveau Design & Ornament: A Pictorial Archive of 577 Illustrations. New York: Dover Publications.

Grahn, Judy
  1982   From Sacred Blood to the Curse and Beyond. In The Politics of Women's Spirituality: Essays on the Rise of Spiritual Power within the Feminist Movement. Charlene Spretnak, ed. Pp. 265–79. Garden City, New York: Anchor Press/Doubleday.

Graves, Robert
  1948   The White Goddess: A Historical Grammar of Poetic Myth. Amended and enlarged ed. New York: Farrar, Straus and Giroux.
  1960   The Greek Myths. 2 vols. Baltimore, Maryland: Penguin Books.

Graves, Robert, and Raphael Patai
  1966   The Hebrew Myths: The Book of Genesis. New York: McGraw-Hill. (First pub. 1963.)

Green, Rayna
  1977   Magnolias Grow in Dirt: The Bawdy Lore of Southern Women. Southern Exposure 4, 4: 29–33.
  1980   Review Essay: Native American Women. Signs 6:248–67.
  1981   (Comp.) Native American Women: A Bibliography. Wichita Falls, Texas: Ohoyo Resource Center.

Greenberg, Caren
  1980   Reading Reading: Echo's Abduction of Language. In Women and Language in Literature and Society. Sally McConnell-Ginet, Ruth Borker, and Nelly Furman, eds. Pp. 300–9. New York: Praeger.

Greenfield, Gloria Z., Judith Antares, and Charlene Spretnak
  1978   The Politics of Women's Spirituality. Chrysalis 6:9–15.

Griffen, Joyce
  1977   A Cross-Cultural Investigation of Behavior Changes at Menopause. Social Science Journal, April, pp. 49–55.

Griffin, Susan
  1978   Woman and Nature: The Roaring Inside Her. New York: Harper & Row.

Grinnell, Robert
  1973   Alchemy in a Modern Woman: A Study in the Contrasexual Archetype. Zürich, Switzerland: Spring Publications.

Gross, Rita, ed.
  1976   Women and Religion II. Missoula, Montana: Scholars' Press and the American Academy of Religion.

Gubar, Susan
  1981   "The Blank Page" and the Issues of Female Creativity. Critical Inquiry 8:243–63.

Guggenbühl-Craig, Adolf
1977 Marriage—Dead or Alive. Murray Stein, trans. Zürich, Switzerland: Spring Publications.

Gulzow, Monte, and Carol Mitchell
1980 "Vagina Dentata" and "Incurable Venereal Disease" Legends from the Viet Nam War. Western Folklore 39:306–16.

Hackett, Amy, and Sarah Pomeroy
1972 Making History: *The First Sex.* Feminist Studies 1, 2:97–108.

Haeberlin, Hermann
1924 Mythology of Puget Sound. Journal of American Folk-Lore 37:371–438.

Haeckel, Ernst
1974 Art Forms in Nature. New York: Dover Publications. (First pub. 1904.)

Hageman, Alice L., ed.
1974 Sexist Religion and Women in the Church—No More Silence. New York: Association Press.

Haining, Peter, ed.
1975 An Illustrated History of Witchcraft. New York: Pyramid Books.

Hale, Horatio
1888 Huron Folk-Lore. Journal of American Folk-Lore 1:177–83.

Hall, Nor
1979 The Goddess in the Consulting Room: A Jungian Perspective. Lady-Unique-Inclination-of-the-Night, Cycle 4, pp. 5–18.
1980 The Moon & the Virgin: Reflections on the Archetypal Feminine. New York: Harper & Row.

Hallett, Judith P.
1979 Sappho and Her Social Context: Sense and Sensuality. Signs 4:447–64.
1979a Response to Stigers. Signs 5:373–74.

Hand, Wayland D.
1957 American Analogues of the Couvade. *In* Studies in Folklore. W. Edson Richmond, ed. Pp. 213–29. Indiana University Publications, Folklore Series No. 9. Bloomington: Indiana University Press.

Hansen, Wm. F.
1978 The Homeric Epics and Oral Poetry. *In* Heroic Epic and Saga: An Introduction to the World's Great Folk Epics. Felix J. Oinas, ed. Pp. 7–26. Bloomington: Indiana University Press.

Harding, M. Esther
1970 The Way of All Women: A Psychological Interpretation. New York: G. P. Putnam's Sons for the C. G. Jung Foundation for Analytical Psychology.
1973 Woman's Mysteries, Ancient and Modern: A Psychological Interpretation of the Feminine Principle as Portrayed in Myth, Story, and Dreams. New York: Bantam Books. (First pub. 1971.)

Harding, Susan
1975 Women and Words in a Spanish Village. *In* Toward an Anthropology of Women. Rayna R. Reiter, ed. Pp. 283–308. New York: Monthly Review Press.
1978 Street Shouting and Shunning: Conflict Between Women in a Spanish Village. Frontiers: a journal of women studies 3, 3:14–18.

Harter, Jim, ed.
1978a Harter's Picture Archive for Collage and Illustration. New York: Dover Publications.
1978b Women: A Pictorial Archive from Nineteenth-Century Sources. New York: Dover Publications.
1979 Food and Drink: A Pictorial Archive from
–80 Nineteenth-Century Sources. 2d rev. ed. New York: Dover Publications.
1980a Men: A Pictorial Archive from Nineteenth-Century Sources. New York: Dover Publications.
1980b Music: A Pictorial Archive of Woodcuts & Engravings. New York: Dover Publications.

Hauptman, Judith
1974 Images of Women in the Talmud. *In* Religion and Sexism: Images of Women in the Jewish and Christian Traditions. Resemary Radford Reuther, ed. Pp. 184–212. New York: Simon and Schuster.

Hawes, Bess Lomax
1968 La Llorona in Juvenile Hall. Western Folklore 27:153–70.

Hays, H. R.
1964 The Dangerous Sex: The Myth of Feminine Evil. New York: G. P. Putnam's Sons.

Heilbrun, Carolyn G.
1973 Toward a Recognition of Androgyny. New York: Alfred A. Knopf.

Henderson, Joseph L.
1964 Ancient Myths and Modern Man. *In* Man and His Symbols, by Carl G. Jung with M.-L. von Franz, Joseph L. Henderson, Jolande Jacobi, and Aniela Jaffé. Pp. 95–156. New York: Dell Publishing.

Heresies Collective
1977 Women's Traditional Arts: The Politics of

−78   Aesthetics. Heresies: A Feminist Publication on Art & Politics, Winter.

1978   The Great Goddess. Heresies: A Feminist Publication on Art & Politics, Spring.

Hess, Thomas B., and Elizabeth C. Baker, eds.
1973   Art and Sexual Politics: Women's Liberation, Women Artists, and Art History. New York: Macmillan.

Heuscher, Julius E.
1974   A Psychiatric Study of Myths and Fairy Tales: Their Origin, Meaning and Usefulness. 2d ed. Springfield, Illinois: Charles C Thomas Publisher.

Hillman, James
1972   The Myth of Analysis: Three Essays in Archetypal Psychology. Evanston, Illinois: Northwestern University Press.

1973   "Anima." Spring, pp. 97–132.
1974   "Anima" (II). Spring, pp. 113–46.
1980   On the Necessity of Abnormal Psychology: Ananke and Athene. In Facing the Gods. James Hillman, ed. Pp. 1–38. Irving, Texas: Spring Publications.

Hine, Daryl, trans.
1972   The Homeric Hymns and The Battle of the Frogs and the Mice. New York: Atheneum.

Hirsch, Marianne
1981   Review Essay: Mothers and Daughters. Signs 7:200–22.

Hoch-Smith, Judith, and Anita Spring, eds.
1978   Women in Ritual and Symbolic Roles. New York: Plenum Press.

Honegger, Claudia
1979   Comment on Garrett's "Women and Witches." Signs 4:792–98.

Horney, Karen
1967   Feminine Psychology. Harold Kelman, ed. New York: W. W. Norton.

Hornung, Clarence P.
1946   Handbook of Designs and Devices. New York: Dover Publications.

Horsley, Richard A.
1979   Further Reflections on Witchcraft and European Folk Religion. History of Religions 19:71–95.

Howe, James, and Lawrence A. Hirschfeld
1981   The Star Girls' Descent: A Myth about Men, Women, Matrilocality, and Singing. Journal of American Folklore 94:292–322.

Hufford, David J.
1976   A New Approach to the "Old Hag": The Nightmare Tradition Reexamined. In American Folk Medicine: A Symposium. Wayland D. Hand, ed. Pp. 73–85. Berkeley: University of California Press.

Hultkrantz, Åke
1961   Bachofen and the Mother Goddess: An Appraisal After One Hundred Years. Ethnos 26:75–85.

1979   The Religions of the American Indians. Monica Setterwall, trans. Berkeley: University of California Press.

Hungry Wolf, Beverly
1980   The Ways of My Grandmothers. New York: William Morrow.

Jackson, Bruce
1971   *Vagina Dentata* and Cystic Teratoma. Journal of American Folklore 84:341–42.

Jacobs, Joseph, coll.
1968   Celtic Fairy Tales. New York: Dover Publications. (First pub. 1892.)

Jacobs, Melville
1958   The Romantic Role of Older Women in a Culture of the Pacific Northwest Coast. Kroeber Anthropological Society Papers 18:79–85.

1959   The Content and Style of an Oral Literature: Clackamas Chinook Myths and Tales. Viking Fund Publications in Anthropology No. 26. New York: Wenner-Gren Foundation for Anthropological Research.

Jacobs, Sue-Ellen
1974   Women in Perspective: A Guide for Cross-Cultural Studies. Urbana: University of Illinois Press.

Janeway, Elizabeth
1980   Powers of the Weak. New York: Alfred A. Knopf.

Jaramillo, Cleofas M.
1972   Shadows of the Past (Sombras del pasado). Santa Fe, New Mexico: Ancient City Press. (First pub. 1941.)

Jewett, Paul K.
1975   Man as Male and Female: A Study in Sexual Relationships from a Theological Point of View. Grand Rapids, Michigan: William B. Eerdmans Publishing.

Johansen, J. Prytz
1975   The Thesmorphia as a Women's Festival. Temenos 11:78–87.

Johnson, Buffie, and Tracy Boyd
1978   The Eternal Weaver. Heresies, Spring, pp. 64–69.

Johnson, Robert A.
1976   She: Understanding Feminine Psychology, An

interpretation based on the myth of Amor and Psyche and using Jungian psychological concepts. King of Prussia, Pennsylvania: Religious Publishing.

Jones, Betty H., and Alberta Arthurs
1978 The American Eve: A New Look at American Heroines and Their Critics. International Journal of Women's Studies 1:1–12.

Jones, David E.
1972 Sanapia: Comanche Medicine Woman. Case Studies in Cultural Anthropology. New York: Holt, Rinehart and Winston.

Jones, Steven
1979 The Pitfalls of Snow White Scholarship. Journal of American Folklore 92:69–73.

Jong, Erica
1981 Witches. New York: Harry N. Abrams.

Jordan (de Caro), Rosan
1973 A Note about Folklore and Literature (The Bosom Serpent Revisited). Journal of American Folklore 86:62–65.

Joyce, Michael, trans.
1961 Symposium. *In* The Collected Dialogues of Plato including the Letters. Edith Hamilton and Huntington Cairns, eds. Pp. 526–74. Bollingen Series 71. New York: Pantheon Books. (First pub. 1935.)

Jung, C. G.
1963 The Psychological Aspects of Kore. *In* Essays on a Science of Mythology: The Myth of the Divine Child and The Mysteries of Eleusis, by C. G. Jung and C. Kerényi. Pp. 156–77. R. F. C. Hull, trans. Bollingen Series 22. Princeton: Princeton University Press.
1968 The Phenomenology of the Spirit in Fairytales. *In* The Archetypes and the Collective Unconscious. 2d ed. R. F. C. Hull, trans. Pp. 207–54. Bollingen Series 20. Princeton: Princeton University Press.
1970 Psychological Reflections: A New Anthology of His Writings 1905–1961. Jolande Jacobi, ed., with R. F. C. Hull. Bollingen Series 31. Princeton: Princeton University Press.

Jung, Emma
1974 On the Nature of the Animus (1931). Cary F. Baynes, trans. *In* Women & Analysis: Dialogues on Psychoanalytic Views of Femininity. Jean Strouse, ed. Pp. 195–226. New York: Grossman Publishers.

Kalčik, Susan
1975 ". . . like Ann's gynecologist or the time I was almost raped": Personal Narratives in Women's Rap Groups. Journal of American Folklore 88:3–11.

Katz, Jane B., ed.
1977 I Am the Fire of Time: The Voices of Native American Women. New York: E. P. Dutton.

Kerényi, C. [or Karl]
1963 Kore. *In* Essays on a Science of Mythology: The Myth of the Divine Child and The Mysteries of Eleusis, by C. G. Jung and C. Kerényi. Pp. 101–55. R. F. C. Hull, trans. Bollingen Series 22. Princeton: Princeton University Press.
1967 Eleusis: Archetypal Image of Mother and Daughter. Ralph Manheim, trans. Bollingen Series 65. Archetypal Images in Greek Religion, vol. 4. New York: Pantheon Books.
1978 Athene: Virgin and Mother, A Study of Pallas Athene. Murray Stein, trans. Irving, Texas: Spring Publications.
1979a Goddesses of Sun and Moon: Circe/Aphrodite/ Medea/Niobe. Murray Stein, trans. Irving, Texas: Spring Publications.
1979 The Gods of the Greeks. Norman Cameron, trans. Great Britain: Thames and Hudson. (First pub. 1951.)
1980 A Mythological Image of Girlhood: Artemis. Hildegard Nagel, trans. *In* Facing the Gods. James Hillman, ed. Pp. 39–45. Irving, Texas: Spring Publications.

Key, Mary Ritchie
1975 Male/Female Language: With a Comprehensive Bibliography. Metuchen, New Jersey: Scarecrow Press.

Kilpatrick, Jack Frederick, and Anna Gritts Kilpatrick
1970 Notebook of a Cherokee Shaman. Smithsonian Contributions to Anthropology, vol. 2, no. 6. Washington: Smithsonian Institution Press.

King, C. W.
1864 The Gnostics and Their Remains, Ancient and Mediaeval. London: Bell and Daldy.

Kirksey, Barbara
1980 Hestia: A Background of Psychological Focusing. *In* Facing the Gods. James Hillman, ed. Pp. 101–13. Irving, Texas: Spring Publications.

Kirtley, Bacil F.
1960 "La Llorona" and Related Themes. Western Folklore 19:155–68.

Kitzinger, Sheila
1979 Women as Mothers. New York: Random House. (First pub. 1978.)

Kluckhohn, Clyde
    1943   Bronislaw Malinowski 1884–1942. Journal of American Folklore 56:208–19.

Kluckhohn, Clyde, and Dorothea Leighton
    1962   The Navaho. Rev. ed. Natural History Library. Garden City, New York: Doubleday. (First pub. 1946.)

Kluger, Rivkah Schärf
    1974   The Queen of Sheba in Bible and Legends. In Psyche and Bible, by Kluger. Pp. 85–144. Zürich, Switzerland: Spring Publications.

Koch, Rudolf
    1955   The Book of Signs. Vyvyan Holland, trans. New York: Dover Publications. (First pub. 1930.)

Kodish, Debora G.
    1980   Moving Toward the Everyday: Some Thoughts on Gossip and Visiting as Secular Procession. Folklore Papers of the University Folklore Association, no. 9, pp. 93–104. Austin: University of Texas.

Kolbenschlag, Madonna
    1979   Kiss Sleeping Beauty Good-Bye: Breaking the Spell of Feminine Myths and Models. Garden City, New York: Doubleday.

Koltun, Elizabeth, ed.
    1976   The Jewish Woman: New Perspectives. New York: Schocken Books.

Kraemer, Ross S.
    1977   Comment on Anne Barstow Driver's "Religion: Review Essay" (vol. 2, no. 2). Signs 3:516–17.
    1980   The Conversion of Women to Ascetic Forms of Christianity. Signs 6:298–307.

Kramer, Samuel Noah
    1944   Sumerian Mythology: A Study of Spiritual and Literary Achievement in the Third Millennium B.C. Memoirs of the American Philosophical Society, vol. 21. Philadelphia: American Philosophical Society.
    1959   History Begins at Sumer. Garden City, New York: Doubleday Anchor Books. (First pub. 1956.)
    1969   The Sacred Marriage Rite: Aspects of Faith, Myth, and Ritual in Ancient Sumer. Bloomington: Indiana University Press.

Kris, Ernst, and Otto Kurz
    1979   Legend, Myth, and Magic in the Image of the Artist. Alastair Lang and Lottie M. Newman, trans. New Haven: Yale University Press. (First pub. 1934.)

Kroeber, A. L.
    1919   Sinkyone Tales. Journal of American Folk-Lore 32:346–51.
    1946   The Chibcha. In The Andean Civilizations. Handbook of South American Indians, vol. 2. Julian H. Steward, ed. Pp. 887–909. Bureau of American Ethnology Bulletin 143. Washington: GPO.

Lacks, Roslyn
    1980   Women and Judaism: Myth, History, and Struggle. Garden City, New York: Doubleday.

Lacourcière, Luc
    1976   A Survey of Folk Medicine in French Canada from Early Times to the Present. In American Folk Medicine: A Symposium. Wayland D. Hand, ed. Pp. 203–14. Berkeley: University of California Press.

Lakoff, Robin
    1975   Language and Woman's Place. New York: Harper & Row. (First pub. 1973.)

Lamphere, Louise
    1977   Review Essay: Anthropology. Signs 2:612–27.

Landes, Ruth
    1968   Ojibwa Religion and the Midéwiwin. Madison: University of Wisconsin Press.
    1971   The Ojibwa Woman. Columbia University Contributions to Anthropology. New York: W. W. Norton. (First pub. 1938.)

Lang, Andrew, ed.
    1965   The Blue Fairy Book. New York: Dover Publications. (First pub. ca. 1889.)
    1965   The Green Fairy Book. New York: Dover Publications. (First pub. ca. 1892.)
    1966   The Red Fairy Book. New York: Dover Publications. (First pub. 1890.)

Langlois, Janet
    1978   Belle Gunness, Lady Bluebeard: Community Legend as Metaphor. Journal of the Folklore Institute 15:147–60.

Lantis, Margaret
    1938   The Mythology of Kodiak, Alaska. Journal of American Folk-Lore 51:123–72.

Lattimore, Richard, trans.
    1951   The Iliad of Homer. Chicago: University of Chicago Press.
    1959   Hesiod: The Works and Days, Theogony, The Shield of Herakles. Ann Arbor: University of Michigan Press.

Laughlin, Whitney
    1977   Female Kachinas. Lady-Unique-Inclination-of-the-Night, Cycle 2, pp. 49–54.

Lauter, Estella
1979   Anne Sexton's "Radical Discontent with the Awful Order of Things." Spring, pp. 77–92.
Lawson, John Cuthbert
1910   Modern Greek Folklore and Ancient Greek Religion: A Study in Survivals. Cambridge: At the University Press.
Layard, John
1972   The Virgin Archetype: Two Papers. Zürich, Switzerland: Spring Publications.
Leach, Maria, ed.
1972   Funk & Wagnalls Standard Dictionary of Folklore, Mythology, and Legend. 1 vol. ed. New York: Funk & Wagnalls. (First pub. 1949, 1950.)
Leavitt, Ruby R.
1975   The Older Woman: Her Status and Role. *In* Humanness: An Exploration into the Mythologies about Women and Men. Ella Lasky, ed. Pp. 495–504. New York: MSS Information Corporation.
Leddy, Betty
1948   La Llorona in Southern Arizona. Western Folklore 7:272–77.
1950   La Llorona Again. Western Folklore 9:363–65.
Lederer, Wolfgang
1968   The Fear of Women. New York: Grune & Stratton.
Lee, Stan
1977   The Superhero Women. New York: Simon and Schuster.
1979   Spider-Woman. Marvel Comics Series. New York: Pocket Books.
Leeming, David Adams
1981   Mythology: The Voyage of the Hero. 2d ed. New York: Harper & Row.
Lefkowitz, Mary R.
1977   *Review of* Females of the Species: Semonides on Women, by Hugh Lloyd-Jones. Signs 2:690–92.
Lefkowitz, Mary R., and Maureen B. Fant
1977   Women in Greece and Rome. Toronto & Sarasota: Samuel-Stevens.
Le Guin, Ursula
1976   The Space Crone. CoEvolution Quarterly, Summer, pp. 108–10.
Lehner, Ernst
1969   Symbols, Signs & Signets. New York: Dover Publications. (First pub. 1950.)
Lehner, Ernst and Johanna

1971   Devils, Demons, Death and Damnation. New York: Dover Publications.
León-Portilla, Miguel
1963   Aztec Thought and Culture: A Study of the Ancient Nahuatl Mind. Jack Emory Davis, trans. Norman: University of Oklahoma Press.
Levi, Peter, trans.
1971   Pausanias, Guide to Greece. Vol. 2: Southern Greece. New York: Penguin Books.
Levi, Steven C.
1977   P. T. Barnum and the Feejee Mermaid. Western Folklore 36:149–54.
Lévi-Strauss, Claude
1973   From Honey to Ashes. Introduction to a Science of Mythology: 2. John and Doreen Weightman, trans. New York: Harper & Row. (First pub. 1966.)
1978   The Origin of Table Manners. Introduction to a Science of Mythology: 3. John and Doreen Weightman, trans. New York: Harper & Row. (First pub. 1968.)
Lewis, C. S.
1956   Till We Have Faces: A Myth Retold. New York: Harcourt, Brace and World.
Lewis, Oscar
1941   Manly-Hearted Women among the North Piegan. American Anthropologist 3:173–87.
Lichtenstein, Grace
1981   Machisma: Women and Daring. Garden City, New York: Doubleday.
Lichtenstein, Marsha
1977   Radical Feminism and Women's Spirituality: Looking Before You Leap. Lady-Unique-Inclination-of-the-Night, Cycle 2, pp. 36–43.
Lieberman, Marcia
1972   Some Day My Prince Will Come. College English, December, pp. 383–95.
Lincoln, Bruce
1981   Emerging from the Chrysalis: Studies in Rituals of Women's Initiation. Cambridge: Harvard University Press.
Lindsay, Jack, trans.
1932   The Golden Ass by Apuleius. Bloomington: Indiana University Press.
Lippard, Lucy R.
1976   From the Center: Feminist Essays on Women's Art. New York: E. P. Dutton.
Lipshitz, Susan, ed.
1978   Tearing the Veil: Essays on Femininity. London: Routledge & Kegan Paul.
Lloyd-Jones, Hugh

1975 Females of the Species: Semonides on Women. With photographs by Don Honeyman of sculptures by Marcelle Quinton. Park Ridge, New Jersey: Noyes Press.

Lopez, Griselda Maria, and Luz Graciela Joly
1981 Singing a Lullaby in Kuna; a Female Verbal Art. Journal of American Folklore 94:351–58.

Lothrop, Samuel Kirkland
1976 Pre-Columbian Designs from Panama: 591 Illustrations of Coclé Poetry. New York: Dover Publications. (First pub. 1942.)

Lowie, Robert H.
1909 The Assiniboine. Anthropological Papers of the American Museum of Natural History, vol. 4, part 1.
1924 Shoshonean Tales. Journal of American Folk-Lore 37:1–242.
1944 (Trans.) Šerente Tales. Journal of American Folklore 57:181–87.

Luke, Helen M.
1980 The Perennial Feminine. Parabola 5, 4:10–23.

Lurie, Nancy Oestreich, ed.
1961 Mountain Wolf Woman, Sister of Crashing Thunder: The Autobiography of a Winnebago Indian. Ann Arbor: University of Michigan Press.

Lüthi, Max
1970 Once Upon a Time: On the Nature of Fairy Tales. Lee Chadeayne and Paul Gottwald, trans. New York: Frederick Ungar. (First pub. 1962.)

MacCormack, Carol P., and Marilyn Strathern, eds.
1980 Nature, Culture and Gender. Cambridge: Cambridge University Press.

Maclagan, David
1977 Creation Myths: Man's Introduction to the World. London: Thames and Hudson.

Malamud, René
1980 The Amazon Problem. Murray Stein, trans. In Facing the Gods. James Hillman, ed. Pp. 47–66. Irving, Texas: Spring Publications.

Malinowski, Bronislaw
1939 The Group and the Individual in Functional Analysis. American Journal of Sociology 44: 938–64.
1948 Myth in Primitive Psychology. In Magic, Science and Religion and Other Essays. Pp. 93–148. Garden City, New York: Doubleday Anchor. (First pub. 1926.)
1961 Argonauts of the Western Pacific: An Account of Native Enterprise and Adventure in the Archipelagoes of Melanesian New Guinea. New York: E. P. Dutton. (First pub. 1922.)

Mallery, Garrick
1893 Picture-Writing of the American Indians. In Tenth Annual Report of the Bureau of Ethnology to the Secretary of the Smithsonian Institution, 1888–89. J. W. Powell, Director. Pp. 3–807. Washington: GPO. (Reprint in 2 vols., New York: Dover Publications, 1972.)

Matalene, Carolyn
1978 Women as Witches. International Journal of Women's Studies 1:53–87.

Matthews, Washington
1887 The Mountain Chant: A Navajo Ceremony. In Fifth Annual Report of the Bureau of Ethnology to the Secretary of the Smithsonian Institution, 1883–1884. J. W. Powell, Director. Pp. 379–467. Washington: GPO.
1902 Myths of Gestation and Parturition. American Anthropologist 4:737–42.

May, Robert
1980 Sex and Fantasy: Patterns of Male and Female Development. New York: W. W. Norton.

Mayerson, Philip
1971 Classical Mythology in Literature, Art, and Music. Lexington, Massachusetts: Xerox College Publishing.

McAllester, David P., and McAllester, Susan W.
1980 Hogans: Navajo Houses & House Songs. Middletown, Connecticut: Wesleyan University Press.

McCall, Dorothy Kaufmann
1979 Simone de Beauvoir, The Second Sex, and Jean-Paul Sartre. Signs 5:209–23.

McClellan, Catharine
1970 The Girl Who Married the Bear: A Masterpiece of Indian Oral Tradition. National Museum of Man Publications in Ethnology, No. 2. Ottawa: National Museums of Canada.

McClelland, David C.
1964a The Harlequin Complex. In The Study of Lives: Essays on Personality in Honor of Henry A. Murray. Robert W. White, ed. Pp. 95–119. New York: Atherton Press.
1964b The Roots of Consciousness. New York: Van Nostrand-Insight.

McConnell-Ginet, Sally
1980 Linguistics and the Feminist Challenge. In Women and Language in Literature and Society. Sally McConnell-Ginet, Ruth Borker,

and Nelly Furman, eds. Pp. 3–25. New York: Praeger.

McConnell-Ginet, Sally, Ruth Borker, and Nelly Furman, eds.
 1980 Women and Language in Literature and Society. New York: Praeger.

Meeks, Wayne A.
 1974 The Image of the Androgyne: Some Uses of a Symbol in Earliest Christianity. History of Religions 13:165–208.

Meinhardt, Lela, and Paul Meinhardt
 1977 Cinderella's Housework Dialectics: Housework as the Root of Human Creation. Nutley, New Jersey: Incunabula Press.

Mellaart, James
 1967 Catal Hüyük: A Neolithic Town in Anatolia. New York: McGraw-Hill.

Meltzer, David, ed.
 1981 Birth: An Anthology of Ancient Texts, Songs, Prayers, and Stories. San Francisco, California: North Point Press.

Mercatante, Anthony S.
 1974 Zoo of the Gods: Animals in Myth, Legend & Fable. New York: Harper & Row.

Merchant, Carolyn
 1980 The Death of Nature: Women, Ecology, and the Scientific Revolution. San Francisco: Harper & Row.

Merck, Mandy
 1978 The City's Achievements: The Patriotic Amazonamachy and Ancient Athens. In Tearing the Veil: Essays on Femininity. Susan Lipshitz, ed. Pp. 95–115. London: Routledge & Kegan Paul.

Mernissi, Fatima
 1977 Women, Saints, and Sanctuaries. Signs 3: 101–12.

Métraux, Alfred
 1943 A Myth of the Chamacoco Indians and Its Social Significance. Journal of American Folklore 56:113–19.
 1946 Myths and Tales of the Toba and Pilagá Indians of the Gran Chaco. Memoirs of the American Folklore Society, vol. 40. Philadelphia: American Folklore Society.

Michelson, Truman
 1925 The Autobiography of a Fox Indian Woman. In Fortieth Annual Report of the Bureau of American Ethnology to the Secretary of the Smithsonian Institution, 1918–1919. J. Walter Fewkes, Chief. Pp. 291–349. Washington: GPO.

Mickley, Niel
 1974 On Hysteria: The Mythical Syndrome. Spring, pp. 147–65.

Miegge, Giovanni
 1955 Virgin Mary. Philadelphia: Westminster Press.

Miller, Casey, and Kate Swift
 1976 Words and Women. Garden City, New York: Anchor Press/Doubleday.

Miller, David L.
 1973 Achelous and the Butterfly: Toward an Archetypal Psychology of Humor. Spring, pp. 1–23.
 1980 Red Riding Hood and Grand Mother Rhea: Images in a Psychology of Inflation. In Facing the Gods. James Hillman, ed. Pp. 87–99. Irving, Texas: Spring Publications.

Millett, Kate
 1970 Sexual Politics. New York: Doubleday.

Minard, Rosemary, ed.
 1975 Womenfolk and Fairy Tales. Boston: Houghton Mifflin.

Mitchell, Juliet
 1974 Psychoanalysis and Feminism. New York: Pantheon Books.

Mitchell, Marilyn Hall
 1978 Sexist Art Criticism: Georgia O'Keeffe—a Case Study. Signs 3:681–87.

Moers, Ellen
 1976 Literary Women. Garden City, New York: Doubleday.

Moia, Nelly
 1979 Comment on Garrett's "Women and Witches." Signs 4:798–802.

Momaday, N. Scott
 1969 The Way to Rainy Mountain. Albuquerque: University of New Mexico Press.

Monaghan, Patricia
 1981 The Book of Goddesses and Heroines. New York: E. P. Dutton.

Montagu, Ashley
 1953 The Natural Superiority of Women. New York: Macmillan.

Mooney, James
 1896 The Ghost-dance Religion and the Sioux Outbreaks of 1890. In Fourteenth Annual Report of the Bureau of Ethnology to the Secretary of the Smithsonian Institution, 1892–1893. J. W. Powell, Director. Part 2, pp. 641–1110. Washington: GPO.
 1900 Myths of the Cherokee. In Nineteenth Annual Report of the Bureau of American Eth-

nology to the Secretary of the Smithsonian Institution, 1897–1898. J. W. Powell, Director. Part 1, pp. 3–548. Washington: GPO.

Mooney, James, and Frans M. Olbrechts, rev. and ed.
1932   The Swimmer Manuscript: Cherokee Sacred Formulas and Medicinal Prescriptions. Bureau of American Ethnology Bulletin 99. Washington: GPO.

Morford, Mark P. O., and Robert J. Lenardon
1977   Classical Mythology. 2d ed. New York: David McKay.

Morgan, Kathryn L.
1966   Caddy Buffers: Legends of a Middle Class Negro Family in Philadelphia. Keystone Folklore Quarterly 2:67–88.
1980   Children of Strangers: The Stories of a Black Family. Philadelphia: Temple University Press.

Morgan, Lewis H.
1881   Houses and House-Life of the American Aborigines. Contributions to North American Ethnology, vol. 4. Washington: GPO.

Mountaingrove, Ruth, and Emily Culpepper
1976   Menstruation: Body and Spirit. Womanspirit, June.

Mullett, G. M., sel. and int.
1979   Spider Woman Stories: Legends of the Hopi Indians. Tucson: University of Arizona Press.

Murphy, Yolanda, and Robert F. Murphy
1974   Women of the Forest. New York: Columbia University Press.

Myerhoff, Barbara
1978a   Number Our Days. New York: E. P. Dutton.
1978   The Older Woman as Androgyne. Parabola 3, 4:75–89.

Mylonas, George E.
1961   Eleusis and the Eleusinian Mysteries. Princeton: Princeton University Press.

Nabokov, Peter
1981   Indian Running. Santa Barbara, California: Capra Press.

Nash, June
1978   The Aztecs and the Ideology of Male Dominance. Signs 4:349–62.

Naylor, Maria
1975   Authentic Indian Designs: 2500 Illustrations from Reports of the Bureau of American Ethnology. New York: Dover Publications.

Nelson, Edward William
1899   The Eskimo About Bering Strait. In Eighteenth Annual Report of the Bureau of American Ethnology to the Secretary of the Smithsonian Institution, 1896–1897. J. W.

Powell, Director. Pp. 3–518. Washington: GPO.

Neumann, Erich
1954   The Origins and History of Consciousness. R. F. C. Hull, trans. Bollingen Series 42. Princeton: Princeton University Press. (Frist pub. 1949.)
1956   Amor and Psyche: The Psychic Development of the Feminine, A Commentary on the Tale by Apuleius. Ralph Manheim, trans. Bollingen Series 54. Princeton: Princeton University Press. (First pub. 1952.)
1959   The Psychological Stages of Feminine Development. Spring, pp. 63–97.
1963   The Great Mother: An Analysis of the Archetype. Ralph Manheim, trans. Bollingen Series 47. Princeton: Princeton University Press. (First pub. 1955.)

Newall, Venetia
1974   The Encyclopedia of Witchcraft & Magic. New York: Dial Press.

Newton, Esther, and Paula Webster
1973   Matriarchy: As Women See It. Aphra 4, 3: 6–22.

Nicholson, Irene
1967   Mexican and Central American Mythology. London: Paul Hamlyn.

Niethammer, Carolyn
1977   Daughters of the Earth: The Lives and Legends of American Indian Women. New York: Collier Books.

Nilsson, Martin P.
1961   Greek Folk Religion. New York: Harper & Row. (First pub. 1940.)
1964   A History of Greek Religion. F. J. Fielden, trans. 2d ed. New York: W. W. Norton. (First pub. 1925.)

Noel, Daniel C.
1981   The Many Guises of the Goddess. Archē: Notes and Papers on Archaic Studies 6:93–111.

Oakley, Ann
1974   Woman's Work: A History of the Housewife. New York: Pantheon Books.

O'Bryan, Aileen
1956   The Dîné: Origin Myths of the Navajo Indians. Smithsonian Institution, Bureau of American Ethnology Bulletin 163. Washington: GPO.

Ochs, Carol
1977   Behind the Sex of God: Toward a New Consciousness—Transcending Matriarchy and Patriarchy. Boston: Beacon Press.

Ochshorn, Judith
1981   The Female Experience and the Nature of the Divine. Bloomington: Indiana University Press.

Oinas, Felix J., ed.
1978   Heroic Epic and Saga: An Introduction to the World's Great Folk Epics. Bloomington: Indiana University Press.

Oliver, Rose
1977   Whatever Became of Goldilocks? Frontiers: a journal of women studies 2, 3:85–93.

Opie, Iona and Peter
1952   (Eds.) The Oxford Dictionary of Nursery Rhymes. Oxford: At the Clarendon Press.
1973   (Eds.) The Oxford Book of Children's Verse. Oxford: Oxford University Press.
1974   The Classic Fairy Tales. London: Oxford University Press.

Otto, Walter F.
1965   Dionysus: Myth and Cult. Robert B. Palmer, trans. Bloomington: Indiana University Press. (First pub. 1933.)

Page, Denys
1973   Folktales in Homer's *Odyssey*. Cambridge: Harvard University Press.

Pagels, Elaine H.
1976   What Became of God the Mother?: Conflicting Images of God in Early Christianity. Signs 2:293–303.
1978   The Gnostic Vision. Parabola 3, 4:6–9.
1979   The Gnostic Gospels. New York: Random House.

Palumbo, Linda, Maurine Renville, Charlene Spretnak, and Terry Wolverton
1978   Women's Spirituality. Chrysalis 6:77–99.

Panofsky, Dora and Erwin
1962   Pandora's Box: The Changing Aspects of a Mythical Symbol. Bollingen Series 52. Princeton: Princeton University Press.

Paredes, Américo, ed. and trans.
1970   Folktales of Mexico. Folktales of the World. Chicago: University of Chicago Press.

Parker, Rozsika, and Griselda Pollock
1981   Old Mistresses: Woman, Art and Ideology. New York: Pantheon Books.

Parkman, E. Breck
1981   The Máien. National Women's Anthropology Newsletter 5, 2:16–22.

Parsons, Elsie Clews
1929   Kiowa Tales. Memoirs of the American Folk-Lore Society, vol. 22. New York: G. E. Stechert.

1932   Zapoteca and Spanish Tales of Mitla, Oaxaca. Journal of American Folk-Lore 45:277–317.
1939   Pueblo Indian Religion. Vol. 1. Chicago: University of Chicago Press.

Patai, Raphael
1964   Lilith. Journal of American Folklore 77:295–314.
1978   The Hebrew Goddess. New York: KTAV Publishing House.

Paul, Lois
1974   The Mastery of Work and the Mystery of Sex in a Guatemalan Village. *In* Woman, Culture, and Society. Michelle Zimbalist Rosaldo and Louise Lamphere, eds. Pp. 281–99. Stanford, California: Stanford University Press.
1978   Careers of Midwives in a Mayan Community. *In* Women in Ritual and Symbolic Roles. Judith Hoch-Smith and Anita Spring, eds. Pp. 129–49. New York: Plenum Press.

Paul, Lois, and Benjamin D. Paul
1975   The Maya Midwife as Sacred Specialist: A Guatemalan Case. American Ethnologist 2:707–26.

Paz, Octavio
1979   Juana Ramírez. Diane Marting, trans. Signs 5:80–97.

Pearson, Carol, and Katherine Pope
1976   (Eds.) Who Am I This Time?: Female Portraits in British and American Literature. New York: McGraw-Hill.
1981   The Female Hero in American and British Literature. Ann Arbor, Michigan: R. R. Bowker.

Peradotto, John, ed.
1978   Women in the Ancient World. Arethusa 11, 1–2. Department of Classics, State University of New York at Buffalo.

Pérez, Soledad
1951   Mexican Folklore from Austin, Texas. *In* The Healer of Los Olmos and Other Mexican Lore. Wilson H. Hudson, ed. Publications of the Texas Folk-Lore Society, No. 24. Pp. 71–127. Dallas: Southern Methodist University Press.

Peterson, Elsa
1980   On the Trail of Red Sky Lady and Other Scholars. Heresies 3, 3: 80–82.

Petroff, Elizabeth
1977   Discovering Biography in Hagiography: Lives of Medieval Saints. Lady-Unique-Inclination-of-the-Night, Cycle 2, pp. 72–86.
1978   Medieval Women Visionaries: Seven Stages

to Power. Frontiers: a journal of women studies 3, 1:34–45.

1981   Transforming the World: The Serpent-Dragon and the Virgin Saint. Archē: Notes and Papers on Archaic Studies 6:53–70.

Phelps, Ethel Johnston, ed.

1978   Tatterhood and Other Tales. Old Westbury, New York: Feminist Press.

1981   The Maid of the North: Feminist Folk Tales from Around the World. New York: Holt, Rinehart and Winston.

Phillips, Rachel

1971   Sor Juana: Dream and Silence. Aphra 3,
–72   1:30–40.

Plaskow, Judith

1979   The Coming of Lilith: Toward a Feminist Theology. In Womanspirit Rising: A Feminist Reader in Religion. Carol P. Christ and Judith Plaskow, eds. Pp. 198–209. San Francisco: Harper & Row.

1979a   Sex, Sin and Grace: Women's Experience and the Theologies of Reinhold Niebuhr and Paul Tillich. Washington, D.C.: University Press of America.

Plaskow, Judith, and Joan A. Romero, eds.

1974   Women and Religion. Missoula, Montana: Scholars' Press.

Pomeroy, Sarah B.

1975   Goddesses, Whores, Wives, and Slaves: Women in Classical Antiquity. New York: Schocken Books.

Pope, Alexander, trans.

1882   The Odyssey of Homer. New York: The American News Company.

Poulsen, Richard C.

1979   Bosom Serpentry among the Puritans and Mormons. Journal of the Folklore Institute 16: 176–89.

Powers, Marla N.

1980   Menstruation and Reproduction: An Oglala Case. Signs 6:54–65.

Preston, James J., ed.

1982   Mother Worship: Theme and Variations. Chapel Hill: University of North Carolina Press.

Puckett, Newbell Niles

1926   Folk Beliefs of the Southern Negro. Chapel Hill: University of North Carolina Press.

Radin, Paul

1957   Primitive Man as Philosopher. 2d rev. ed. New York: Dover Publications. (First pub. 1927.)

Ramsey, Jarold

1977   The Bible in Western Indian Mythology. Journal of American Folklore 90:442–54.

1977a   Coyote Was Going There: Indian Literature of the Oregon Country. Seattle: University of Washington Press.

Randolph, Vance

1947   Ozark Superstitions. New York: Columbia University Press.

Rapp, Rayna

1979   Review Essay: Anthropology. Signs 4:497–513.

Rasmussen, Knud

1931   The Netsilik Eskimos: Social Life and Spiritual Culture. Report of the Fifth Thule Expedition 1921–24, vol. 8, 1/2. Copenhagen: Gyldendal Bughandel, Nordisk Forlag.

Raven, Susan, and Alison Weir

1981   Women of Achievement: Thirty-five Centuries of History. New York: Harmony Books.

Ray, Dorothy Jean

1967   Eskimo Masks: Art and Ceremony. Seattle: University of Washington Press.

Reed, Evelyn

1975   Woman's Evolution: From Matriarchal Clan to Patriarchal Family. New York: Pathfinder Press.

Reichard, Gladys A.

1934   Spider Woman: A Story of Navajo Weavers and Chanters. New York: Macmillan.

1947   An Analysis of Coeur d'Alene Indian Myths. Memoirs of the American Folklore Society, vol. 41. Philadelphia: American Folklore Society.

Reichel-Dolmatoff, Gerardo

1971   Amazonian Cosmos: The Sexual and Religious Symbolism of the Tukano Indians. Chicago: Univeristy of Chicago Press. (First pub. 1968.)

Reik, Theodor

1960   The Creation of Woman: A Psychoanalytic Inquiry into the Myth of Eve. New York: McGraw-Hill.

Reiter, Rayna R., ed.

1975   Toward an Anthropology of Women. New York: Monthly Review Press.

Rhoads, Ellen

1973   Little Orphan Annie and Lévi-Strauss: The Myth and the Method. Journal of American Folklore 86:345–57.

Rhode Island Feminist Theatre

1978   Persephone's Return. Frontiers: a journal of women studies 3, 2:60–74.

Rice, Don
1979 Animals: A Picture Sourcebook. New York: Van Nostrand Reinhold.

Rich, Adrienne
1976 Of Woman Born: Motherhood as Experience and Institution. New York: W. W. Norton.
1978 The Dream of a Common Language: Poems 1974–1977. New York: W. W. Norton.

Rich, George W.
1971 Rethinking the "Star Husbands." Journal of American Folklore 84:436–41.

Rickels, Patricia K.
1979 Some Accounts of Witch Riding. In Readings in American Folklore. Jan Harold Brunvand, ed. Pp. 53–63. New York: W. W. Norton. (First pub. 1961.)

Rigby, Peter
1970 The Structural Context of Girls' Puberty Rites. Man 2:434–44.

Rivlin, Lily
1972 Lilith. Ms. Magazine, December, pp. 92–97, 114–15.

Roach, Susan, and Lorre M. Weidlich
1974 Quilt Making in America: A Selected Bibliography. Folklore Feminists Communication 3:17–28.

Robbins, Rossell Hope
1959 The Encyclopedia of Witchcraft and Demonology. New York: Crown Publishers.

Robinson, James M., ed.
1977 The Nag Hammadi Library in English. San Francisco: Harper & Row.

Rogers, Susan Carol
1975 Female Forms of Power and the Myth of Male Dominance: A Model of Female-Male Interaction in Peasant Society. American Ethnologist 2:727–56.

Róheim, Géza
1972 The Panic of the Gods and Other Essays. Werner Muensterberger, ed. New York: Harper & Row. ("Aphrodite, or the Woman with a Penis" first pub. in Psychoanalytic Quarterly 14, 13 [July 1945]:350–90.)

Rohrlich, Ruby, and June Nash
1981 Patriarchal Puzzle: State Formation in Mesopotamia and Mesoamerica. Heresies 4, 1: 60–65.

Rooth, Anna Birgitta
1957 The Creation Myths of the North American Indians. Anthropos 52:497–508.

Rosaldo, M. Z.
1980 The Use and Abuse of Anthropology: Reflections on Feminism and Cross-cultural Understanding. Signs 5:389–417.

Rosaldo, Michelle Zimbalist, and Jane Monnig Atkinson
1975 Man the Hunter and Woman: Metaphors for the Sexes in Ilongot Magical Spells. In The Interpretation of Symbolism. Roy Willis, ed. Pp. 43–75. New York: John Wiley & Sons.

Rosaldo, Michelle Zimbalist, and Louise Lamphere, eds.
1974 Woman, Culture, and Society. Stanford, California: Stanford University Press.

Ross, Joe
1980 Hags Out of Their Skins. Journal of American Folklore 93:183–86.

Rothgeb, Carrie Lee, ed.
1971 Abstracts of The Standard Edition of the Complete Psychological Works of Sigmund Freud. Rockville, Maryland: U.S.D.H.E.W., National Institute of Mental Health.

Ruether, Rosemary Radford
1974 (Ed.) Religion and Sexism: Images of Woman in the Jewish and Christian Traditions. New York: Simon and Schuster.
1975 New Woman/New Earth: Sexist Ideologies and Human Liberation. New York: Seabury Press.
1977 Mary—The Feminine Face of the Church. Philadelphia: Westminster.

Ruether, Rosemary, and Eleanor McLaughlin, eds.
1979 Women of Spirit: Female Leadership in the Jewish and Christian Traditions. New York: Simon and Schuster.

Rupprecht, Carol Schreier
1974 The Martial Maid and the Challenge of Androgyny (Notes on an Unbefriendable Archetype). Spring, pp. 269–93.

Rush, Anne Kent
1976 Moon, Moon. New York: Random House and Berkeley, California: Moon Books.
1979 Meditation: Moon Body. Lady-Unique-Inclination-of-the-Night, Cycle 4, p. 19.

Russ, L. Daniel
1980 Song of Songs: A World Infolded by the Lovers' Embrace. Dragonflies: Studies in Imaginal Psychology, Summer, pp. 93–122.

Russell, Frank
1975 The Pima Indians. Bernard L. Fontana, ed. Tucson: University of Arizona Press. (First pub. 1908.)

Russell, Letty M.
1973 Human Liberation in a Feminist Perspective: A Theology. Philadelphia: Westminster Press.

Sanday, Peggy Reeves

1981 Female Power and Male Dominance: On the Origins of Sexual Inequality. Cambridge: Cambridge University Press.

Sandner, Donald
1979 Navaho Symbols of Healing. New York: Harcourt Brace Jovanovich.

Sapir, Edward
1910 Yana Texts. University of California Publica--11 tions in American Archaeology and Ethnology, vol. 9, no. 1.

Schlegel, Alice
1972 Male Dominance and Female Autonomy: Domestic Authority in Matrilineal Societies. New Haven: HRAF Press.

Schulz, Muriel R.
1975 The Semantic Derogation of Women. *In* Language and Sex: Difference and Dominance. Barrie Thorne and Nancy Henley, eds. Pp. 64–75. Rowley, Massachusetts: Newbury House Publishers.

Sexton, Anne
1971 Transformations. Boston: Houghton Mifflin.

Shaffer, Frederick W.
1979 Indian Designs from Ancient Ecuador. New York: Dover Publications.

Sheehan, Carol
1978a A Sketch for a Reading of The Homeric Hymn to Demeter. Archē: Notes and Papers on Archaic Studies 1:29–53.

1978b Demeter and the Making of Soul. Archē: Notes and Papers on Archaic Studies 2:64–79.

Shelley, Percy Bysshe, trans.
1895 The Banquet of Plato. Chicagoway and Williams.

Shepard, Odell
1979 The Lore of the Unicorn. New York: Harper & Row.

Shimony, Annemarie
1980 Women of Influence and Prestige Among the Native American Iroquois. *In* Unspoken Worlds: Women's Religious Lives in Non-Western Cultures. Nancy Auer Falk and Rita M. Gross, eds. Pp. 243–59. San Francisco: Harper & Row.

Shuttle, Penelope, and Peter Redgrove
1978 The Wise Wound: Eve's Curse and Everywoman. New York: Richard Marek Publishers.

Sides, Dorothy Smith
1961 Decorative Art of the Southwestern Indians. New York: Dover Publications. (First pub. 1936.)

Simmer, Stephen
1980 The Net of Artemis: Text, Complex. Dragonflies: Studies in Imaginal Psychology, Summer, pp. 55–65.

Simmons, Leo W., ed.
1942 Sun Chief: The Autobiography of a Hopi Indian. New Haven: Yale University Press.

Singer, June
1976 Androgyny: Toward a New Theory of Sexuality. Garden City, New York: Anchor Press/Doubleday.

Sjöö, Monica, with Barbara Mor, ed. and extender
1981 The Ancient Religion of The Great Cosmic Mother of All. Trondheim, Norway: Rainbow Press.

Skinner, Charles M.
1896 Myths & Legends of Our Own Land. Vol. 2. Philadelphia: J. B. Lippincott.

Skov, G. E.
1975 The Priest of Demeter and Kore and Her Role in the Initiation of Women at the Festival of the Haloa at Eleusis. Temenos 11: 136–47.

Slater, Philip E.
1968 The Glory of Hera: Greek Mythology and the Greek Family. Boston: Beacon Press.

Smith, Harlan I.
1894 Notes on Eskimo Traditions. Journal of American Folk-Lore 7:209–16.

Snow, Loudell F., and Shirley M. Johnson
1978 Myths about Menstruation: Victims of Our Own Folklore. International Journal of Women's Studies 1:64–72.

Snyder-Ott, Joelynn
1978 Women and Creativity. Millbrae, California: Les Femmes Publishing.

Sobol, Donald J.
1972 The Amazons of Greek Mythology. New York: A. S. Barnes.

Sojourner, Sabrina
1982 From the House of Yemanja: The Goddess Heritage of Black Women. *In* The Politics of Spirituality: Essays on the Rise of Spiritual Power within the Feminist Movement. Charlene Spretnak, ed. Pp. 57–63. Garden City, New York: Anchor Press/Doubleday.

Sontag, Susan
1975 The Double Standard of Aging. *In* Humanness: An Exploration into the Mythologies about Women and Men. Ella Lasky, ed. Pp. 479–94. New York: MSS Information Corporation.

Speck, Frank G.
1909   Ethnology of the Yuchi Indians. University of Pennsylvania, Anthropological Publications of the University Museum, vol. 1, no. 1. Philadelphia.

Spencer, J.
1909   Shawnee Folk-Lore. Journal of American Folk-Lore 22:319–26.

Spitze, Glennys
1981   Syzygy: A Symbol of Maturation. The American Theosophist 69:323–29. (First pub. 1964.)

Spretnak, Charlene
1978   Lost Goddesses of Early Greece: A Collection of Pre-Hellenic Mythology. Berkeley, California: Moon Books.
1982   (Ed.) The Politics of Women's Spirituality: Essays on the Rise of Spiritual Power within the Feminist Movement. Garden City, New York: Anchor Press/Doubleday.

Sproul, Barbara C.
1979   Primal Myths: Creating the World. San Francisco: Harper & Row.

Stack, Carol B., Mina Davis Caulfield, Valerie Estes, Susan Landes, Karen Larson, Pamela Johnson, Juliet Rake, and Judith Shirek
1975   Review Essay: Anthropology. Signs 1:147–59.

Stannard, Una
1977   Mrs Man. San Francisco, California: Germainbooks.

Stanton, Elizabeth Cady
1968   The Matriarchate, or Mother-Age. In Up from the Pedestal. Aileen S. Kraditor, ed. Pp. 140–47. Chicago: Quadrangle Books.

Stanton, Elizabeth Cady, and the Revising Committee
1974   The Woman's Bible: Part I The Pentateuch, Part II Judges, Kings, Prophets and Apostles. Seattle: Coalition Task Force on Women and Religion.

Starhawk
1979   The Spiral Dance: A Rebirth of the Ancient Religion of the Great Goddess. San Francisco: Harper & Row.

Stein, Murray
1977   Hera: Bound and Unbound. Spring, pp. 105–19.

Stein, Robert M.
1981   Coupling/Uncoupling: Reflections on the Evolution of the Marriage Archetype. Spring, pp. 205–14.

Steinem, Gloria, Phyllis Chesler, and Bea Feitler
1972   Wonder Woman. A Ms. Book. New York: Holt, Rinehart and Winston and Warner Books.

Steiner, Stan, ed.
1980   Spirit Woman: The Diaries and Paintings of Bonita Wa Wa Calachaw Nuñez. San Francisco: Harper & Row.

Stern, Susan
1981   Arachne. Parabola 6, 4:45–47.

Stevens, Evelyn P.
1973   Marianismo: The Other Face of Machismo in Latin American. In Female and Male in Latin America. Ann Pescatello, ed. Pp. 89–101. Pittsburg: University of Pittsburgh Press.

Stevenson, Burton, ed.
1948   The Macmillan Book of Proverbs, Maxims, and Famous Phrases. New York: Macmillan.

Stigers, Eve Stehle
1979   Romantic Sensuality, Poetic Sense: A Response to Hallett on Sappho. Signs 4:465–71.

Stirling, Matthew W.
1942   Origin Myth of Acoma and Other Records. Bureau of American Ethnology Bulletin 135. Washington: GPO.

Stone, Kay F.
1975   Things Walt Disney Never Told Us. Journal of American Folklore 88:42–50.
1980   Fairy Tales for Adults: Walt Disney's Americanization of the Märchen. In Folklore of Two Continents: Essays in Honor of Linda Dégh. Nikolai Burlakoff and Carl Lindahl, eds. Pp. 40–48. Bloomington, Indiana: Trickster Press.
1981   Märchen to Fairy Tale: An Unmagical Transformation. Western Folklore 40:232–44.

Stone, Merlin
1976   When God Was a Woman. New York: Harcourt Brace Jovanovich.
1979   Ancient Mirrors of Womanhood: Our Goddess and Heroine Heritage. 2 vols. New York: New Sibylline Books.

Stroud, Joanne, and Gail Thomas, eds.
1982   Images of the Untouched: Virginity in Psyche, Myth and Community. The Pegasus Foundation I. Dallas, Texas: Spring Publications.

Strouse, Jean, ed.
1974   Women & Analysis: Dialogues on Psychoanalytic Views of Femininity. New York: Grossman Publishers.

Suhr, Elmer G.
1969   The Spinning Aphrodite: The Evolution of the Goddess from Earliest Pre-Hellenic Sym-

bolism through Late Classical Times. New York: Helios Books.

Summers, Rev. Montague, trans. and ed.
1971   The Malleus Maleficarum of Heinrich Kramer and James Sprenger. New York: Dover Publications. (First pub. 1928.)

Swanton, John R.
1909   Tlingit Myths and Texts. Bureau of American Ethnology Bulletin 39. Washington: GPO.
1911   Indian Tribes of the Lower Mississippi Valley and Adjacent Coast of the Gulf of Mexico. Bureau of American Ethnology Bulletin 43. Washington: GPO.
1929   Myths and Tales of the Southeastern Indians. Bureau of American Ethnology Bulletin 88. Washington: GPO.

Tafoya, Terry
1981   Dancing with Dash-Kayah: The Mask of the Cannibal Woman. Parabola 6, 3:6–11.

Taggart, James M.
1979   Men's Changing Image of Women in Nahuat Oral Tradition. American Ethnologist 6: 723–41.

Taylor, Archer
1964   The Biographical Pattern in Traditional Narrative. Journal of the Folklore Institute 1: 114–29.

Teit, James A.
1912   Mythology of the Thompson Indians. Publications of the Jessup North Pacific Expedition 8. New York: Brill.
1917   Coeur d'Alène Tales. In Folk-Tales of Salishan and Sahaptin Tribes. Franz Boas, ed. Memoirs of the American Folk-Lore Society, vol. 11. Lancaster, Pennsylvania and New York: G. E. Stechert.

Thiébaux, Marcelle
1978   A Mythology for Women: Monique Wittig's Les Guérillères. 13th Moon: A Literary Magazine Publishing Women 4, 1:37–45.

Thompson, J. Eric
1939   The Moon Goddess in Middle America. Carnegie Institute of Washington, Publication 509, Contribution 29.

Thompson, Stith
1929   Tales of the North American Indians. Bloomington: Indiana University Press.
1946   The Folktale. New York: Holt, Rinehart and Winston.
1958   Myth and Folktales. In Myth: A Symposium. Thomas A. Sebeok, ed. Pp. 169–80. Bloom-

ington: Indiana University Press. (First pub. 1955.)
1965   The Star Husband Tale. In The Study of Folklore. Alan Dundes, ed. Pp. 414–74. Englewood Cliffs, New Jersey: Prentice-Hall. (First pub. 1953.)
1973   (Trans. and ed., with Antti Aarne) The Types of the Folktale: A Classification and Bibliography. 2d rev. Folklore Fellows Communications No. 184. Helsinki.

Thorne, Barrie, and Nancy Henley, eds.
1975   Language and Sex: Difference and Dominance. Rowley, Massachusetts: Newbury House Publishers.

Thorsten, Geraldine
1980   God Herself: The Feminist Roots of Astrology. Garden City, New York: Doubleday.

Toelken, Barre
1979   The Dynamics of Folklore. Boston: Houghton Mifflin.

Travers, P. L.
1975   About the Sleeping Beauty. New York: McGraw-Hill.

Trejo, Judy
1974   Coyote Tales: A Paiute Commentary. Journal of American Folklore 87:66–71.

Trible, Phyllis
1976   Depatriarchalizing in Biblical Interpretation. In The Jewish Woman: New Perspectives. Elizabeth Koltun, ed. Pp. 217–40. New York: Schocken Books.

Turner, John D., trans.
1977   Trimorphic Protennoia (XIII, 1). In The Nag Hammadi Library. James M. Robinson, ed. Pp. 461–70. San Francisco: Harper & Row.

Turner, Kay
1976   Ixchel: Biography of a Mayan Moon Goddess. Lady-Unique-Inclination-of-the-Night, Cycle 1, pp. 41–51.
1976a   Why we are so inclined. . . . Lady-Unique-Inclination-of-the-Night, Cycle 1, pp. 2–4.
1978   Contemporary Feminist Rituals. Heresies, Spring, pp. 20–26.
1981   The Virgin of Sorrows Procession: Mothers, Movement, and Transformation. Archē: Notes and Papers on Archaic Studies 6:71–92.

Tyson, Katherine
1980   Medea: Priestess Who Guards the Dark Door. Dragonflies: Studies in Imaginal Psychology, Summer, pp. 67–92.

Ulanov, Anna Belford
1971   The Feminine in Jungian Psychology and in

Christian Theology. Evanston, Illinois: North-western University Press.

1981　Receiving Woman: Studies in the Psychology and Theology of the Feminine. Philadelphia: Westminster Press.

Underhill, Ruth M.

1965　Red Man's Religion: Beliefs and Practices of the Indians North of Mexico. Chicago: University of Chicago Press.

1973　Singing for Power: The Song Magic of the Papago Indians of Southern Arizona. New York: Ballantine Books. (First pub. 1938.)

1979　Papago Woman. Case Studies in Cultural Anthropology. New York: Holt, Rinehart and Winston. (First pub. 1936.)

Utley, Francis Lee

1945　The Bible of the Folk. California Folklore Quarterly 4:1–17.

1957　Abraham Lincoln's *When Adam Was Created*. *In* Studies in Folklore. W. Edson Richmond, ed. Pp. 187–212. Indiana University Publications, Folklore Series, No. 9. Bloomington: Indiana University Press.

Vaillant, George C.

1962　Aztecs of Mexico: Origin, Rise, and Fall of the Aztec Nation. Suzannah B. Vaillant, rev. Baltimore, Maryland: Penguin Books. (First pub. 1944.)

Van Over, Raymond, ed.

1980　Sun Songs: Creation Myths from Around the World. New York: New American Library.

Van Vuuren, Nancy

1973　The Subversion of Women as Practiced by Churches, Witch-Hunters and Other Sexists. Philadelphia: Westminster Press.

Vennum, Thomas, Jr.

1978　Ojibwa Origin-Migration Songs of the *mitewiwin*. Journal of American Folklore 91: 753–91.

Vickers, Nancy J.

1981　Diana Described: Scattered Woman and Scattered Rhyme. Critical Inquiry 8:265–79.

Villas Boas, Orlando, and Villas Boas, Claudio

1973　Xingu: The Indians, Their Myths. Susana Hertelendy Rudge, trans. New York: Farrar, Straus and Giroux. (First pub. 1970.)

Voegelin, C. F.

1936　The Shawnee Female Deity. Yale University Publications in Anthropology, No. 10. New Haven.

Voegelin, C. F. and E. W.

1944　The Shawnee Female Deity in Historical Perspective. American Anthropologist 46: 370–75.

Vogel, Virgil J.

1970　American Indian Medicine. Norman: University of Oklahoma Press.

von Franz, Marie-Louise

1964　The Process of Individuation. *In* Man and His Symbols, by Carl G. Jung with M.-L. von Franz, Joseph L. Henderson, Jolande Jacobi, Aniela Jaffé. Pp. 157–254. New York: Dell Publishing.

1970　A Psychological Interpretation of The Golden Ass of Apuleius. Zürich, Switzerland: Spring Publications.

1972　Problems of the Feminine in Fairytales. New York: Spring Publications.

1973　An Introduction to the Interpretation of Fairy Tales. Zürich, Switzerland: Spring Publications. (First pub. 1970.)

1978　Time: Rhythm and Repose. Great Britain: Thames and Hudson.

1980　The Passion of Perpetua. Elizabeth Welsh, trans. Irving, Texas: Spring Publications.

Wagley, Charles, and Eduardo Galvão

1949　The Tenetehara Indians of Brazil: A Culture in Transition. Columbia University Contributions to Anthropology, No. 35. New York: Columbia University Press.

Wald, Carol, with text by Judith Papachristou

1975　Myth America: Picturing Women, 1865–1945. New York: Pantheon Books.

Walker, Gail

1976　Moon Changes. Lady-Unique-Inclination-of-the-Night, Cycle 1, pp. 5–10.

Wallace, Anthony F. C.

1966　Religion: An Anthropological View. New York: Random House.

Ward, Marilynn I.

1978　The Feminist Crisis of Sor Juana Ines de la Cruz. International Journal of Women's Studies 1:475–81.

Wardle, H. Newell

1900　The Sedna Cycle: A Study in Myth Evolution. American Anthropologist 2:568–80.

Warner, Marina

1976　Alone of All Her Sex: The Myth and the Cult of the Virgin Mary. New York: Alfred A. Knopf.

1981　Joan of Arc: The Image of Female Heroism. New York: Alfred A. Knopf.

Washbourn, Penelope
1977   Becoming Woman: The Quest for Wholeness in Female Experience. New York: Harper & Row.
1979   (Ed.) Seasons of Woman: Song, Poetry, Ritual, Prayer, Myth, Story. San Francisco: Harper & Row.

Watts, A. E., trans.
1980   The Metamorphoses of Ovid. With etchings by Pablo Picasso. San Francisco, California: North Point Press. (First pub. 1954.)

Watts, Alan W.
1968   Myth and Ritual in Christianity. Boston: Beacon Press.

Weaver, Rix
1973   The Old Wise Woman: A Study of Active Imagination. New York: G. P. Putnam's Sons for the C. G. Jung Foundation for Analytical Psychology.

Webster, Paula
1975   Matriarchy: A Vision of Power. *In* Toward an Anthropology of Women. Rayna R. Reiter, ed. Pp. 141–56. New York: Monthly Review Press.
1978   Politics of Rape in Primitive Society. Heresies, Summer, pp. 16–18, 20, 22.

Weideger, Paula
1976   Menstruation and Menopause: The Physiology and Psychology, the Myth and the Reality. New York: Alfred A. Knopf.

Weigle, Marta
1978   Women as Verbal Artists: Reclaiming the Sisters of Enheduanna. Frontiers: a journal of women studies 3, 3:1–9.

Weigle, Marta, and David Johnson
1980   At the Beginning: American Creation Myths. Albuquerque: University of New Mexico, Department of English.

Wheeler-Voegelin, Erminie, and Remedios W. Moore
1957   The Emergence Myth in Native North America. *In* Studies in Folklore. W. Edson Richmond, ed. Pp. 66–91. Indiana University Publications, Folklore Series, No. 9. Bloomington: Indiana University Press.

White, Leslie A.
1932   The Acoma Indians. *In* Forty-seventh Annual Report of the Bureau of American Ethnology to the Secretary of the Smithsonian Institution, 1929–1930. M. W. Stirling, Chief. Pp. 17–192. Washington: GPO.

White, Newman Ivey, gen. ed.
1952   North Carolina Folklore. Stith Thompson, ed. Vol. 1. Durham, North Carolina: Duke University Press.

White, T. H., trans. and ed.
1954   The Bestiary: A Book of Beasts, being a Translation from a Latin Bestiary of the Twelfth Century. New York: G. P. Putnam's Sons.

Widdowson, John
1973   The Witch as a Frightening and Threatening Figure. *In* The Witch Figure. Venetia Newall, ed. Pp. 200–20. London: Routledge & Kegan Paul.

Willard, Nancy
1981   Goddess in the Belfrey. Parabola 6, 3:90–94.

Willeford, William
1969   The Fool and His Scepter: A Study in Clowns and Jesters and Their Audience. Evanston, Illinois: Northwestern University Press.

Williams, Juanita H.
1978   Woman: Myth and Stereotype. International Journal of Women's Studies 1:221–47.

Witherspoon, Gary
1977   Language and Art in the Navajo Universe. Ann Arbor: University of Michigan Press.

Wolf, Eric
1958   The Virgin of Guadalupe: A Mexican National Symbol. Journal of American Folklore 71: 34–39.

Wyman, Leland C.
1970   Blessingway: With Three Versions of the Myth Recorded and Translated from the Navajo by Father Berard Haile, O.F.M. Tucson: University of Arizona Press.
1975   The Mountainway of the Navajo: With a Myth of the Female Branch Recorded and Translated by Father Berard Haile, O.F.M. Tucson: University of Arizona Press.

Yeats, William Butler
1928   The Collected Poems of W. B. Yeats. New York: Macmillan.

Yerkovich, Sally
1976   Gossiping; or, The Creation of Fictional Lives, Being a Study of the Subject in an Urban American Setting Drawing Upon Vignettes from Upper Middle Class Lives. Diss. University of Pennsylvania.

Young, Frank W.
1970   A Fifth Analysis of the Star Husband Tale. Ethnology 9:389–413.
1978   Folktales and Social Structure: A Comparison

of Three Analyses of the Star-Husband Tale.
Journal of American Folklore 91:691–99.

Zahler, Leah
    1973   Matriarchy and Myth. Aphra 4, 3:25–31.

Zipes, Jack
    1979   Breaking the Magic Spell: Radical Theories of Folk and Fairy Tales. Austin: University of Texas Press.

Zolla, Elémire
    1981   The Androgyne: Reconciliation of male and female. New York: Crossroad.

Zuntz, Günther
    1971   Persephone: Three Essays on Religion and Thought in Magna Graecia. Oxford: Oxford University Press.

Sources

Continued from page iv

J. J. Bachofen, *Myth, Religion, and Mother Right*, trans. Ralph Manheim. Bollingen Series LXXXIV. Copyright © 1967 by Princeton University Press. Excerpts reprinted by permission.

Joan Bamberger. Excerpted from "The Myth of Matriarchy: Why Men Rule in Primitive Society," by Joan Bamberger, in *Woman, Culture, and Society*, edited by Michelle Zimbalist Rosaldo and Louise Lamphere, with the permission of the publishers, Stanford University Press. © 1974 by the Board of Trustees of the Leland Stanford Junior University.

Sharon Barba, "A Cycle of Women." All rights reserved. Reprinted by permission of the author.

Patricia Berry, "The Rape of Demeter/Persephone and Neurosis." Copyright © 1975 The Analytical Psychology Club of New York, Inc. Used with permission of Spring Publications Inc., P.O. Box 222069, Dallas, Texas 75222.

Bruno Bettelheim. From *The Uses of Enchantment: The Meaning and Importance of Fairy Tales*, by Bruno Bettelheim. Copyright © 1976 by Bruno Bettelheim. Reprinted by permission of Alfred A. Knopf, Inc. Portions of this book originally appeared in *The New Yorker*.

John Bierhorst. Reprinted by permission of Farrar, Straus and Giroux, Inc. "Earth Goddess," an Aztec myth from *The Red Swan: Myths and Tales of the American Indians* by John Bierhorst. Copyright © 1976 by John Bierhorst.

Dorothy Bloch, from *"So the Witch Won't Eat Me"*. Reprinted by permission of Dorothy Bloch and her agent, Raines & Raines, 475 Fifth Avenue, New York 10017. Copyright © 1978 by Dorothy Bloch.

Elizabeth Brandon, "Folk Medicine in French Louisiana," from *American Folk Medicine: A Symposium*, edited by Wayland D. Hand, University of California Press. Essay originally presented at a UCLA conference in 1973. Copyright © 1976 by The Regents of the University of California.

Phyllis Chesler. Excerpt from *Women and Madness* by Phyllis Chesler. Copyright © 1972 by Phyllis Chesler. Reprinted by permission of Doubleday & Company, Inc.

Mary Daly. From *Beyond God the Father: Toward a Philosophy of Women's Liberation* by Mary Daly. Copyright © 1973 by Mary Daly. Reprinted by permission of Beacon Press and the author.

Mary Daly. Specified excerpt from pp. 22–23 in *The Church and the Second Sex* by Mary Daly. Copyright © 1975 by Mary Daly. Reprinted by permission of Harper & Row, Publishers, Inc.

Mary Daly. From *Gyn/Ecology: The Metaethics of Radical Feminism* by Mary Daly. Copyright © 1978 by Mary Daly. Reprinted by permission of Beacon Press and the author.

Elizabeth Gould Davis, from *The First Sex*, G. P. Putnam's Sons. Copyright © Elizabeth Gould Davis, 1971. By permission of The Putnam Publishing Group.

Hall. Reprinted by permission of Harper & Row, Publishers, Inc.

Judith P. Hallett, "Sappho and Her Social Context." Reprinted from *Signs: Journal of Women in Culture and Society* 1979, vol. 4, no. 3, by permission of The University of Chicago Press. © 1979 by The University of Chicago.

M. Esther Harding, from *Woman's Mysteries, Ancient and Modern*. New York: C. G. Jung Foundation for Analytical Psychology, 1971. Used with permission.

Susan Harding, from "Women and Words in a Spanish Village," in *Toward an Anthropology of Women*, edited by Rayna R. Reiter. Copyright © 1975 by Rayna R. Reiter. Reprinted by permission of Monthly Review Press.

H. R. Hays, *The Dangerous Sex*. Copyright © 1964. Used by permission of the author and the Ann Elmo Agency, Inc.

Julius E. Heuscher. From Julius E. Heuscher, *A Psychiatric Study of Myths and Fairy Tales*, second edition, 1974. Courtesy of Charles C Thomas, Publisher, Springfield, Illinois.

James Hillman, " 'Anima'." Copyright © 1973 Analytical Psychology Club of New York, Inc. Used with permission of Spring Publications, Inc., P.O. Box 222069, Dallas, Texas 75222.

Daryl Hine. From Daryl Hine (Translator) *The Homeric Hymns and The Battle of the Frogs and the Mice*. Copyright © 1972 by Daryl Hine. (New York: Atheneum, 1972). Reprinted with the permission of Atheneum Publishers.

Mary Howitt, "The Spider and the Fly," from Iona and Peter Opie, eds., *The Oxford Book of Children's Verse*, © Oxford University Press 1973. By permission of Oxford University Press.

Åke Hultkrantz, *The Religions of the American Indians*, translated by Monica Setterwall, The University of California Press. This translation copyright © 1979 by The Regents of the University of California. Used with permission.

Beverly Hungry Wolf. Excerpt from p. 33 "A few years ago . . . necklace around me," in *The Ways of My Grandmothers* by Beverly Hungry Wolf. Copyright © 1980 by Beverly Hungry Wolf. By permission of William Morrow & Co.

Melville Jacobs. Reprinted from *The Content and Style of an Oral Literature* by Melville Jacobs by permission of The University of Chicago Press. © 1959 by Wenner-Gren Foundation for Anthropological Research, Inc.

David E. Jones. From *Sanapia: Comanche Medicine Woman* by David E. Jones. Copyright © 1972 by Holt, Rinehart and Winston, Inc. Reprinted by permission of Holt, Rinehart and Winston.

Rosan Jordan de Caro, "A Note about Folklore and Literature (The Bosom Serpent Revisited)." Reproduced by permission of the American Folklore Society from the *Journal of American Folklore* 86:64–5, 1973.

C. G. Jung. *The Collected Works of C. G. Jung*, trans. R. F. C. Hull, Bollingen Series XX, Vol. 9, 1, *The Archetypes and the Collective Unconscious*, copyright © 1959, 1969 by Princeton University Press. Excerpts reprinted by permission.

C. G. Jung, *Psychological Reflections: A New Anthology of His Writings, 1905–1961*, ed. Jolande Jacobi and R. F. C. Hull, Bollingen Series XXXI, Copyright 1953 by Princeton University Press; new edition copyright © 1970 by Princeton University Press. Excerpts reprinted by permission.

C. G. Jung and C. Kerenyi, *Essays on a Science of Mythology*, trans. R. F. C. Hull, Bollingen Series XXII. Copyright © 1949, 1959, 1963 by Princeton University Press. Excerpts reprinted by permission.

Emma Jung, "On the Nature of the Animus," translated by Cary F. Baynes. Copyright © 1957, 1972 by The Analytical Psychology Club of New York, Incorporated. Used with permission of Spring Publications Inc., P.O. Box 222069, Dallas, Texas 75222.

C. Kerényi, *Eleusis: Archetypal Image of Mother and Daughter*, trans. Ralph Manheim. Bollingen Series LXV, 4. Copyright © 1967 by Princeton University Press. Used with permission.

Mary Ritchie Key. Reprinted by permission from *Male/Female Language* by Mary Ritchie Key (Metuchen, N.J.: Scarecrow Press, 1974). Copyright © 1974 by Mary Ritchie Key.

Barbara Kirksey, "Hestia: a Background of Psychological Focusing." Copyright © 1980, Spring Publications, Inc. Used with permission of Spring Publications Inc., P.O. Box 222069, Dallas, Texas 75222.

Madonna Kolbenschlag. Excerpts from *Kiss Sleeping Beauty Good-Bye* by Madonna Kolbenschlag. Copyright © 1979 by Madonna Kolbenschlag. Reprinted by permission of Doubleday & Company, Inc.

Roslyn Lacks. Excerpt from *Women and Judaism* by Roslyn Lacks. Copyright © 1979 by Roslyn Lacks. Reprinted by permission of Doubleday & Company, Inc.

lady-unique-inclination-of-the-night. Drawing of Ix Chel in chapter four. All rights reserved. Reprinted by permission of Kay Turner.

Ruth Landes, from *The Ojibwa Woman*, Columbia University Press, 1938. Used with permission of the publisher.

Richard Lattimore, translator, from *Hesiod*, The University of Michigan Press. Copyright © by The University of Michigan 1959. Used with permission.

John Layard, *The Virgin Archetype: Two Essays*. Copyright ©

1978 by Raphael Patai. Reprinted by permission of KTAV Publishing House, Inc.

Lois Paul, from "Careers of Midwives in a Mayan Community," in Judith Hoch-Smith and Anita Spring, eds., *Women in Ritual and Symbolic Roles*, Plenum Press, 1978. Reprinted by permission from Dr. Benjamin Paul, Dr. Anita Spring, and Plenum Publishing Corporation.

Judith Plaskow. Specified excerpt from p. 205 in *Womanspirit Rising*. Specified excerpt from "The Coming of Lilith: Toward a Feminist Theology" (p. 205) by Judith Plaskow in *Womanspirit Rising*, edited by Carol P. Christ and Judith Plaskow, 1979. Reprinted by permission of Harper & Row, Publishers, Inc.

Sarah B. Pomeroy. Reprinted by permission of Schocken Books Inc. from *Goddesses, Whores, Wives and Slaves* by Sarah B. Pomeroy. Copyright © 1975 by Sarah B. Pomeroy.

Marla N. Powers, "Menstruation and Reproduction." Reprinted from *Signs: Journal of Women in Culture and Society* 1980, vol. 6, no. 1, by permission of The University of Chicago Press. © 1980 by The University of Chicago.

Vance Randolph, from *Ozark Superstitions*. Copyright © 1947 by Columbia University Press. Used with permission of the publisher.

Gerardo Reichel-Dolmatoff. Reprinted from *Amazonian Cosmos: The Sexual and Religious Symbolism of the Tukano Indians* by Gerardo Reichel-Dolmatoff, trans. by the author, by permission of The University of Chicago Press. © 1971 by The University of Chicago.

James M. Robinson, ed. Specified excerpts from pp. 206, 217–217, 461, 465–466, 467 in *The Nag Hammadi Library*, edited by James M. Robinson. English language copyright © 1977 by E. J. Brill. Reprinted by permission of Harper & Row, Publishers, Inc.

M. Z. Rosaldo, "The Use and Abuse of Anthropology." Reprinted from *Signs: Journal of Women in Culture and Society* 1980, vol. 5, no. 3, by permission of The University of Chicago Press. © 1980 by The University of Chicago.

Christina Rosetti, "Lady Moon," from Iona and Peter Opie, eds., *The Oxford Book of Children's Verse*, © Oxford University Press 1973. By permission of Oxford University Press.

Carol Schreier Rupprecht, "The Martial Maid and the Challenge of Androgyny." Copyright © 1974 by The Analytical Psychology Club of New York, Inc. Used with permission of Spring Publications Inc., P.O. Box 222069, Dallas, Texas 75222.

Anne Sexton, from "Briar Rose (Sleeping Beauty)," from *Transformations* by Anne Sexton. Copyright © 1971 by Anne Sexton. Reprinted by permission of Houghton Mifflin Company.

Penelope Shuttle and Peter Redgrove, from *The Wise Wound: Eve's Curse and Everywoman*, Richard Marek Publishers. Copyright © 1978 by Penelope Shuttle and Peter Redgrove. Used with permission from Richard Marek Publishers, Inc.

Lee W. Simmons, from *Sun Chief*, Yale University Press. Copyright 1942 by Yale University Press. Used with permission.

June Singer. Excerpt from *Androgyny: Toward a New Theory of Sexuality* by June Singer. Copyright © 1976 by June Singer. Reprinted by permission of Doubleday & Company, Inc.

Philip E. Slater, from *The Glory of Hera: Greek Mythology and the Greek Family*. Copyright © 1968 by Philip E. Slater. Reprinted by permission of Beacon Press, Boston.

Murray Stein, "Hera Bound and Unbound." Copyright © 1977 The Analytical Psychology Club of New York, Inc. Used with permission of Spring Publications Inc., P.O. Box 222069, Dallas, Texas 75222.

Murray Stein, "Translator's Afterthoughts," from Karl Kerényi, *Athene: Virgin and Mother*. Translation Copyright © 1978, Spring Publications, Postfach, 8024 Zürich. Used with permission of Spring Publications Inc., P.O. Box 222069, Dallas, Texas 75222.

Gloria Steinem, from "Wonder Woman: An Introduction" to *Wonder Woman*, Ms./Holt, Rinehart and Winston. Reprinted with permission. Copyright © 1972, Gloria Steinem.

Stan Steiner. Specified excerpts from pp. xvi–xvii, xvii–xviii in *Spirit Woman*, edited by Stan Steiner. Copyright © 1980 by Stan Steiner. Reprinted by permission of Harper & Row, Publishers, Inc., and Stan Steiner.

Burton Stevenson. Reprinted by permission of Macmillan Publishing Co., Inc., from *The Macmillan Book of Proverbs, Maxims, and Famous Phrases*, selected and arranged by Burton Stevenson. Copyright 1948, by The Macmillan Company.

Kay Stone, "Things Walt Disney Never Told Us." Reproduced by permission of the American Folklore Society from the *Journal of American Folklore* 88:43–44, 1975.

Merlin Stone, from *When God was a Woman*. Copyright © 1976 by Merlin Stone. Permission granted by The Dial Press.

Geraldine Thorsten. Excerpt from *God Herself* by Geraldine Thorsten. Copyright © 1980 by Geraldine Thorsten. Reprinted by permission of Doubleday & Company, Inc.

Barre Toelken, *The Dynamics of Folklore*. Copyright © 1979

Index

Printed in the United Kingdom by
Lightning Source UK Ltd., Milton Keynes
137615UK00001BB/6/A